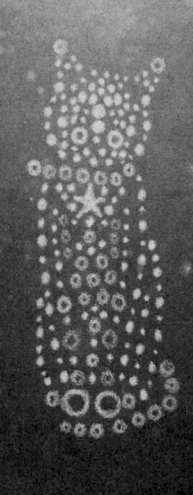

Because little children aren't able to speak well, they say it's
important to get them to express the emotions that are deep in
their hearts through activities such as drawing.

I believe some grown-ups need to do the same, myself
included.

Thank goodness for manga.

—Hiroyuki Asada, 2013

Hiroyuki Asada made his debut in *Monthly Shonen Jump* in
1986. He's best known for his basketball manga *I'll*.
He's a contributor to artist Range Murata's quarterly manga
anthology *Robot*. *Tegami Bachi: Letter Bee*
is his most recent series.

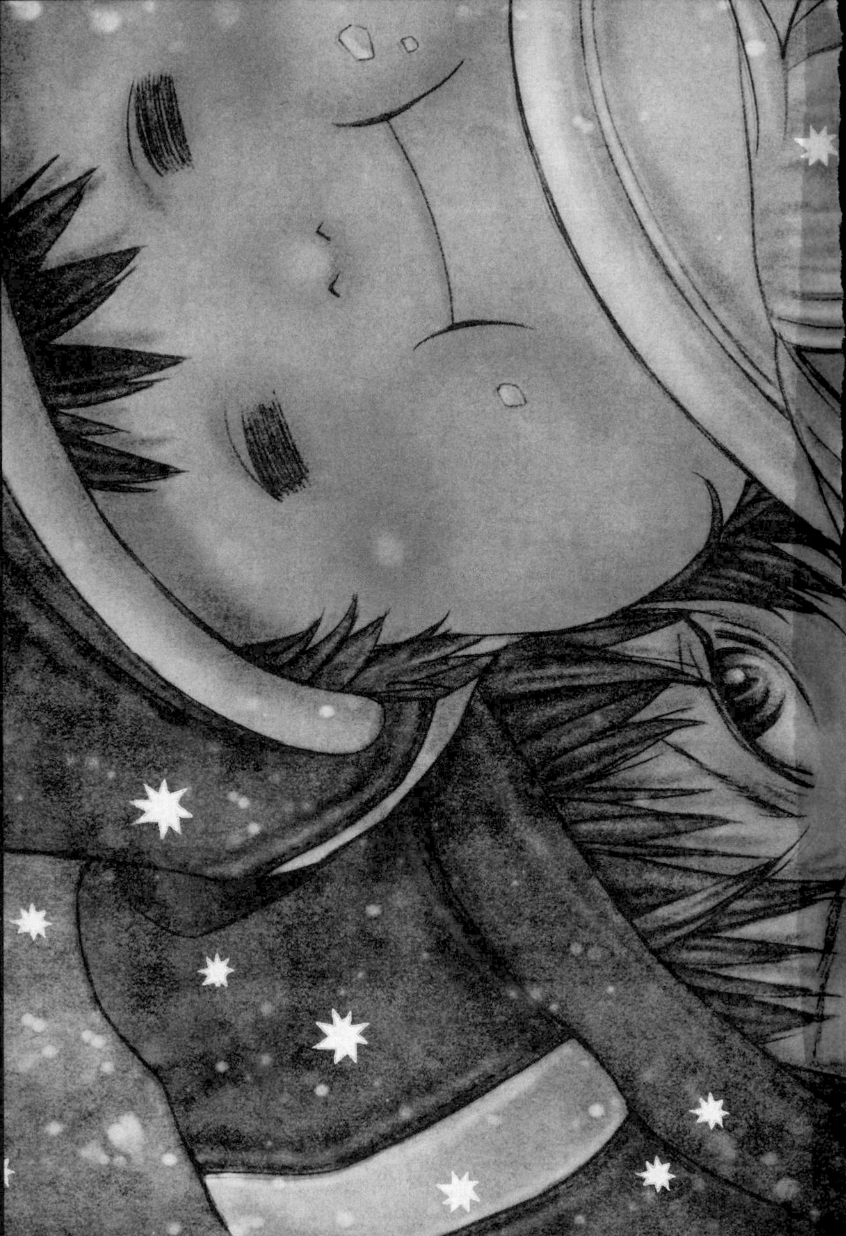

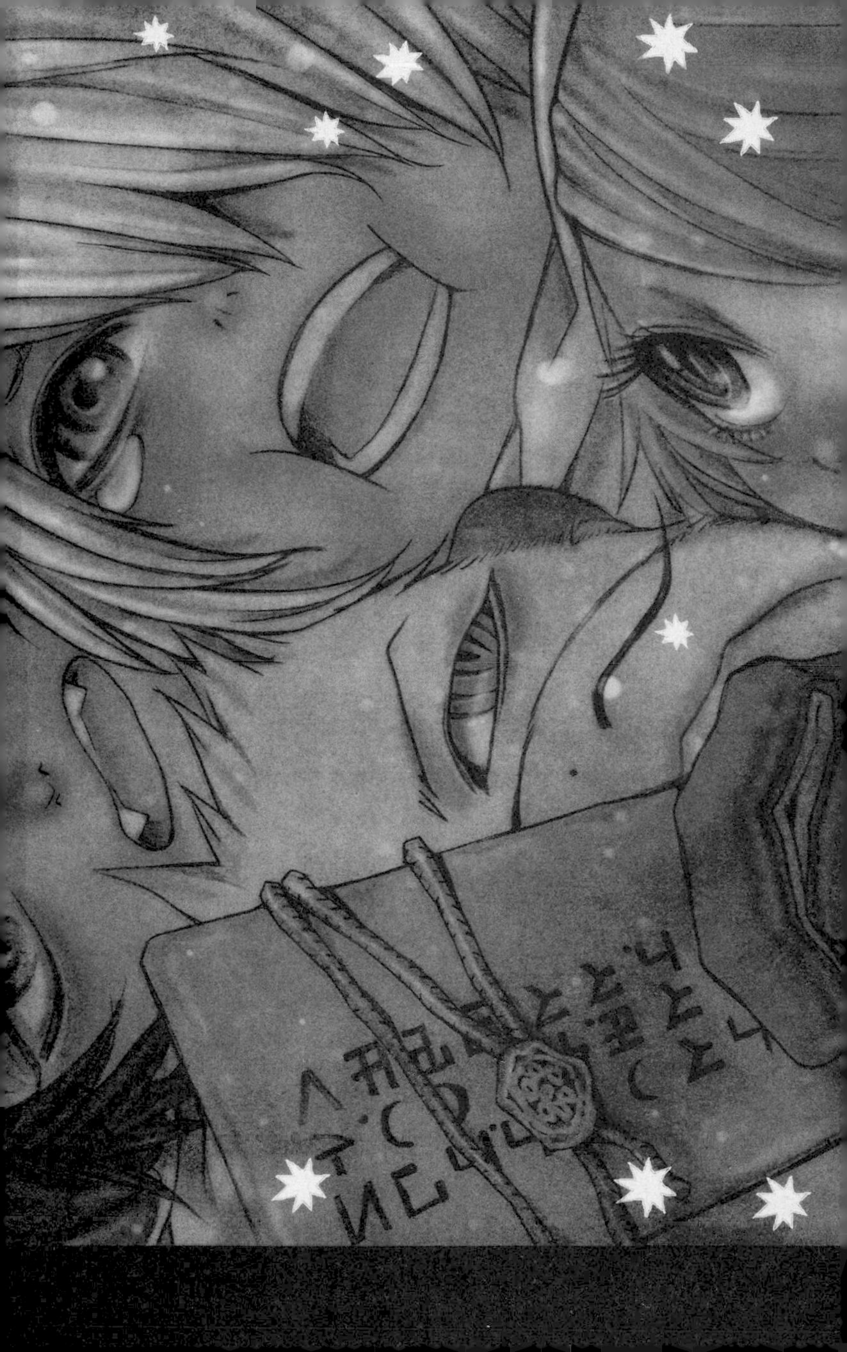

Tegami Bachi
LETTER · BEE

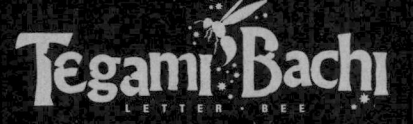

Volume 16

SHONEN JUMP Manga Edition

Story and Art by Hiroyuki Asada

English Adaptation/Rich Amtower
Translation/JN Productions
Touch-up & Lettering/Annaliese Christman
Design/Amy Martin
Editor/Shaenon K. Garrity

Printed in Canada

Published by VIZ Media, LLC
P.O. Box 77010
San Francisco, CA 94107

10 9 8 7 6 5 4 3 2 1
First printing, March 2014

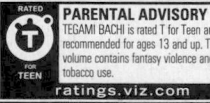

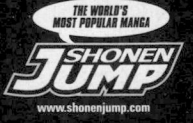

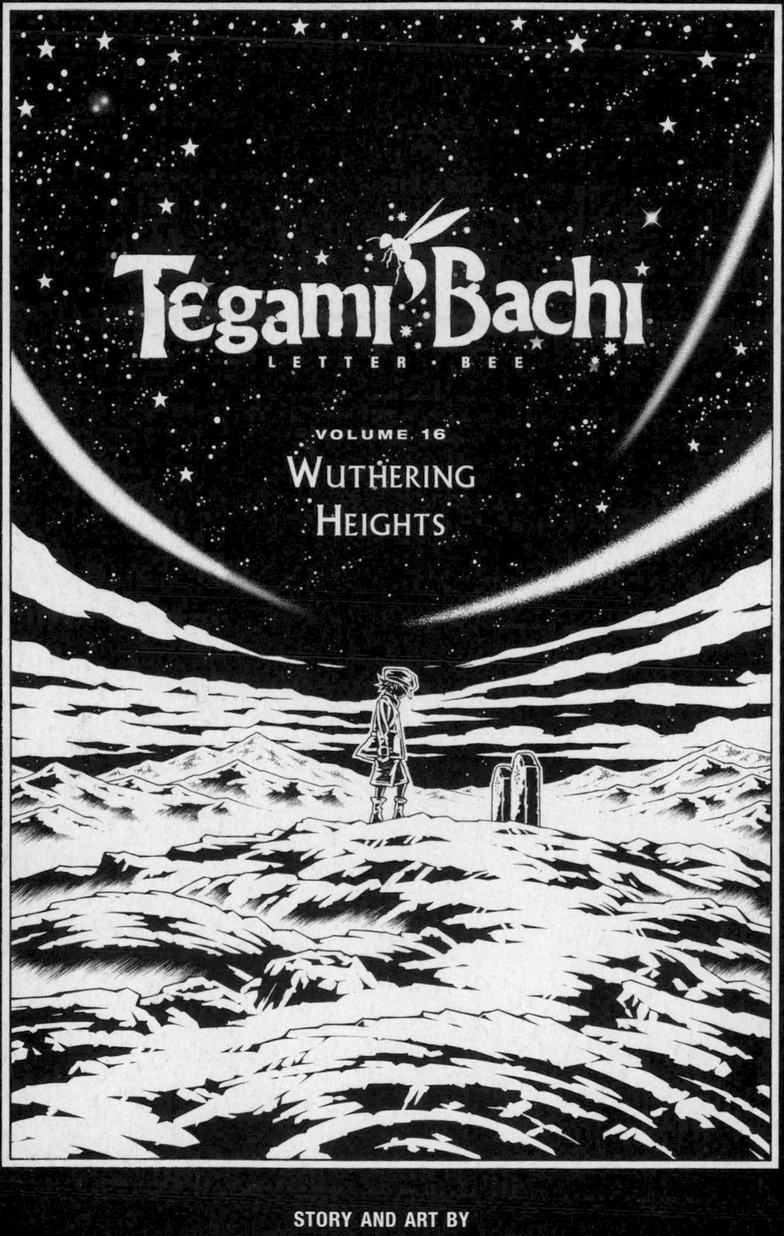
Tegami Bachi
LETTER • BEE
VOLUME 16
Wuthering
Heights

STORY AND ART BY

HIROYUKI ASADA

This is a country known as Amberground, where night never ends.

Its capital, Akatsuki, is illuminated by a man-made sun. The farther one strays from the capital, the weaker the light. The Yuusari region is cast in twilight; the Yodaka region survives only on pale moonlight.

Letter Bee Gauche Suede and young Lag Seeing meet in the Yodaka region—a postal worker and the "letter" he must deliver. In their short time together, they form a fast friendship, but when the journey ends, each departs down his own path. Gauche longs to become Head Bee, while Lag himself wants to be a Letter Bee, like Gauche.

In time, Lag becomes a Letter Bee. But Gauche has lost his *heart* and become a Marauder named Noir, working for the rebel organization Reverse.

Lag learns about the secret of his birth from Sabrina Mary, the woman who raised him. What's more, Sabrina gives him a letter from his mother revealing that she is the Empress of Akatsuki. To learn the truth about Amberground and change the world, Lag must find the five children, including himself, who were born on the "Day of the Flicker," when the sun almost went out.

Meanwhile, while making his deliveries, the Letter Bee Zazie comes across signs of his sworn enemy, the Gaichuu Laphroaig, which devoured his parents' *hearts...*

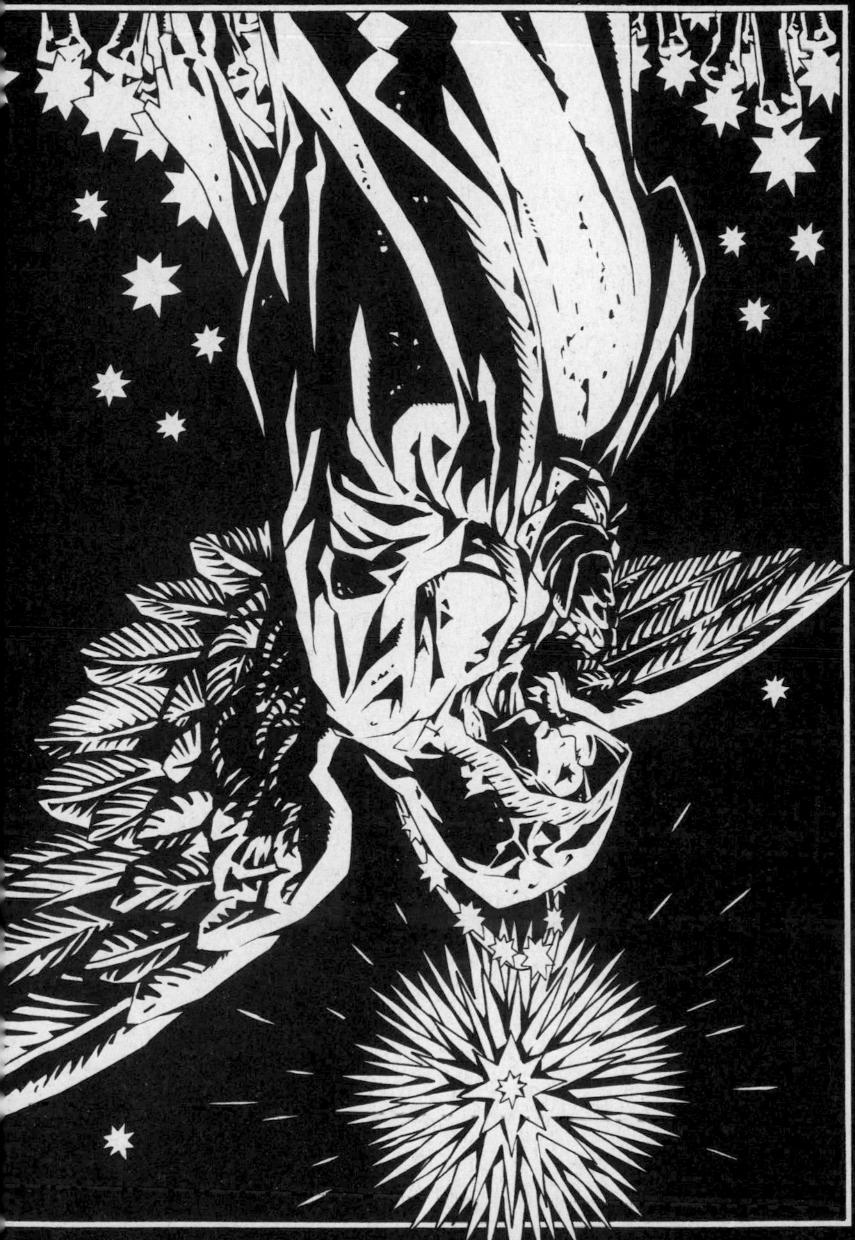

List of Characters

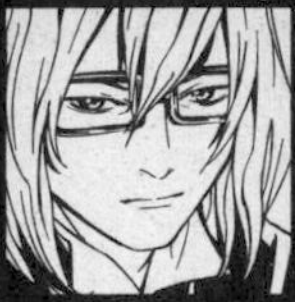

LARGO LLOYD
Ex-Beehive Director

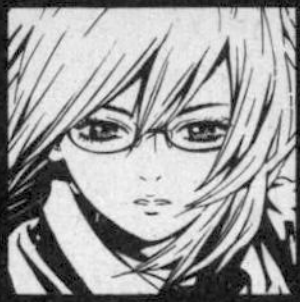

ARIA LINK
Section Chief of the Dead Letter Office

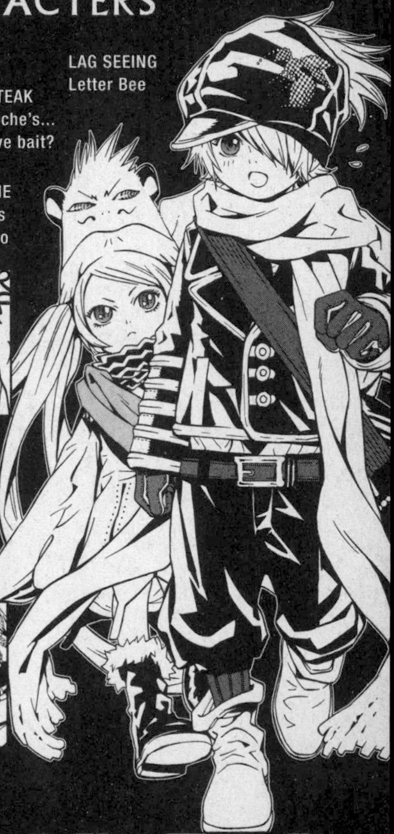

LAG SEEING
Letter Bee

STEAK
Niche's... live bait?

NICHE
Lag's Dingo

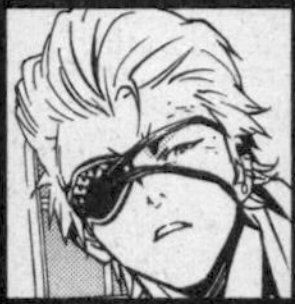

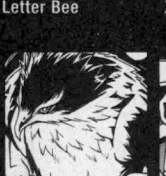

DR. THUNDERLAND, JR.
Member of the AG Biological Science Advisory Board, Third Division and head doctor at the Beehive

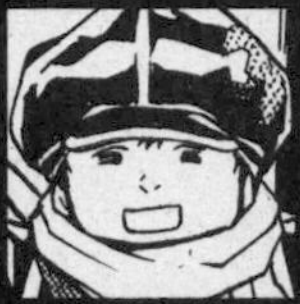

CONNOR KLUFF
Letter Bee

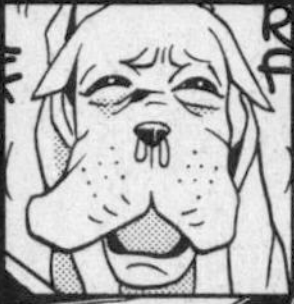

GUS
Connor's Dingo

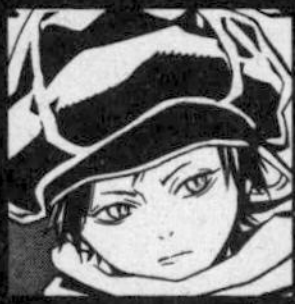

ZAZIE
Letter Bee

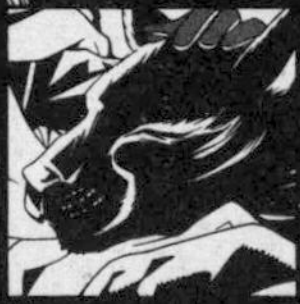

WASIOLKA
Zazie's Dingo

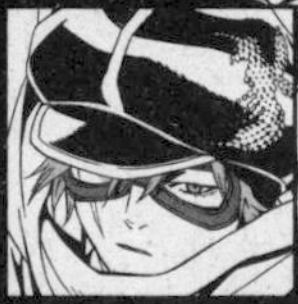

JIGGY PEPPER
Express Delivery Letter Bee

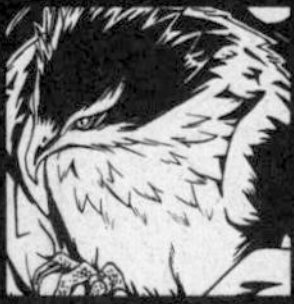

HARRY
Jiggy's Dingo

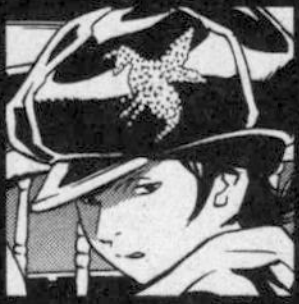

MOC SULLIVAN
Letter Bee

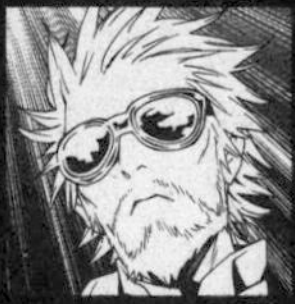

CHALYBS GARRARD
Inspector and ex-Letter Bee

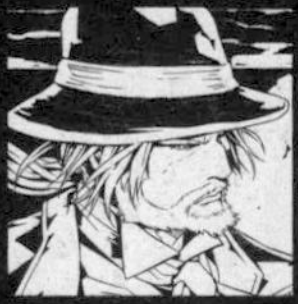

HAZEL VALENTINE
Inspector and Garrard's ex-Dingo

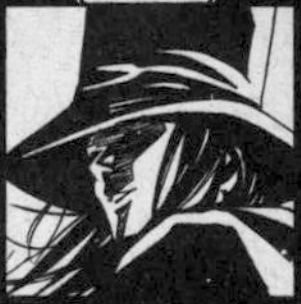

LAWRENCE
The ringleader of Reverse

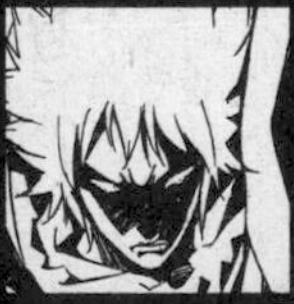

ZEAL
Marauder for Reverse

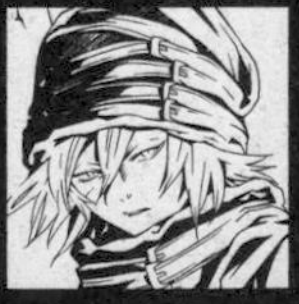

NOIR (FORMERLY GAUCHE SUEDE)
Marauder for Reverse and an ex–Letter Bee

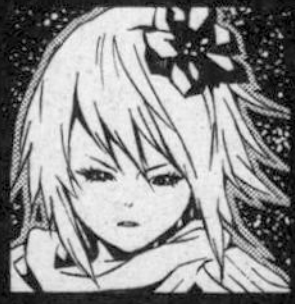

RODA
Noir's Dingo

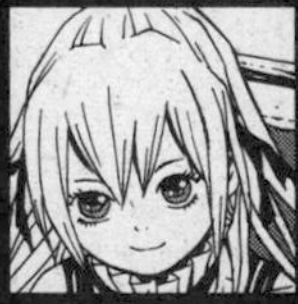

SYLVETTE SUEDE
Gauche's Sister

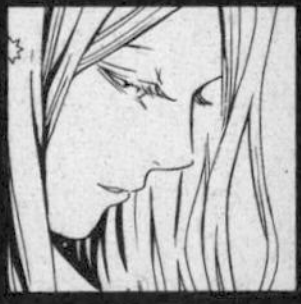

ANNE SEEING
Lag's Mother (Missing)

Tegami Bachi
LETTER · BEE

WUTHERING HEIGHTS

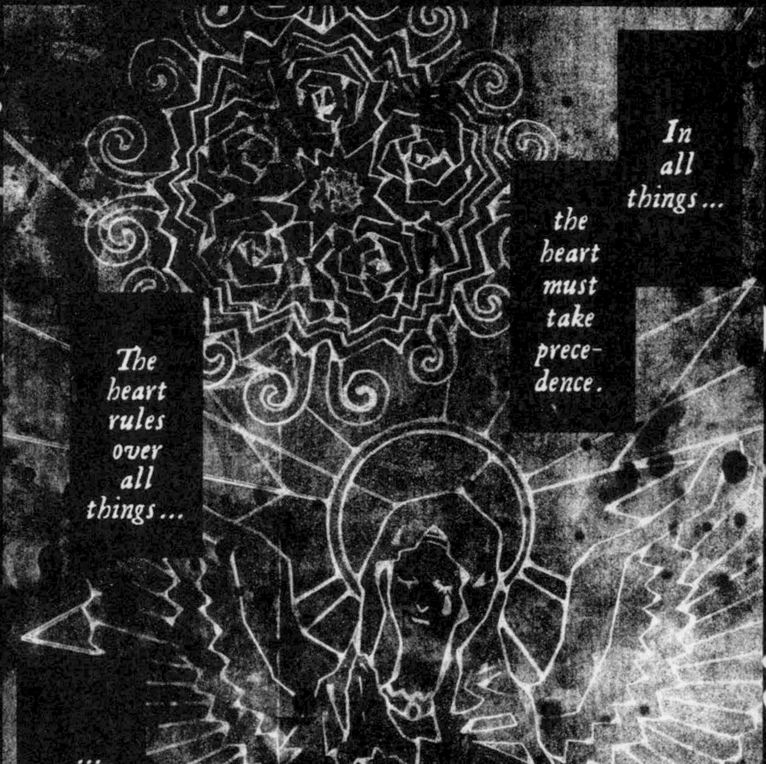
In all things...
the heart must take precedence.
The heart rules over all things...
... and all things come from the heart.
–THE SCRIPTURES OF AMBERGROUND, 1st verse

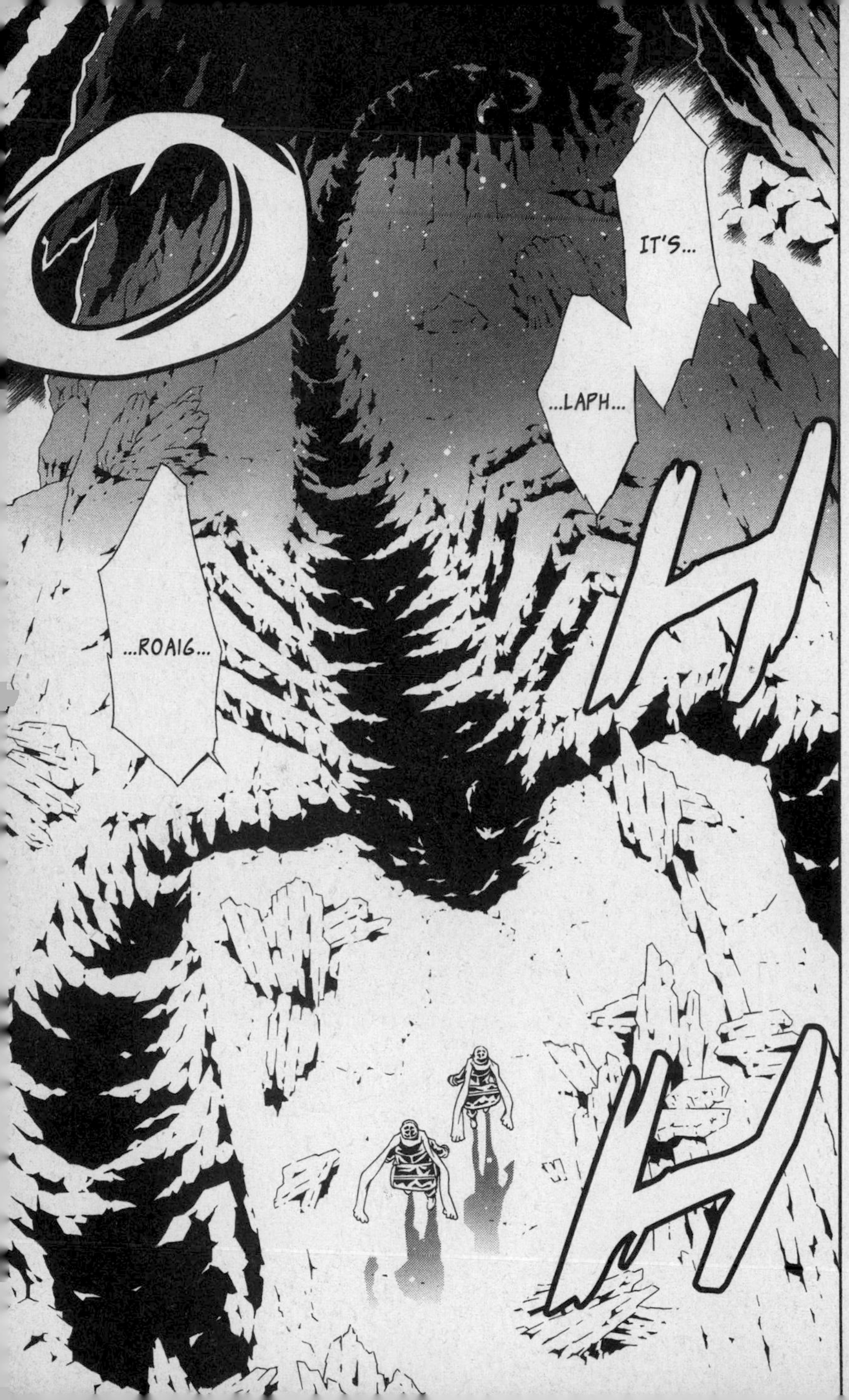
IT'S...
...LAPH...
...ROAIG...

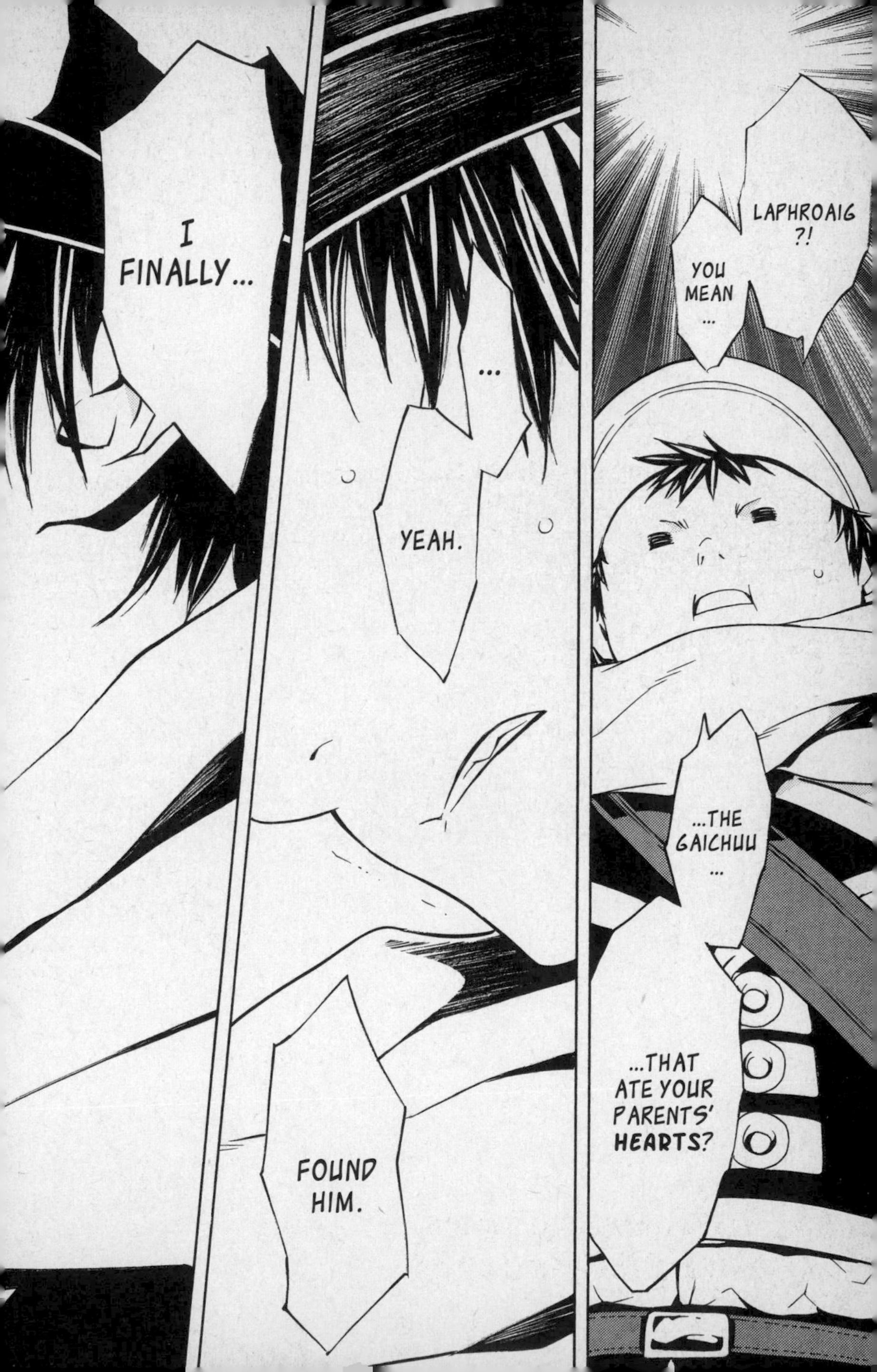
LAPHROAIG ?!
YOU MEAN ...
...THE GAICHUU ...
...THAT ATE YOUR PARENTS' HEARTS?
...
YEAH.
FOUND HIM.
I FINALLY...

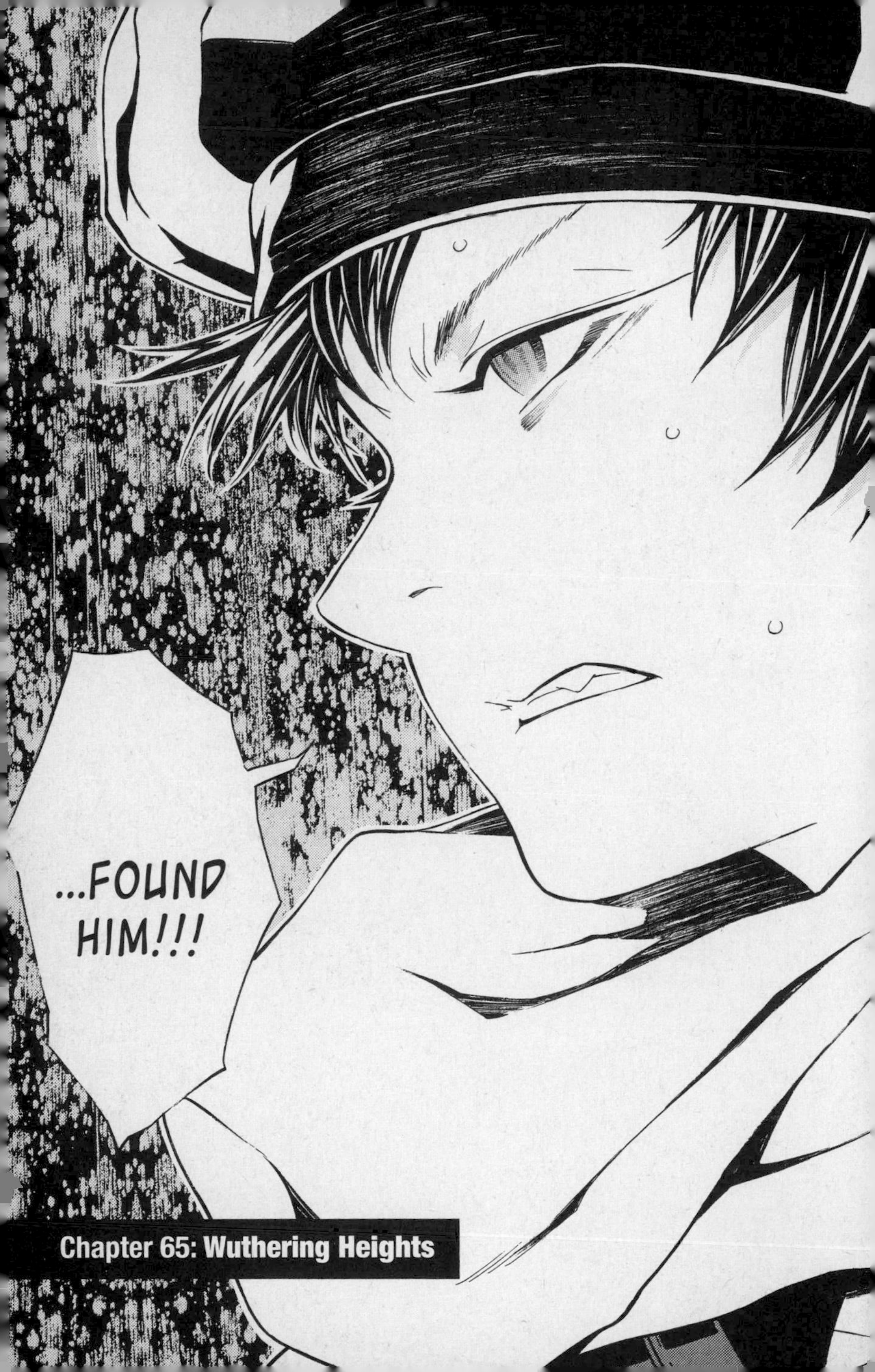
...FOUND HIM!!!
Chapter 65: Wuthering Heights

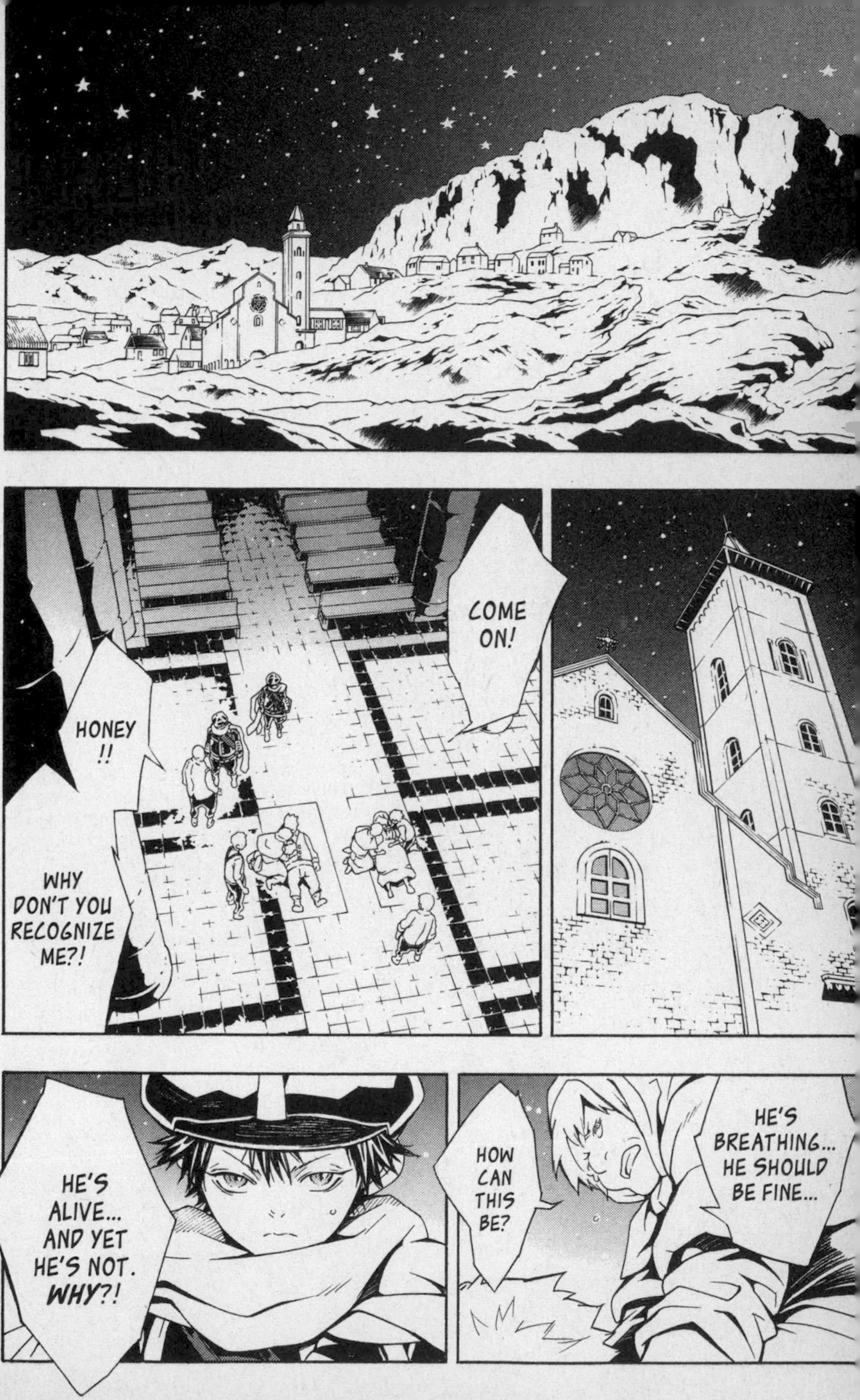
COME ON!
HONEY!!
WHY DON'T YOU RECOGNIZE ME?!
HE'S BREATHING... HE SHOULD BE FINE...
HOW CAN THIS BE?
HE'S ALIVE... AND YET HE'S NOT. *WHY?!*

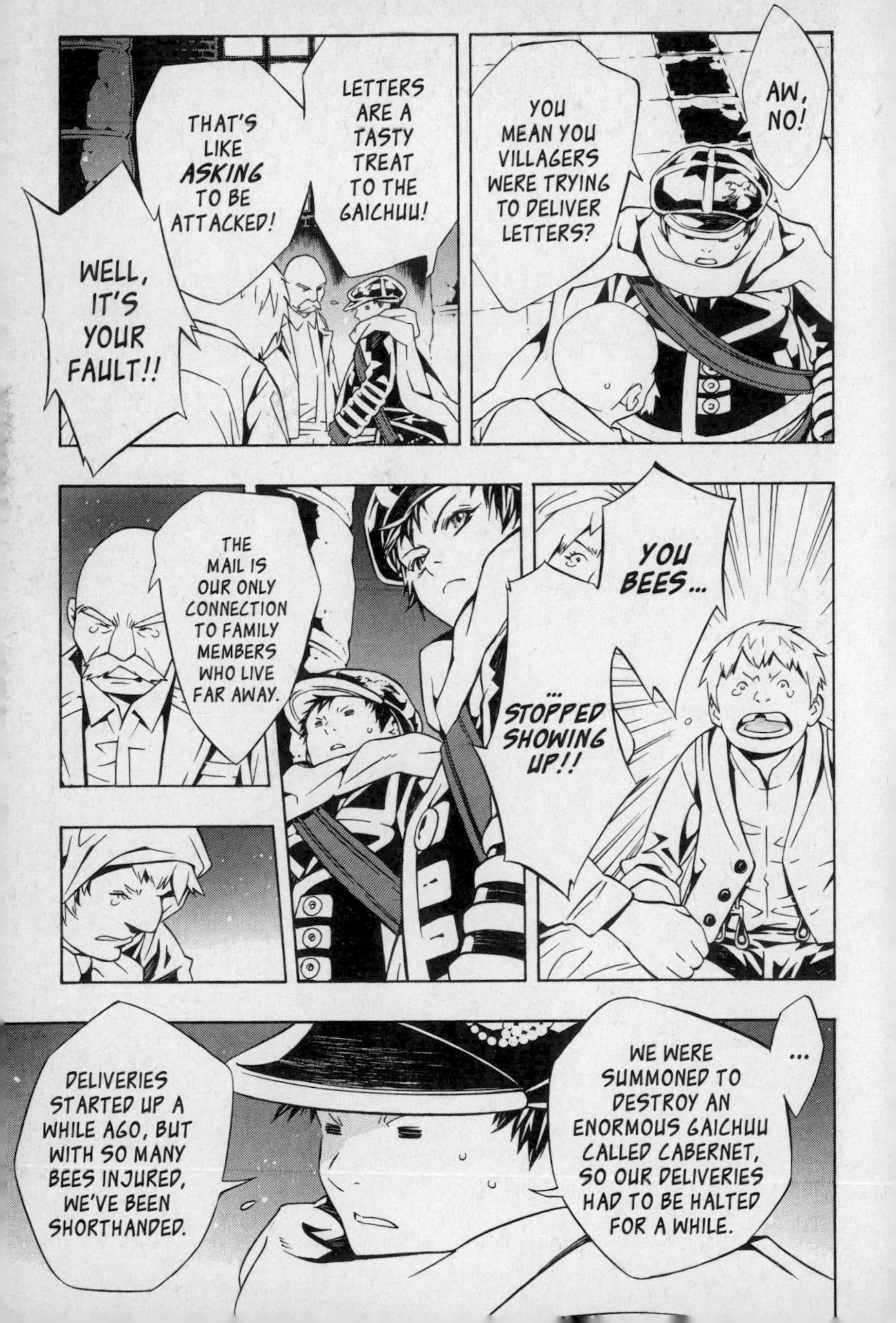
AW, NO!
YOU MEAN YOU VILLAGERS WERE TRYING TO DELIVER LETTERS?
LETTERS ARE A TASTY TREAT TO THE GAICHUU!
THAT'S LIKE *ASKING* TO BE ATTACKED!
WELL, IT'S YOUR FAULT!!
YOU BEES...
...STOPPED SHOWING UP!!
THE MAIL IS OUR ONLY CONNECTION TO FAMILY MEMBERS WHO LIVE FAR AWAY.
...
WE WERE SUMMONED TO DESTROY AN ENORMOUS GAICHUU CALLED CABERNET, SO OUR DELIVERIES HAD TO BE HALTED FOR A WHILE.
DELIVERIES STARTED UP A WHILE AGO, BUT WITH SO MANY BEES INJURED, WE'VE BEEN SHORTHANDED.

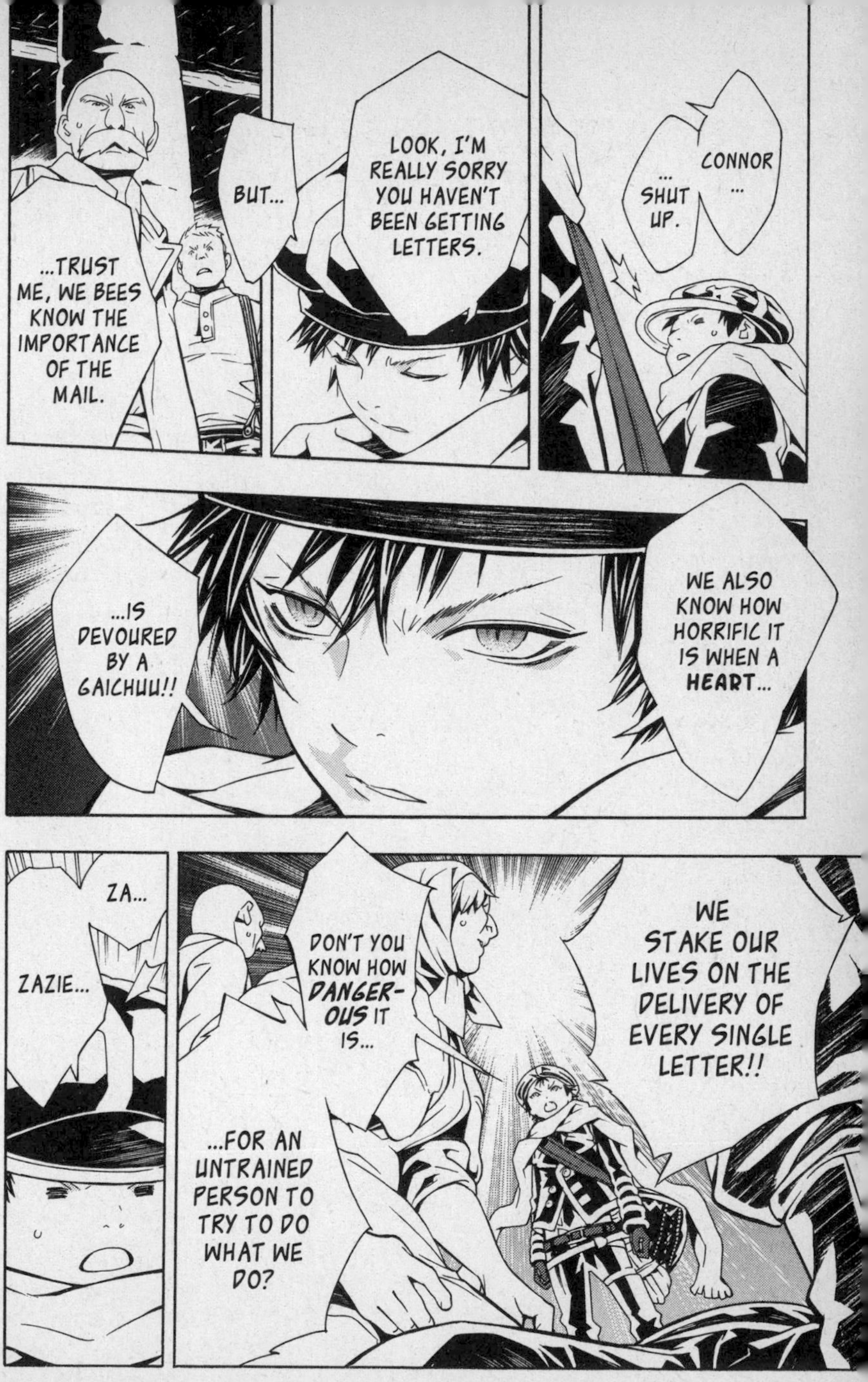
CONNOR ...
... SHUT UP.
LOOK, I'M REALLY SORRY YOU HAVEN'T BEEN GETTING LETTERS.
BUT...
...TRUST ME, WE BEES KNOW THE IMPORTANCE OF THE MAIL.
WE ALSO KNOW HOW HORRIFIC IT IS WHEN A **HEART**...
...IS DEVOURED BY A GAICHUU!!
WE STAKE OUR LIVES ON THE DELIVERY OF EVERY SINGLE LETTER!!
DON'T YOU KNOW HOW ***DANGEROUS*** IT IS...
...FOR AN UNTRAINED PERSON TO TRY TO DO WHAT WE DO?
ZA...
ZAZIE...

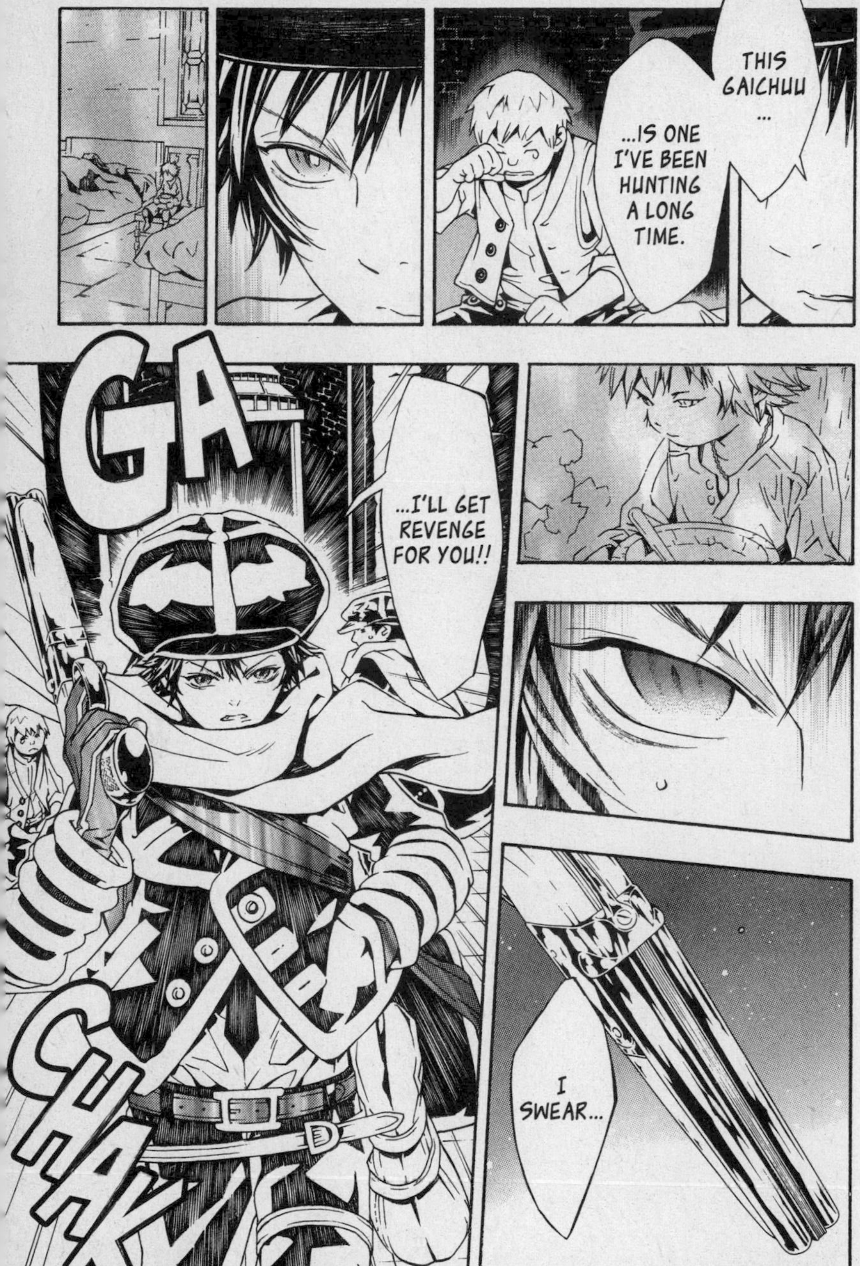
THIS GAICHUU ...
...IS ONE I'VE BEEN HUNTING A LONG TIME.
I SWEAR...
GA
...I'LL GET REVENGE FOR YOU!!
CHAK

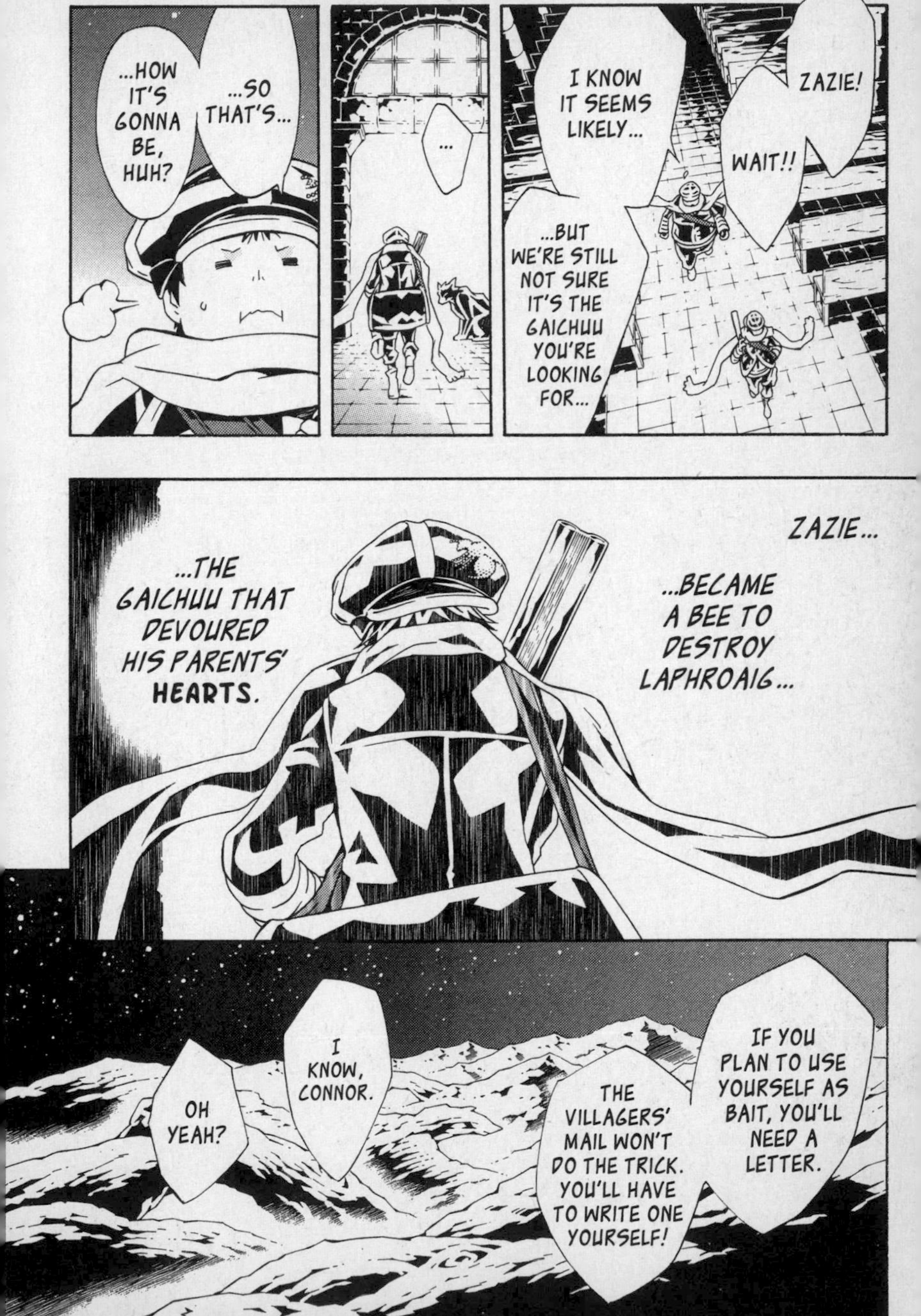
ZAZIE!
WAIT!!
I KNOW IT SEEMS LIKELY...
...BUT WE'RE STILL NOT SURE IT'S THE GAICHUU YOU'RE LOOKING FOR...
...
...SO THAT'S...
...HOW IT'S GONNA BE, HUH?
ZAZIE...
...BECAME A BEE TO DESTROY LAPHROAIG...
...THE GAICHUU THAT DEVOURED HIS PARENTS' HEARTS.
IF YOU PLAN TO USE YOURSELF AS BAIT, YOU'LL NEED A LETTER.
THE VILLAGERS' MAIL WON'T DO THE TRICK. YOU'LL HAVE TO WRITE ONE YOURSELF!
I KNOW, CONNOR.
OH YEAH?

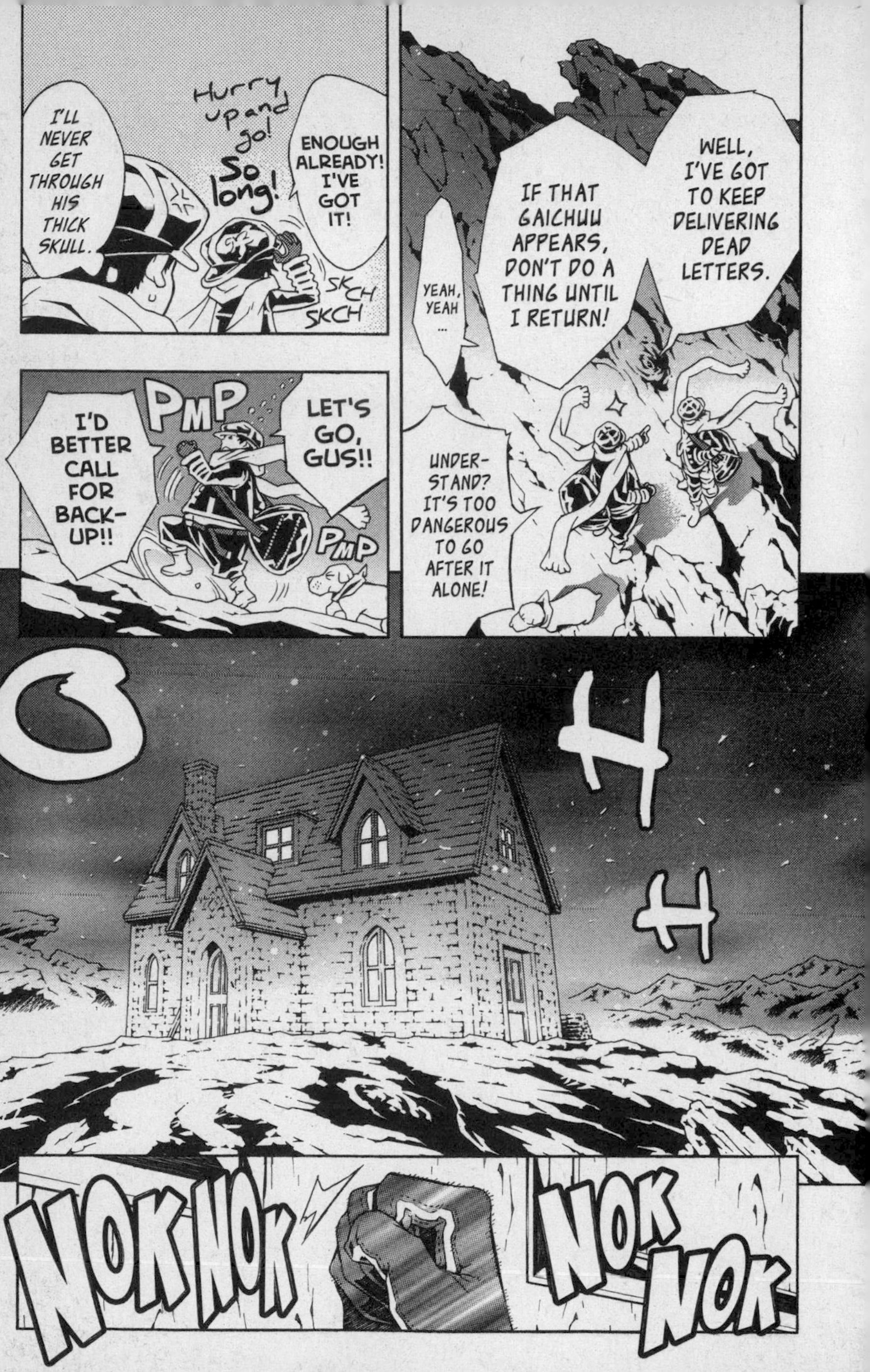
WELL, I'VE GOT TO KEEP DELIVERING DEAD LETTERS.
IF THAT GAICHUU APPEARS, DON'T DO A THING UNTIL I RETURN!
YEAH, YEAH ...
UNDER-STAND? IT'S TOO DANGEROUS TO GO AFTER IT ALONE!
ENOUGH ALREADY! I'VE GOT IT!
So long!
Hurry up and go!
I'LL NEVER GET THROUGH HIS THICK SKULL.
SKCH SKCH
LET'S GO, GUS!!
PMP
I'D BETTER CALL FOR BACK-UP!!
PMP
NOK NOK
NOK NOK

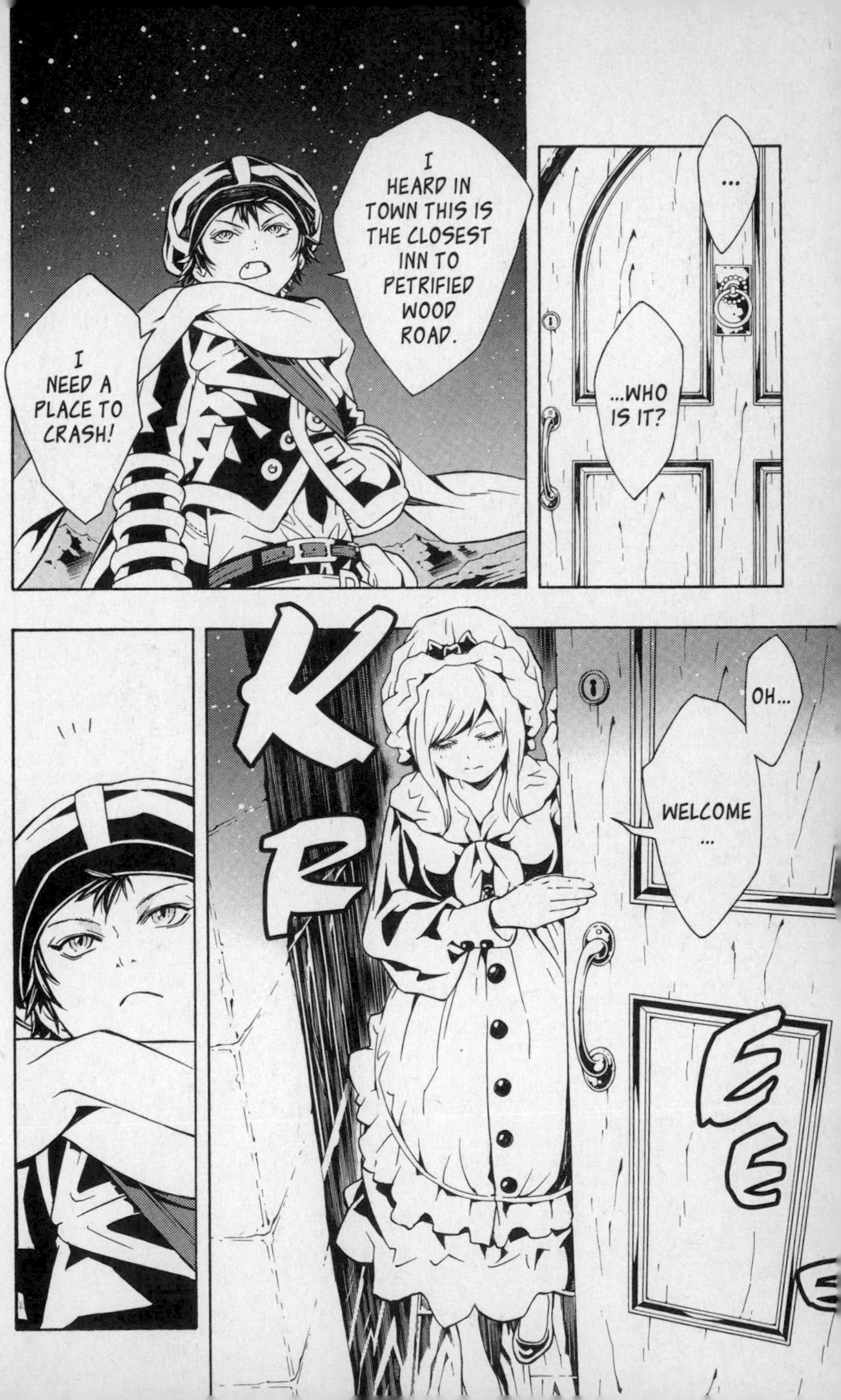
...
...WHO IS IT?
I HEARD IN TOWN THIS IS THE CLOSEST INN TO PETRIFIED WOOD ROAD.
I NEED A PLACE TO CRASH!
KREEE
OH...
WELCOME
...

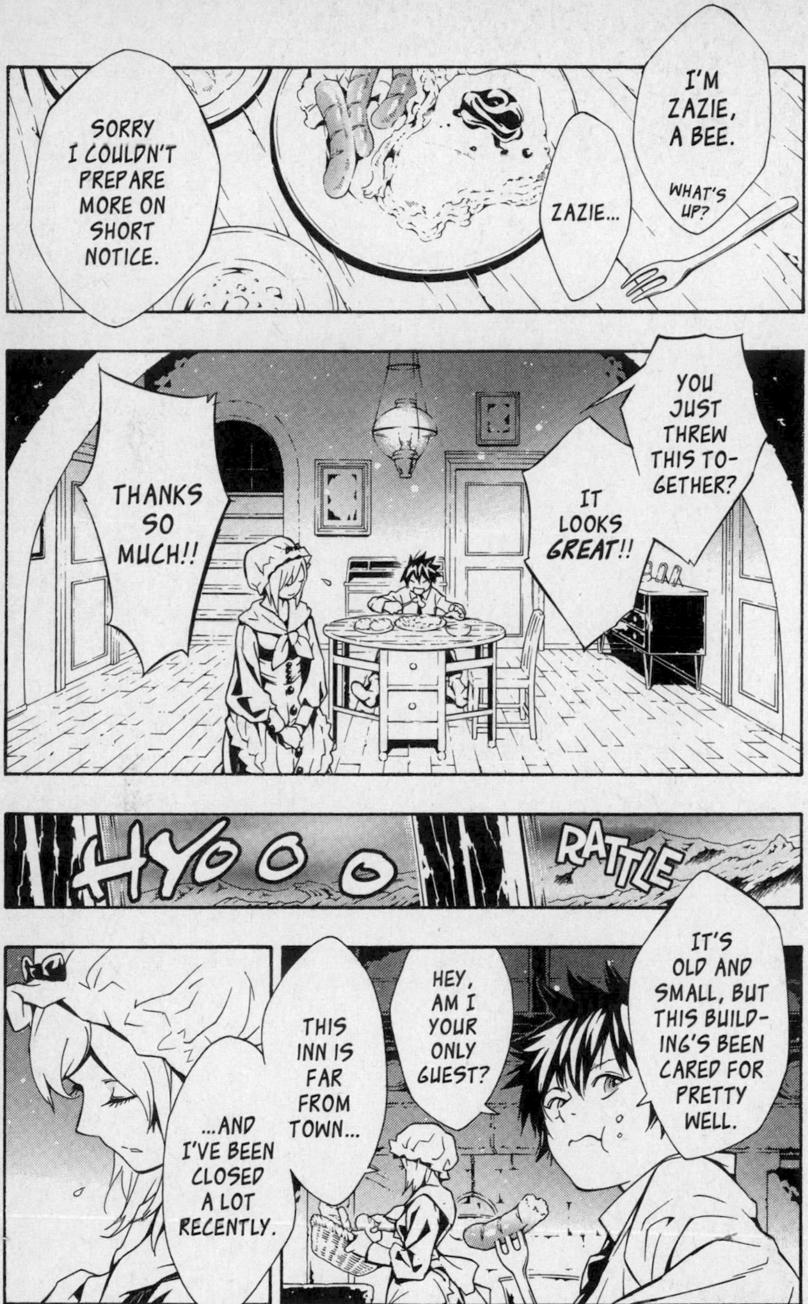
I'M ZAZIE, A BEE.
WHAT'S UP?
ZAZIE...
SORRY I COULDN'T PREPARE MORE ON SHORT NOTICE.
YOU JUST THREW THIS TO-GETHER?
IT LOOKS GREAT!!
THANKS SO MUCH!!
RATTLE
HYOOO
IT'S OLD AND SMALL, BUT THIS BUILD-ING'S BEEN CARED FOR PRETTY WELL.
HEY, AM I YOUR ONLY GUEST?
THIS INN IS FAR FROM TOWN...
...AND I'VE BEEN CLOSED A LOT RECENTLY.

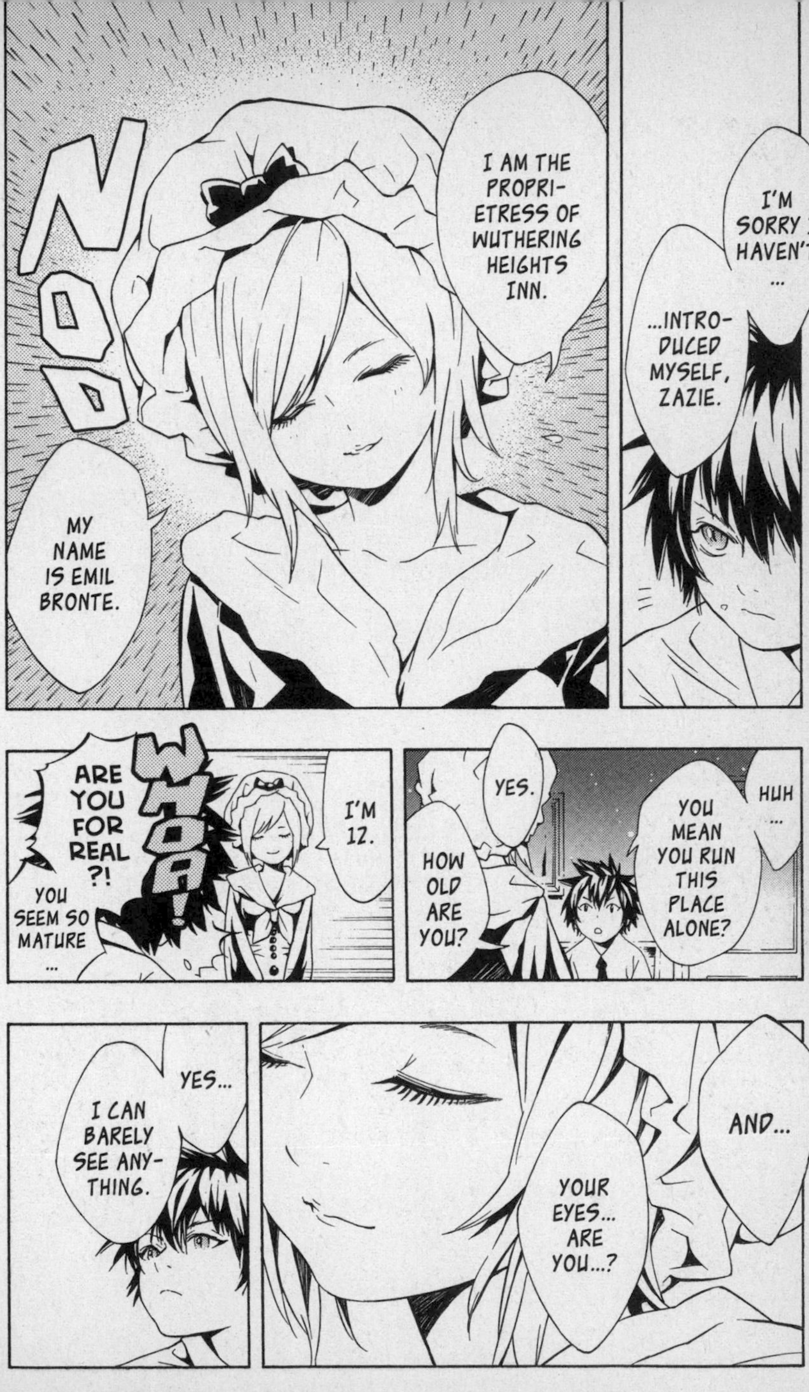
I'M SORRY I HAVEN'T ...
...INTRODUCED MYSELF, ZAZIE.
I AM THE PROPRIETRESS OF WUTHERING HEIGHTS INN.
NOD
MY NAME IS EMIL BRONTE.
HUH ...
YOU MEAN YOU RUN THIS PLACE ALONE?
YES.
HOW OLD ARE YOU?
I'M 12.
WHOA!
ARE YOU FOR REAL ?!
YOU SEEM SO MATURE ...
AND...
YOUR EYES... ARE YOU...?
YES...
I CAN BARELY SEE ANYTHING.

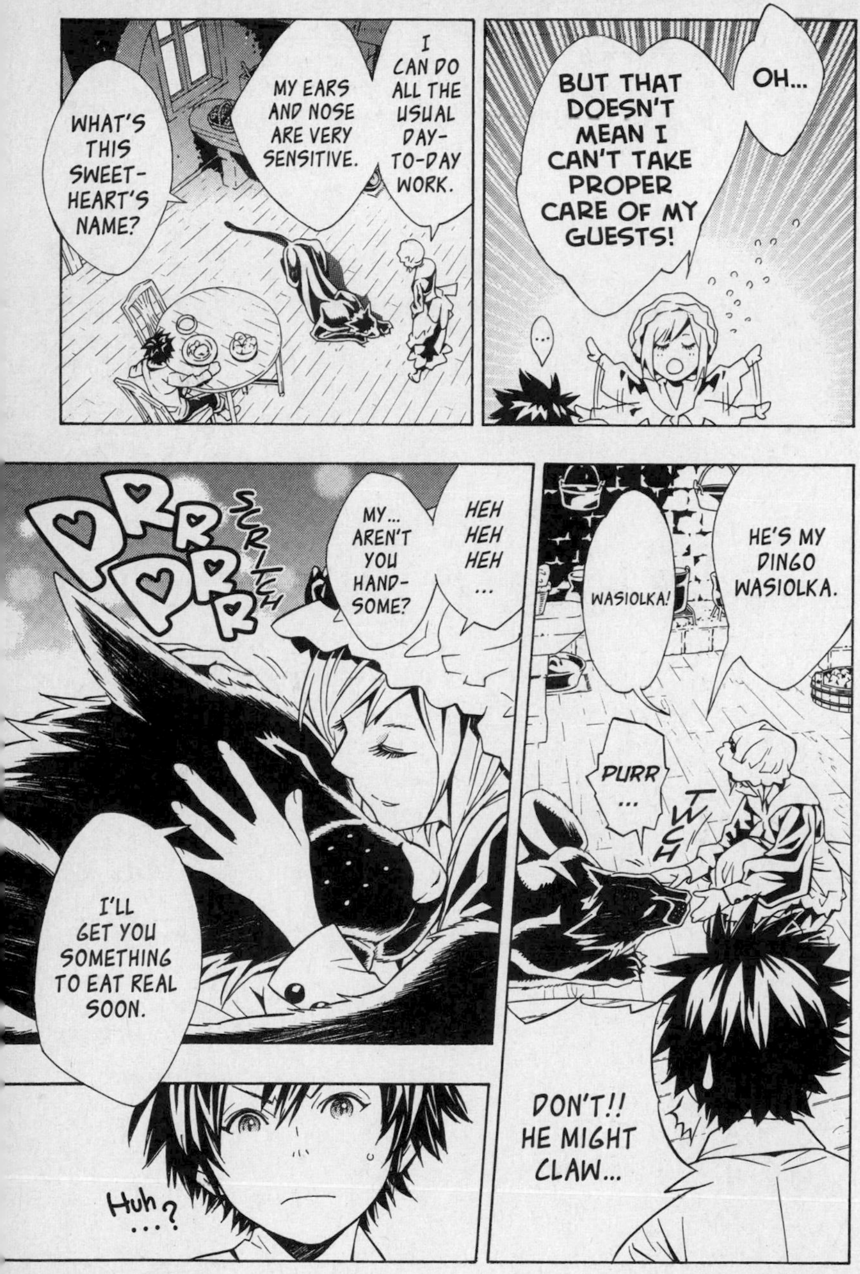
OH...
BUT THAT DOESN'T MEAN I CAN'T TAKE PROPER CARE OF MY GUESTS!
...
I CAN DO ALL THE USUAL DAY-TO-DAY WORK.
MY EARS AND NOSE ARE VERY SENSITIVE.
WHAT'S THIS SWEET-HEART'S NAME?
HE'S MY DINGO WASIOLKA.
WASIOLKA!
PURR ...
TWITCH
DON'T!! HE MIGHT CLAW...
HEH HEH HEH ...
MY... AREN'T YOU HAND-SOME?
SCRITCH
PRR PRR
I'LL GET YOU SOMETHING TO EAT REAL SOON.
Huh ...?

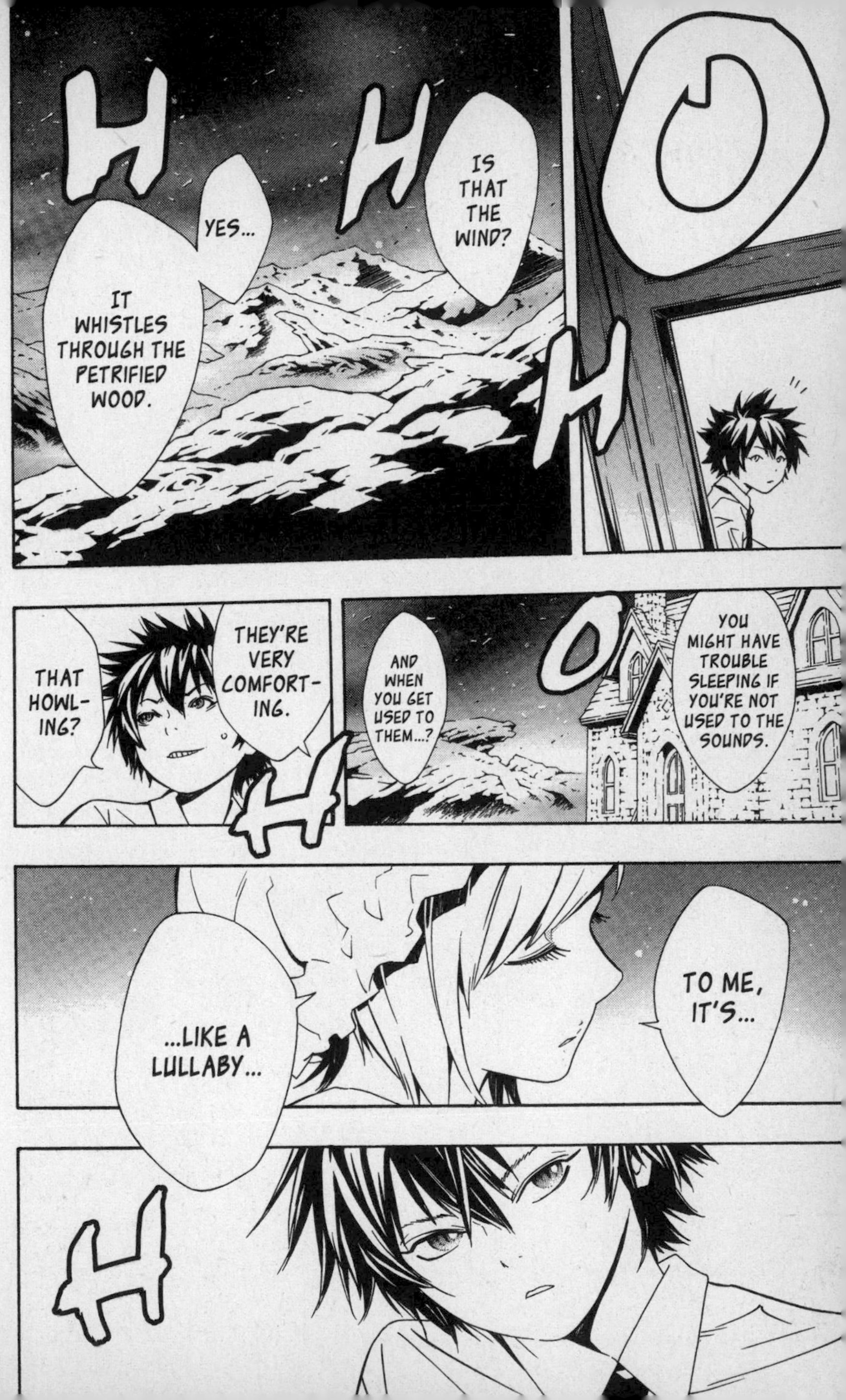

O
H
H
IS THAT THE WIND?
H
YES...
IT WHISTLES THROUGH THE PETRIFIED WOOD.
O
YOU MIGHT HAVE TROUBLE SLEEPING IF YOU'RE NOT USED TO THE SOUNDS.
AND WHEN YOU GET USED TO THEM...?
H
THEY'RE VERY COMFORT-ING.
THAT HOWL-ING?
TO ME, IT'S...
...LIKE A LULLABY...
H

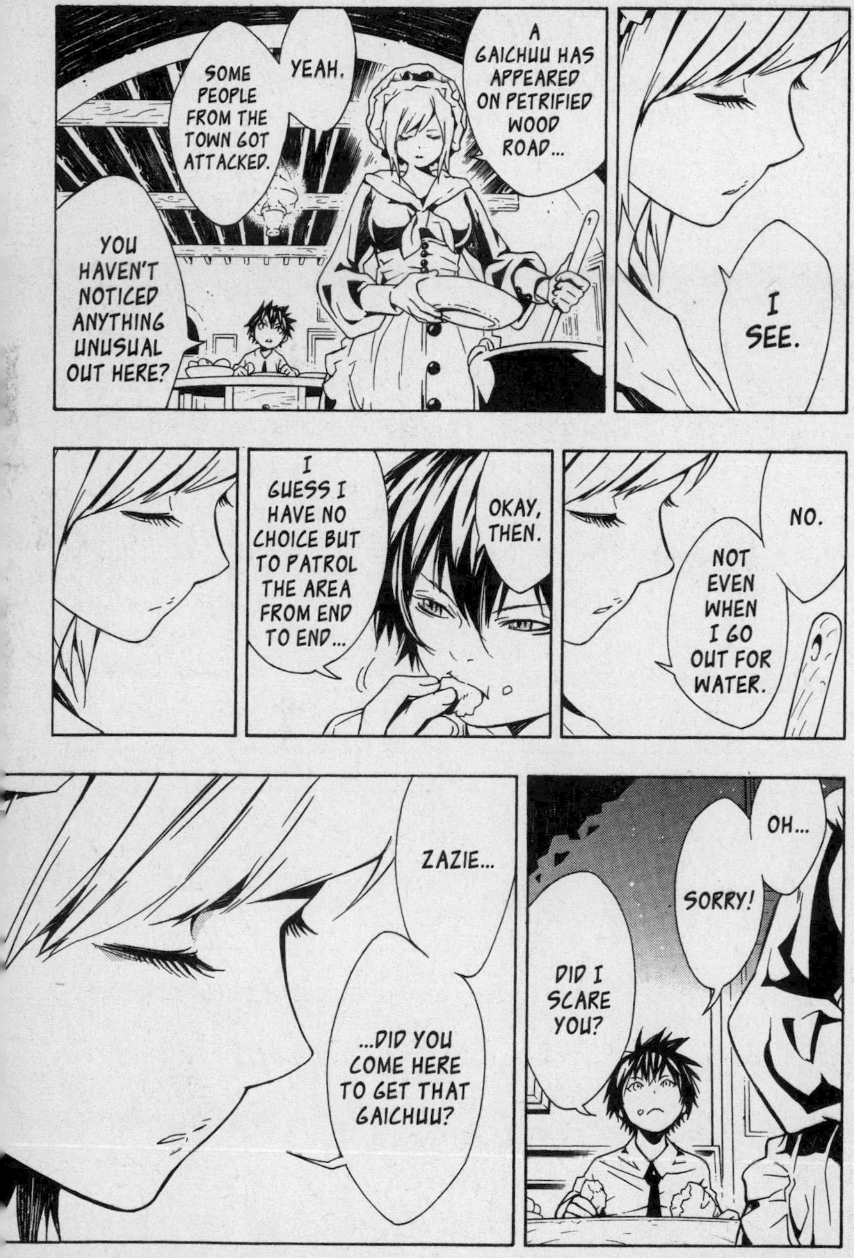
I SEE.
A GAICHUU HAS APPEARED ON PETRIFIED WOOD ROAD...
YEAH.
SOME PEOPLE FROM THE TOWN GOT ATTACKED.
YOU HAVEN'T NOTICED ANYTHING UNUSUAL OUT HERE?
NO.
NOT EVEN WHEN I GO OUT FOR WATER.
OKAY, THEN.
I GUESS I HAVE NO CHOICE BUT TO PATROL THE AREA FROM END TO END...
OH...
SORRY!
DID I SCARE YOU?
ZAZIE...
...DID YOU COME HERE TO GET THAT GAICHUU?

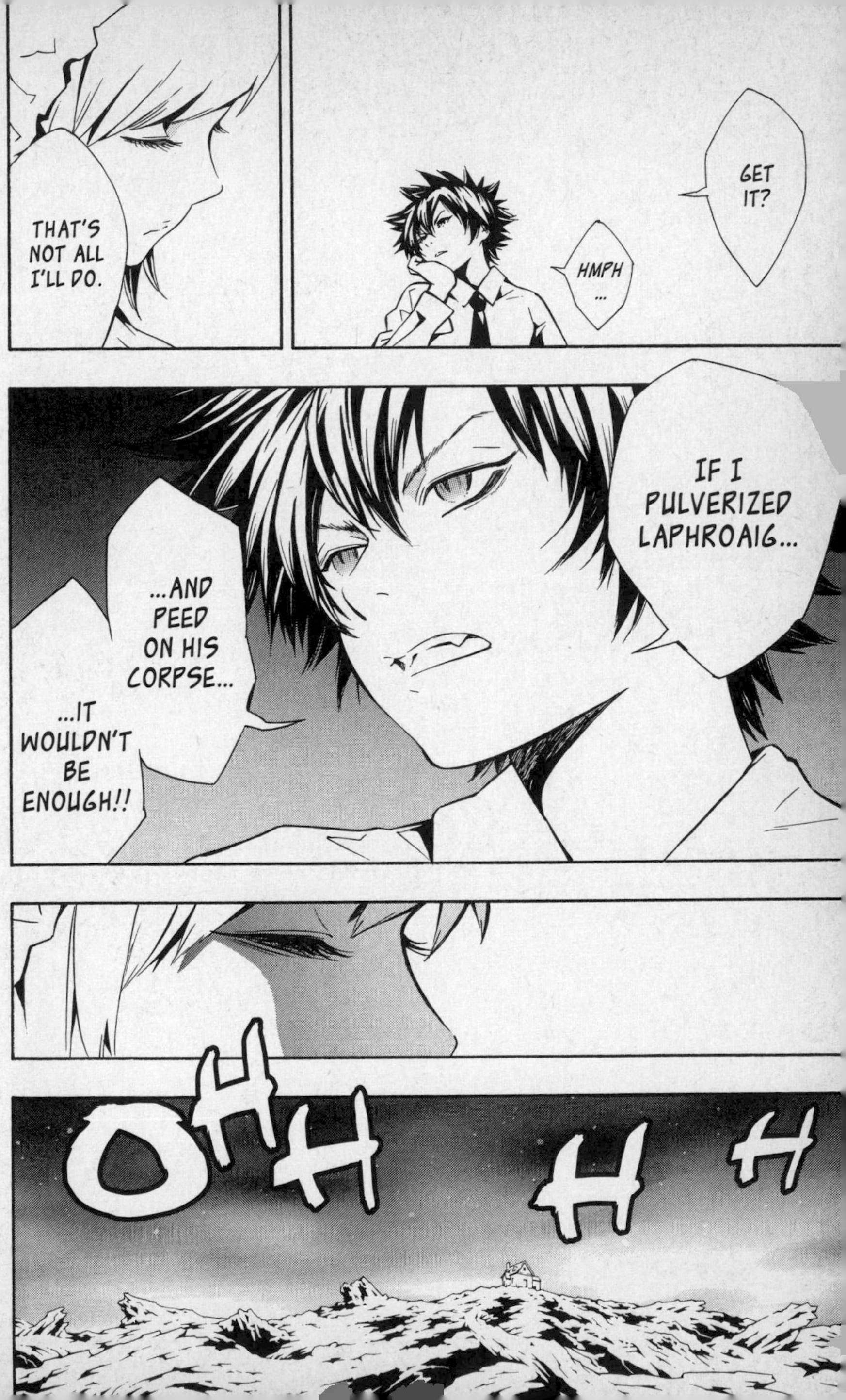
GET IT?
HMPH...
THAT'S NOT ALL I'LL DO.
IF I PULVERIZED LAPHROAIG...
...AND PEED ON HIS CORPSE...
...IT WOULDN'T BE ENOUGH!!
OHH H H

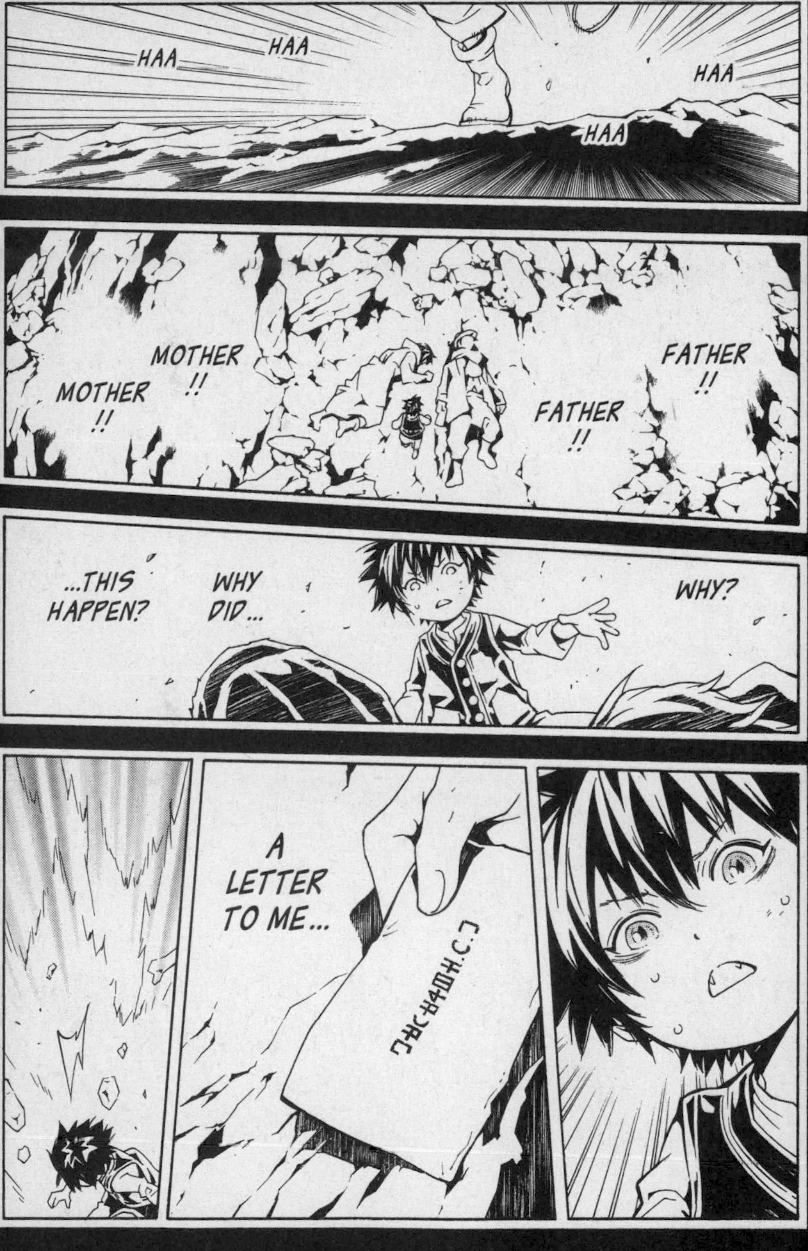
HAA
HAA
HAA
HAA
FATHER !!
FATHER !!
MOTHER !!
MOTHER !!
WHY?
WHY DID...
...THIS HAPPEN?
A LETTER TO ME...

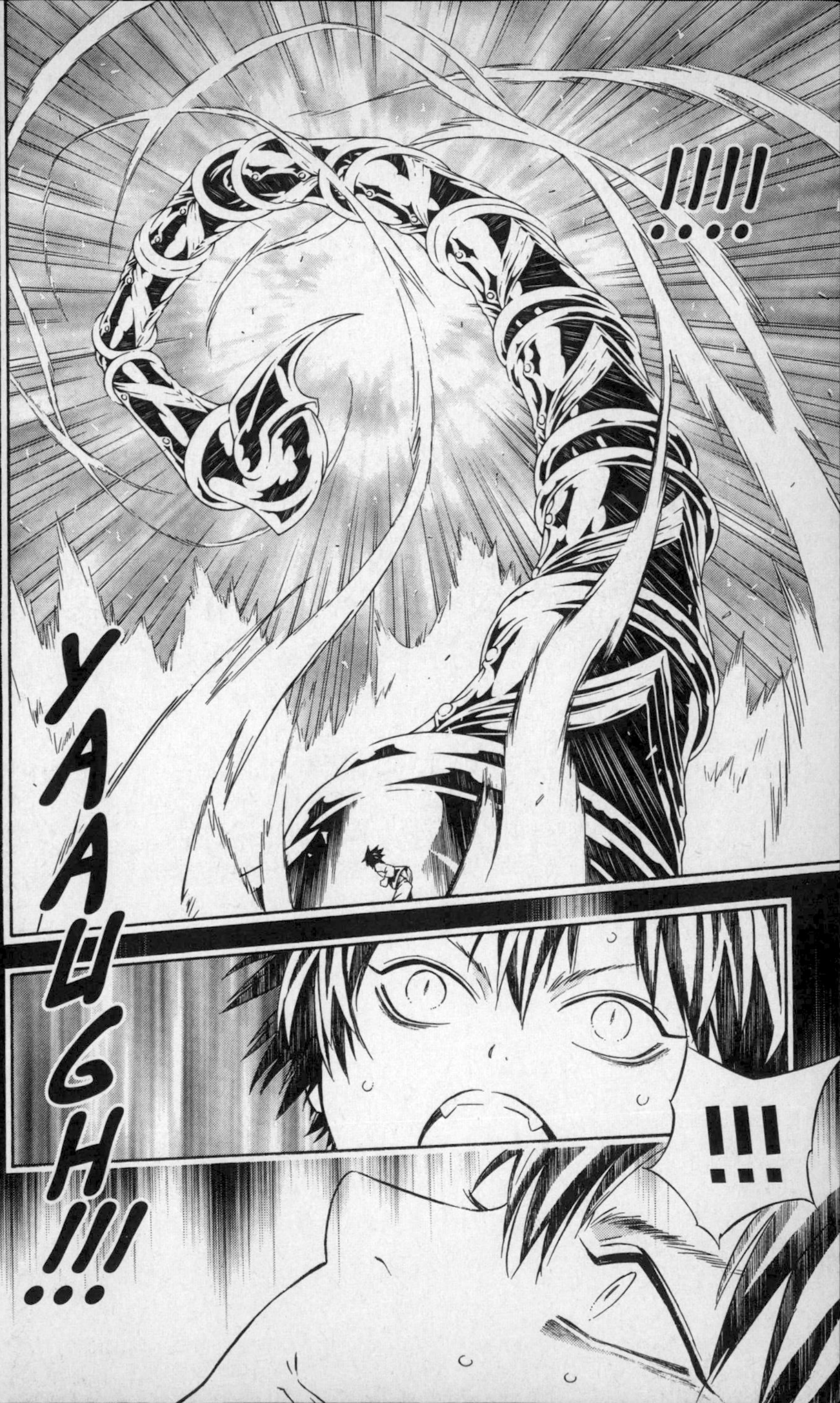

!!!!
YAAUGH!!!
!!!

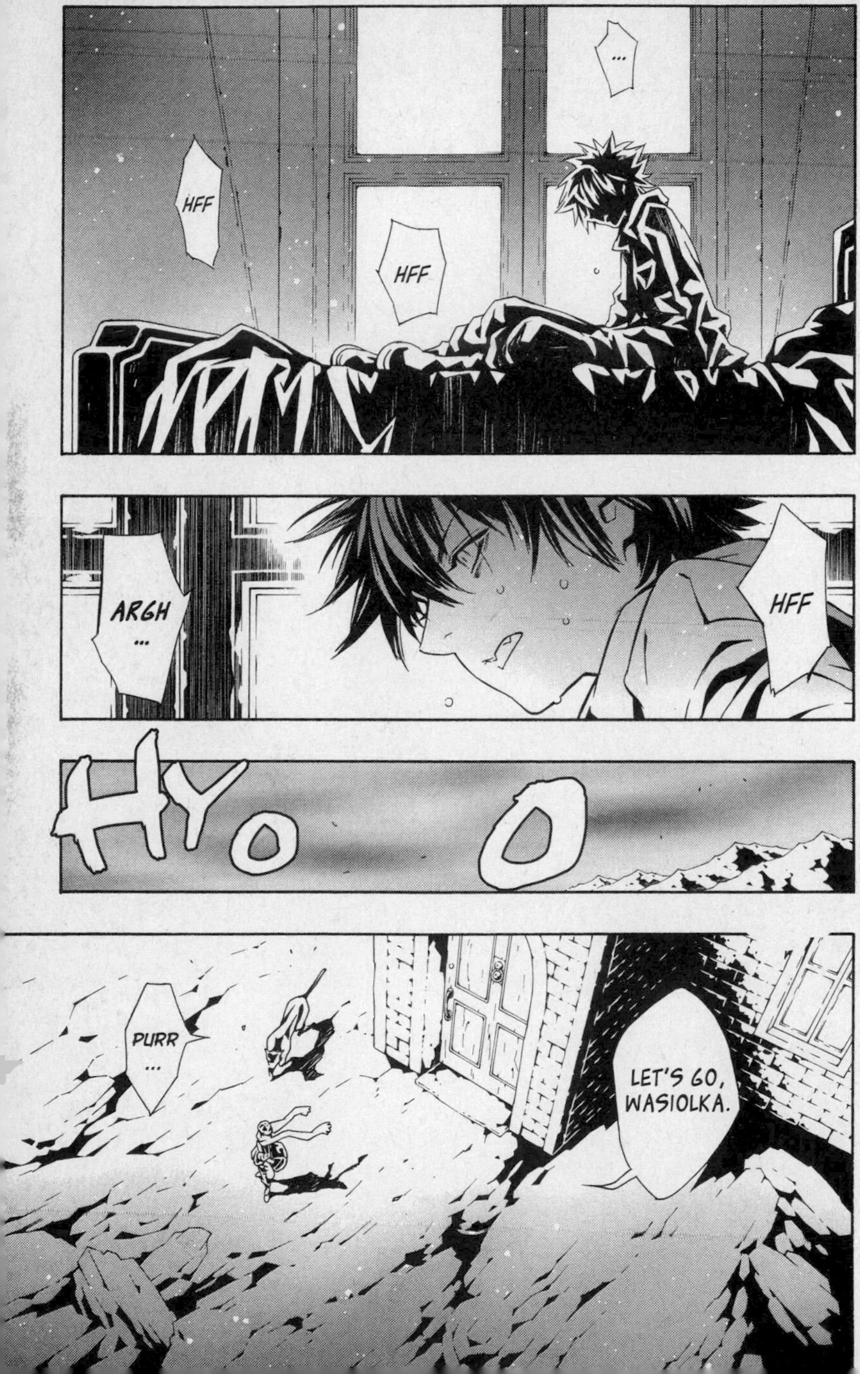
...
HFF
HFF
HFF
ARGH ...
HYO O
LET'S GO, WASIOLKA.
PURR ...

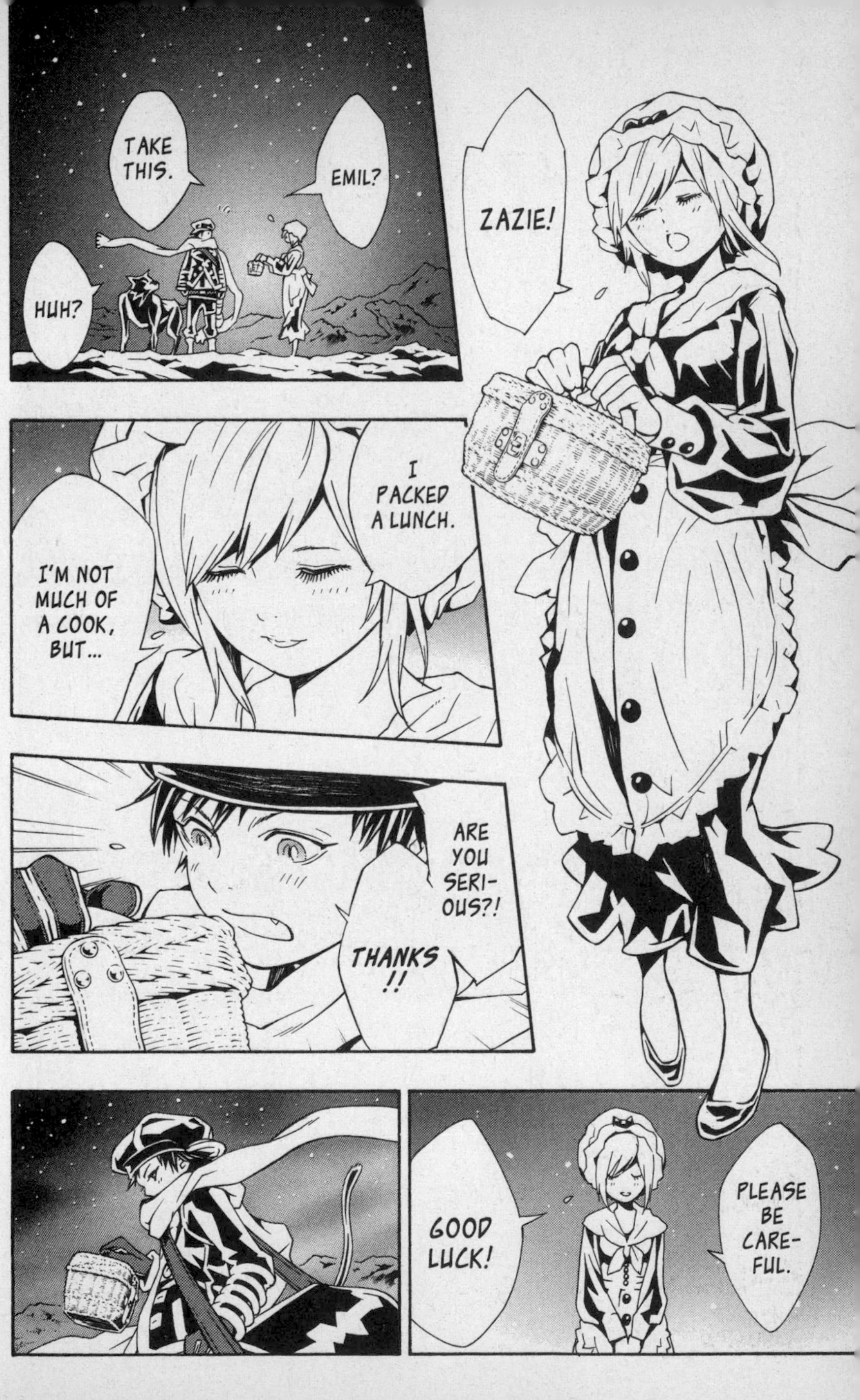
ZAZIE!
EMIL?
TAKE THIS.
HUH?
I PACKED A LUNCH.
I'M NOT MUCH OF A COOK, BUT...
ARE YOU SERI-OUS?!
THANKS!!
PLEASE BE CARE-FUL.
GOOD LUCK!

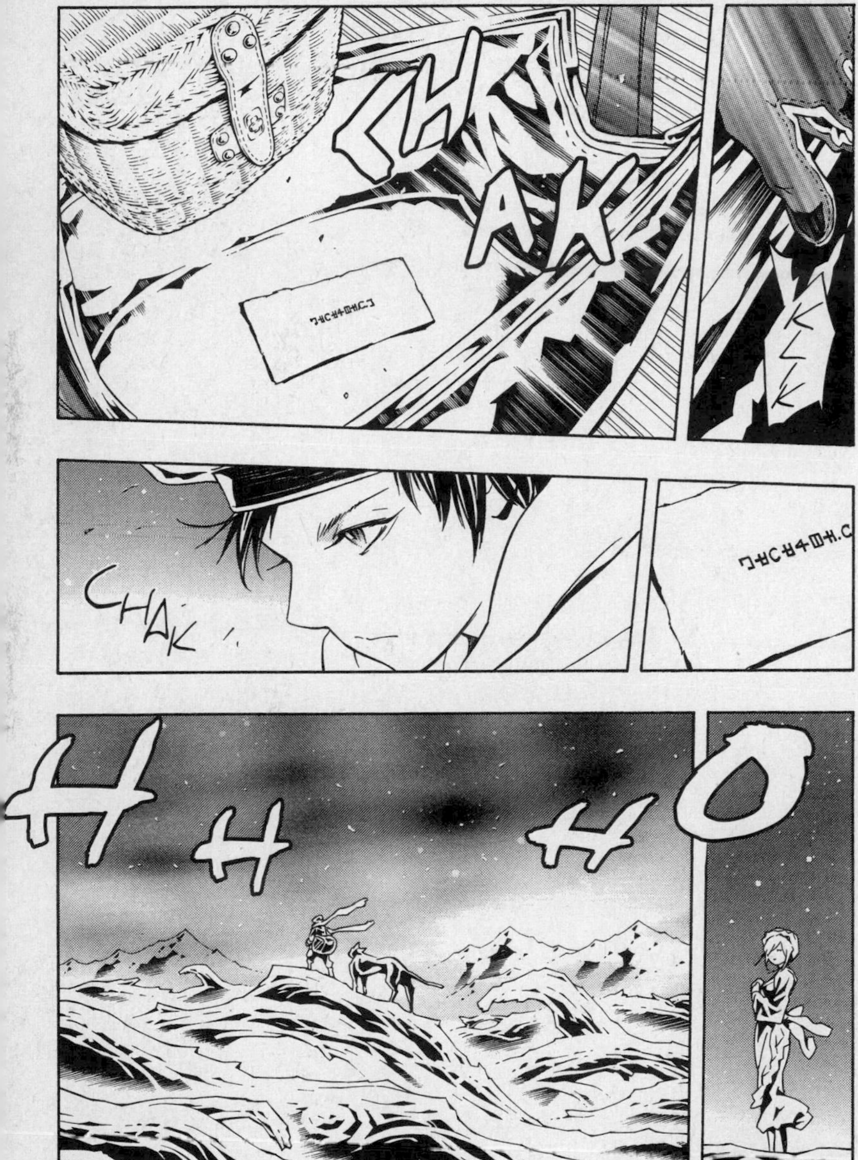
KLIK
CHAK
CHAK
HHHO

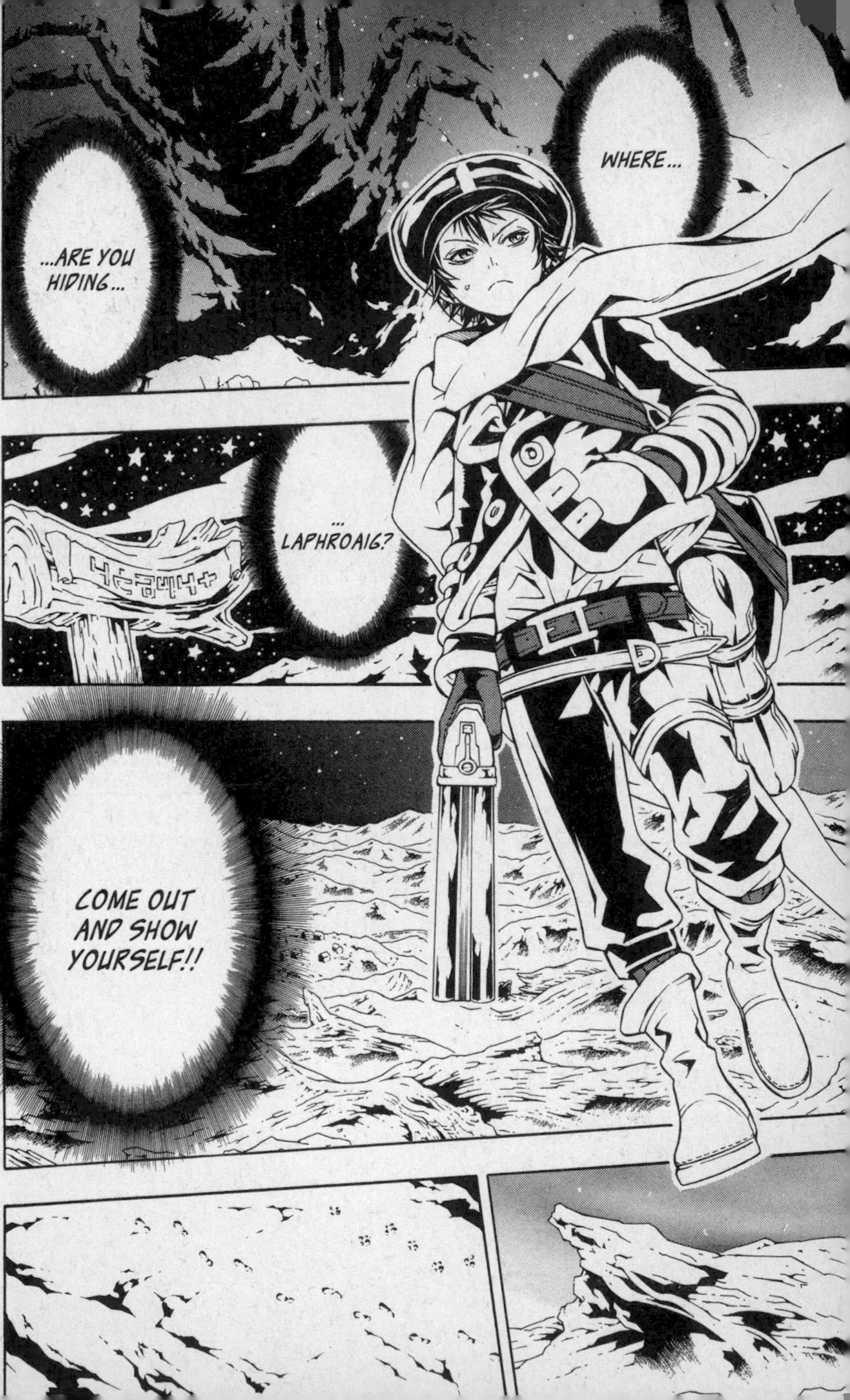
WHERE...
...ARE YOU HIDING...
... LAPHROAIG?
COME OUT AND SHOW YOURSELF!!

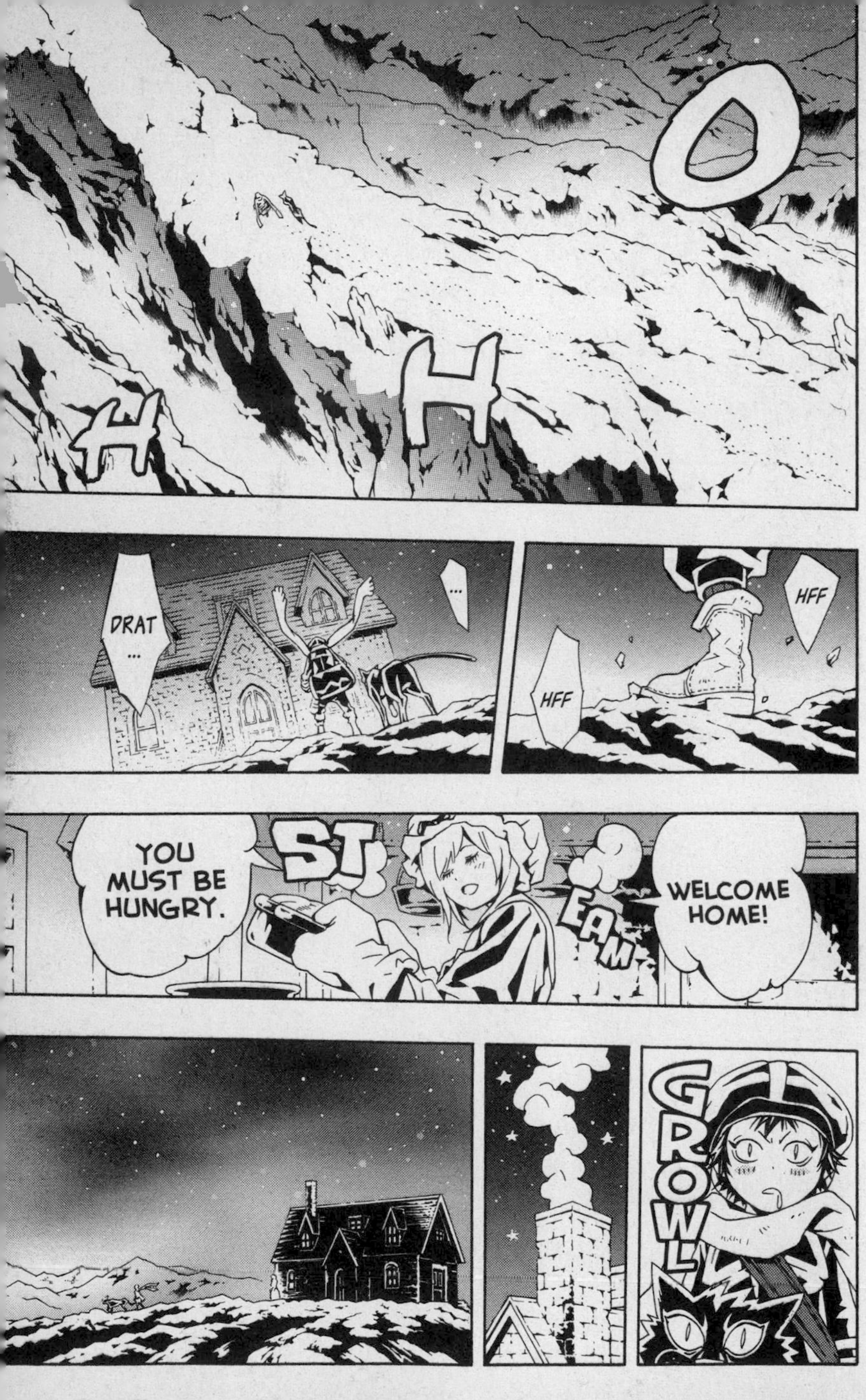
O
H
H
HFF
HFF
...
DRAT ...
WELCOME HOME!
ST
EAM
YOU MUST BE HUNGRY.
GROWL

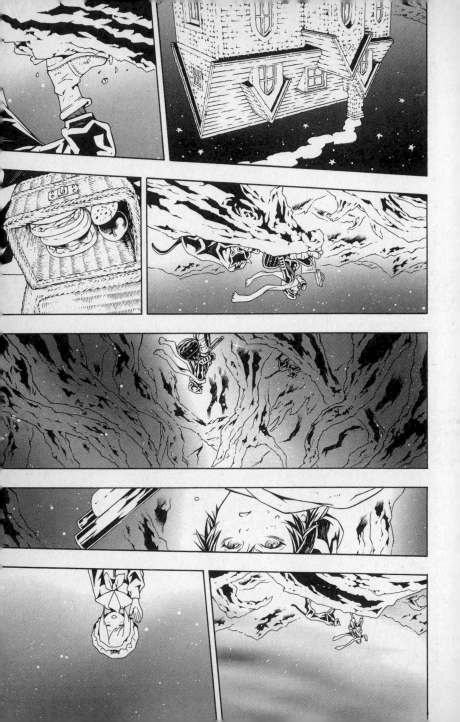

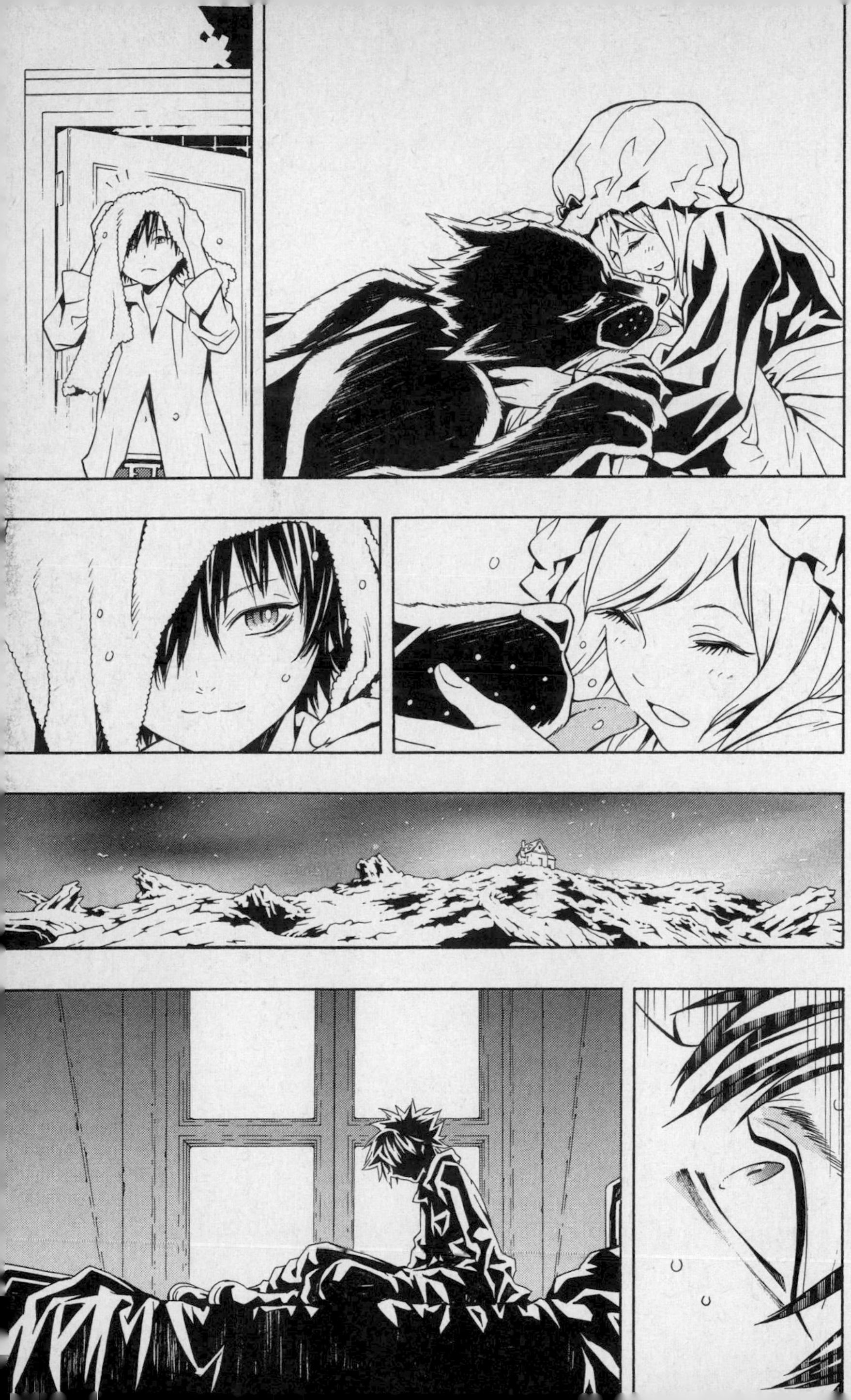

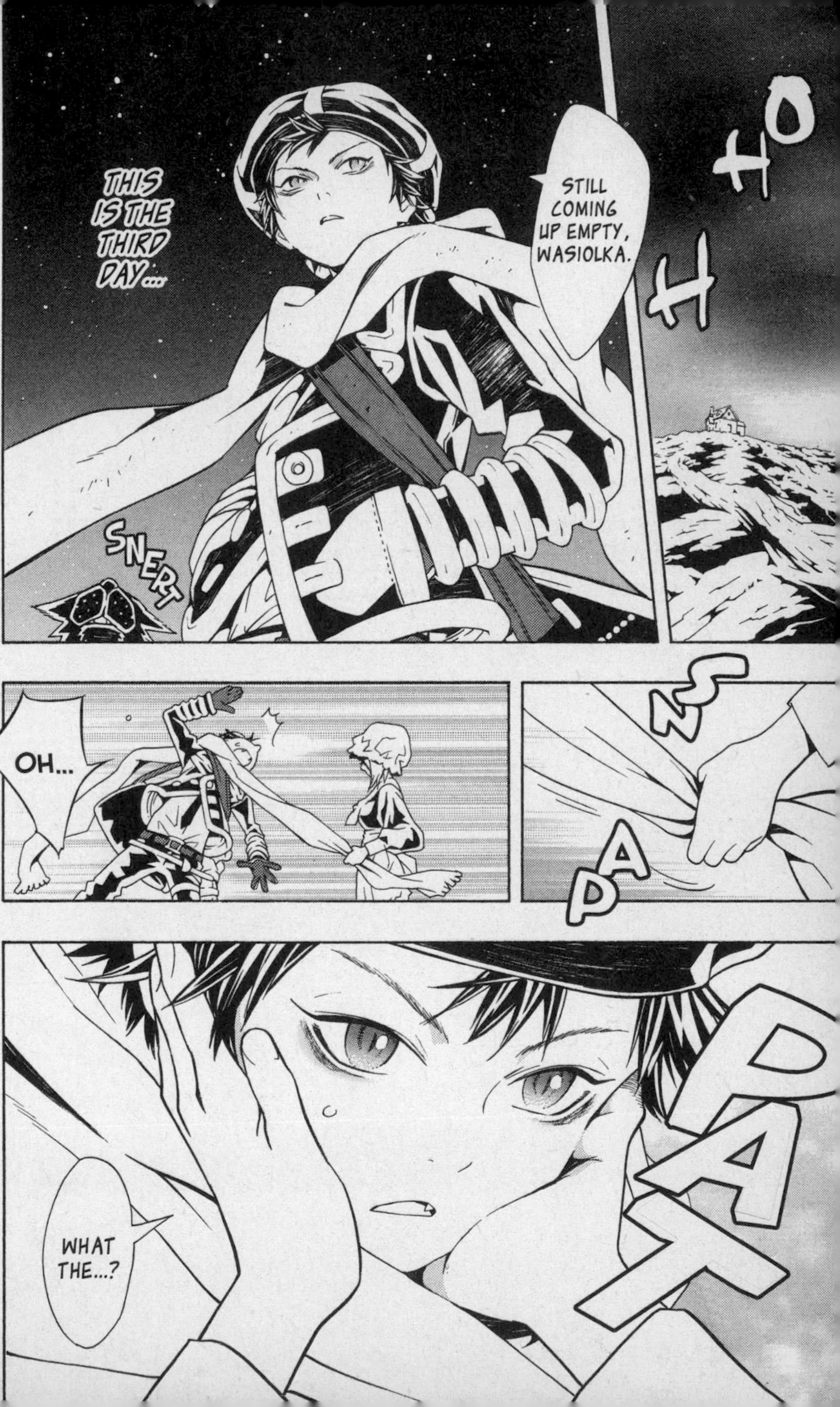
HO
H
STILL COMING UP EMPTY, WASIOLKA.
THIS IS THE THIRD DAY...
SNERT
SNAP
OH...
PAT
WHAT THE...?

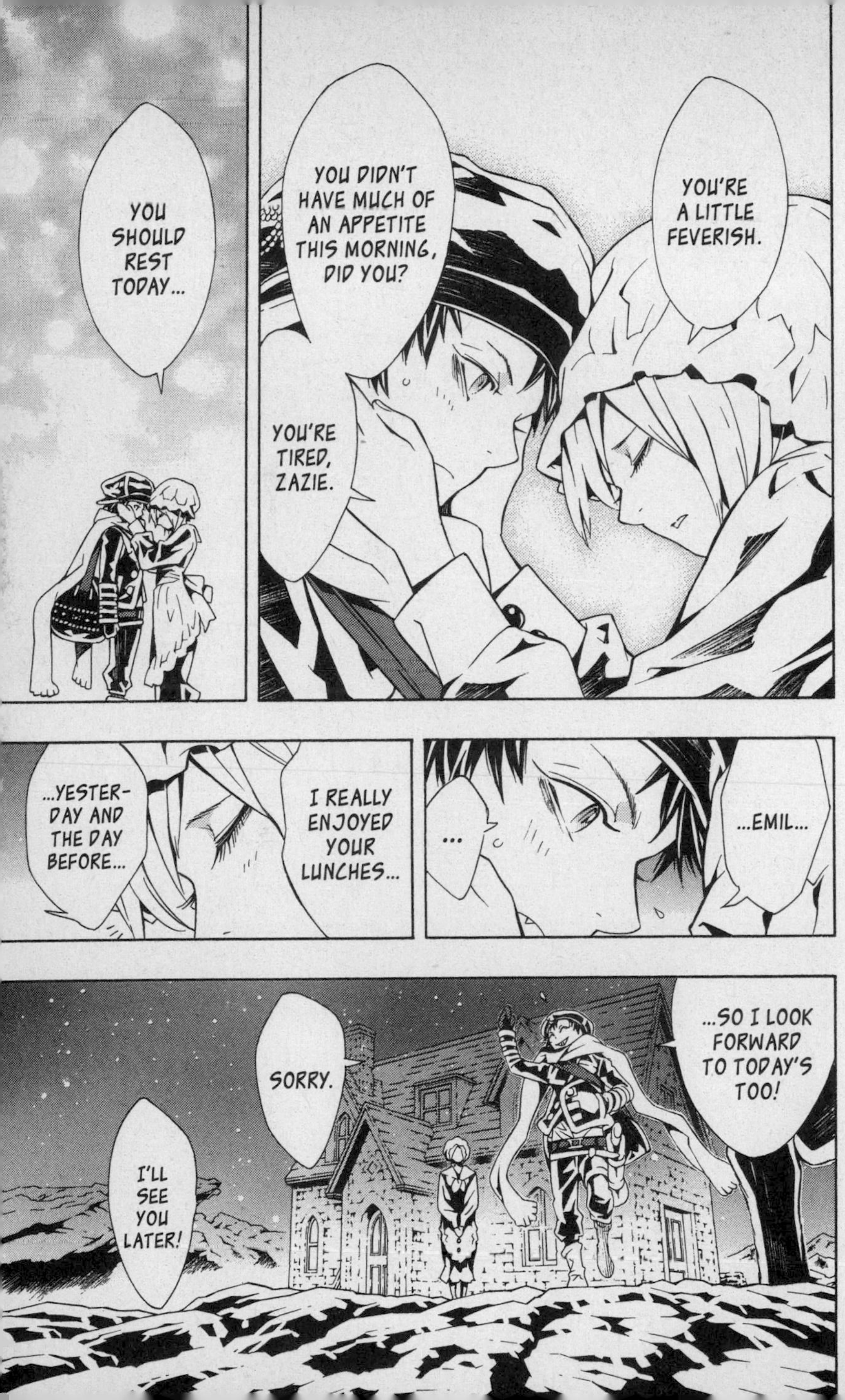
YOU'RE A LITTLE FEVERISH.
YOU DIDN'T HAVE MUCH OF AN APPETITE THIS MORNING, DID YOU?
YOU'RE TIRED, ZAZIE.
YOU SHOULD REST TODAY...
...EMIL...
...
I REALLY ENJOYED YOUR LUNCHES...
...YESTER-DAY AND THE DAY BEFORE...
...SO I LOOK FORWARD TO TODAY'S TOO!
SORRY.
I'LL SEE YOU LATER!

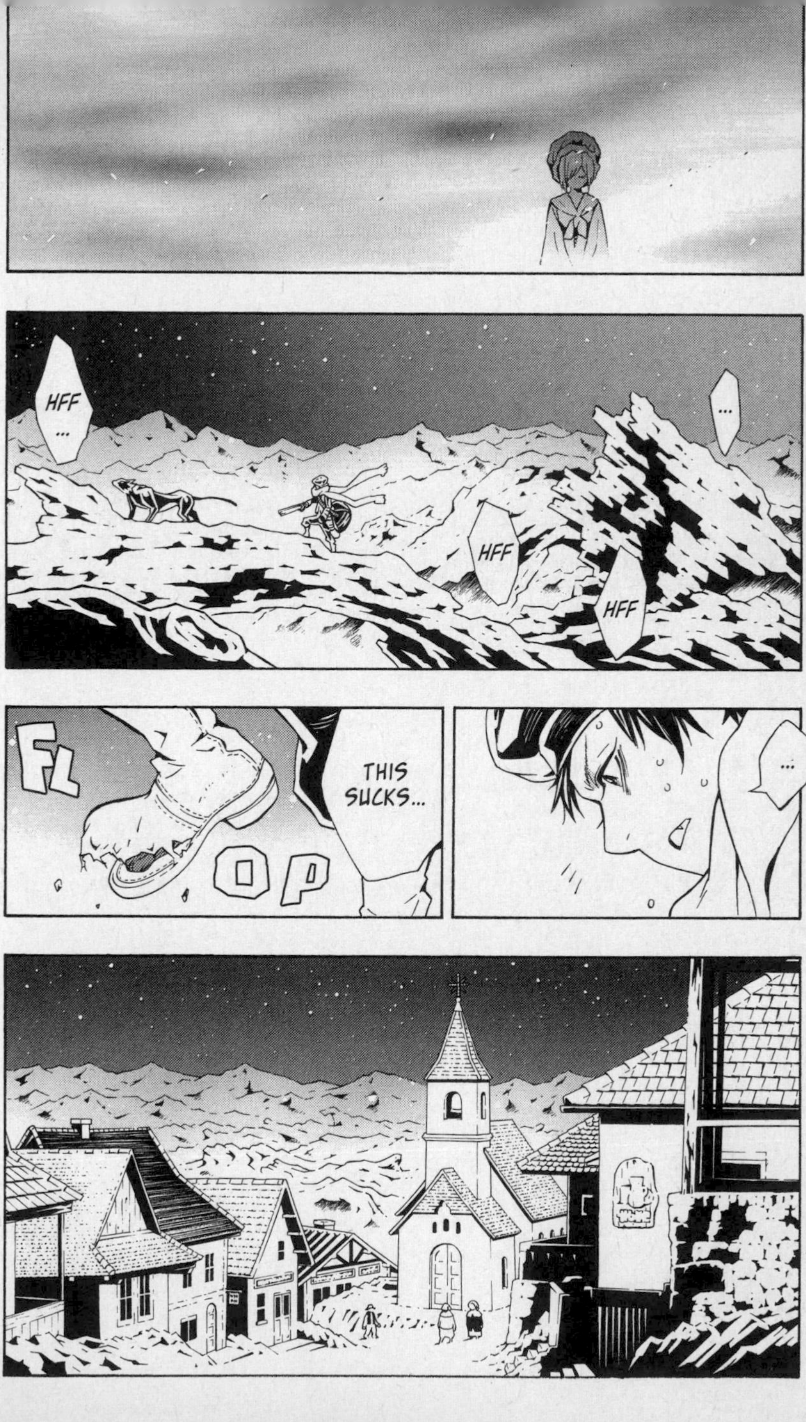
...
HFF
HFF
HFF
...
...
THIS
SUCKS...
FL
OP

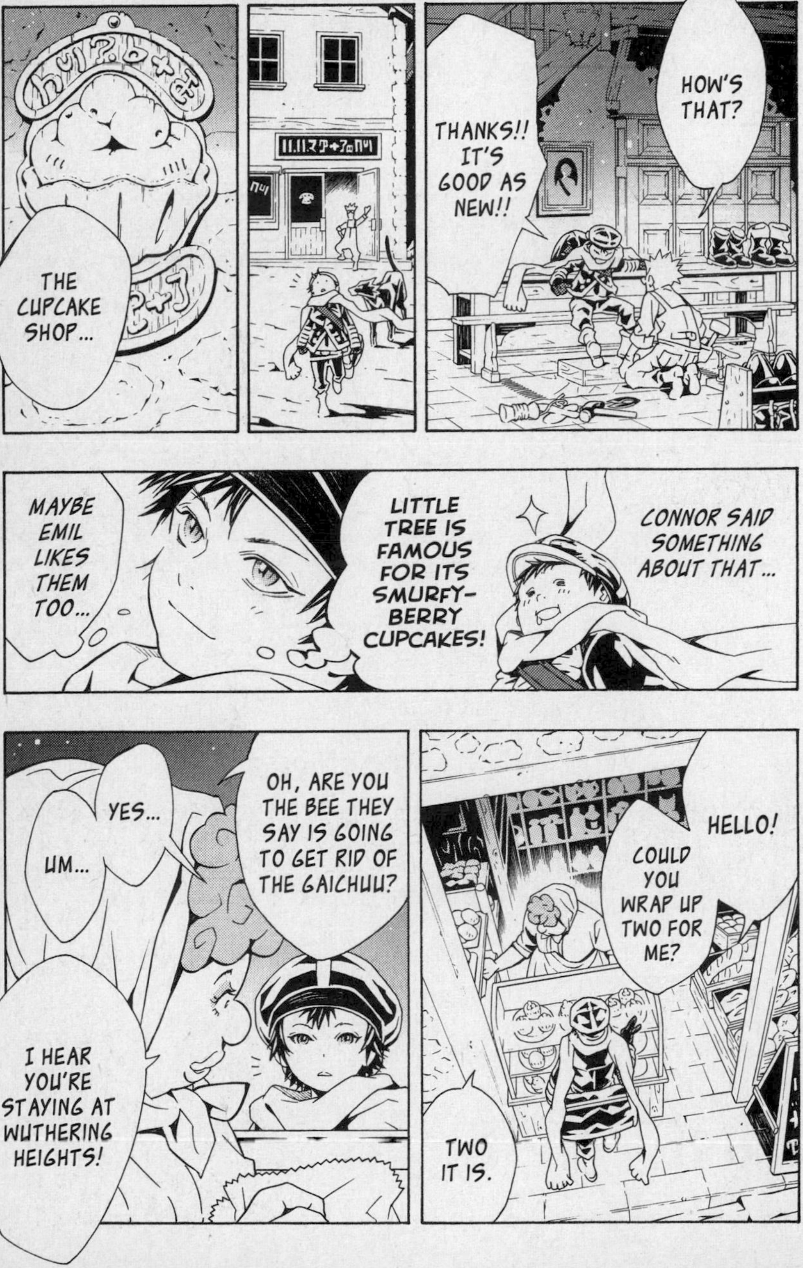
HOW'S THAT?
THANKS!! IT'S GOOD AS NEW!!
THE CUPCAKE SHOP...
CONNOR SAID SOMETHING ABOUT THAT...
LITTLE TREE IS FAMOUS FOR ITS SMURFY-BERRY CUPCAKES!
MAYBE EMIL LIKES THEM TOO...
HELLO!
COULD YOU WRAP UP TWO FOR ME?
TWO IT IS.
OH, ARE YOU THE BEE THEY SAY IS GOING TO GET RID OF THE GAICHUU?
YES...
UM...
I HEAR YOU'RE STAYING AT WUTHERING HEIGHTS!

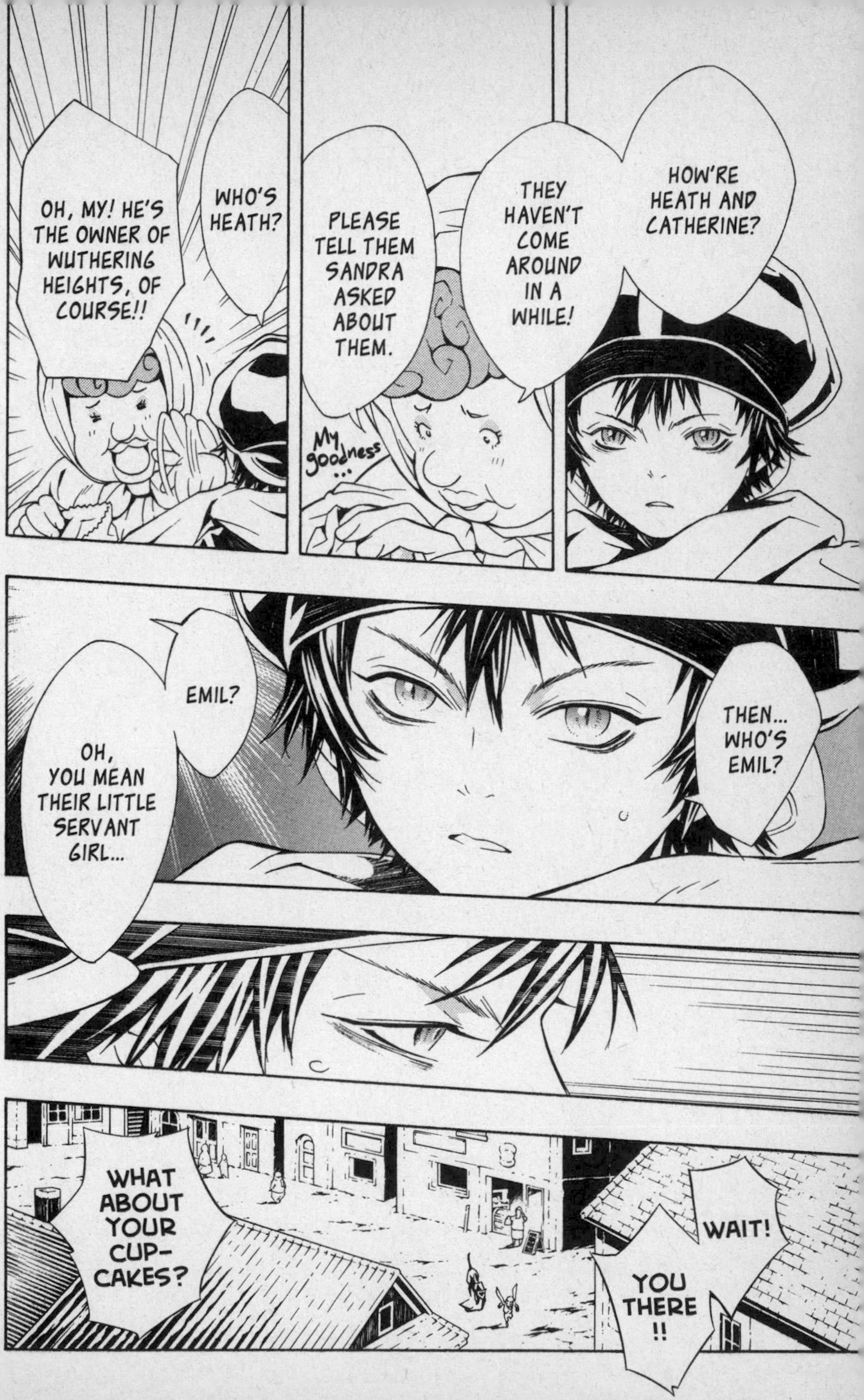
HOW'RE HEATH AND CATHERINE?
THEY HAVEN'T COME AROUND IN A WHILE!
PLEASE TELL THEM SANDRA ASKED ABOUT THEM.
My goodness...
WHO'S HEATH?
OH, MY! HE'S THE OWNER OF WUTHERING HEIGHTS, OF COURSE!!
THEN... WHO'S EMIL?
EMIL?
OH, YOU MEAN THEIR LITTLE SERVANT GIRL...
WAIT!
YOU THERE !!
WHAT ABOUT YOUR CUP-CAKES?

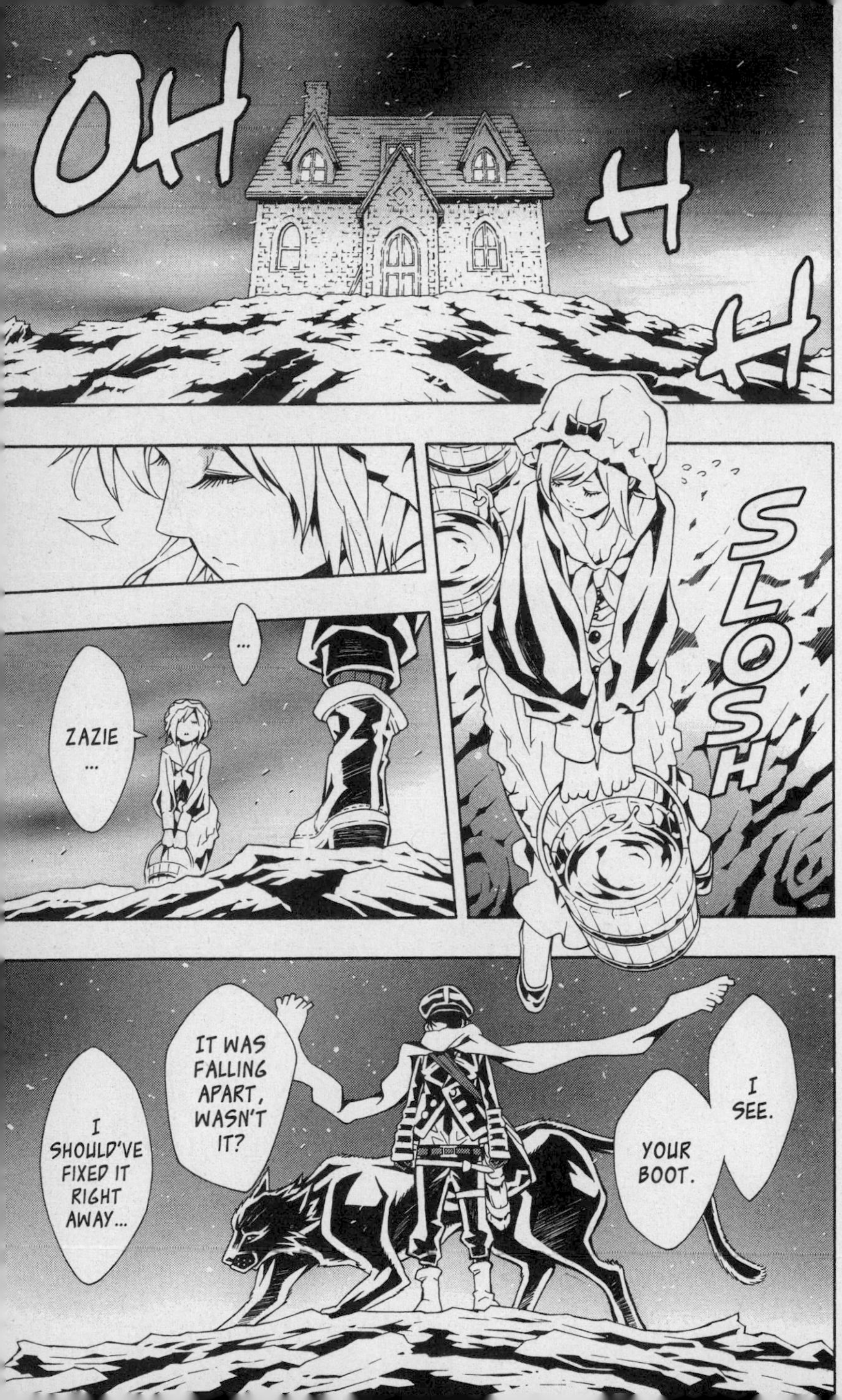
OHHH
SLOSH
...
ZAZIE ...
I SEE.
YOUR BOOT.
IT WAS FALLING APART, WASN'T IT?
I SHOULD'VE FIXED IT RIGHT AWAY...

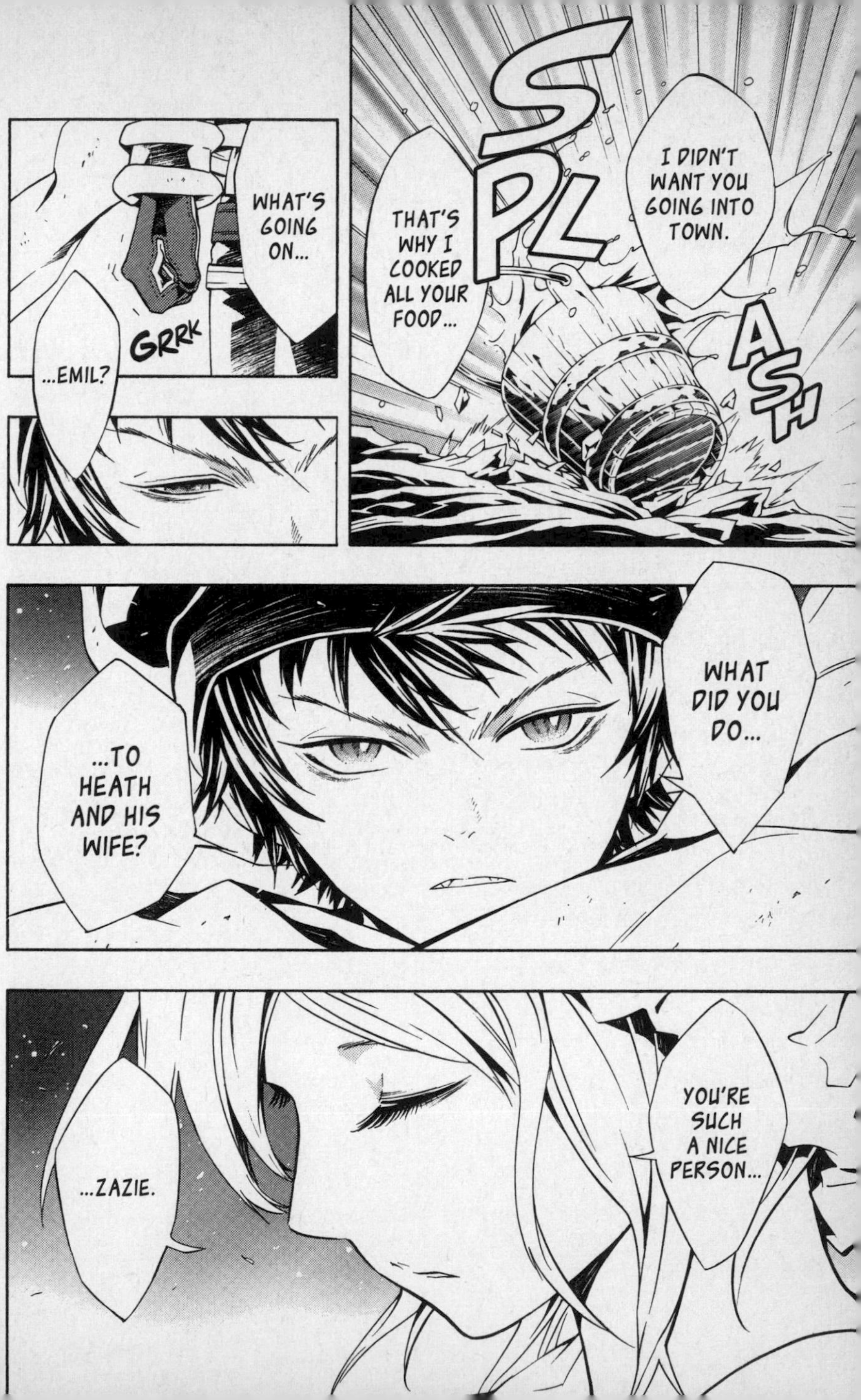
I DIDN'T WANT YOU GOING INTO TOWN.
SPLASH
THAT'S WHY I COOKED ALL YOUR FOOD...
WHAT'S GOING ON...
GRRK
...EMIL?
WHAT DID YOU DO...
...TO HEATH AND HIS WIFE?
YOU'RE SUCH A NICE PERSON...
...ZAZIE.

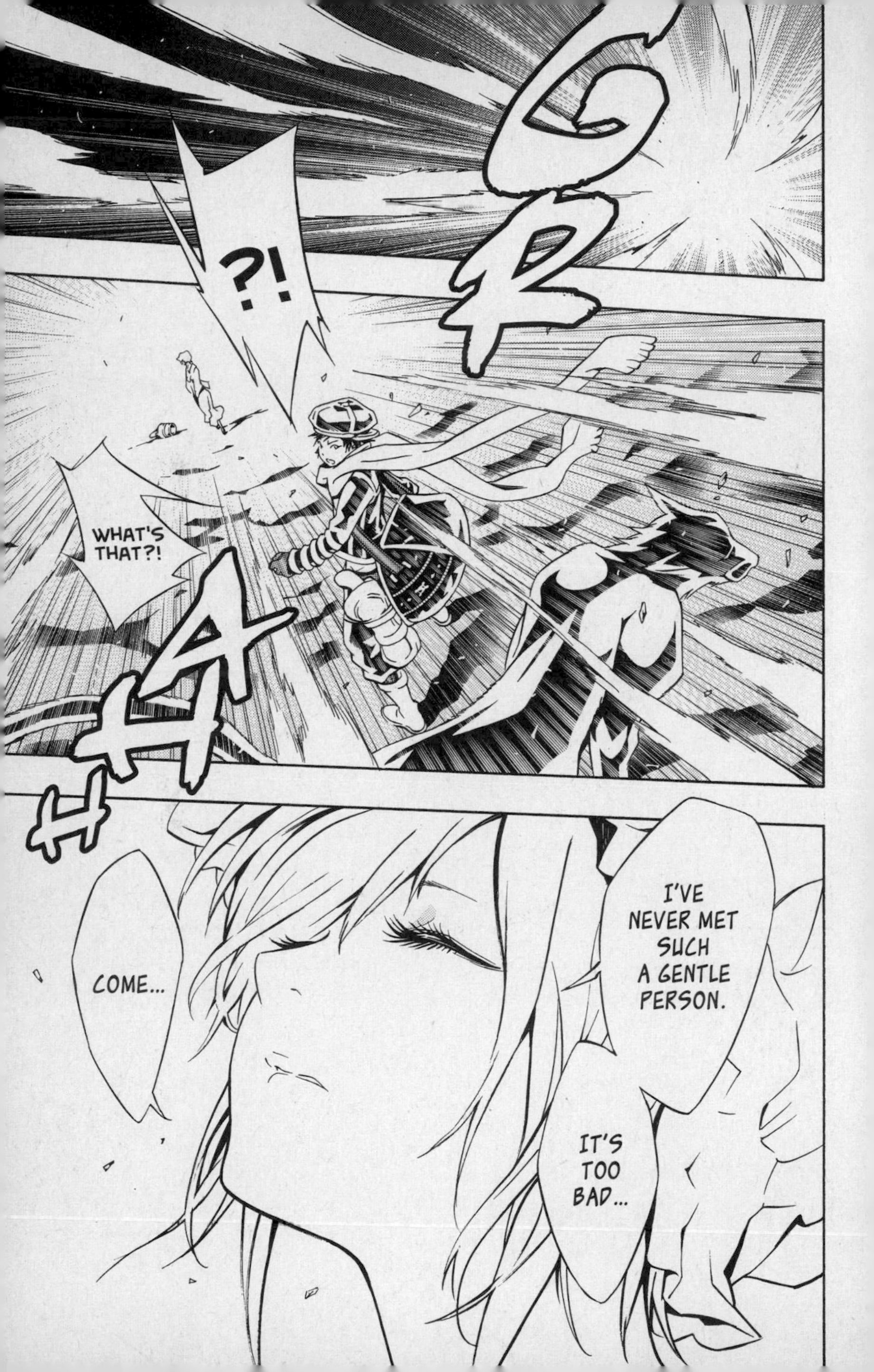
?!
WHAT'S THAT?!
I'VE NEVER MET SUCH A GENTLE PERSON.
IT'S TOO BAD...
COME...

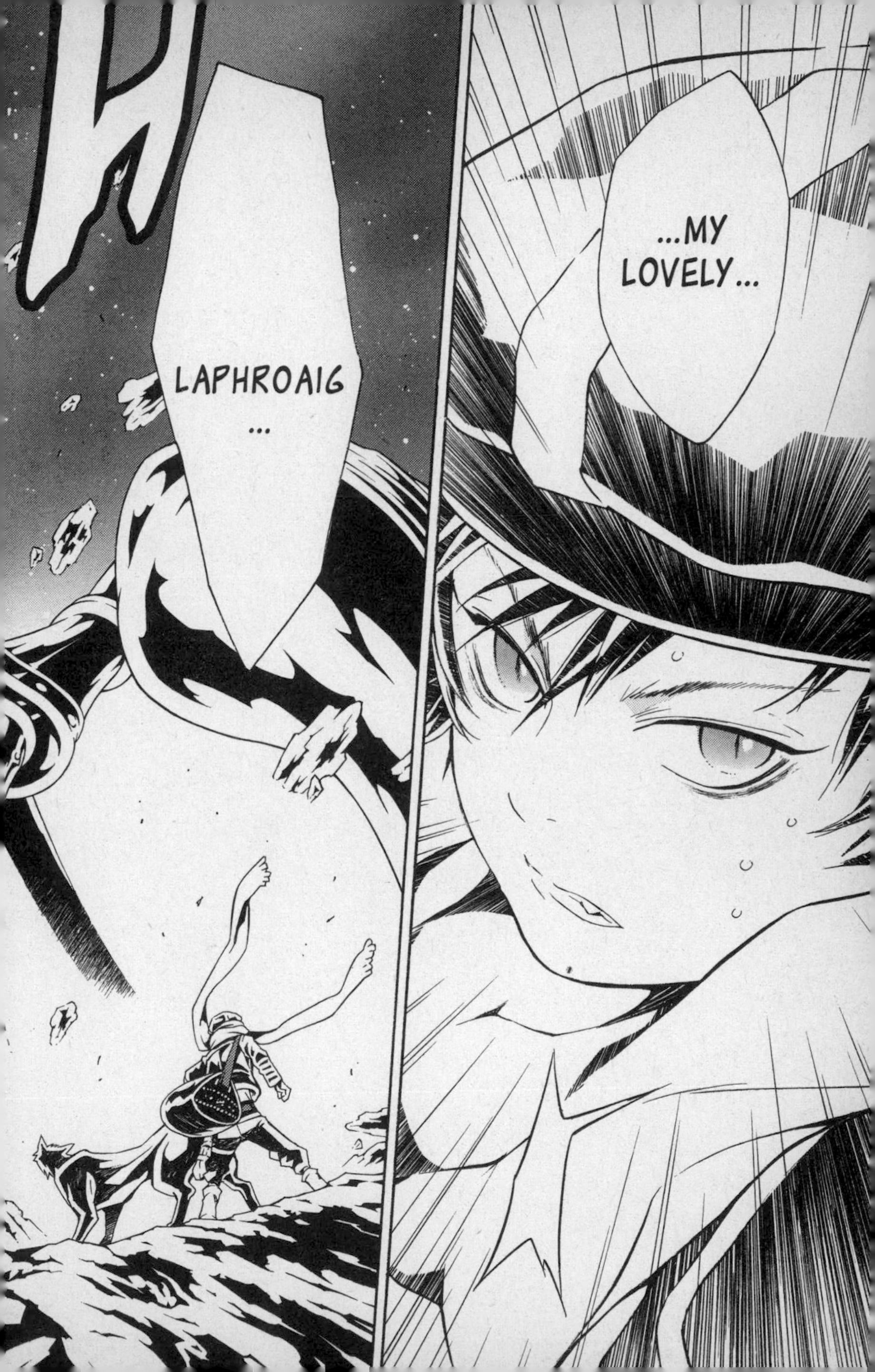
...MY LOVELY...
LAPHROAIG ...

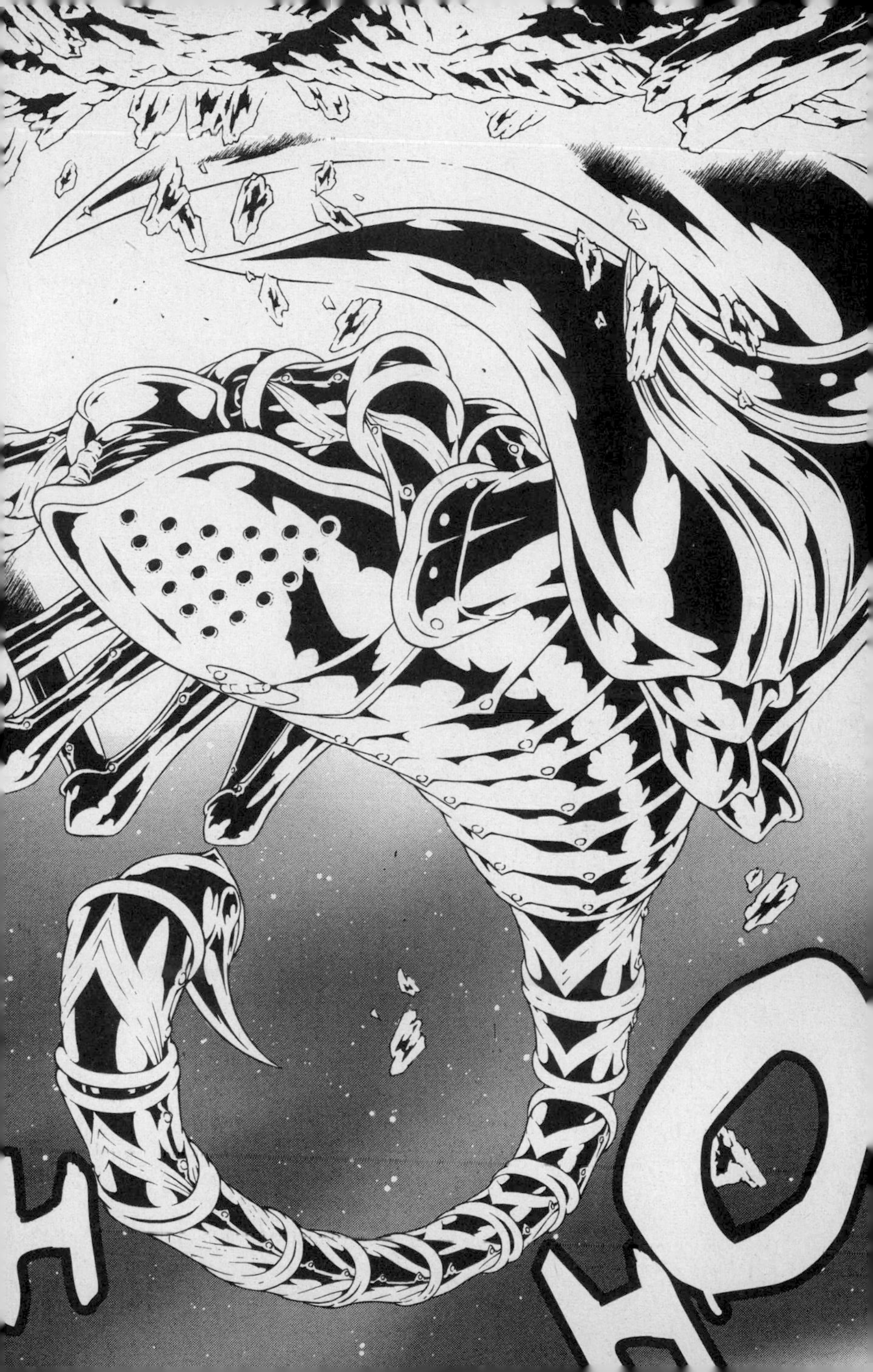

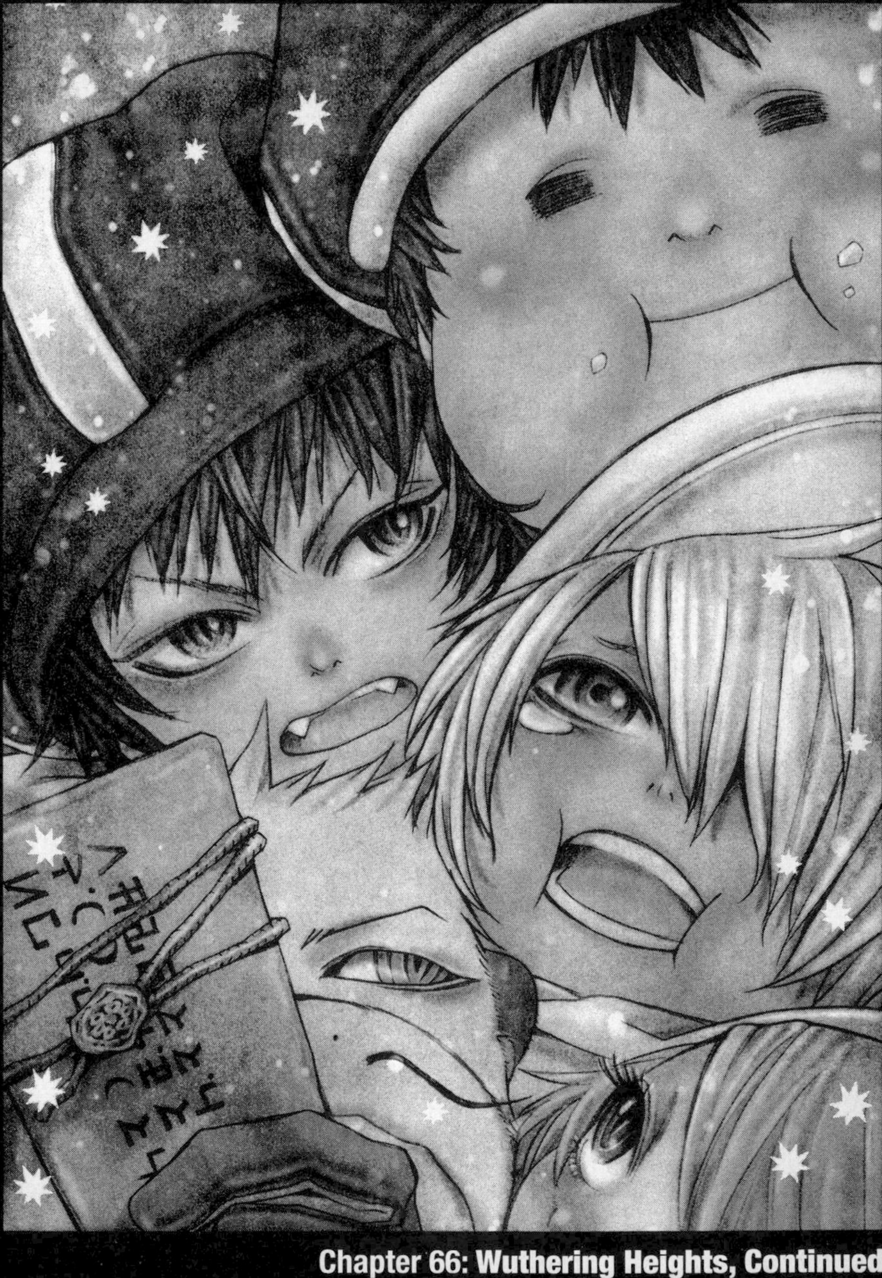

Chapter 66: Wuthering Heights, Continued

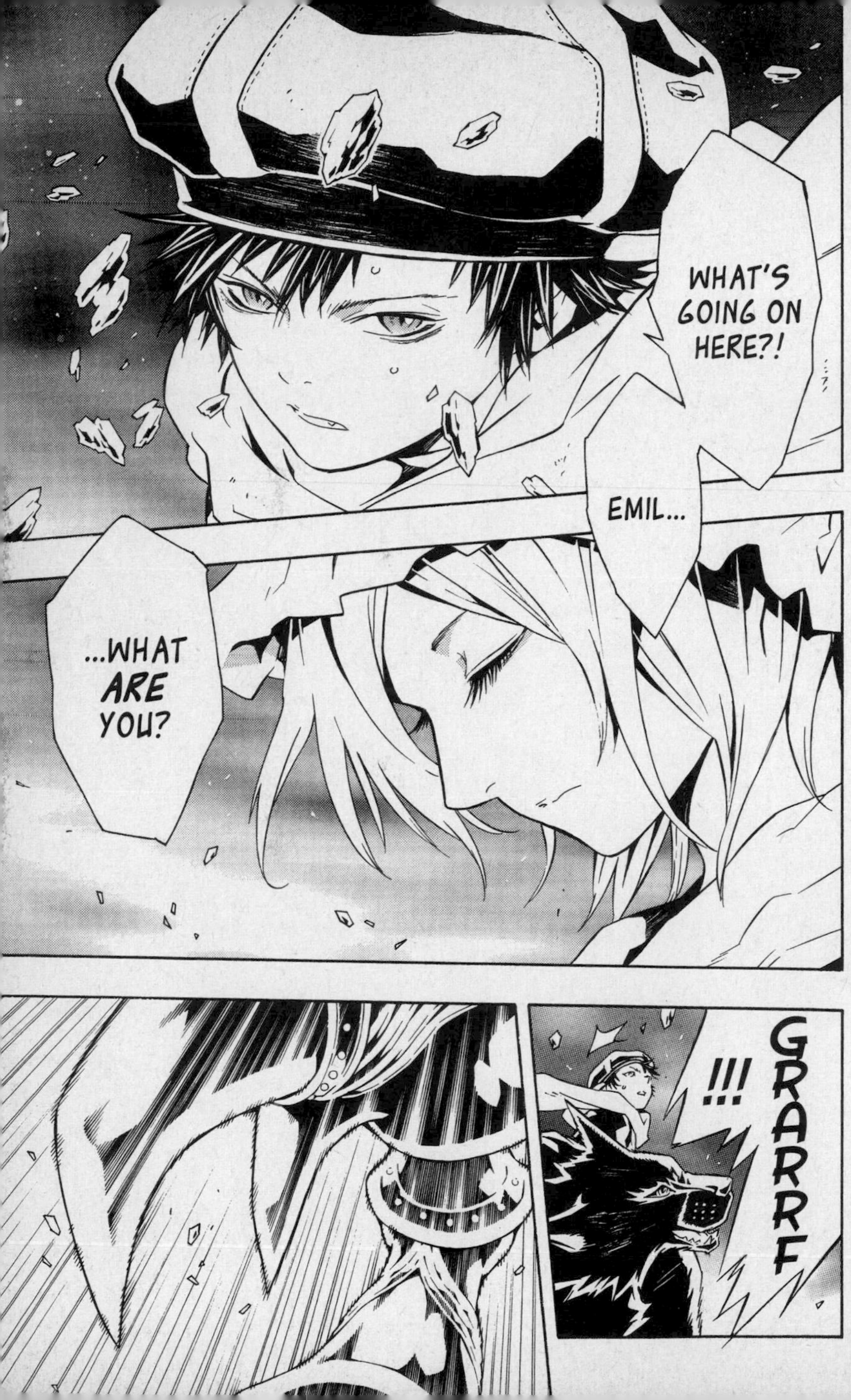
WHAT'S GOING ON HERE?!
EMIL...
...WHAT ARE YOU?
GRARRF
!!!

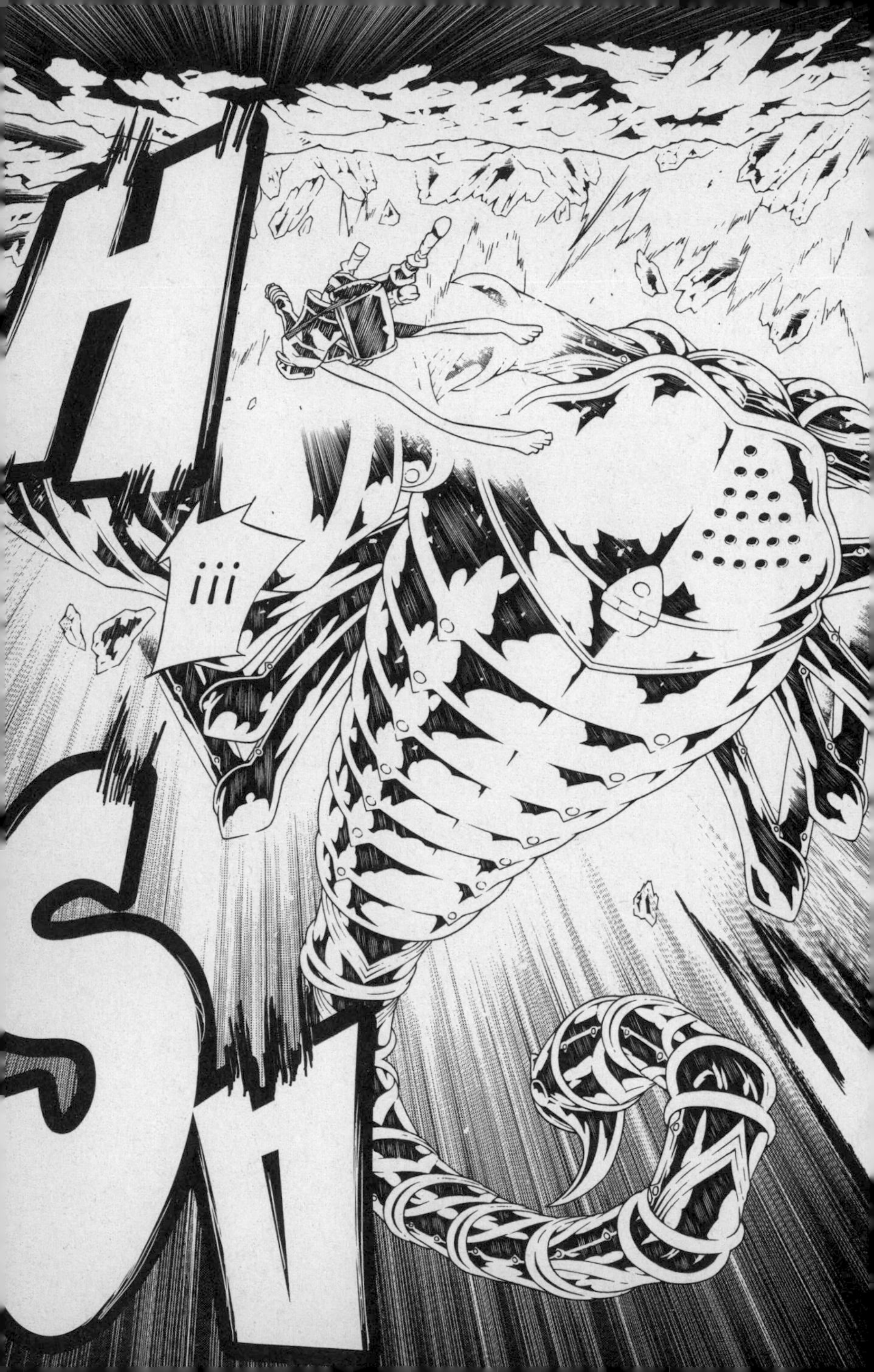
ASH

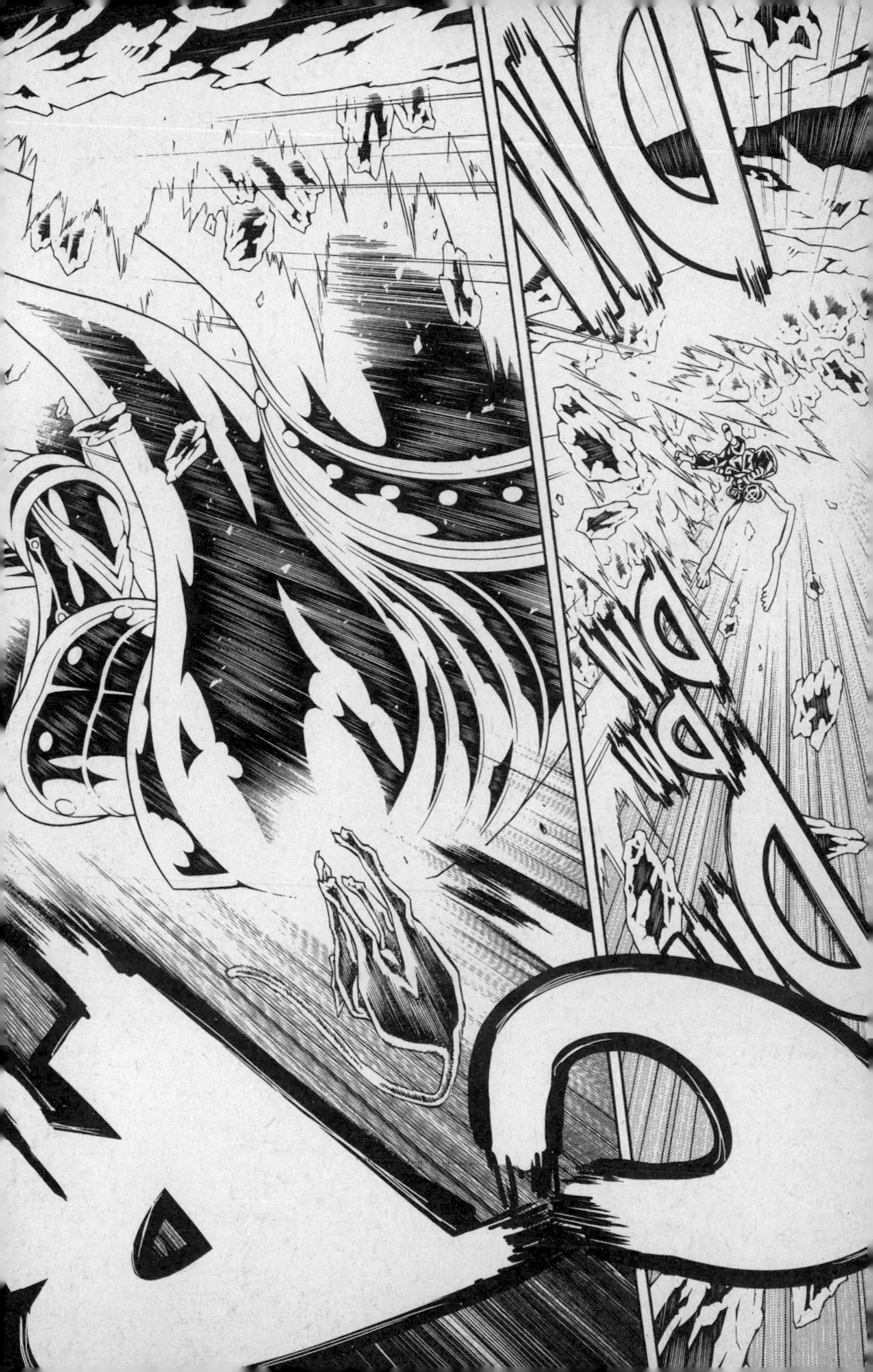

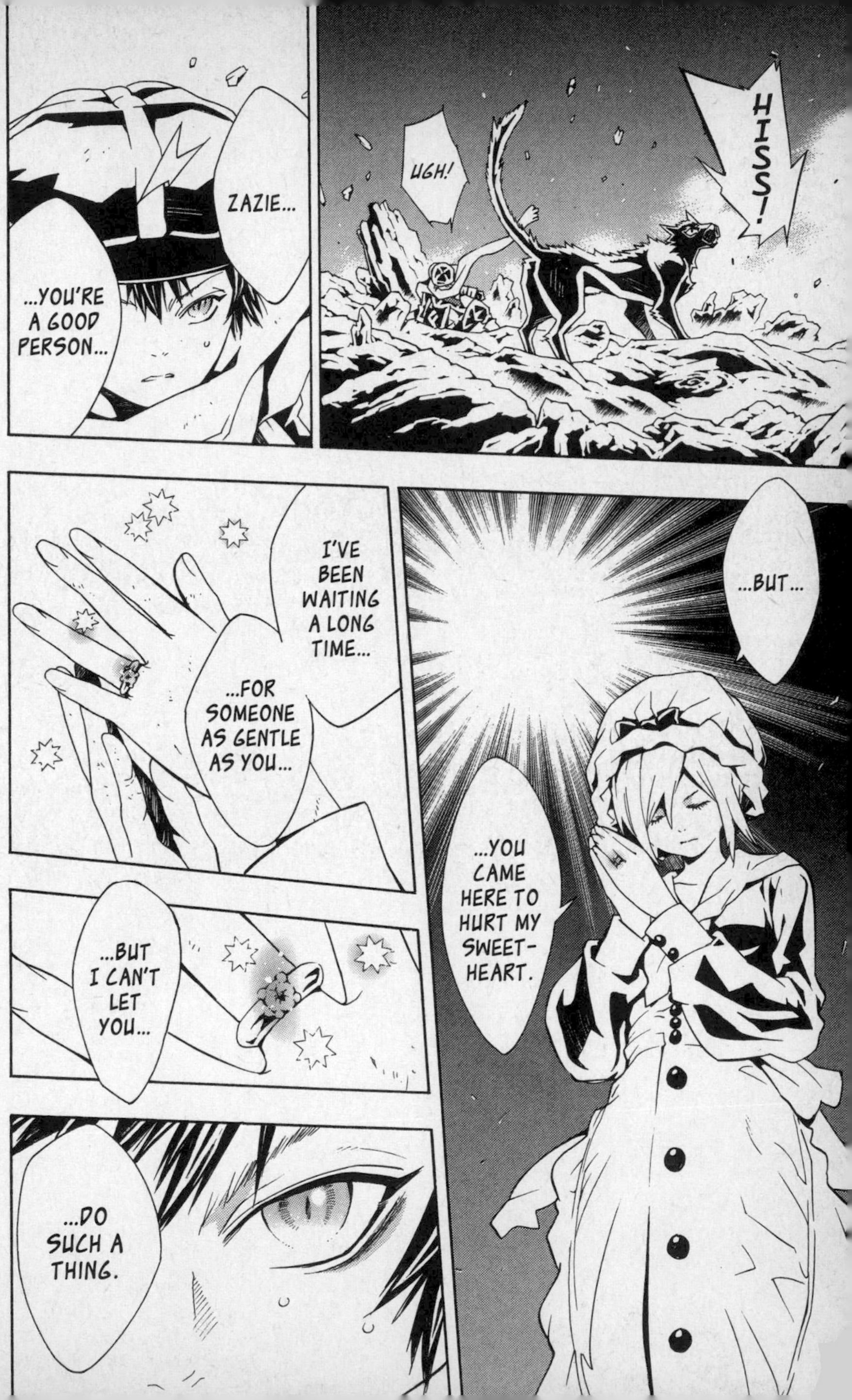
HISS!
UGH!
ZAZIE...
...YOU'RE A GOOD PERSON...
...BUT...
...YOU CAME HERE TO HURT MY SWEET-HEART.
I'VE BEEN WAITING A LONG TIME...
...FOR SOMEONE AS GENTLE AS YOU...
...BUT I CAN'T LET YOU...
...DO SUCH A THING.

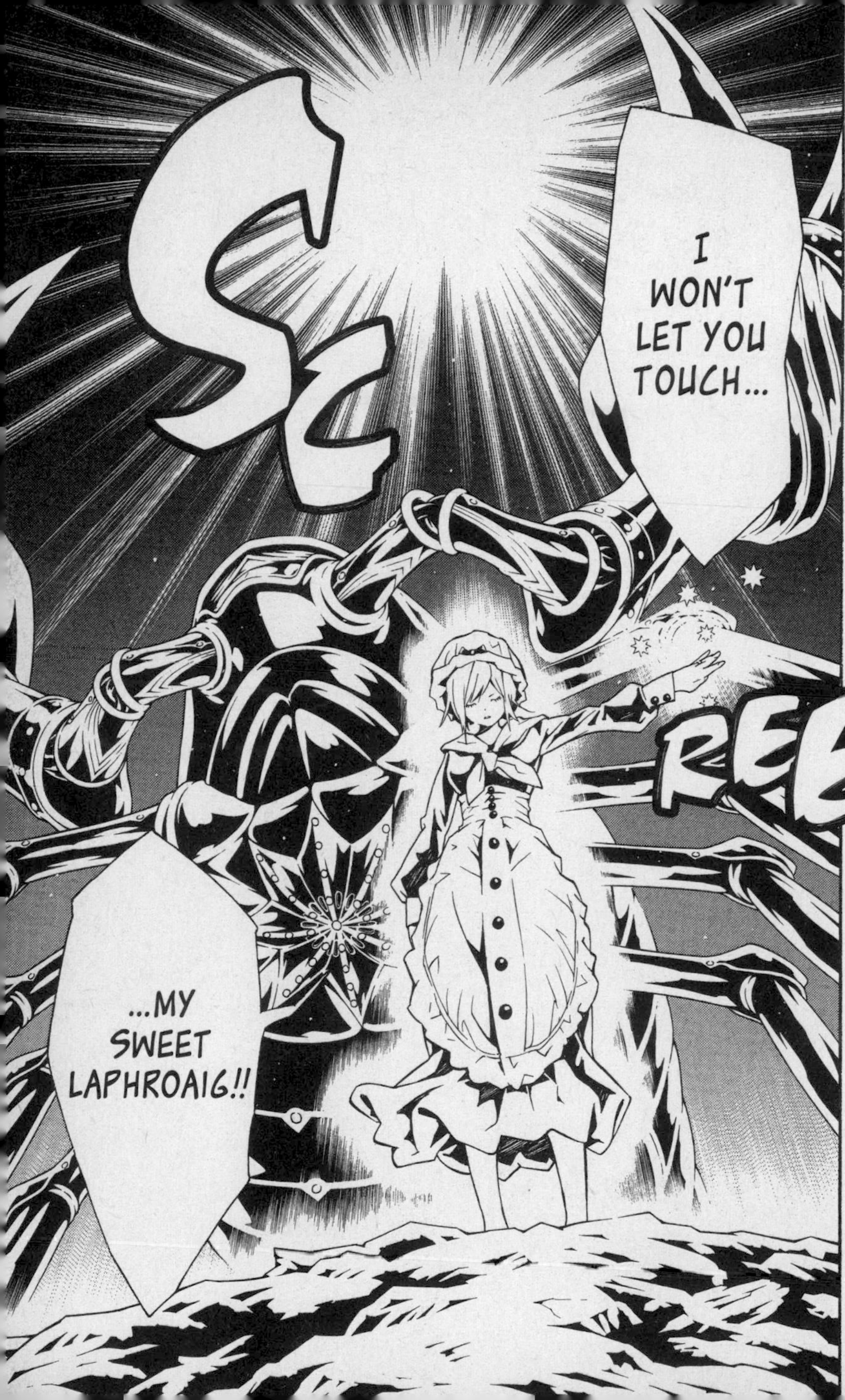
I WON'T LET YOU TOUCH...
SC
REE
...MY SWEET LAPHROAIG!!

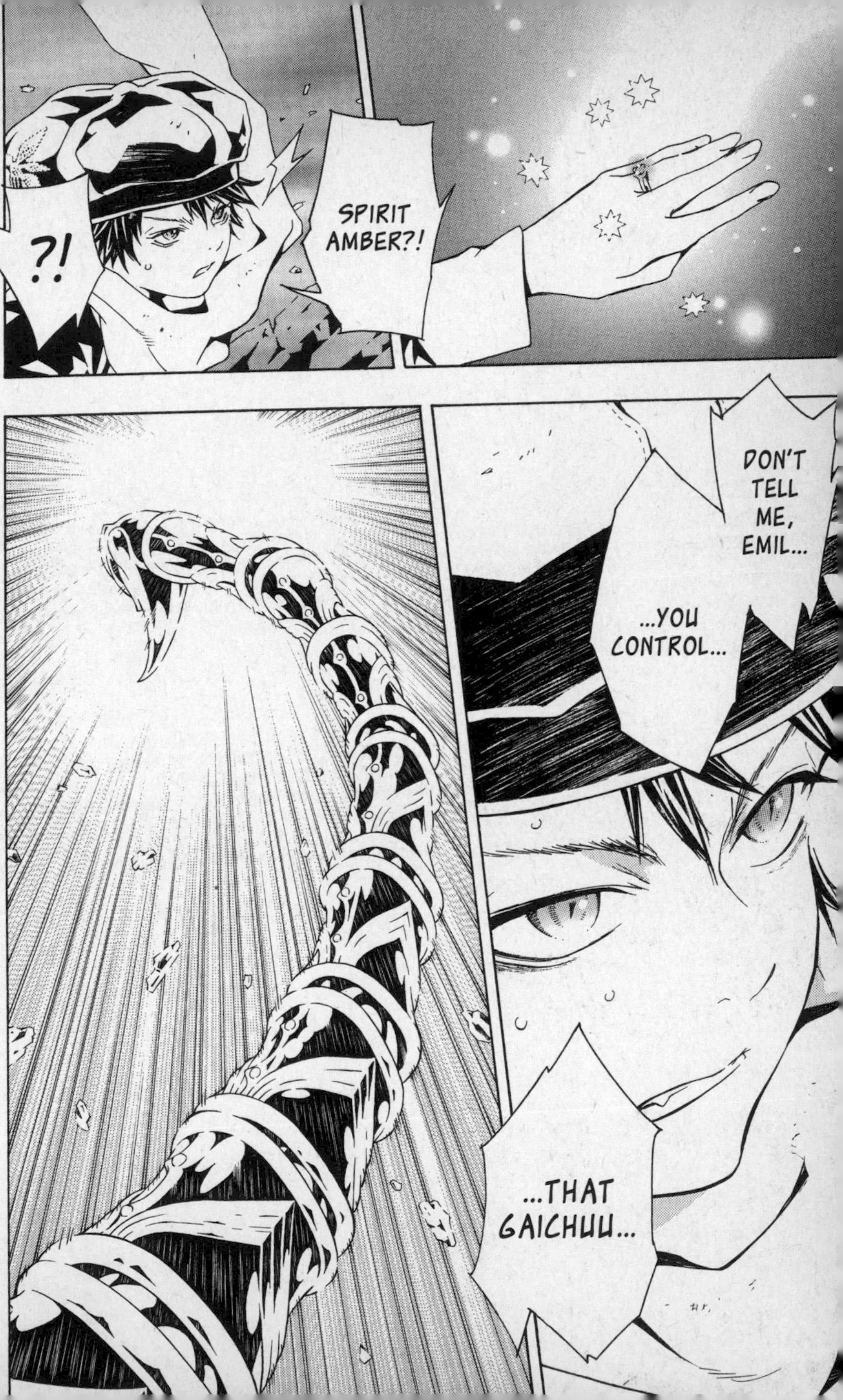
?!
SPIRIT AMBER?!
DON'T TELL ME, EMIL...
...YOU CONTROL...
...THAT GAICHUU...

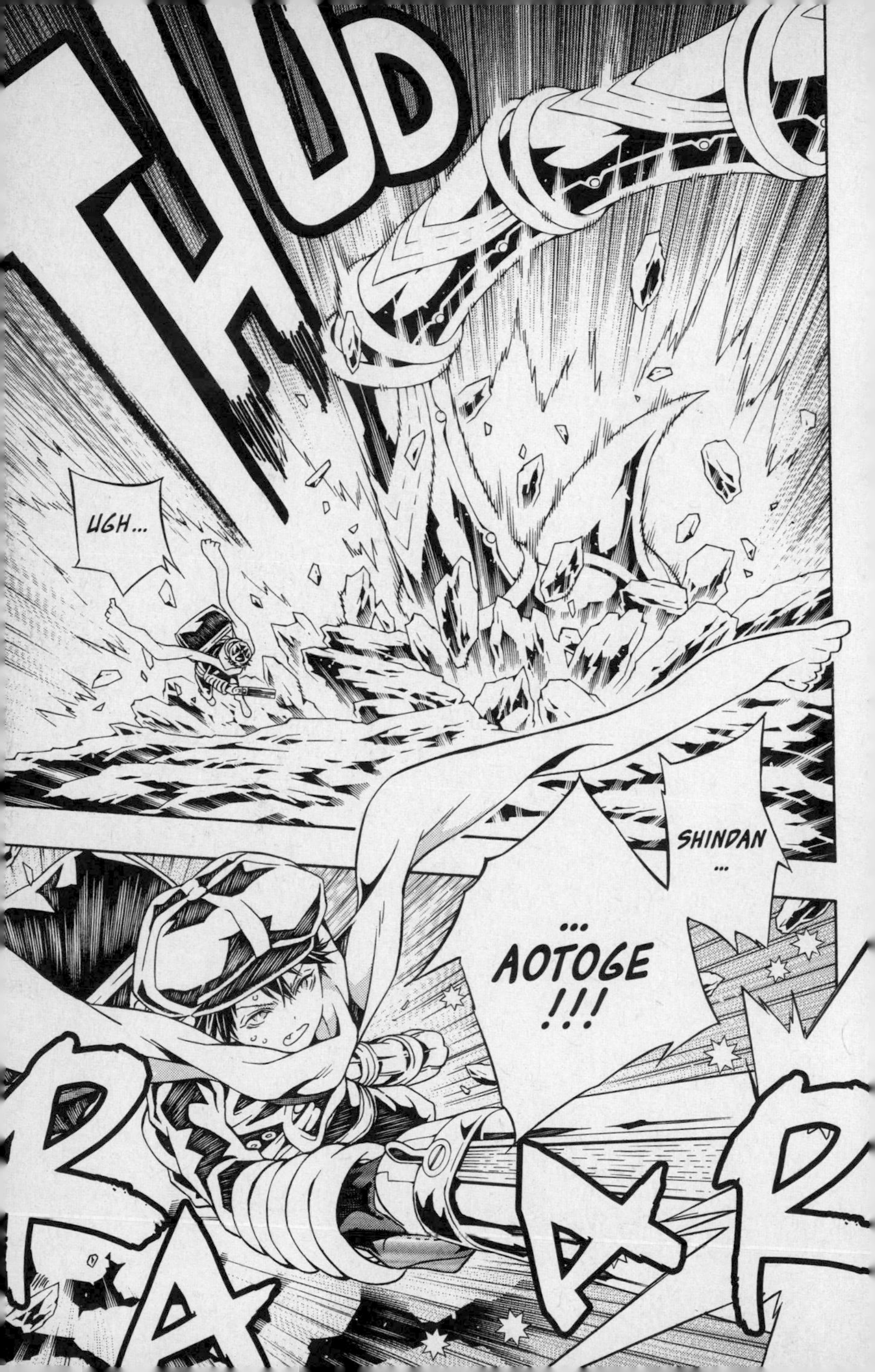
THUD
UGH...
SHINDAN...
...AOTOGE!!!
RAAR

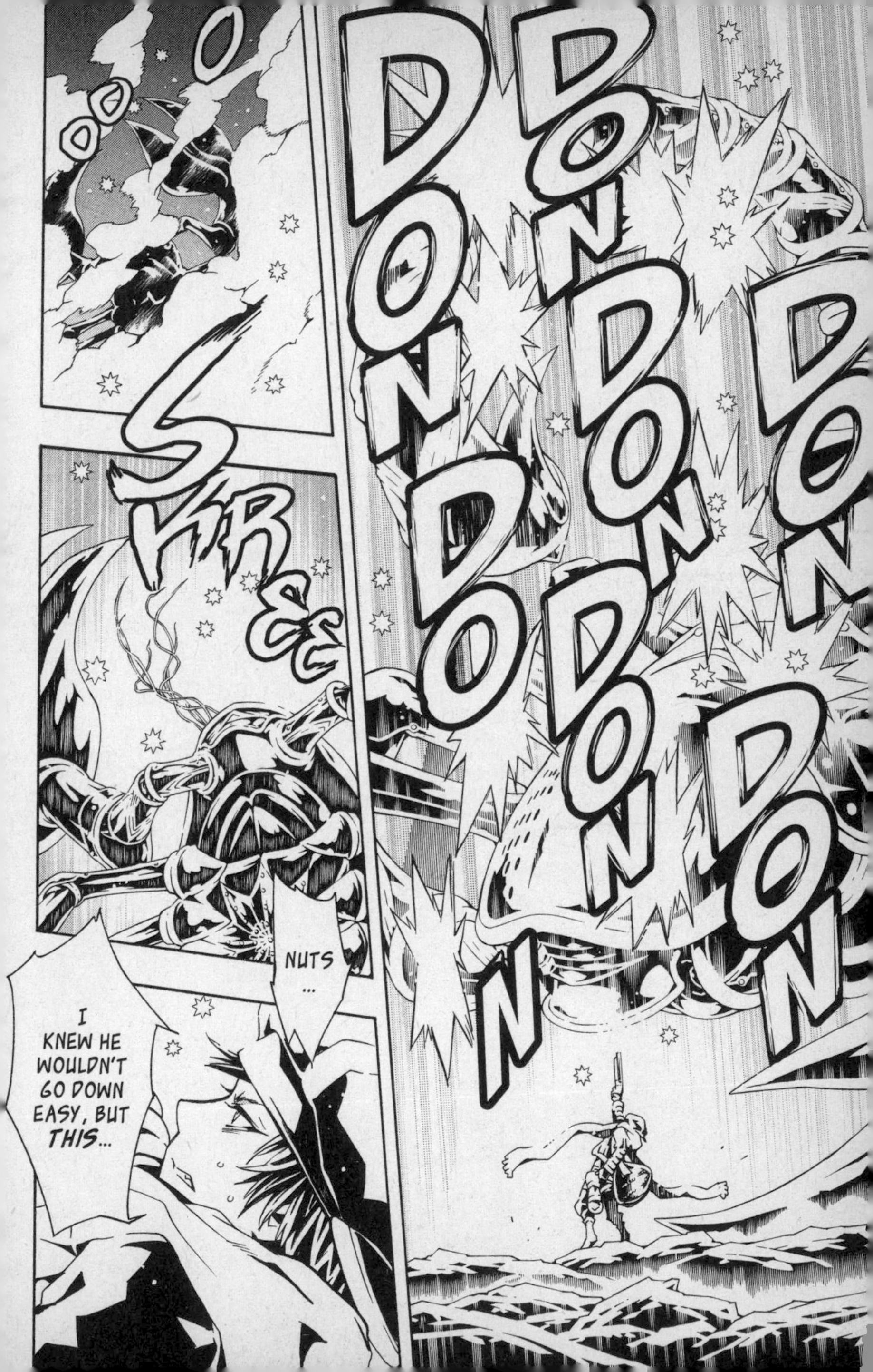
DON DON
DON DON
DON DON
DON DON
O O O
SKREEE
NUTS...
I KNEW HE WOULDN'T GO DOWN EASY, BUT *THIS*...

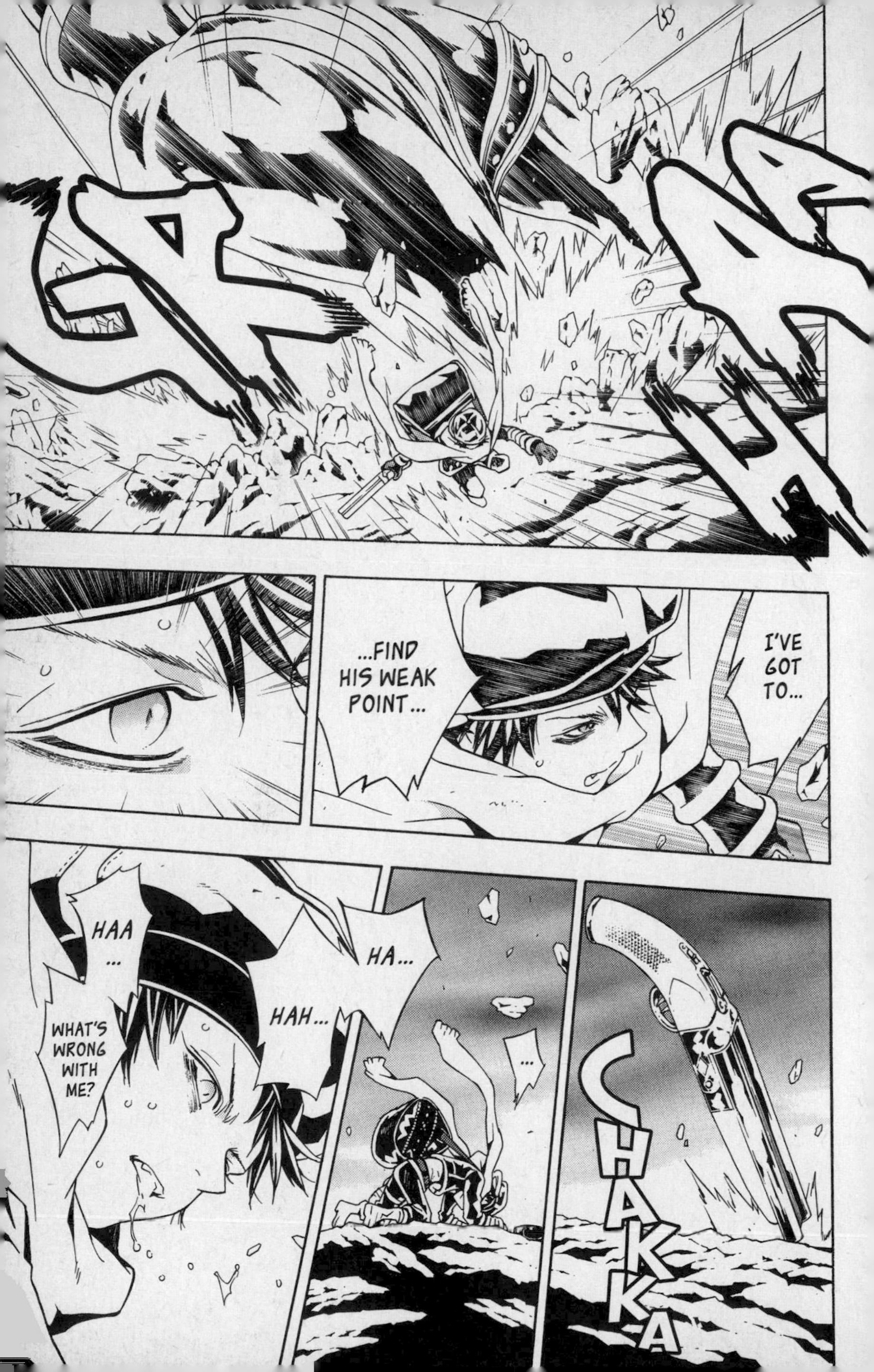
I'VE GOT TO...
...FIND HIS WEAK POINT...
CHAKA
...
HA...
HAA...
HAH...
WHAT'S WRONG WITH ME?

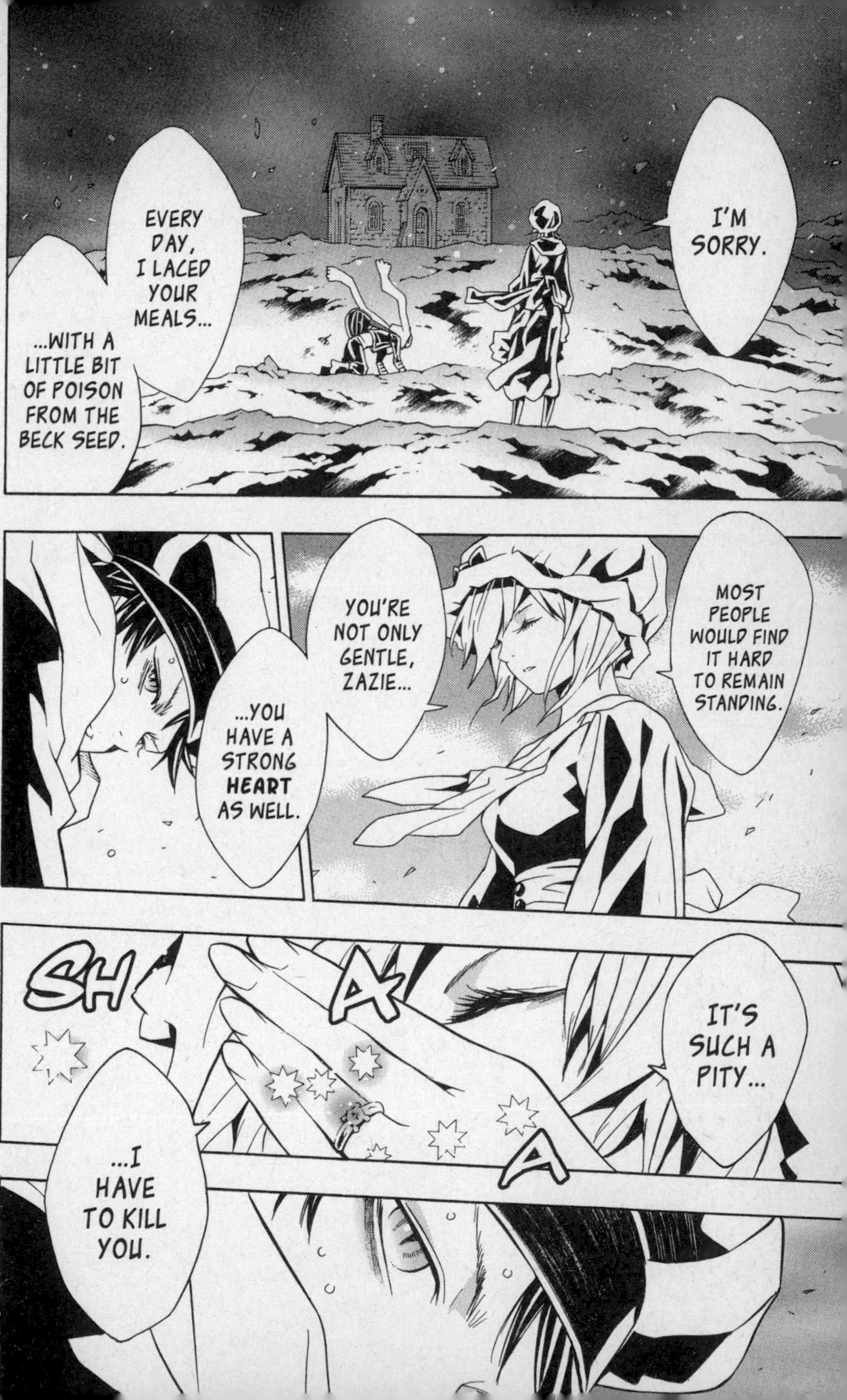
I'M SORRY.
EVERY DAY, I LACED YOUR MEALS...
...WITH A LITTLE BIT OF POISON FROM THE BECK SEED.
MOST PEOPLE WOULD FIND IT HARD TO REMAIN STANDING.
YOU'RE NOT ONLY GENTLE, ZAZIE...
...YOU HAVE A STRONG **HEART** AS WELL.
IT'S SUCH A PITY...
SH
A
A
...I HAVE TO KILL YOU.

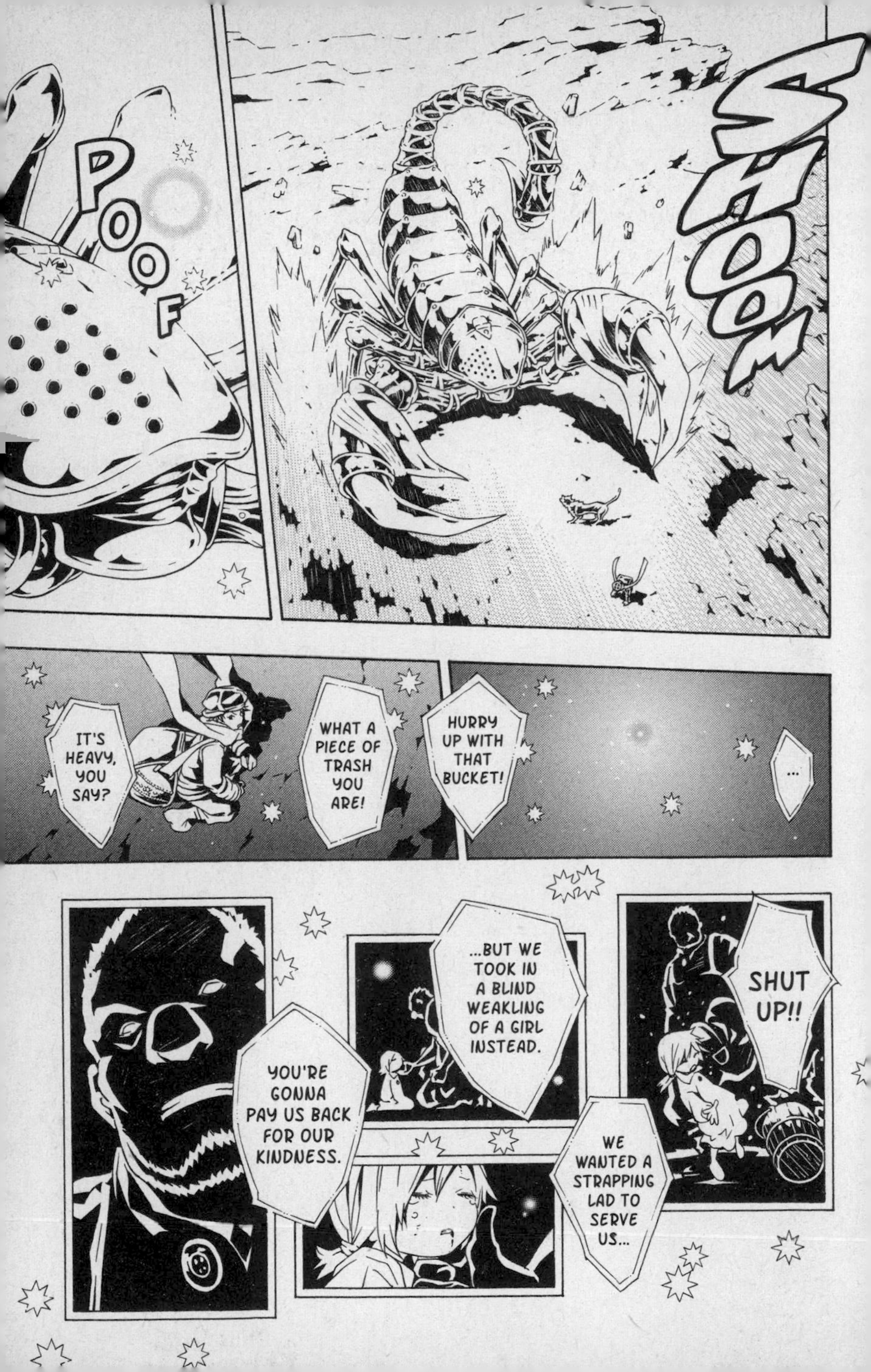
SHOOM
POOF
...
HURRY UP WITH THAT BUCKET!
WHAT A PIECE OF TRASH YOU ARE!
IT'S HEAVY, YOU SAY?
SHUT UP!!
WE WANTED A STRAPPING LAD TO SERVE US...
...BUT WE TOOK IN A BLIND WEAKLING OF A GIRL INSTEAD.
YOU'RE GONNA PAY US BACK FOR OUR KINDNESS.

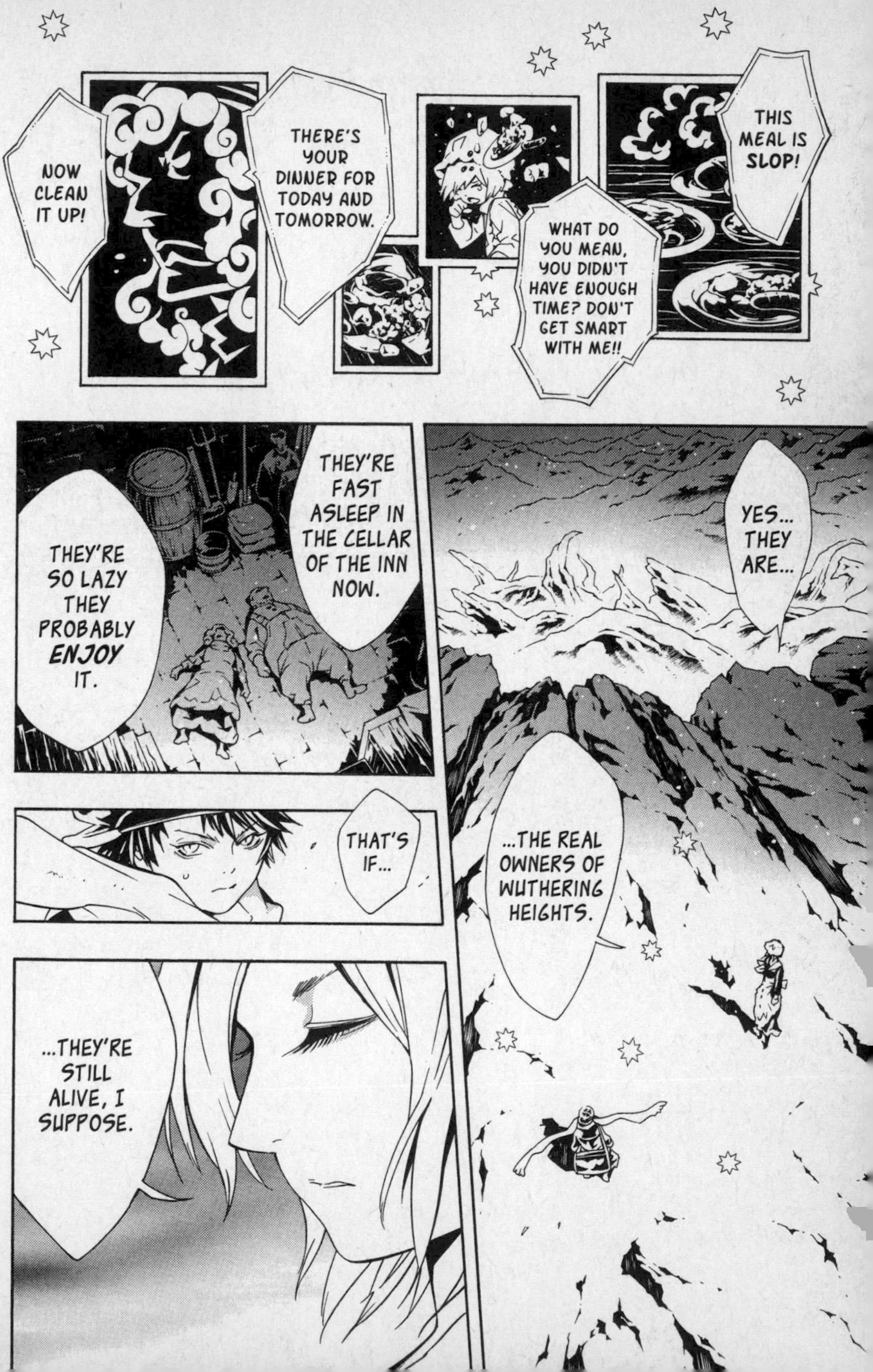
THIS MEAL IS SLOP!
WHAT DO YOU MEAN, YOU DIDN'T HAVE ENOUGH TIME? DON'T GET SMART WITH ME!!
THERE'S YOUR DINNER FOR TODAY AND TOMORROW.
NOW CLEAN IT UP!
YES... THEY ARE...
...THE REAL OWNERS OF WUTHERING HEIGHTS.
THEY'RE FAST ASLEEP IN THE CELLAR OF THE INN NOW.
THEY'RE SO LAZY THEY PROBABLY *ENJOY* IT.
THAT'S IF...
...THEY'RE STILL ALIVE, I SUPPOSE.

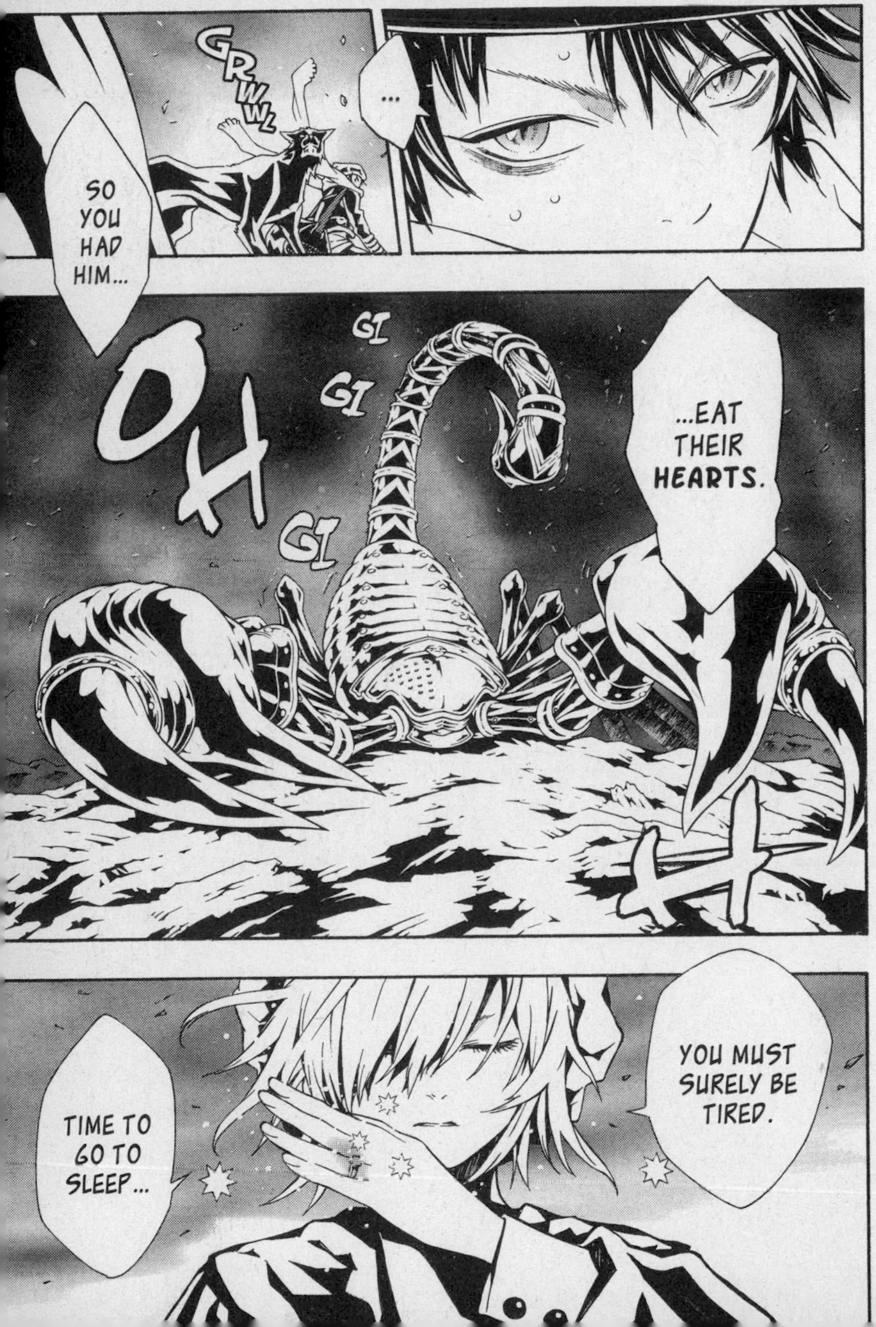
...
GRWL
SO YOU HAD HIM...
...EAT THEIR HEARTS.
OH
GI
GI
GI
YOU MUST SURELY BE TIRED.
TIME TO GO TO SLEEP...

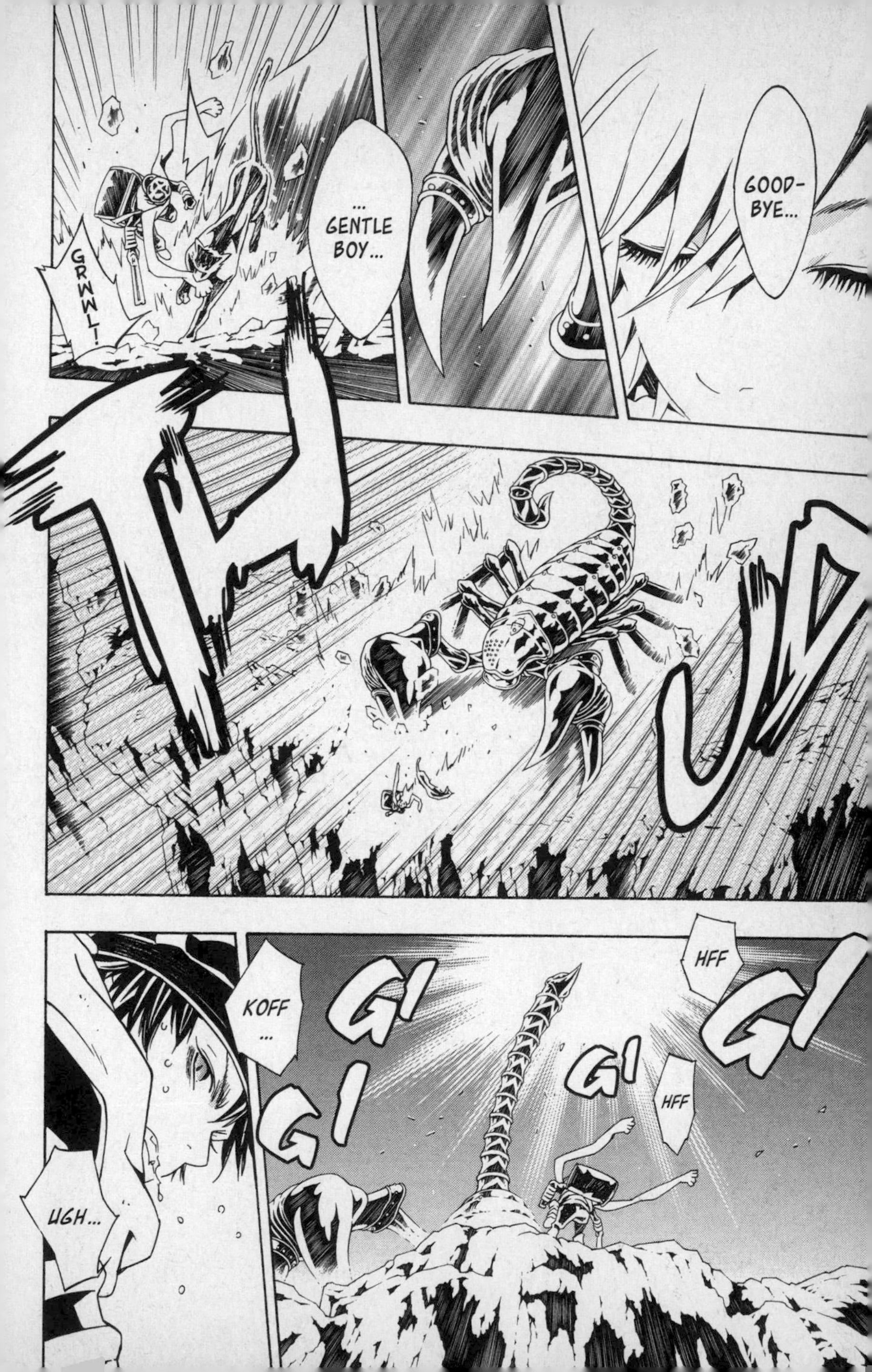
GOOD-BYE...
...GENTLE BOY...
GRWWL!
HFF
GI
GI
GI
HFF
GI
KOFF...
UGH...

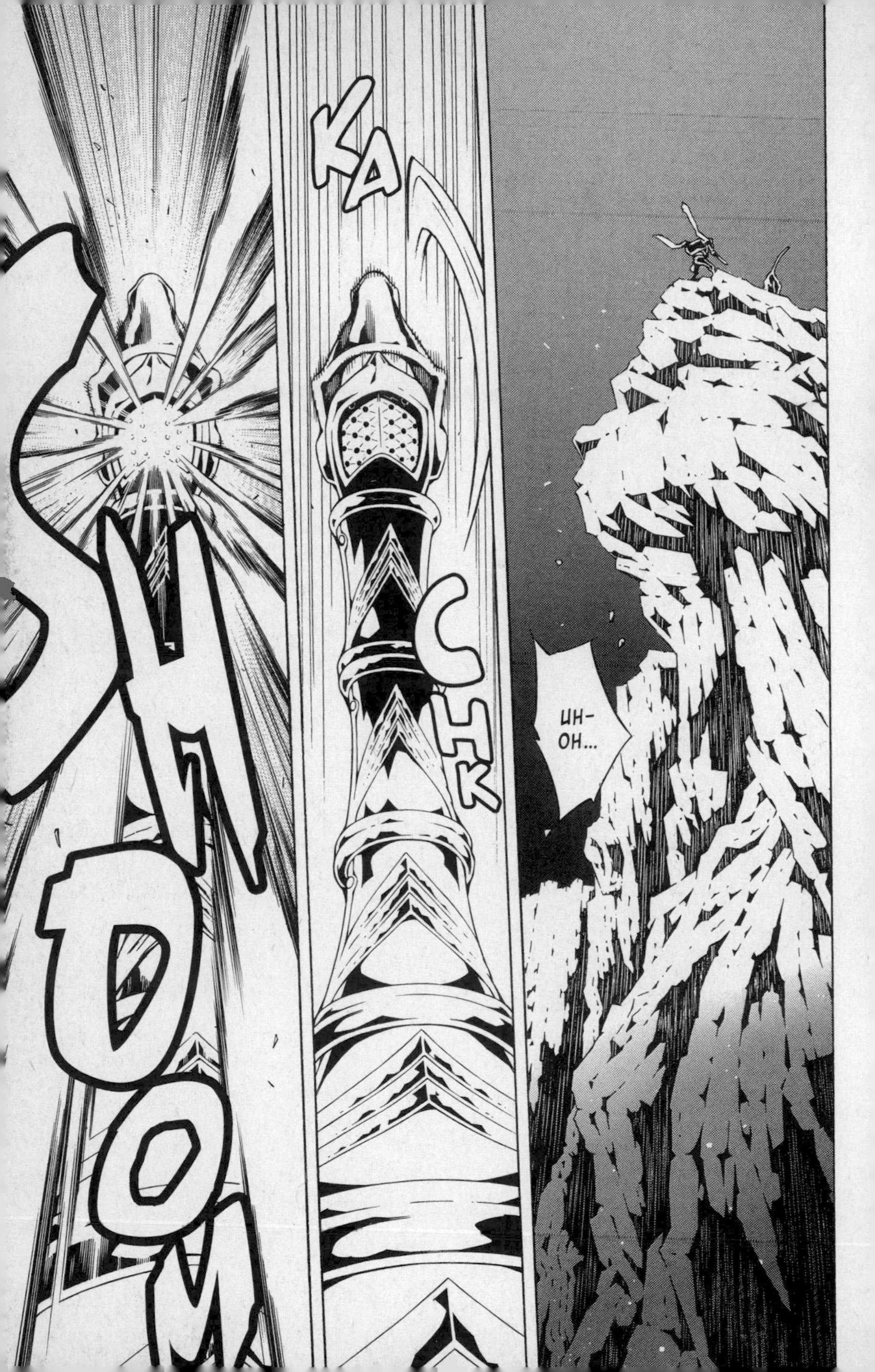
UH-
OH...
KA
CHK

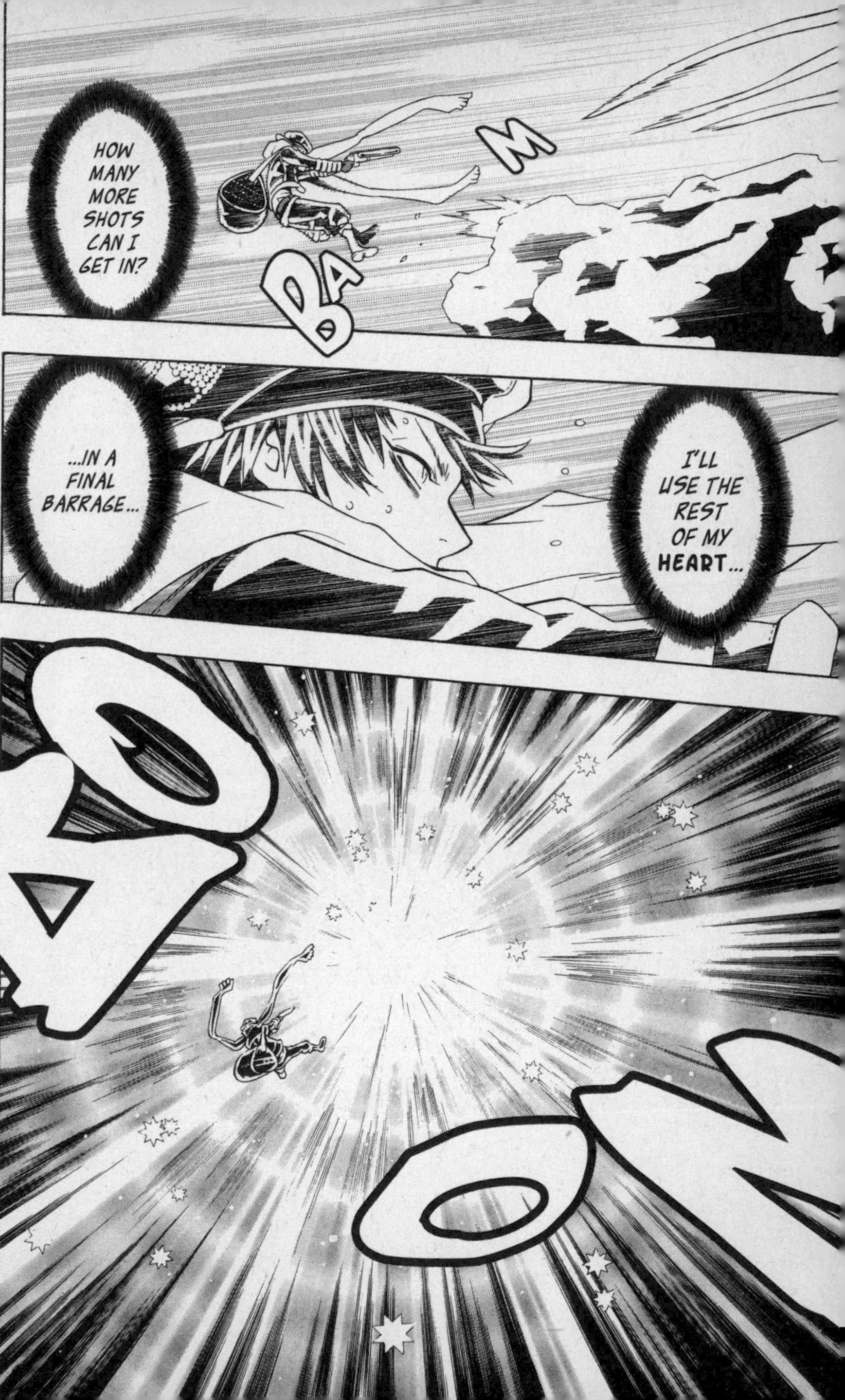
BAM
HOW MANY MORE SHOTS CAN I GET IN?
I'LL USE THE REST OF MY HEART...
...IN A FINAL BARRAGE...

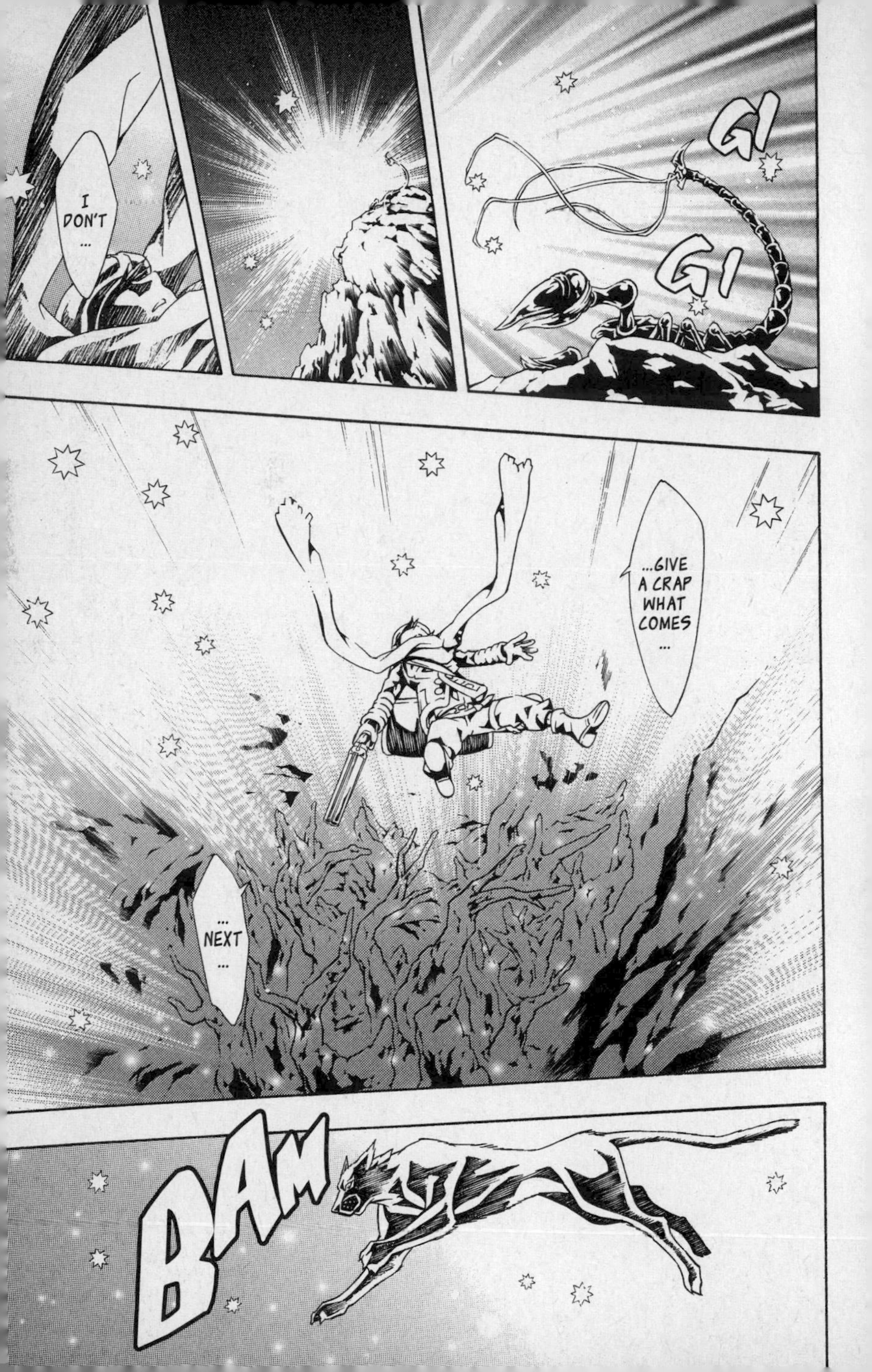
GI
GI
I DON'T ...
...GIVE A CRAP WHAT COMES ...
... NEXT ...
BAM

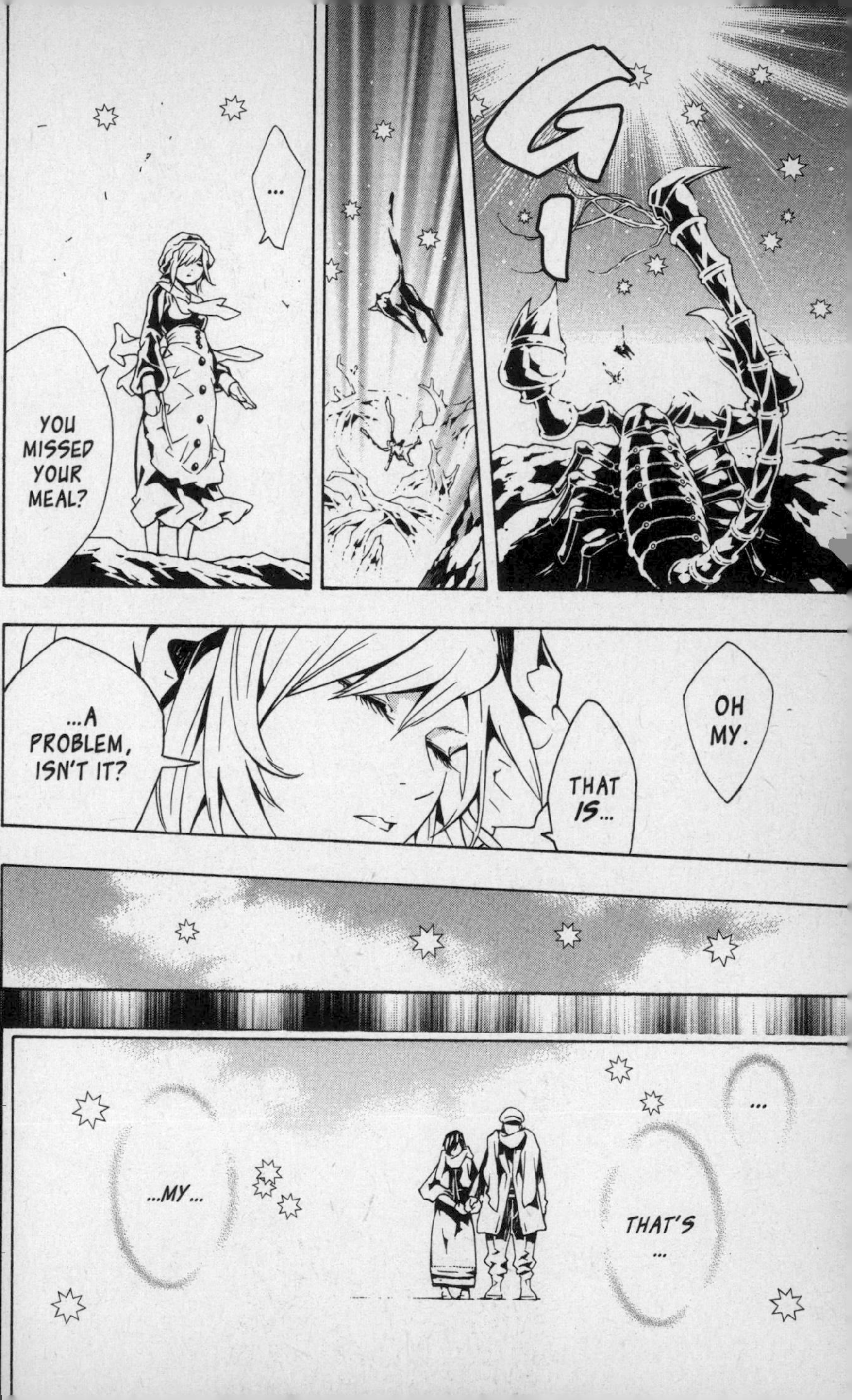
G
...
YOU MISSED YOUR MEAL?
OH MY.
THAT IS...
...A PROBLEM, ISN'T IT?
...
THAT'S ...
...MY...

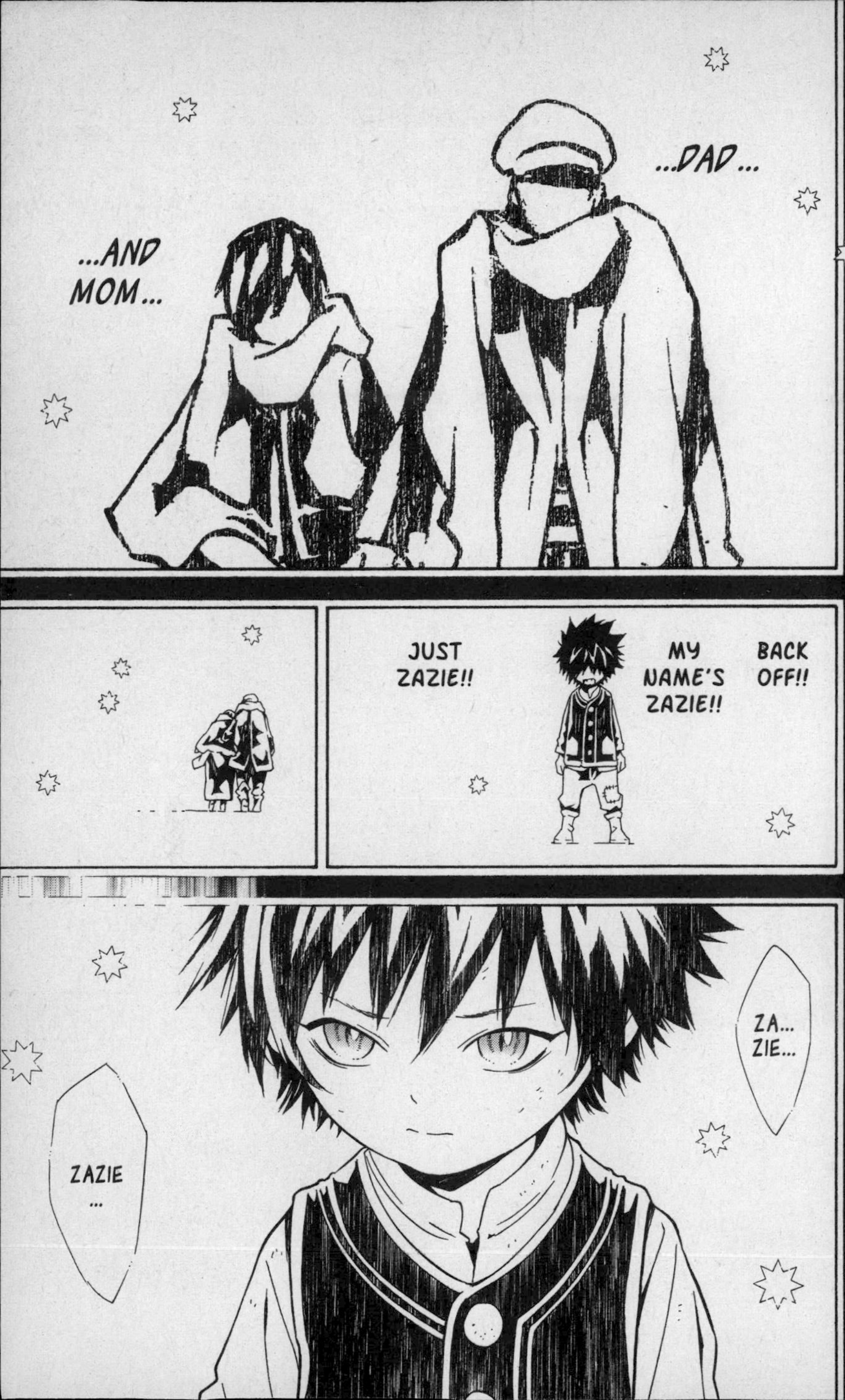
...DAD...
...AND MOM...
BACK OFF!!
MY NAME'S ZAZIE!!
JUST ZAZIE!!
ZA... ZIE...
ZAZIE ...

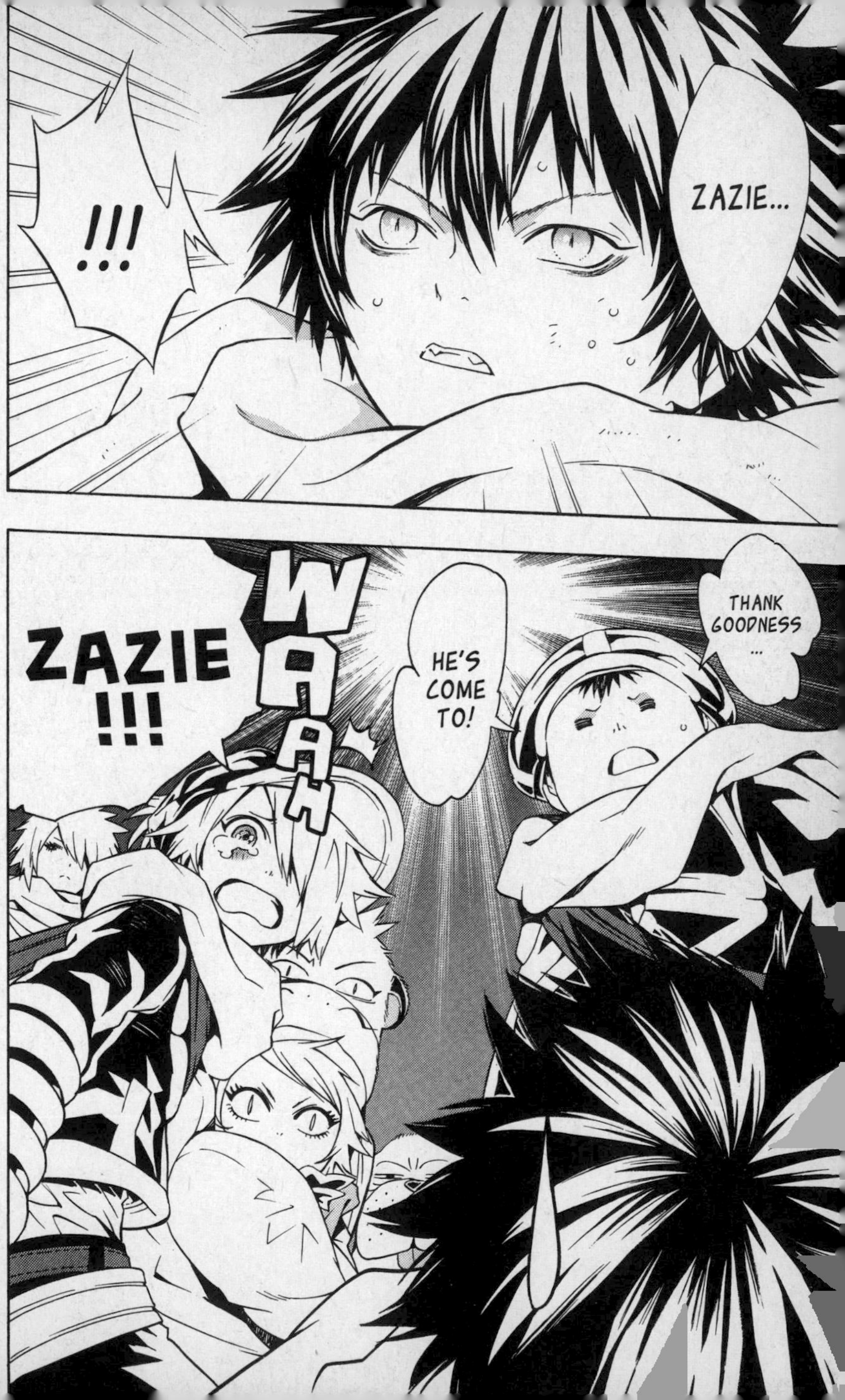
ZAZIE...
!!!
THANK GOODNESS ...
HE'S COME TO!
WAAAH
ZAZIE !!!

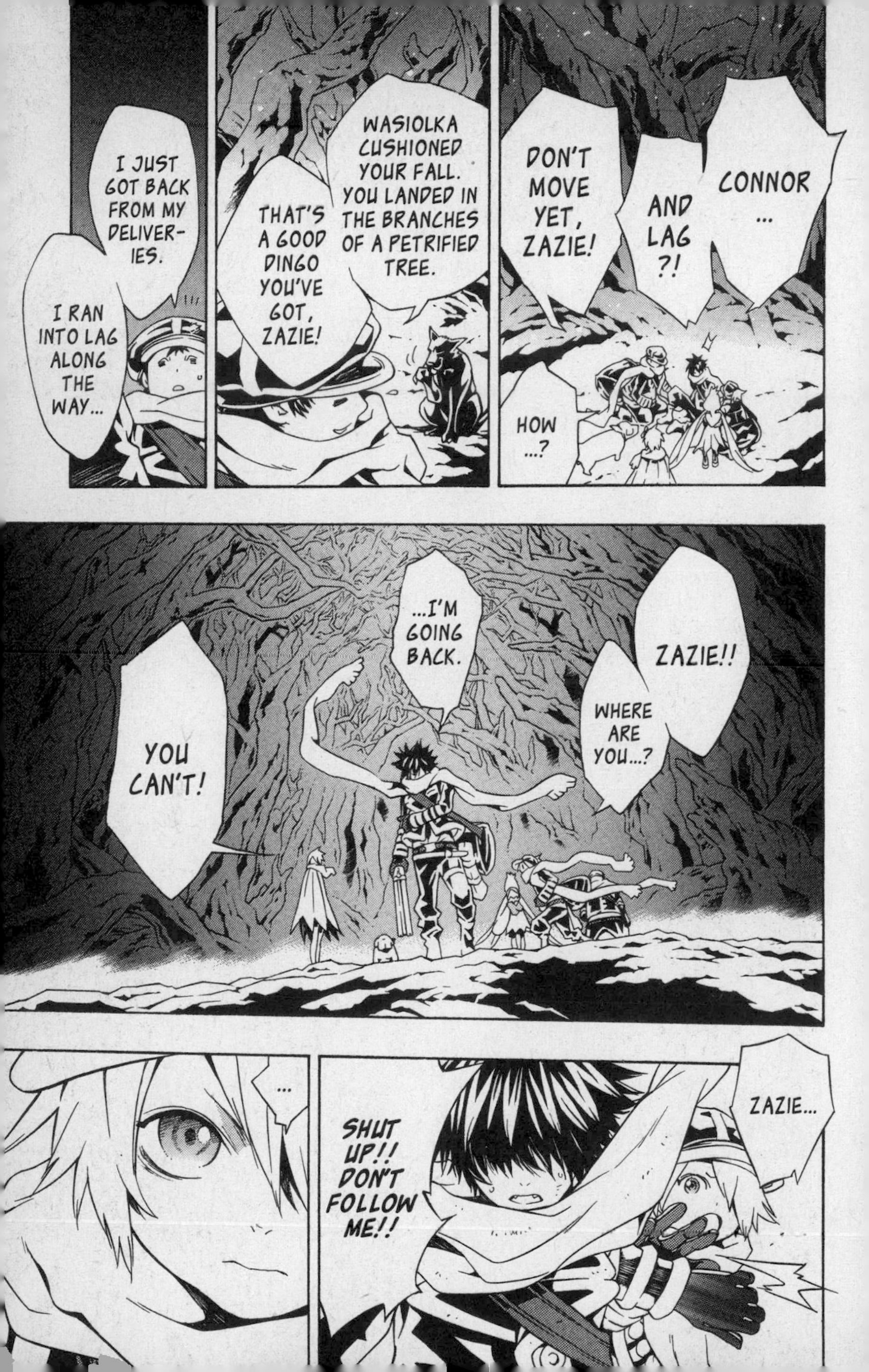
CONNOR ...
AND LAG ?!
DON'T MOVE YET, ZAZIE!
HOW ...?
WASIOLKA CUSHIONED YOUR FALL. YOU LANDED IN THE BRANCHES OF A PETRIFIED TREE.
THAT'S A GOOD DINGO YOU'VE GOT, ZAZIE!
I JUST GOT BACK FROM MY DELIVER-IES.
I RAN INTO LAG ALONG THE WAY...
ZAZIE!!
WHERE ARE YOU...?
...I'M GOING BACK.
YOU CAN'T!
ZAZIE...
SHUT UP!! DON'T FOLLOW ME!!
...

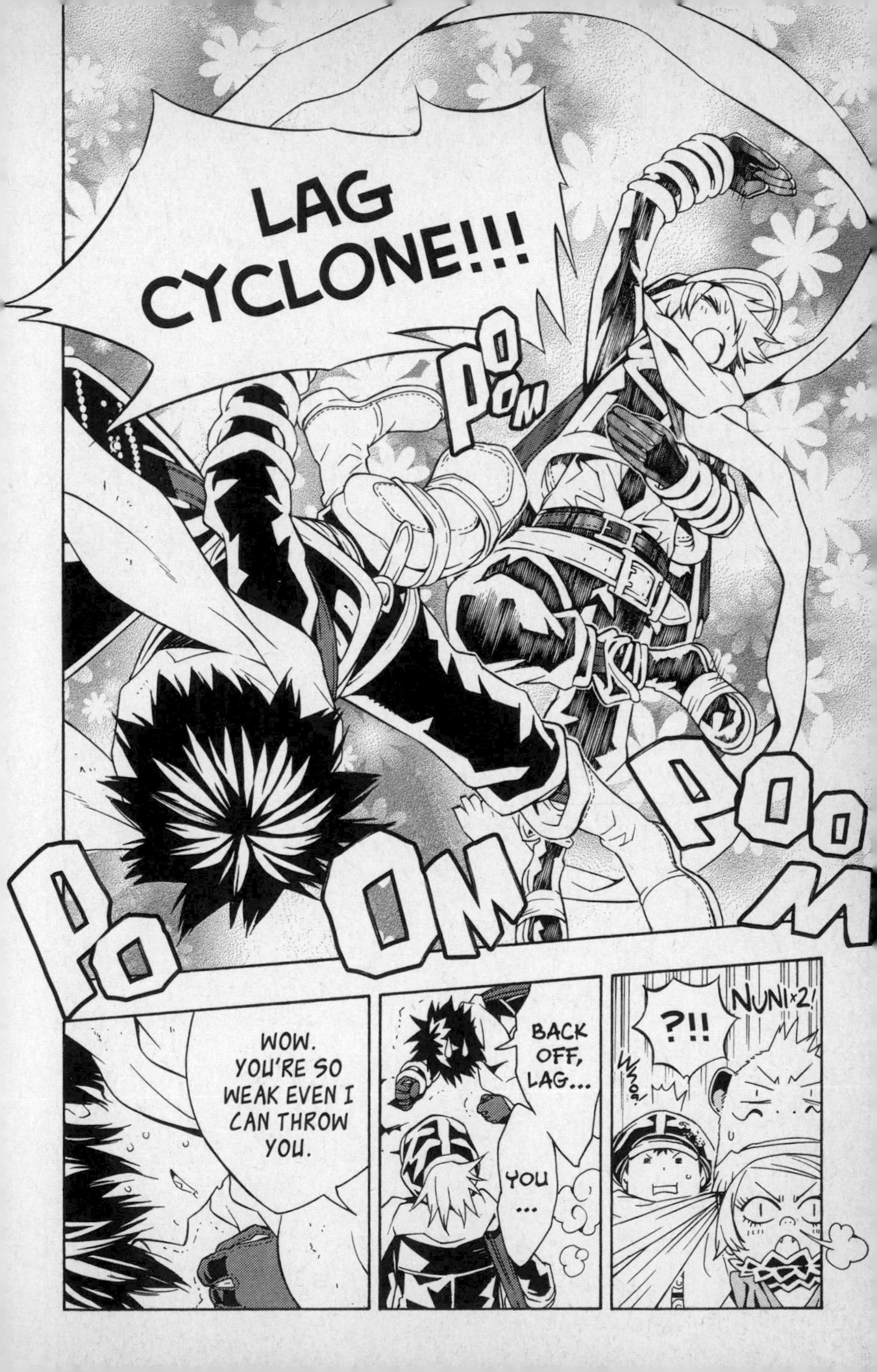
LAG CYCLONE!!!
POOM
POOM
POOM
?!!
NUNI×2!
BACK OFF, LAG...
YOU...
WOW. YOU'RE SO WEAK EVEN I CAN THROW YOU.

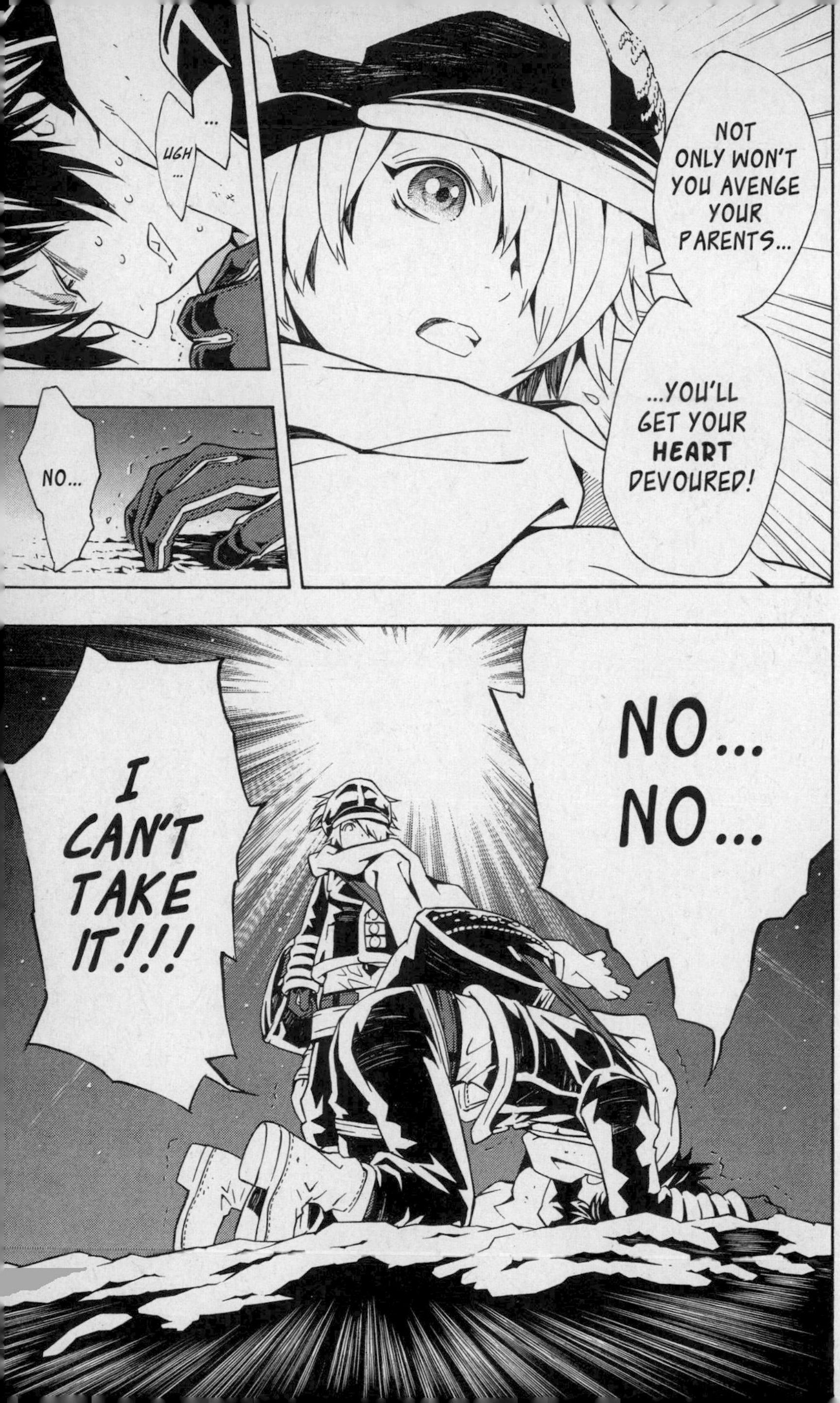
NOT ONLY WON'T YOU AVENGE YOUR PARENTS...
...YOU'LL GET YOUR **HEART** DEVOURED!
... UGH ...
NO...
NO... NO...
I CAN'T TAKE IT!!!

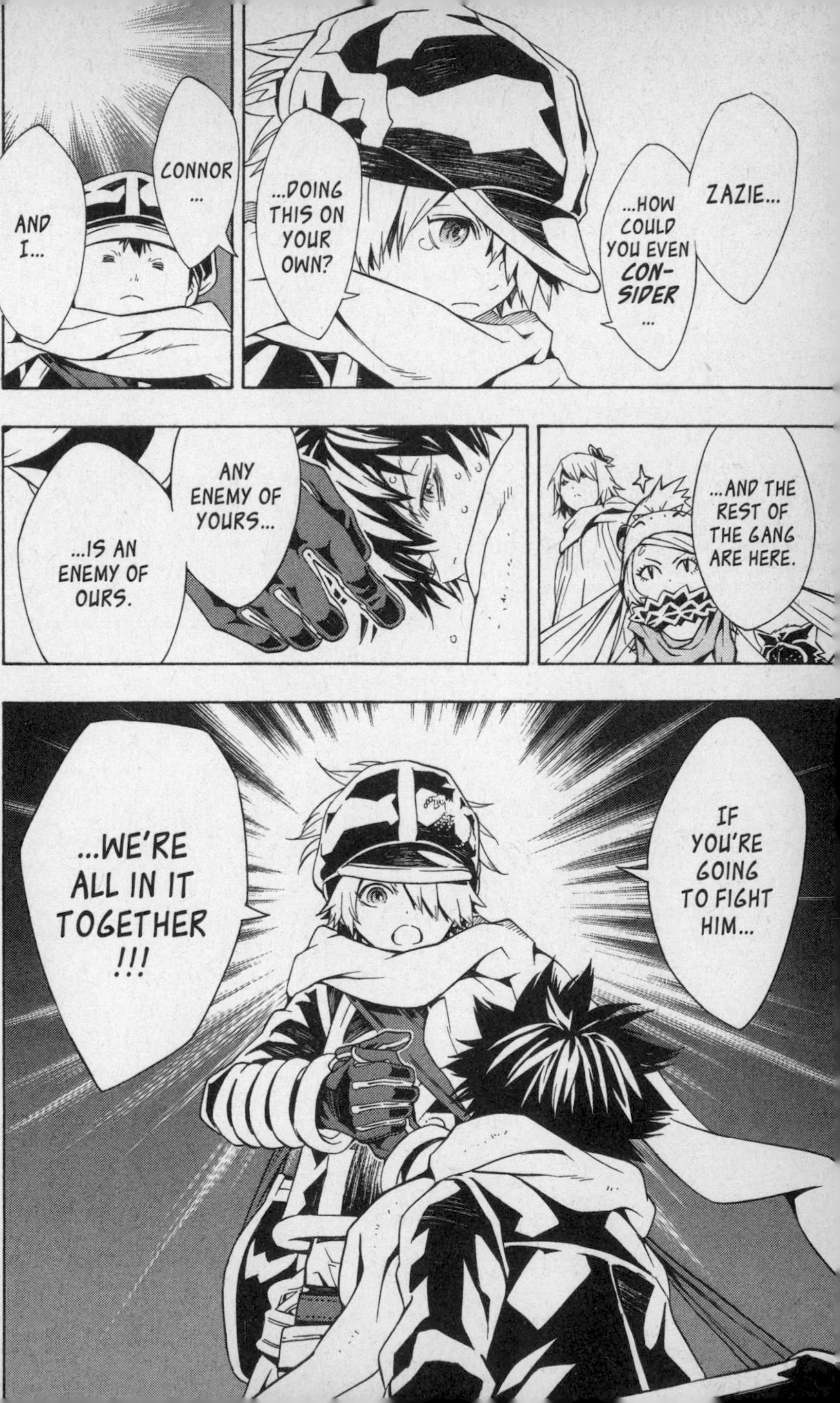
ZAZIE...
...HOW COULD YOU EVEN CON-SIDER...
...DOING THIS ON YOUR OWN?
CONNOR...
AND I...
...AND THE REST OF THE GANG ARE HERE.
ANY ENEMY OF YOURS...
...IS AN ENEMY OF OURS.
IF YOU'RE GOING TO FIGHT HIM...
...WE'RE ALL IN IT TOGETHER!!!

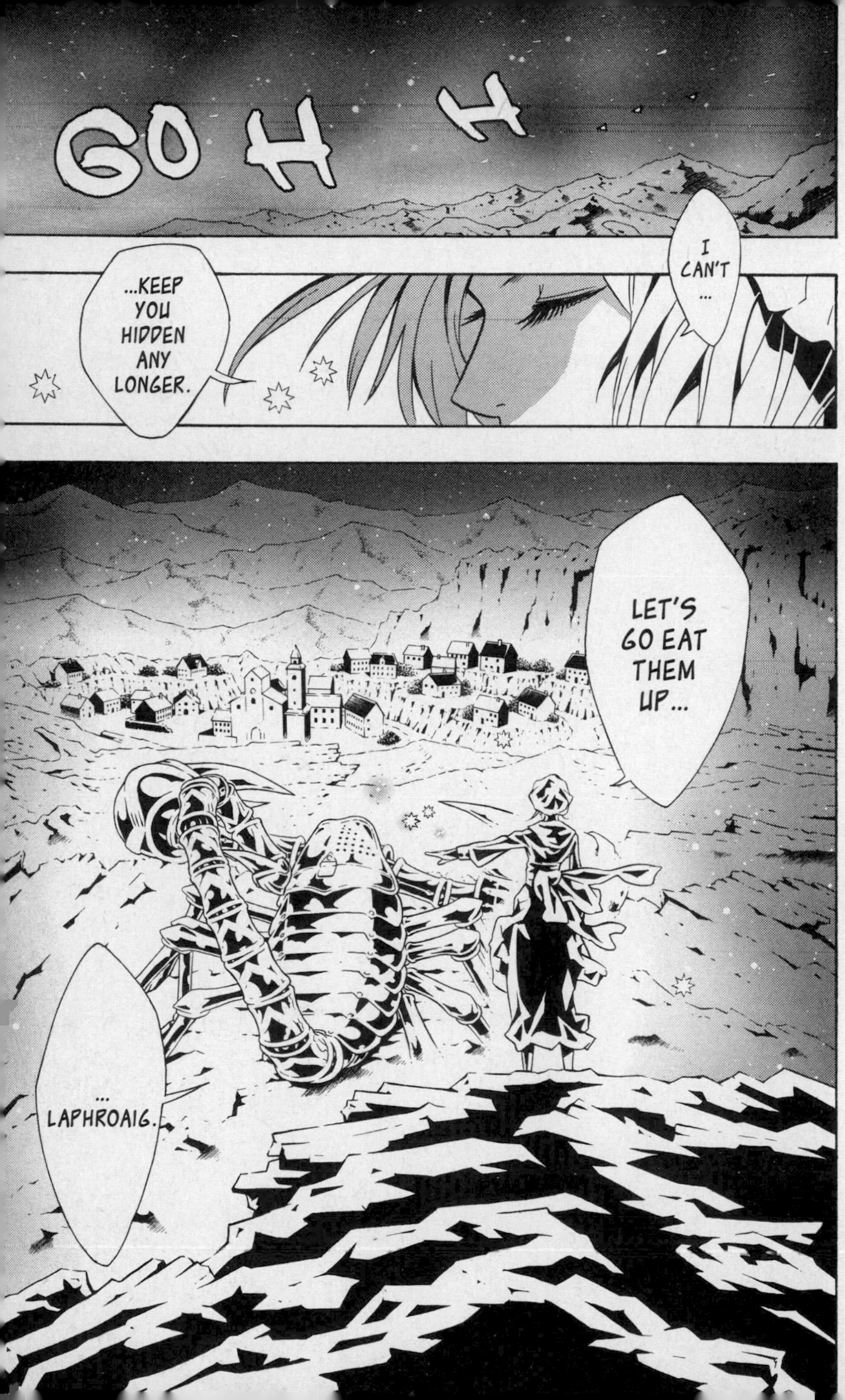
GO H H
I CAN'T ...
...KEEP YOU HIDDEN ANY LONGER.
LET'S GO EAT THEM UP...
... LAPHROAIG.

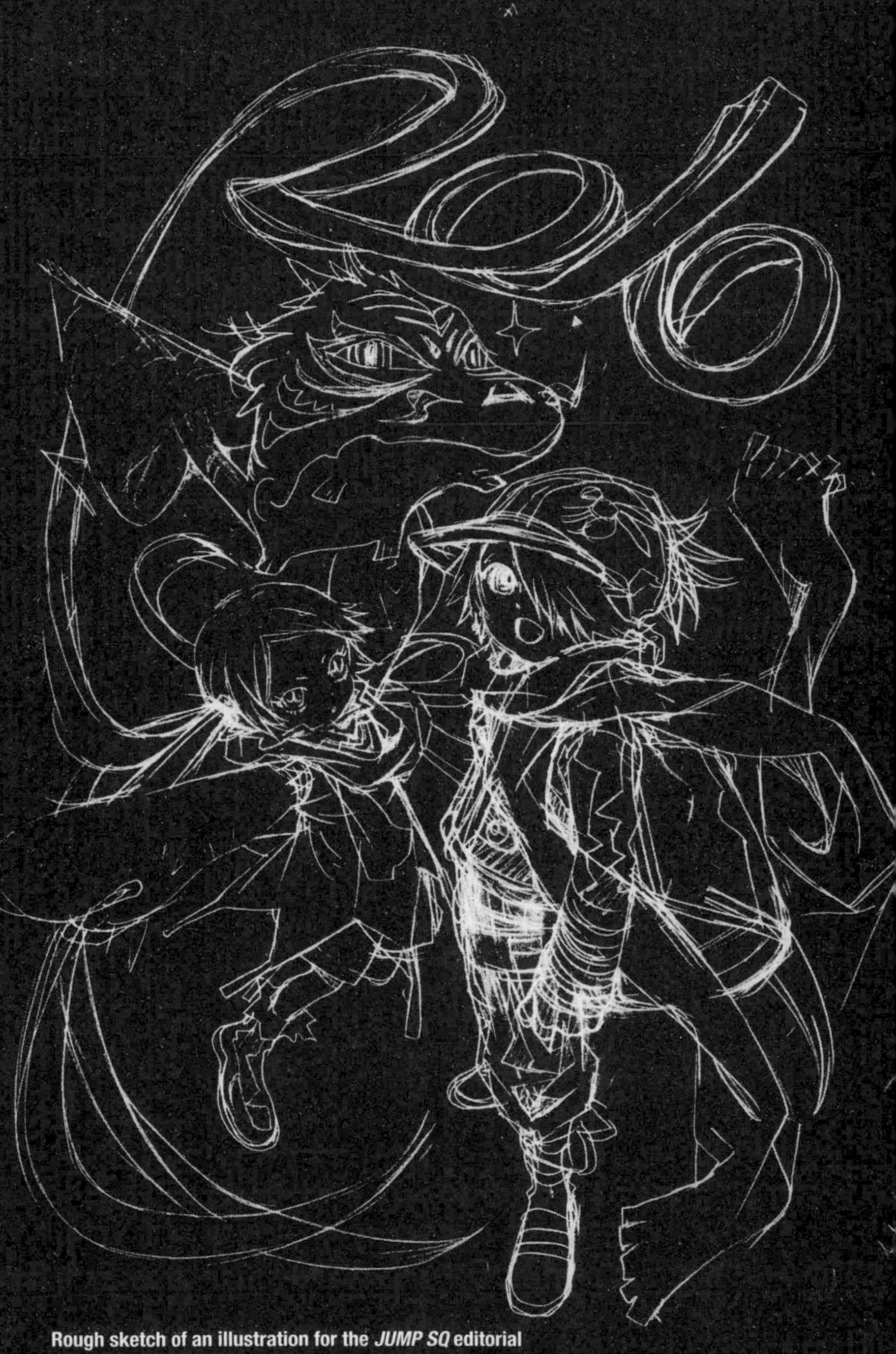

Rough sketch of an illustration for the *JUMP SQ* editorial department's 2010 New Year's card.

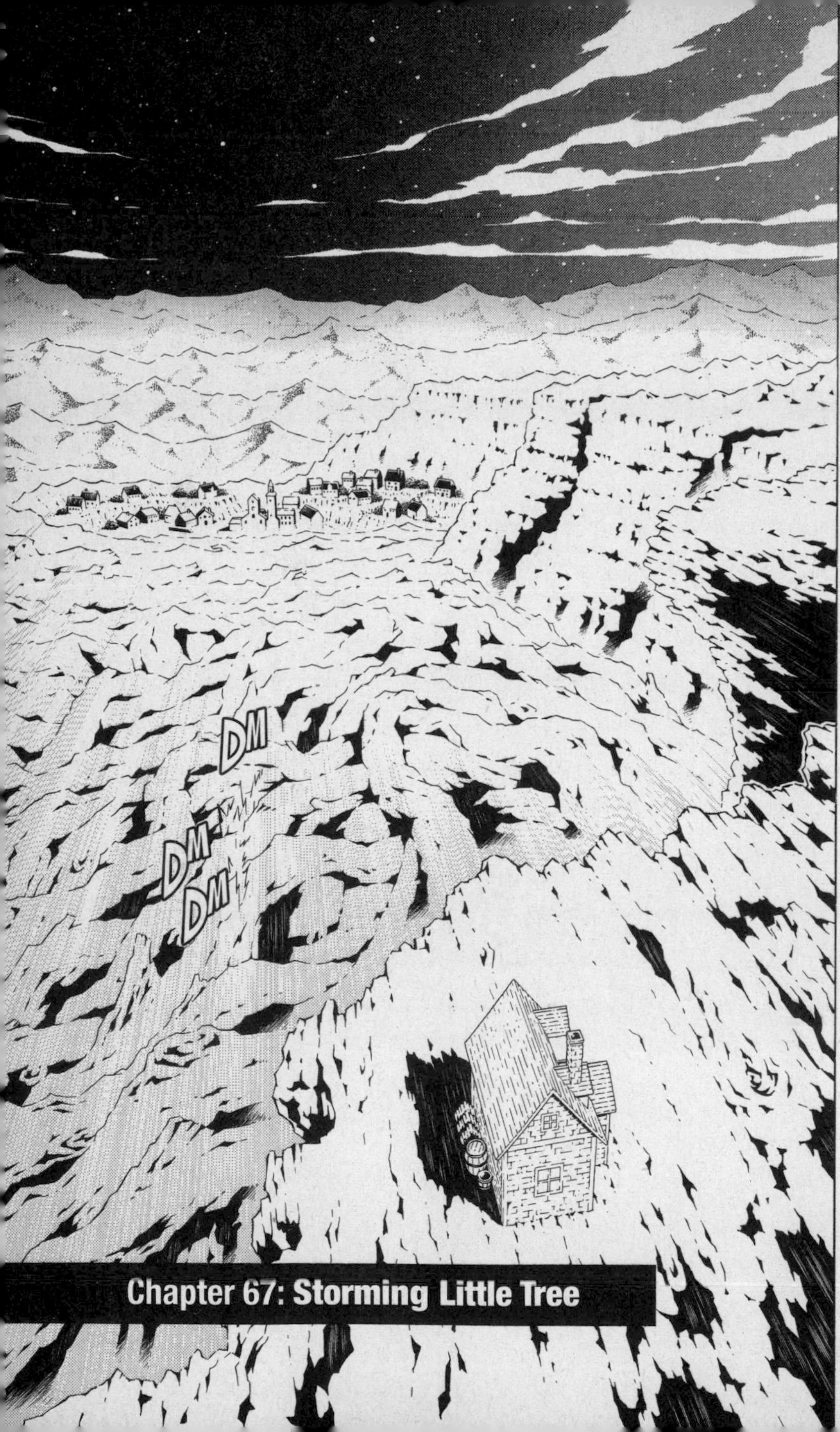
DM
DM
DM
Chapter 67: Storming Little Tree

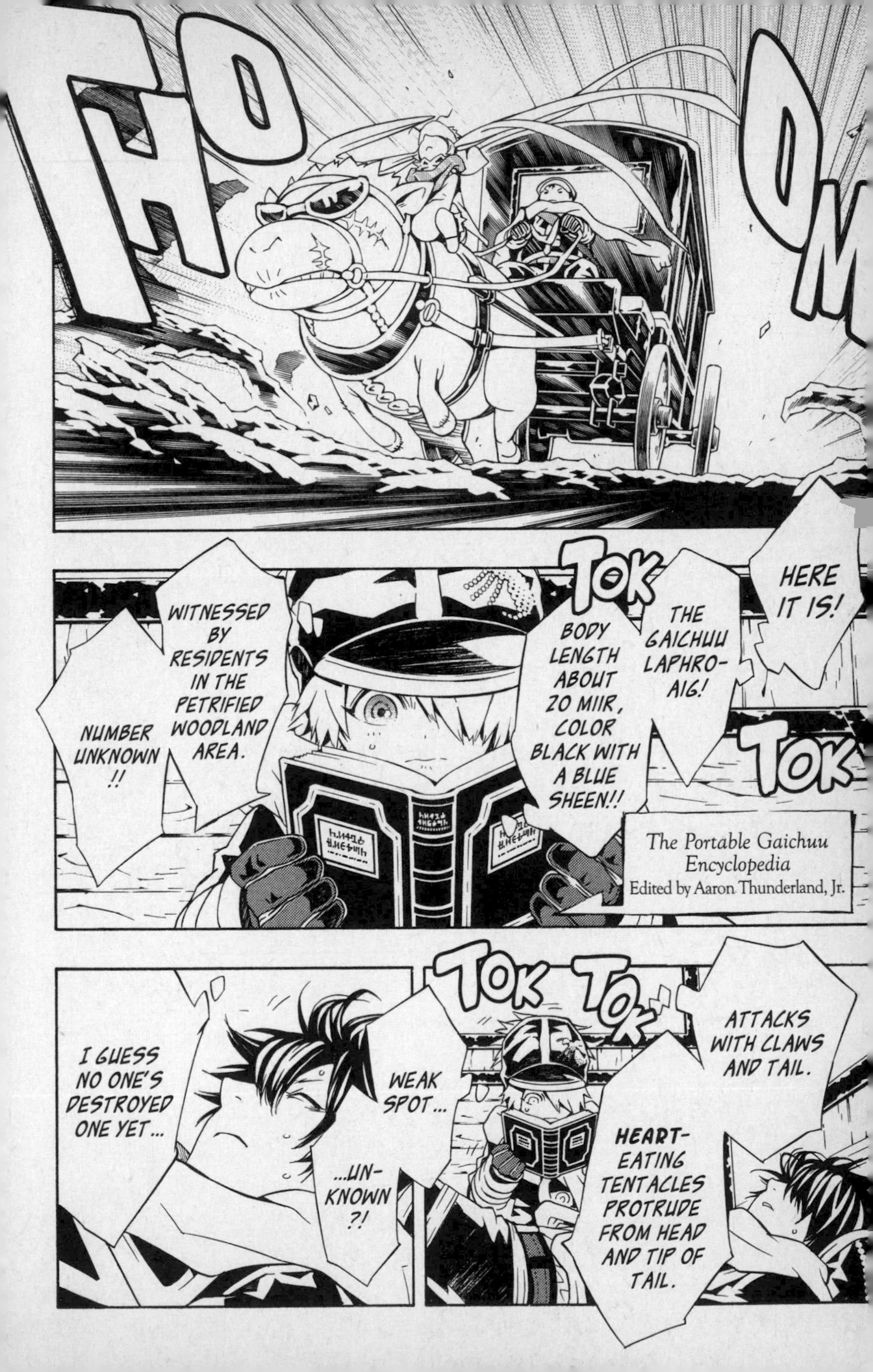
FHOOM
HERE IT IS!
THE GAICHUU LAPHRO-AIG!
TOK
BODY LENGTH ABOUT 20 MIIR, COLOR BLACK WITH A BLUE SHEEN!!
TOK
The Portable Gaichuu Encyclopedia
Edited by Aaron Thunderland, Jr.
WITNESSED BY RESIDENTS IN THE PETRIFIED WOODLAND AREA.
NUMBER UNKNOWN !!
ATTACKS WITH CLAWS AND TAIL.
TOK TOK
HEART-EATING TENTACLES PROTRUDE FROM HEAD AND TIP OF TAIL.
WEAK SPOT...
...UN-KNOWN ?!
I GUESS NO ONE'S DESTROYED ONE YET...

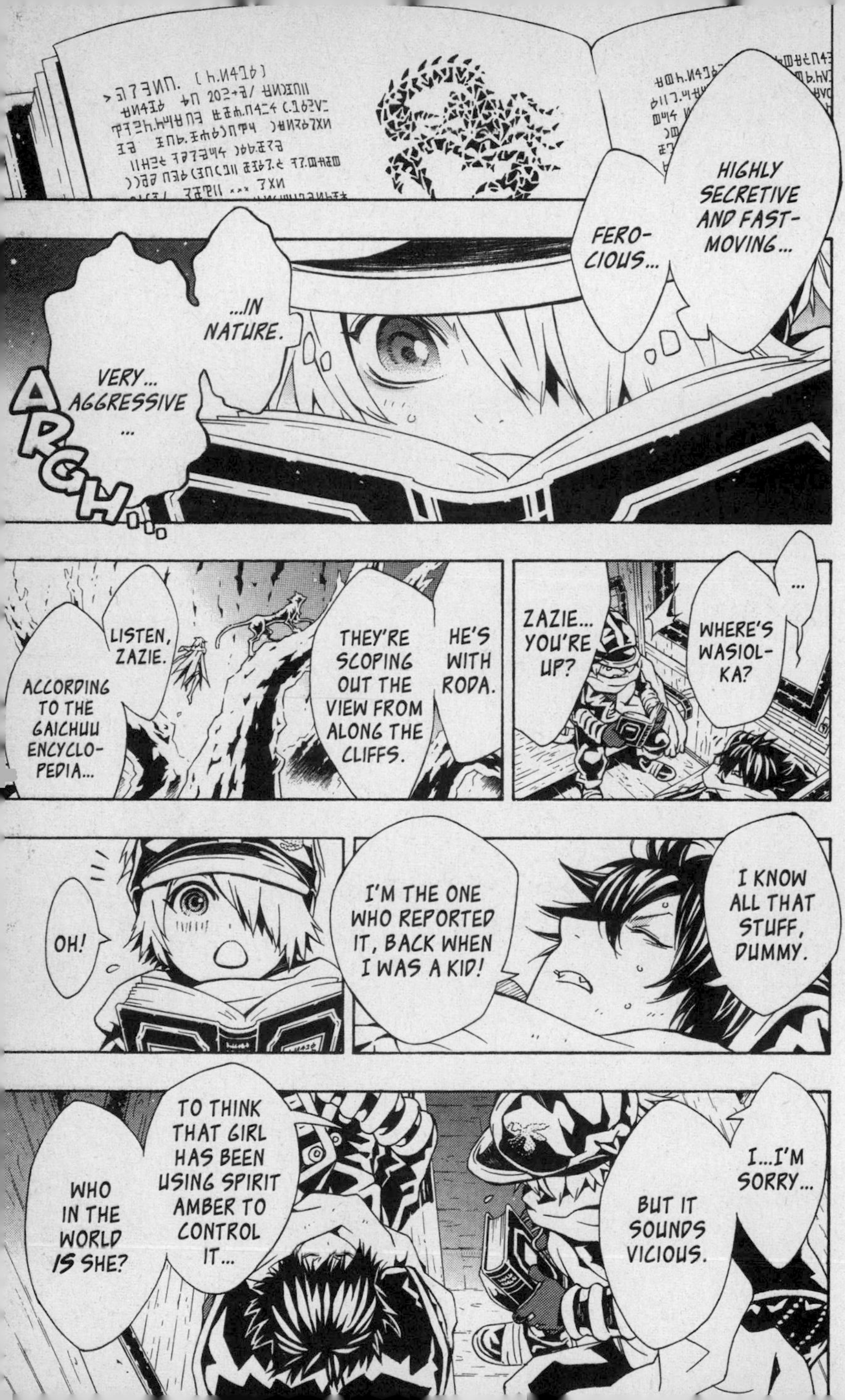
HIGHLY SECRETIVE AND FAST-MOVING...
FERO-CIOUS...
...IN NATURE.
VERY... AGGRESSIVE ...
ARGH...
...
WHERE'S WASIOL-KA?
ZAZIE... YOU'RE UP?
HE'S WITH RODA.
THEY'RE SCOPING OUT THE VIEW FROM ALONG THE CLIFFS.
LISTEN, ZAZIE.
ACCORDING TO THE GAICHUU ENCYCLO-PEDIA...
I KNOW ALL THAT STUFF, DUMMY.
I'M THE ONE WHO REPORTED IT, BACK WHEN I WAS A KID!
OH!
I...I'M SORRY...
BUT IT SOUNDS VICIOUS.
TO THINK THAT GIRL HAS BEEN USING SPIRIT AMBER TO CONTROL IT...
WHO IN THE WORLD IS SHE?

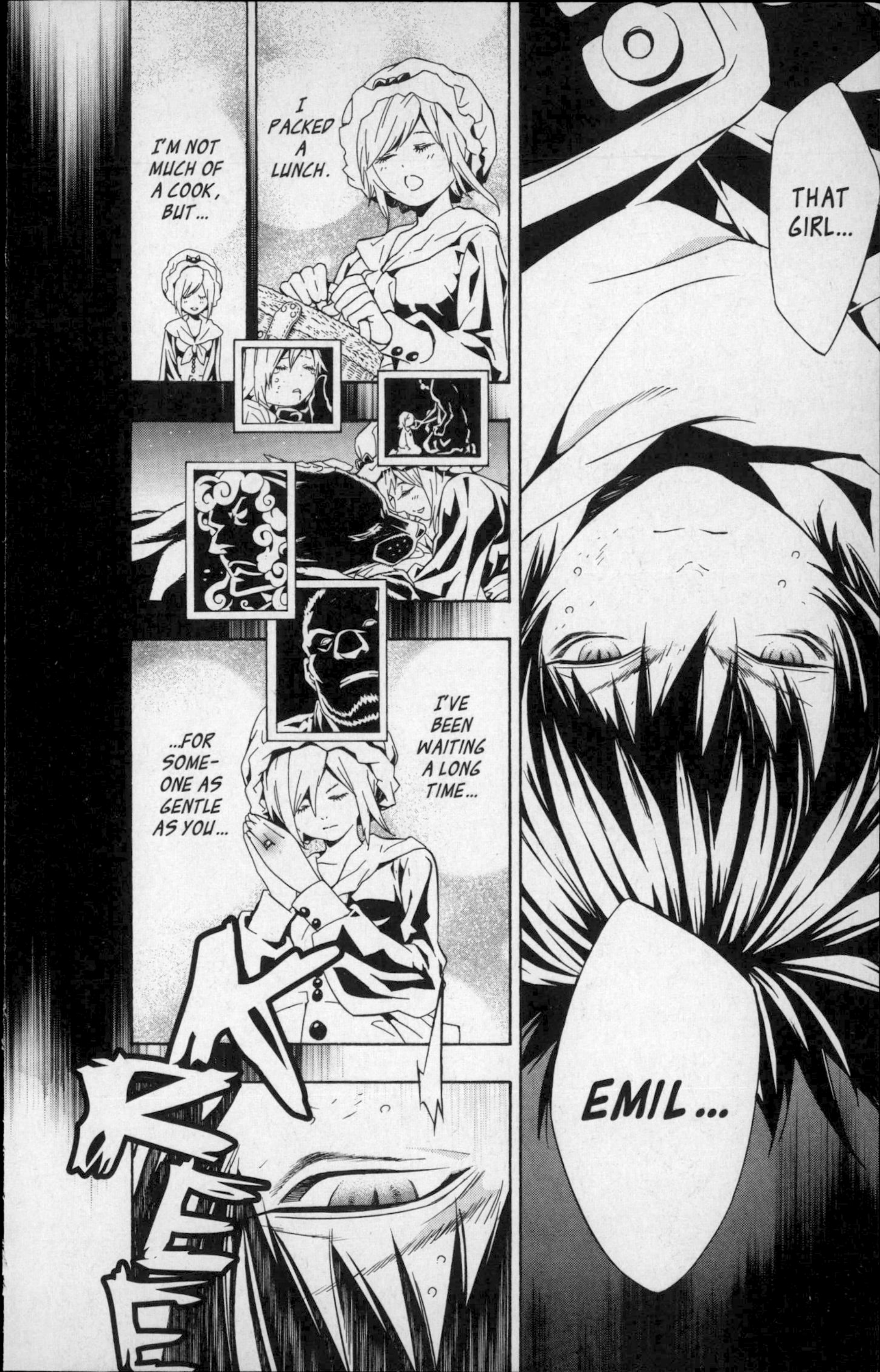
THAT GIRL...
EMIL...
I PACKED A LUNCH.
I'M NOT MUCH OF A COOK, BUT...
I'VE BEEN WAITING A LONG TIME...
...FOR SOME-ONE AS GENTLE AS YOU...

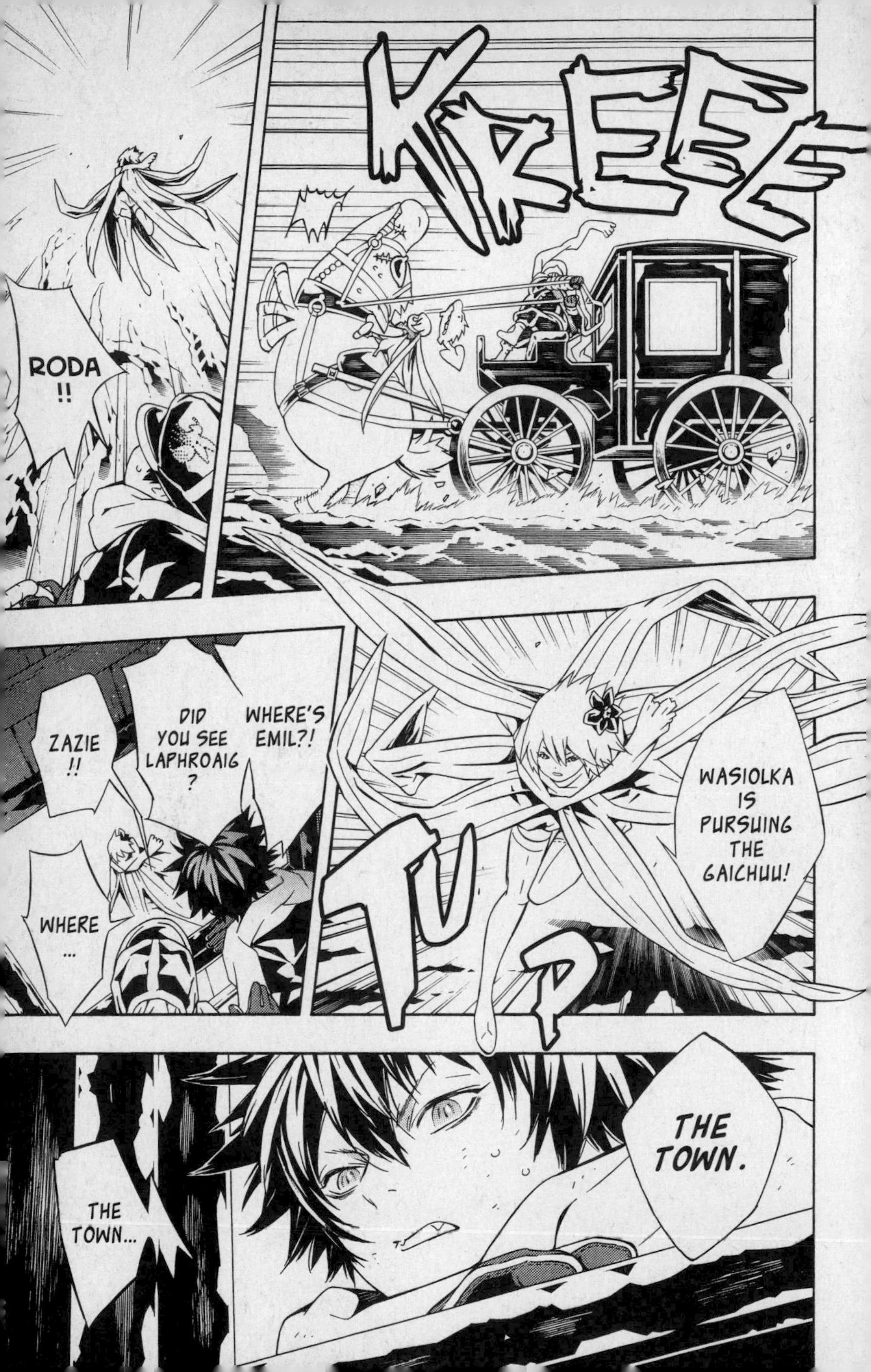
KREEE
RODA !!
WASIOLKA IS PURSUING THE GAICHUU!
TUP
WHERE'S EMIL?!
DID YOU SEE LAPHROAIG ?
ZAZIE !!
WHERE ...
THE TOWN.
THE TOWN...

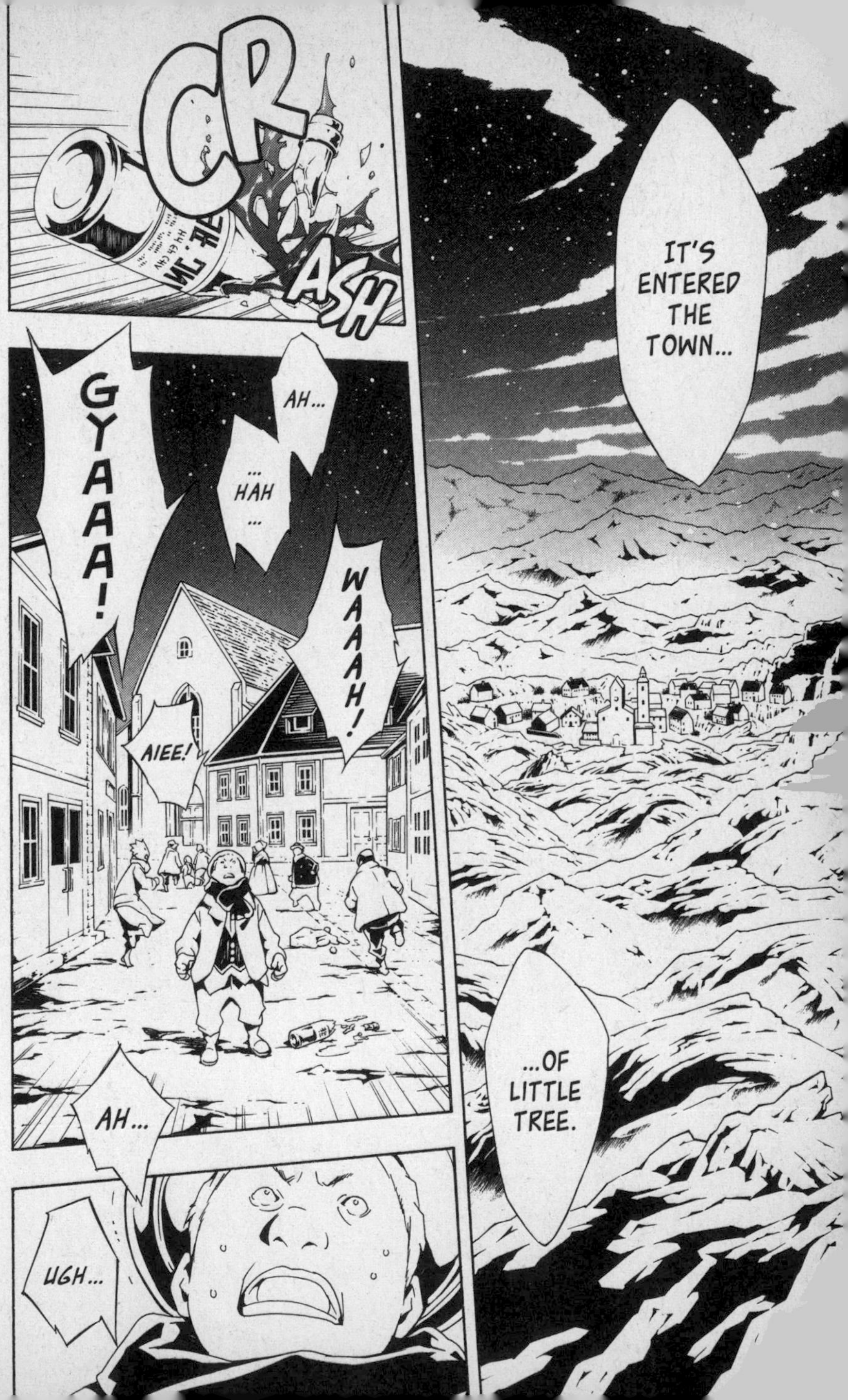
IT'S ENTERED THE TOWN...
...OF LITTLE TREE.
CRASH
GYAAAA!
AH...
...HAH...
WAAAAH!
AIEE!
AH...
UGH...

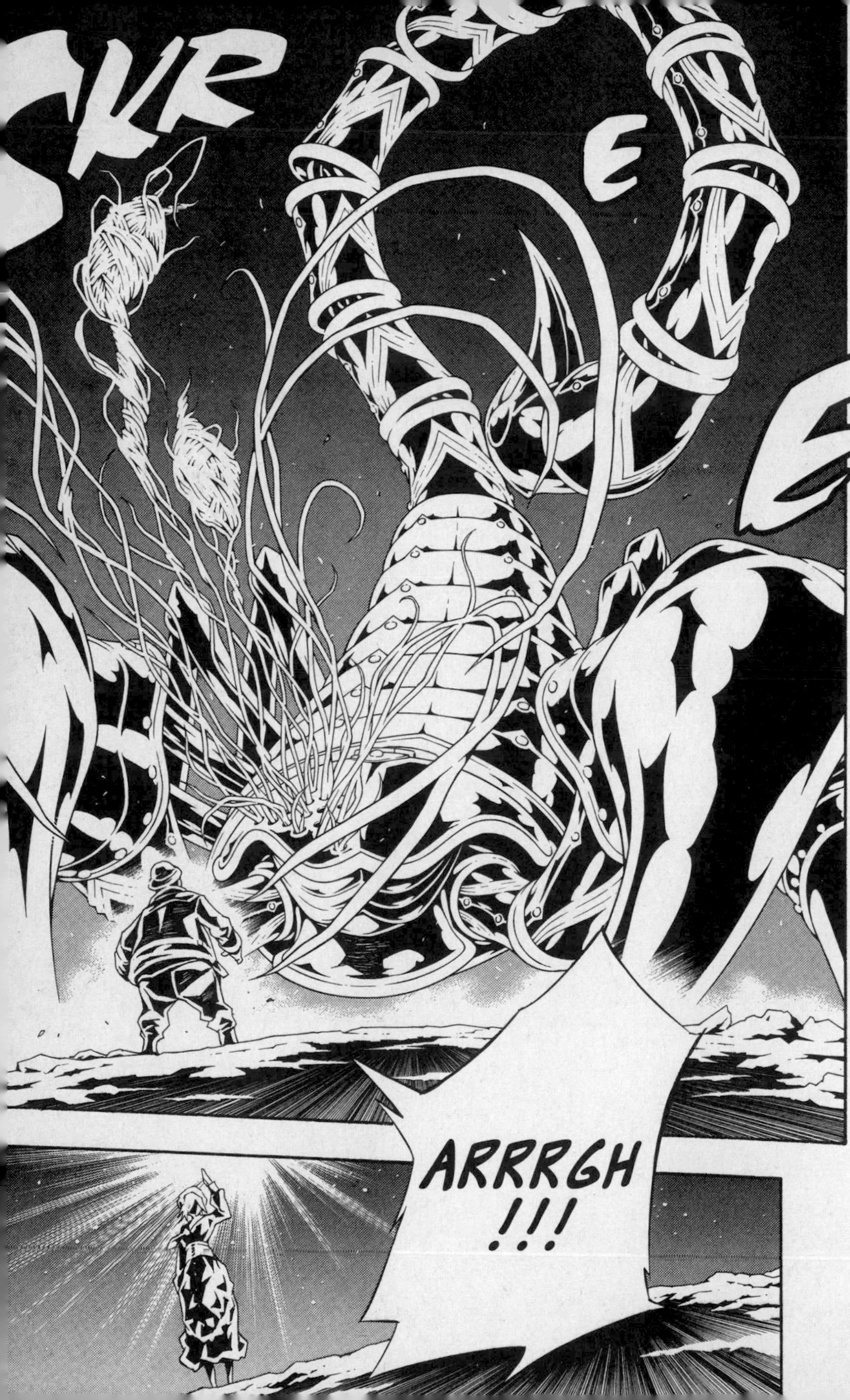
SKR
E
E
ARRRGH!!!

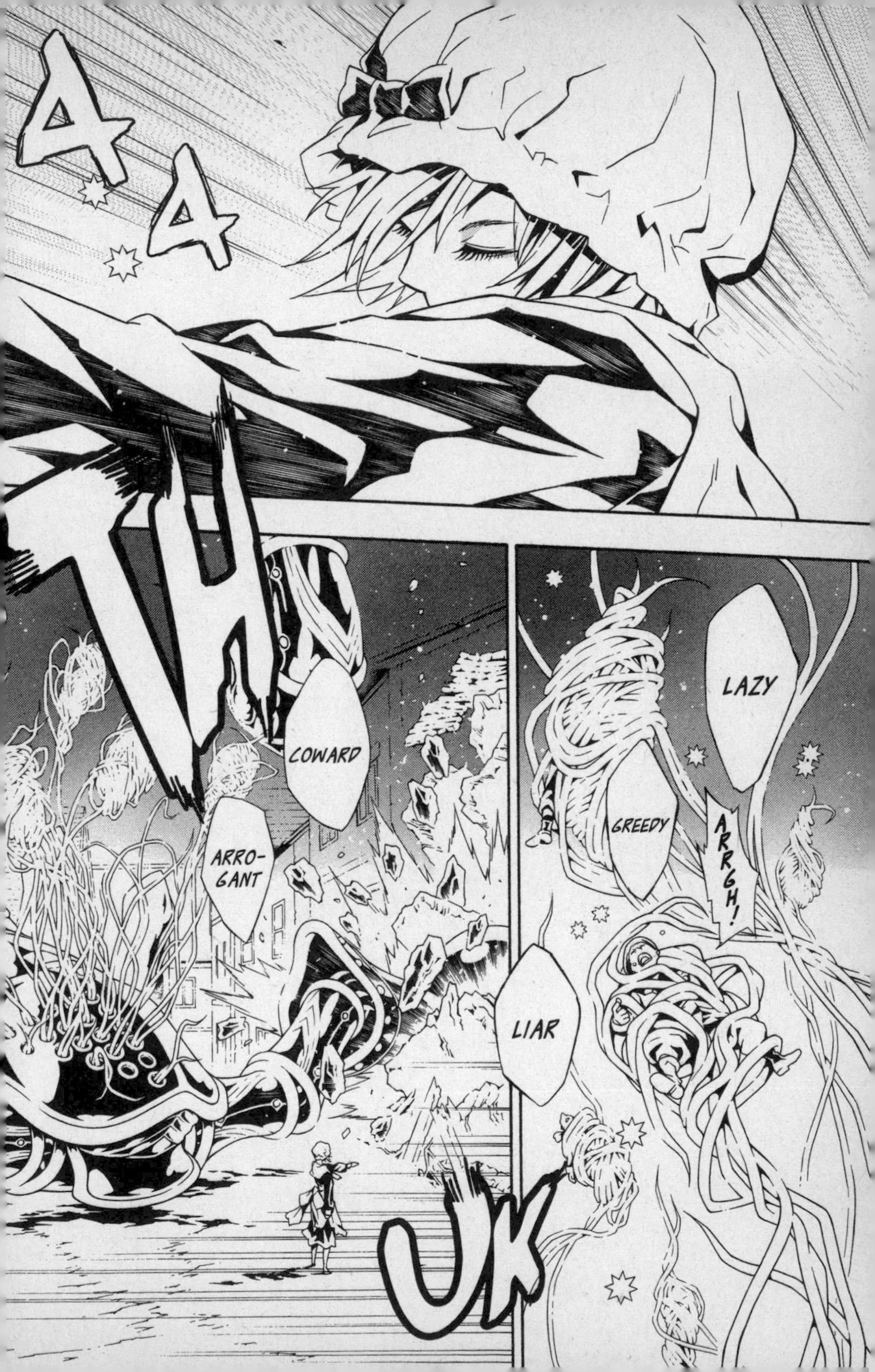
A
A
LAZY
GREEDY
ARRGH!
LIAR
COWARD
ARRO-GANT
TH
UK

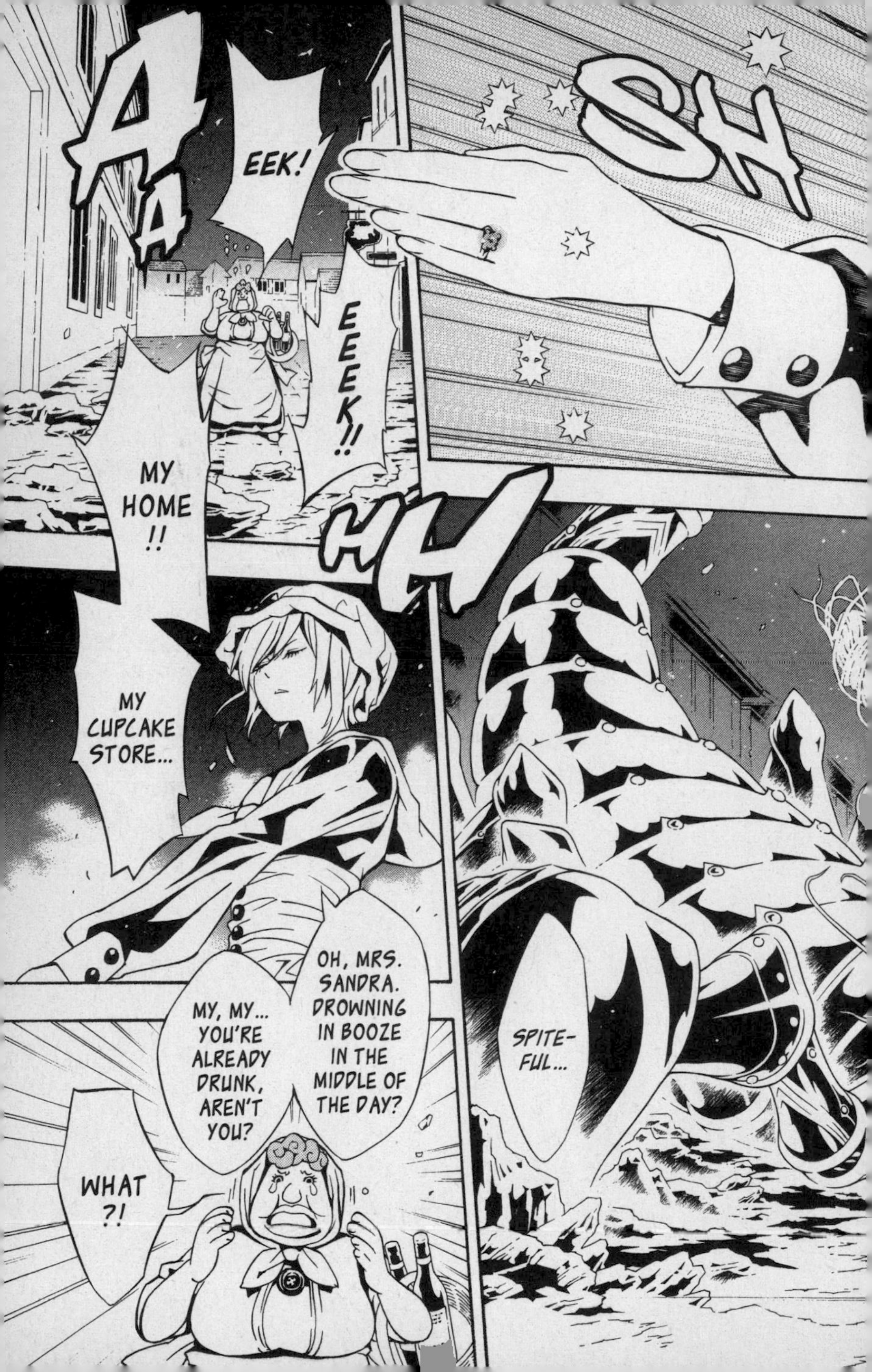
SHH
AA
EEK!
EEEEK!!
MY HOME!!
SPITE-FUL...
MY CUPCAKE STORE...
OH, MRS. SANDRA. DROWNING IN BOOZE IN THE MIDDLE OF THE DAY?
MY, MY... YOU'RE ALREADY DRUNK, AREN'T YOU?
WHAT?!

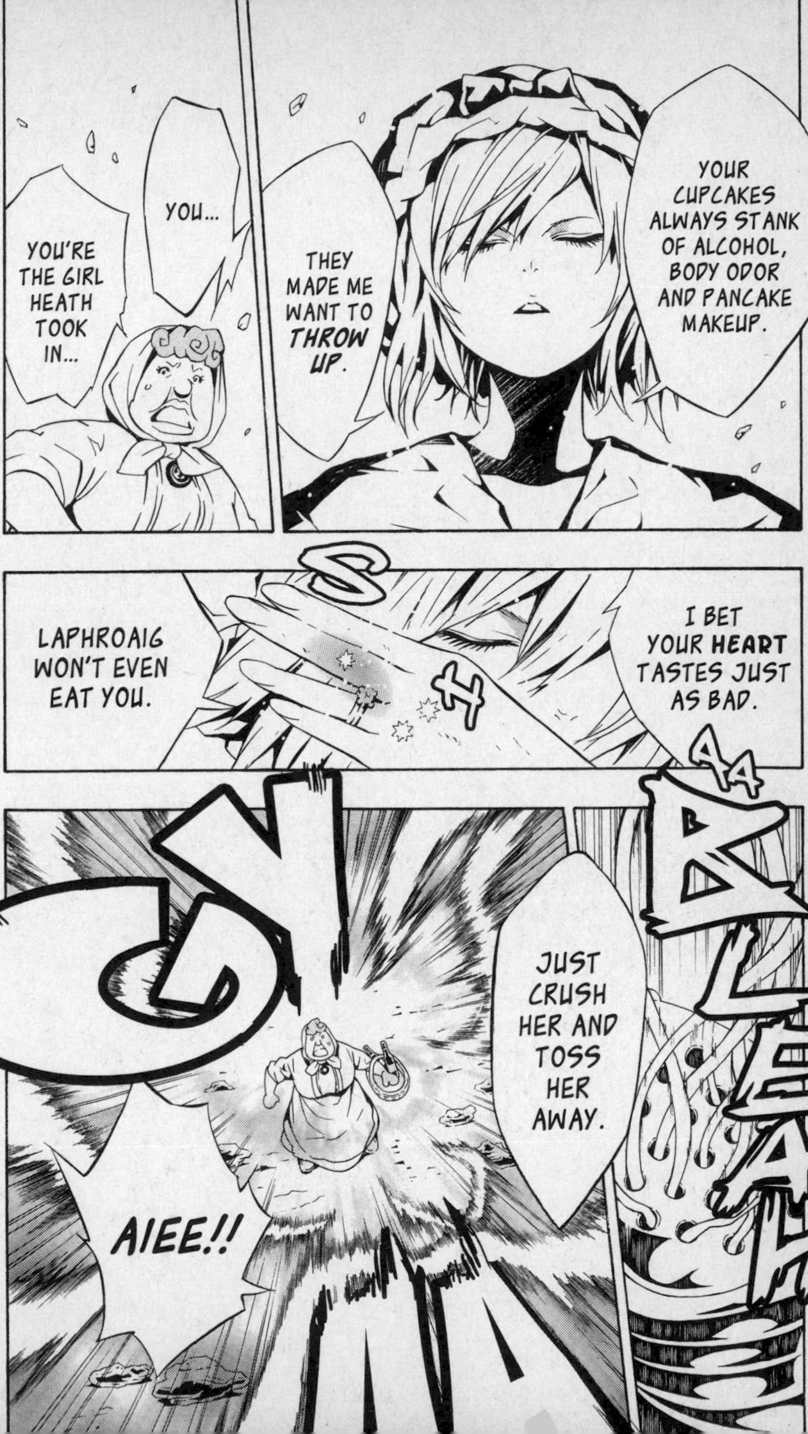
YOUR CUPCAKES ALWAYS STANK OF ALCOHOL, BODY ODOR AND PANCAKE MAKEUP.
THEY MADE ME WANT TO **THROW UP**.
YOU...
YOU'RE THE GIRL HEATH TOOK IN...
I BET YOUR **HEART** TASTES JUST AS BAD.
LAPHROAIG WON'T EVEN EAT YOU.
JUST CRUSH HER AND TOSS HER AWAY.
AIEE!!

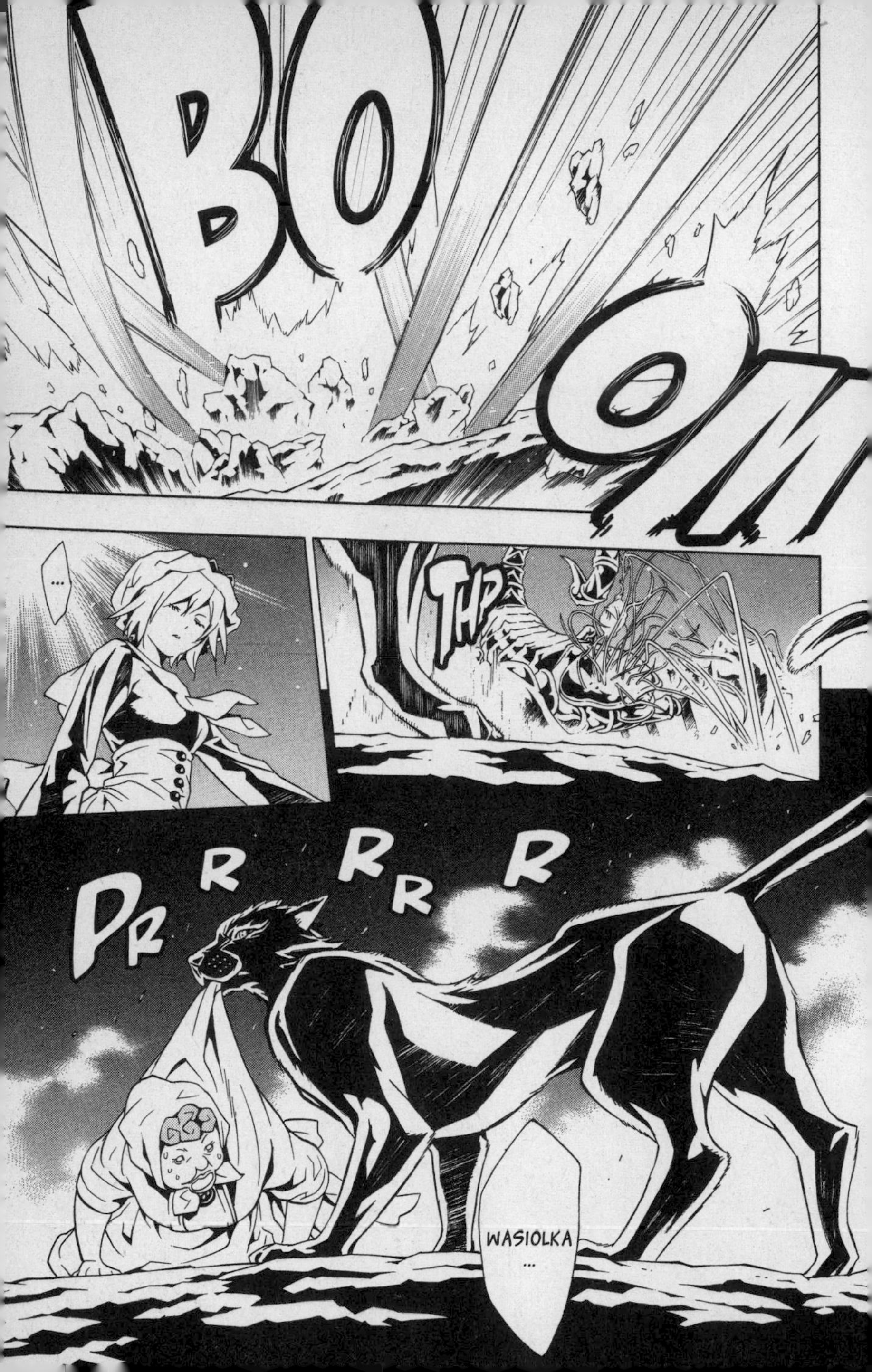
BOOM
THP
...
PRRRR
WASIOLKA
...

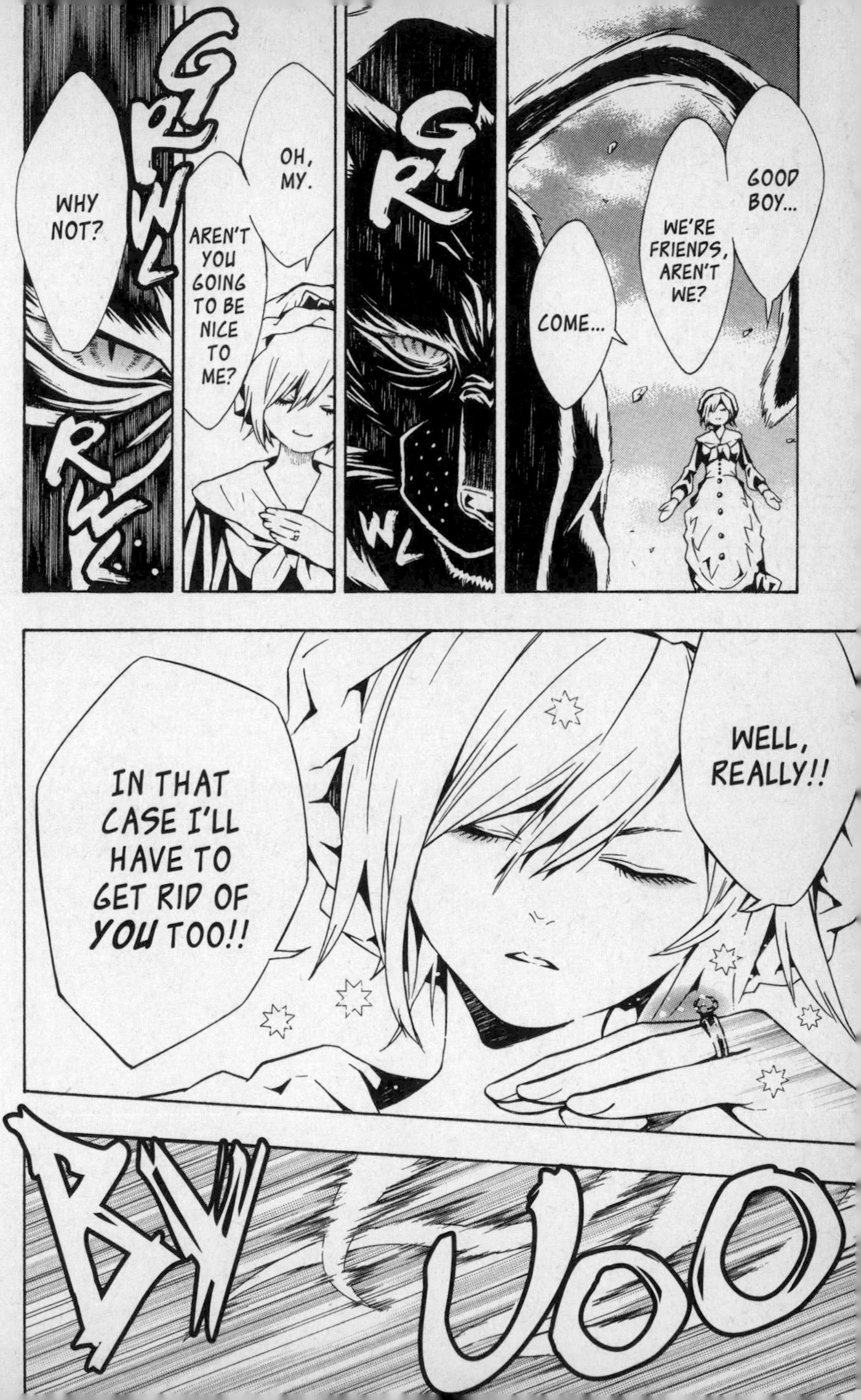
GOOD BOY...
WE'RE FRIENDS, AREN'T WE?
COME...
OH, MY.
AREN'T YOU GOING TO BE NICE TO ME?
WHY NOT?
WELL, REALLY!!
IN THAT CASE I'LL HAVE TO GET RID OF YOU TOO!!
BYUOO

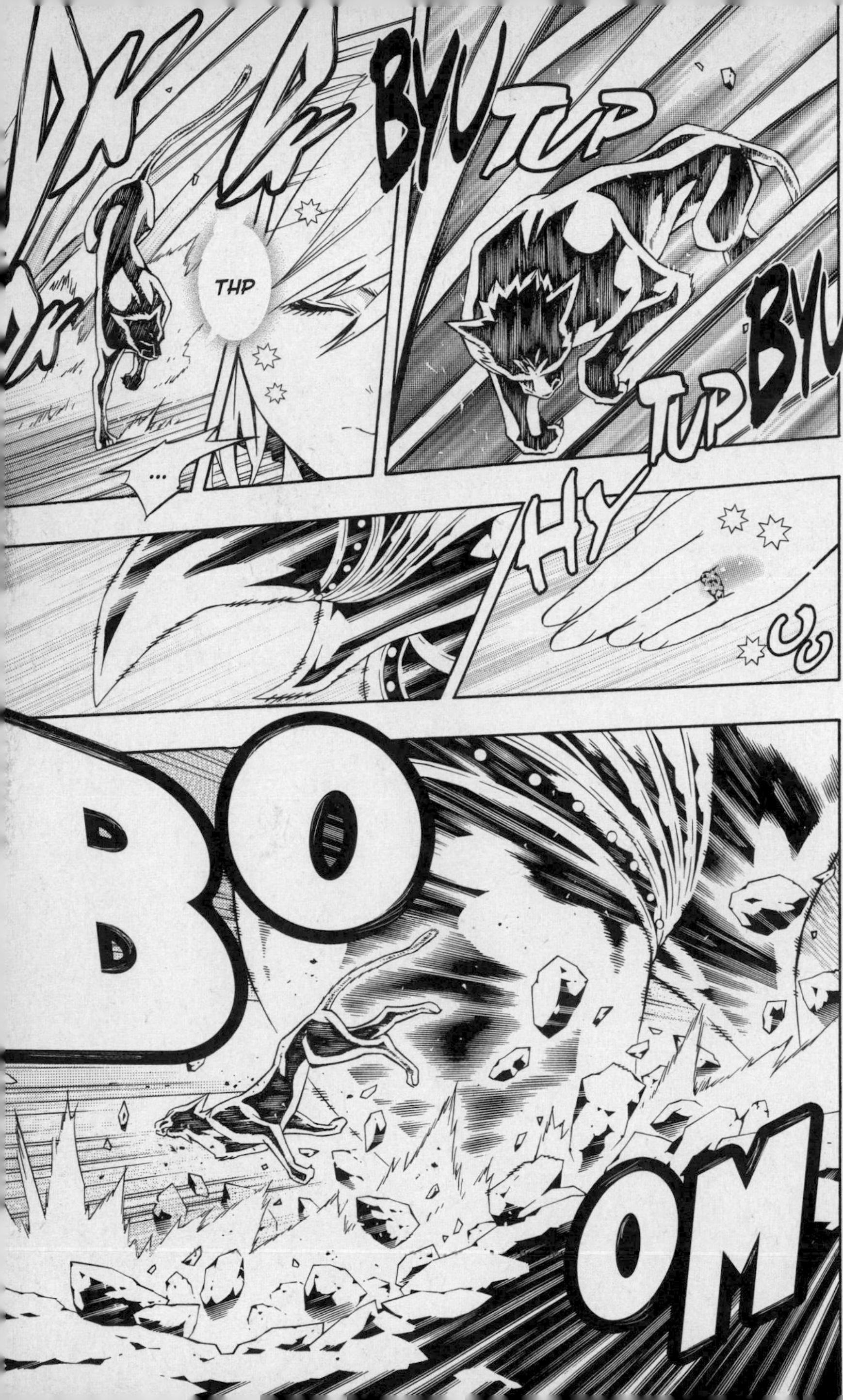
BYU TUP
TUP BYU
THP
...
HY
BOOM

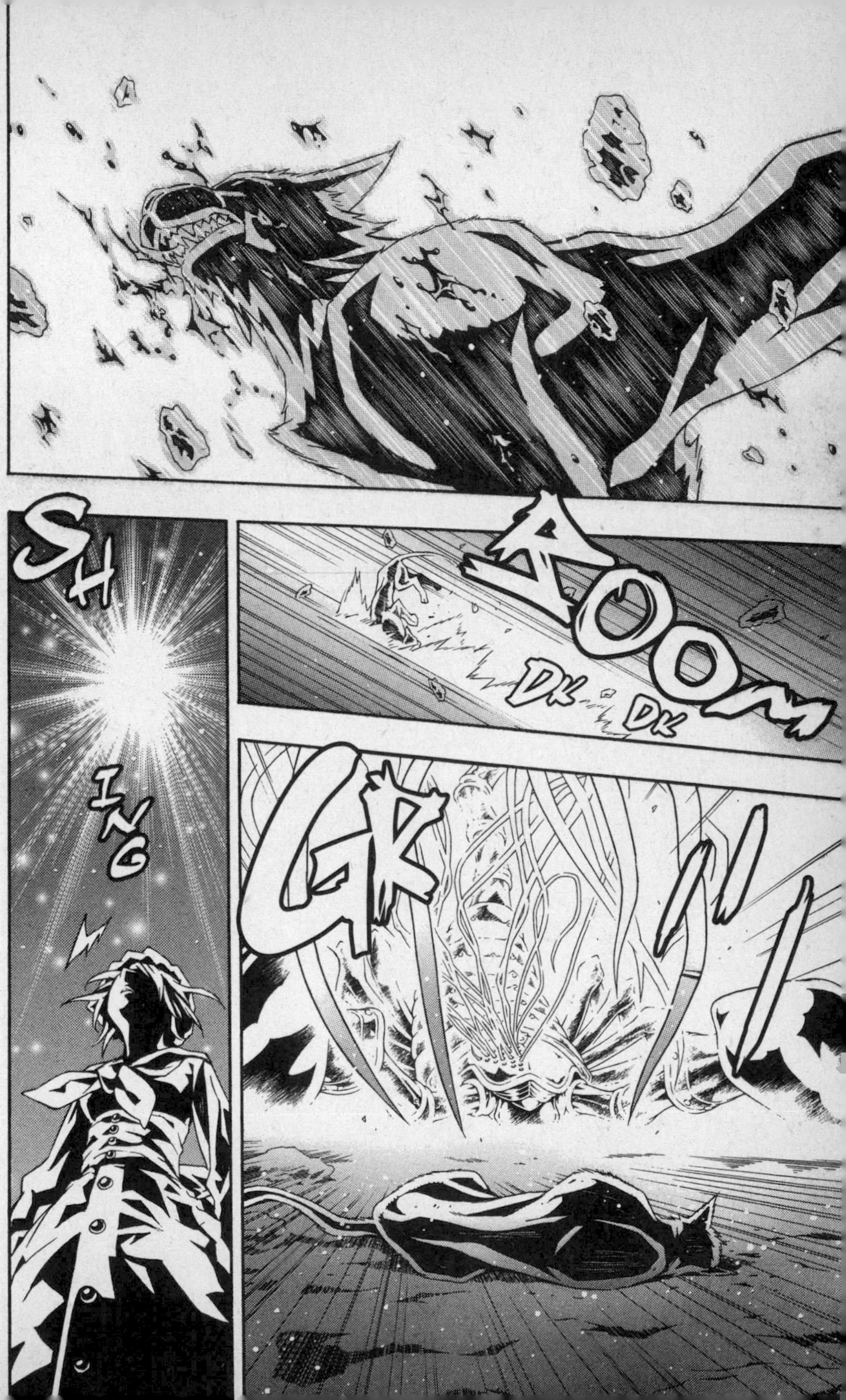
BOOM
DK DK
GRNN
SHING

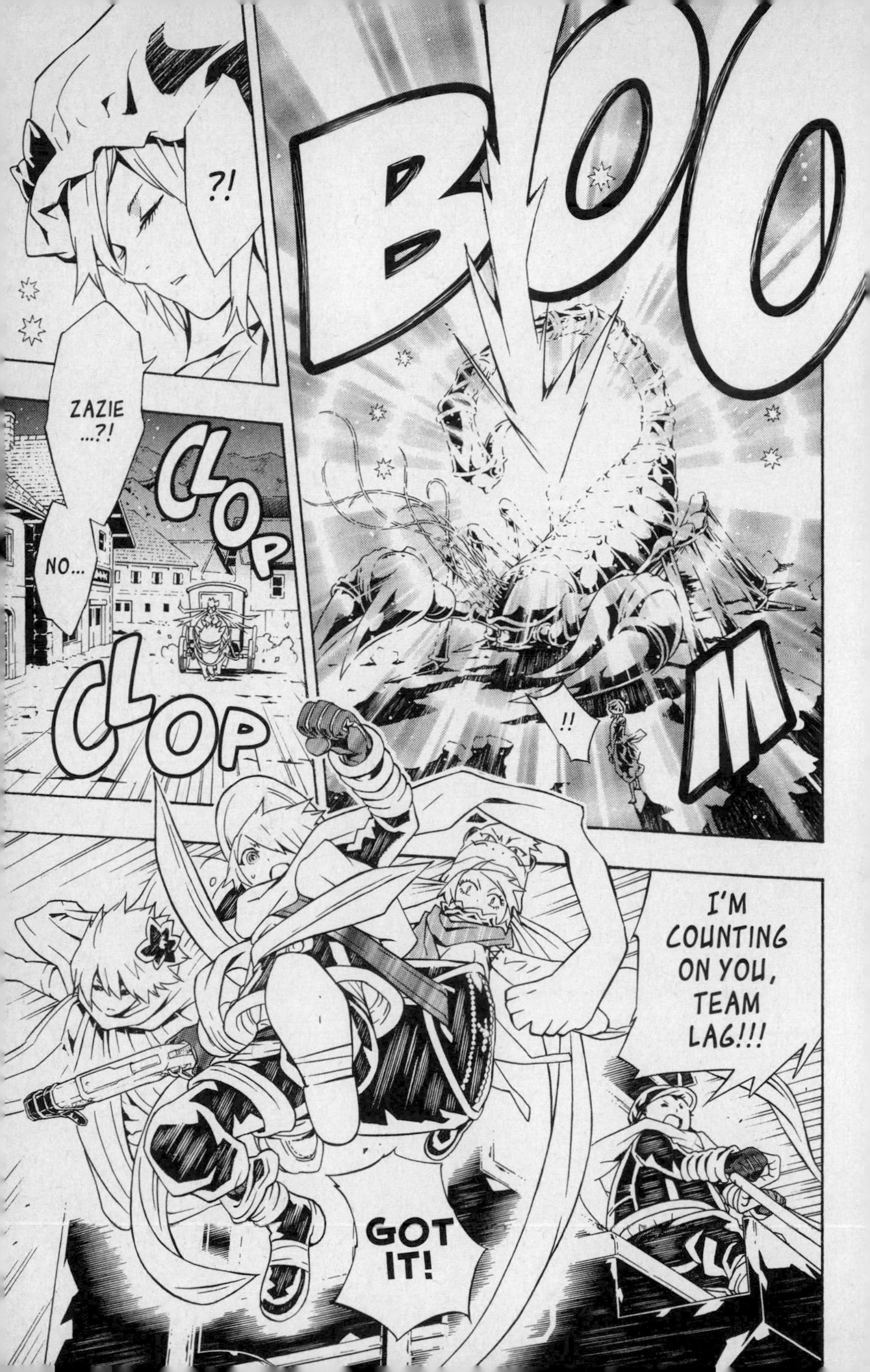
BOOOM
!!
?!
ZAZIE ...?!
CLOP
CLOP
NO...
I'M COUNTING ON YOU, TEAM LAG!!!
GOT IT!

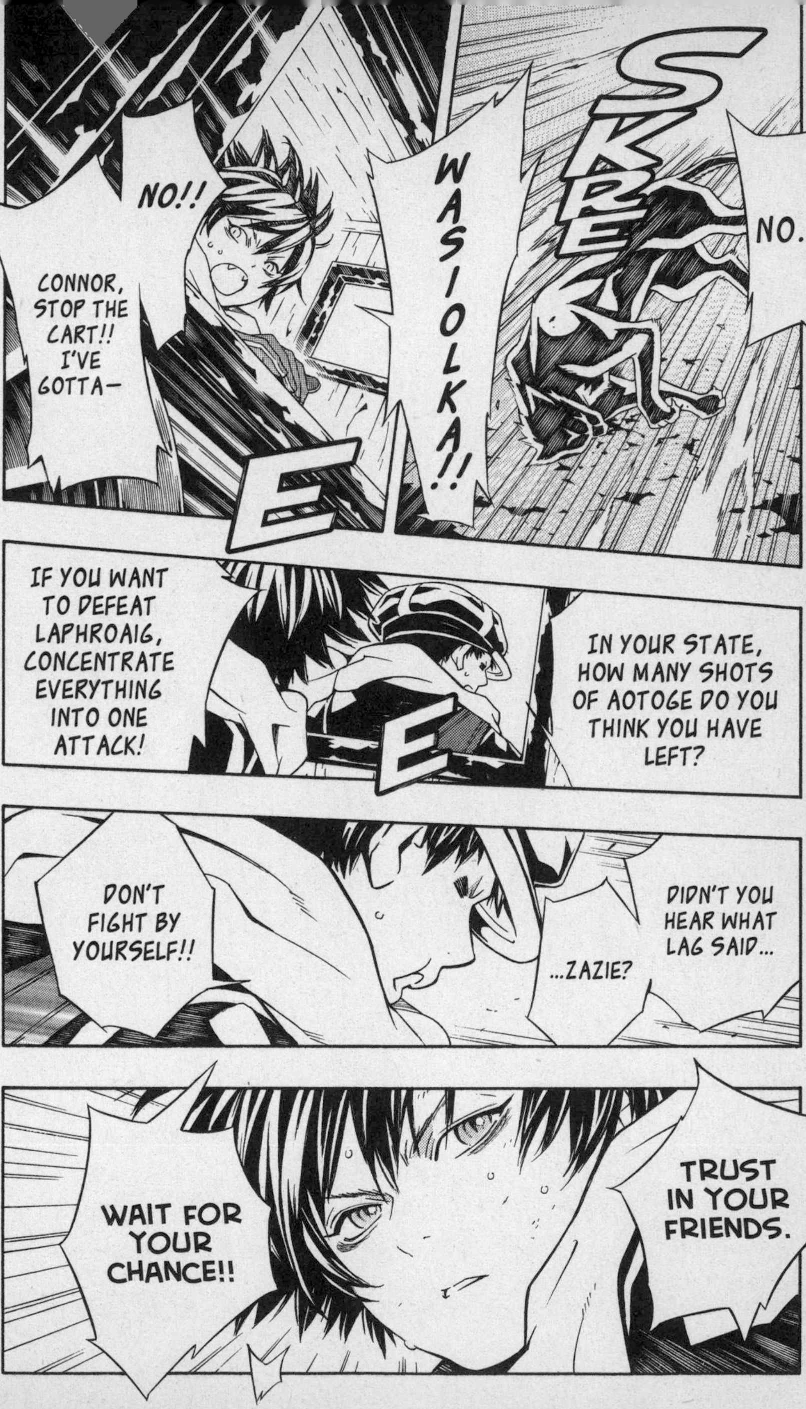
NO...
SKREE
WASIOLKA!!
NO!!
CONNOR, STOP THE CART!! I'VE GOTTA—
IN YOUR STATE, HOW MANY SHOTS OF AOTOGE DO YOU THINK YOU HAVE LEFT?
IF YOU WANT TO DEFEAT LAPHROAIG, CONCENTRATE EVERYTHING INTO ONE ATTACK!
DIDN'T YOU HEAR WHAT LAG SAID...
...ZAZIE?
DON'T FIGHT BY YOURSELF!!
TRUST IN YOUR FRIENDS.
WAIT FOR YOUR CHANCE!!

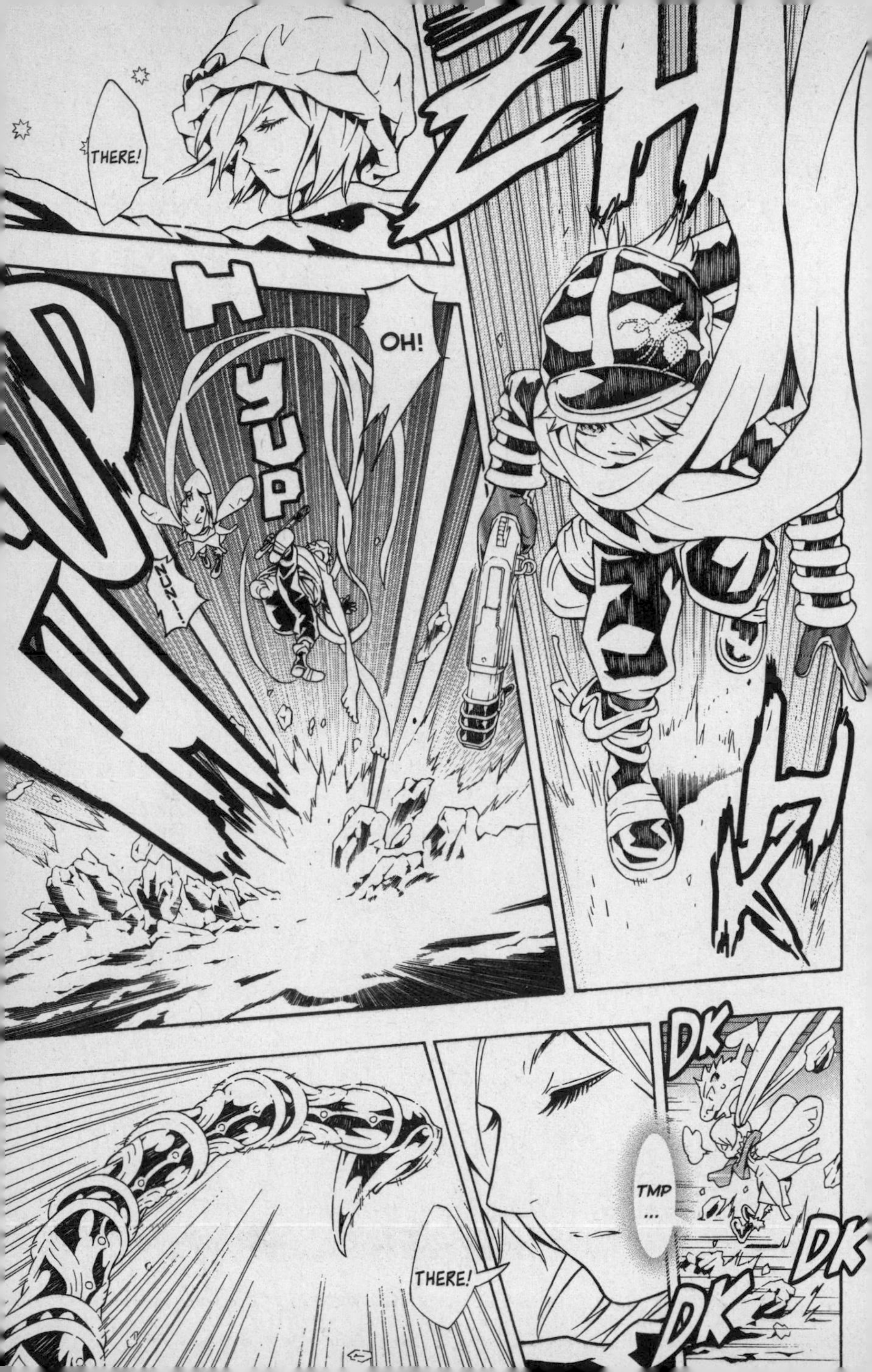
THERE!
OH!
HYUP
NUN!!
DK
DK
DK
TMP ...
THERE!

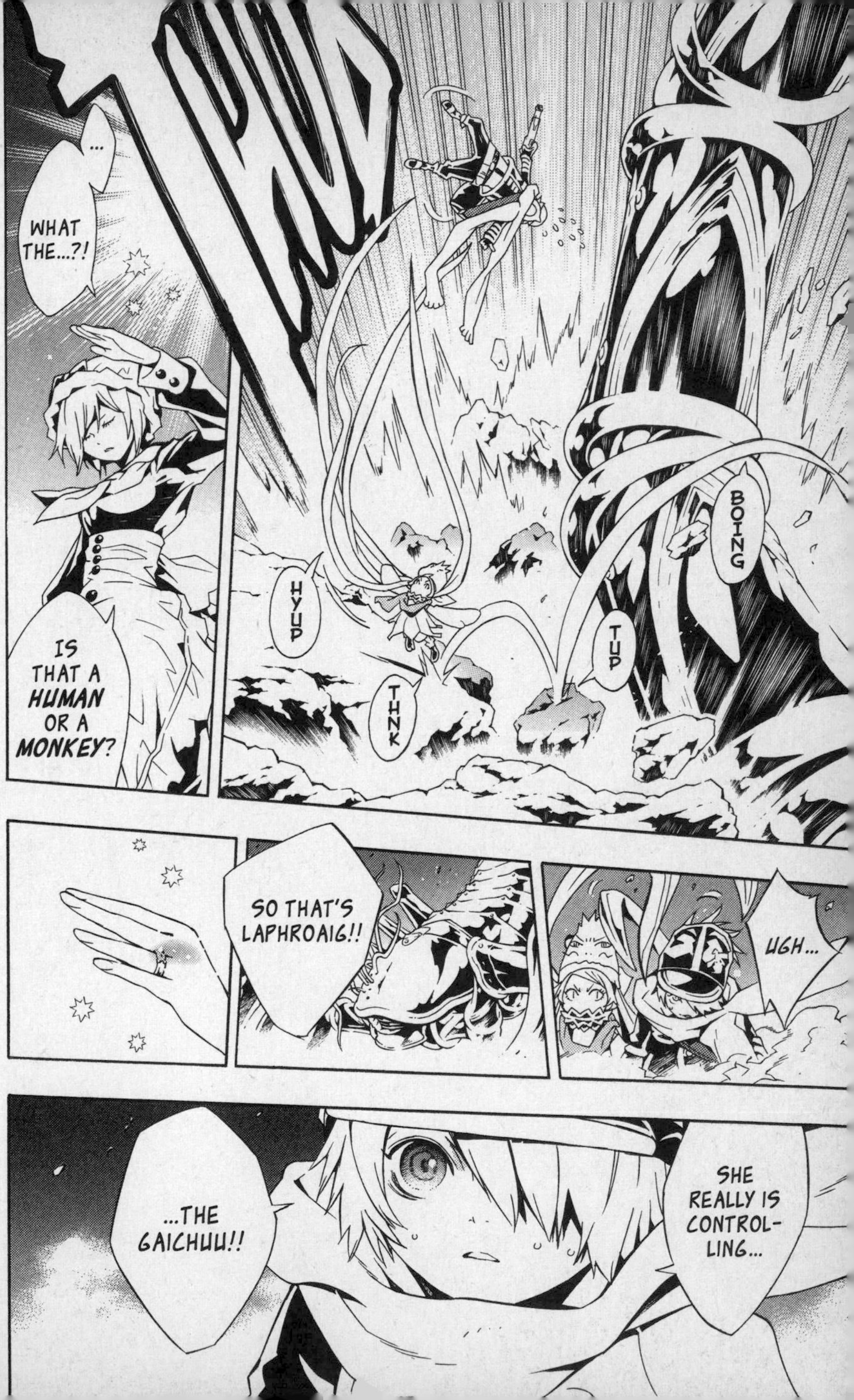
BOING
TUP
HYUP
THNK
THUD
...
WHAT THE...?!
IS THAT A *HUMAN* OR A *MONKEY*?
UGH...
SO THAT'S LAPHROAIG!!
SHE REALLY IS CONTROL-LING...
...THE GAICHUU!!

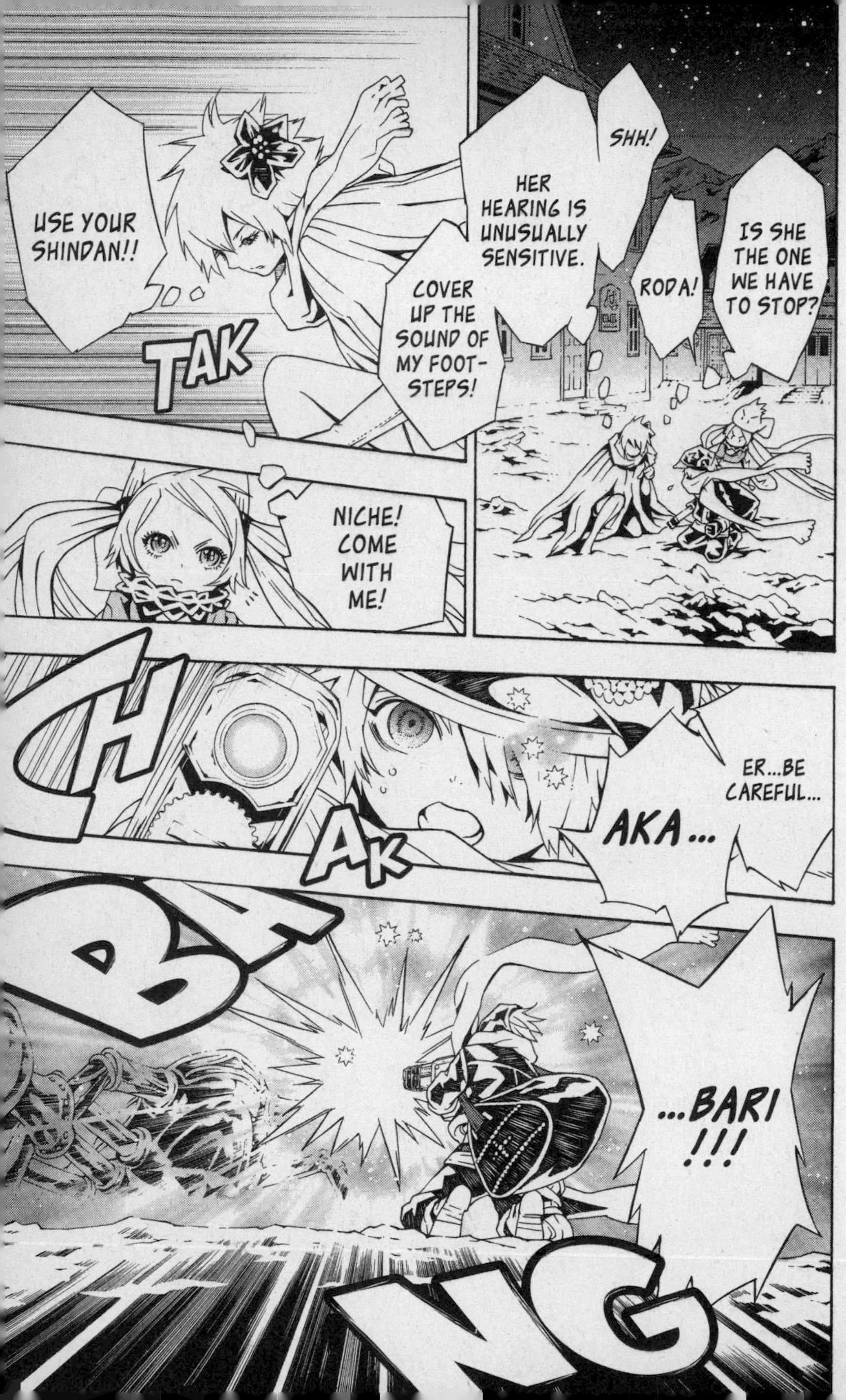
IS SHE THE ONE WE HAVE TO STOP?
RODA!
SHH!
HER HEARING IS UNUSUALLY SENSITIVE.
COVER UP THE SOUND OF MY FOOT-STEPS!
USE YOUR SHINDAN!!
TAK
NICHE! COME WITH ME!
ER...BE CAREFUL...
AKA...
WH
AK
...BARI !!!
BA
NG

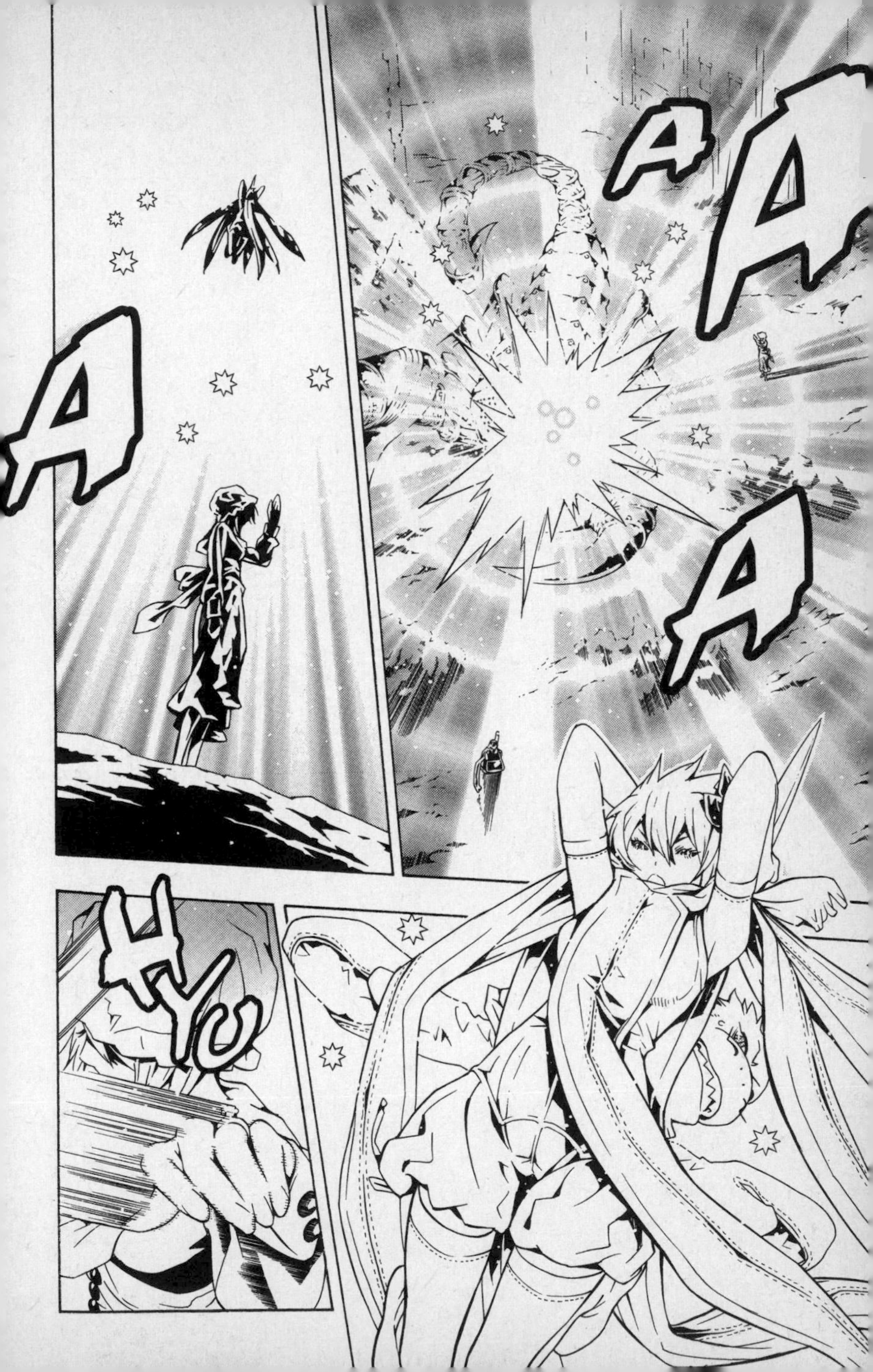
AAA
A
HYU

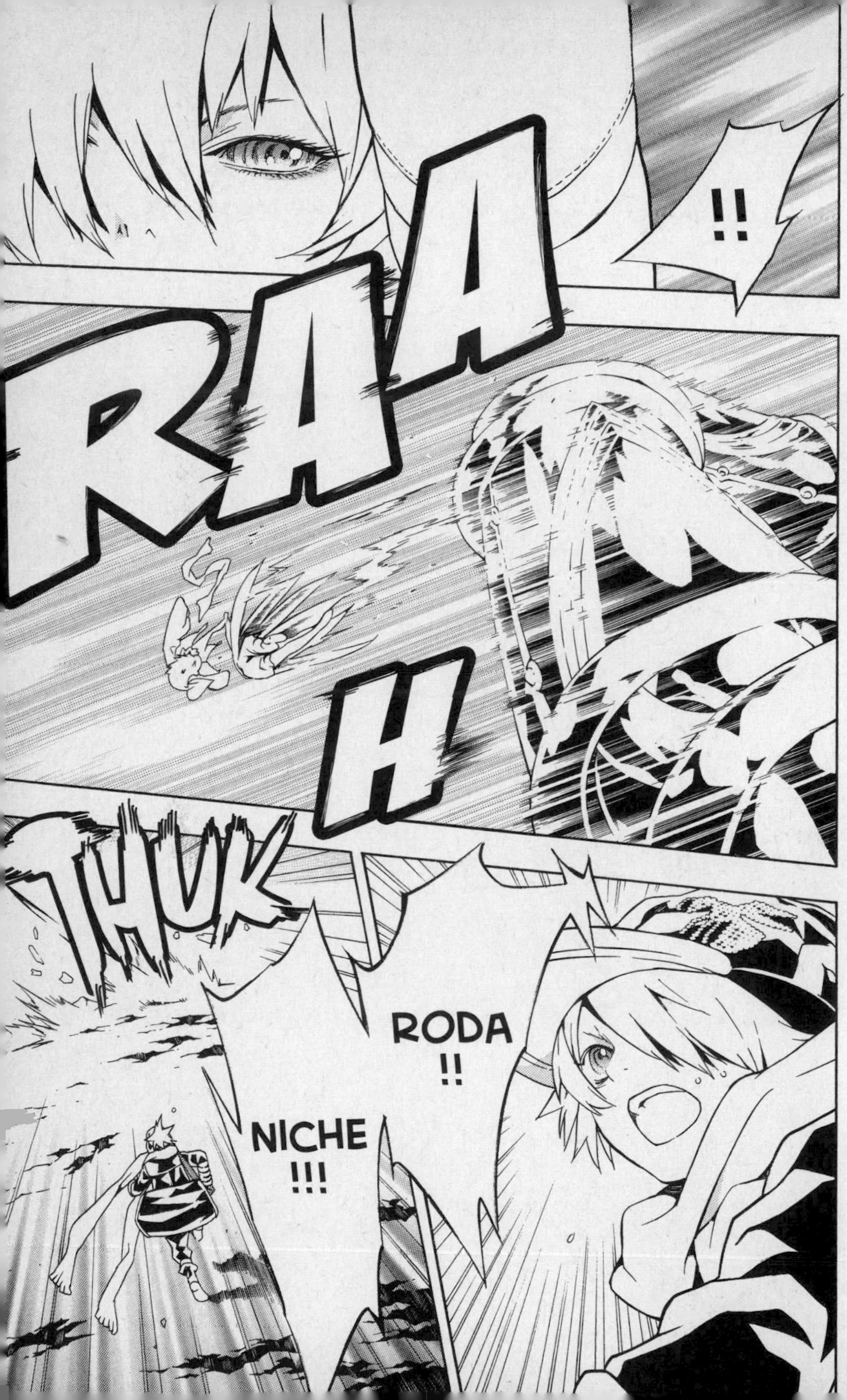
!!
RAAH
THUK
RODA !!
NICHE !!!

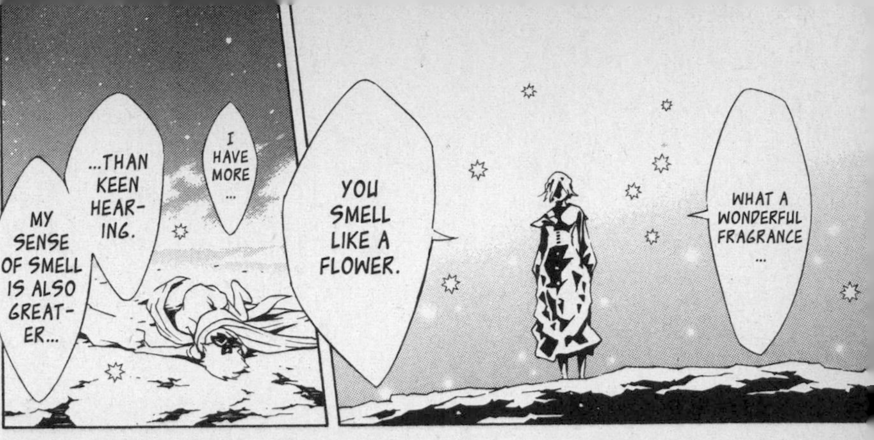
WHAT A WONDERFUL FRAGRANCE ...
YOU SMELL LIKE A FLOWER.
I HAVE MORE ...
...THAN KEEN HEAR-ING.
MY SENSE OF SMELL IS ALSO GREAT-ER...

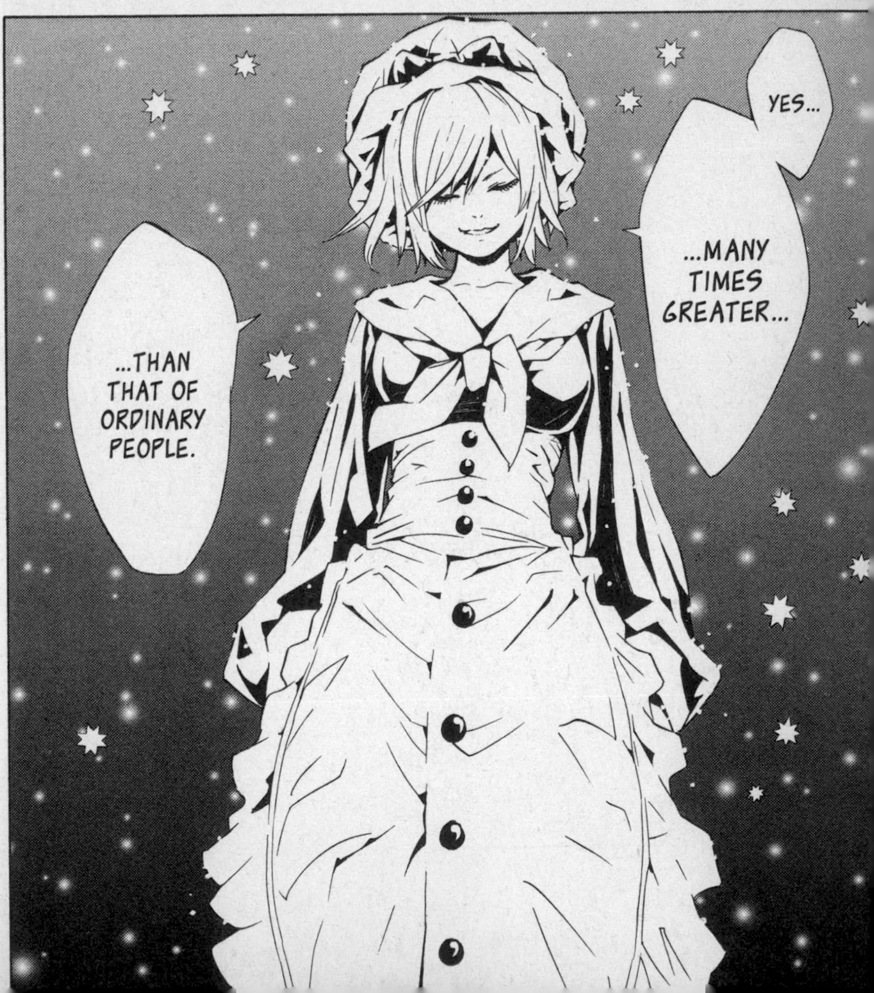
YES...
...MANY TIMES GREATER...
...THAN THAT OF ORDINARY PEOPLE.

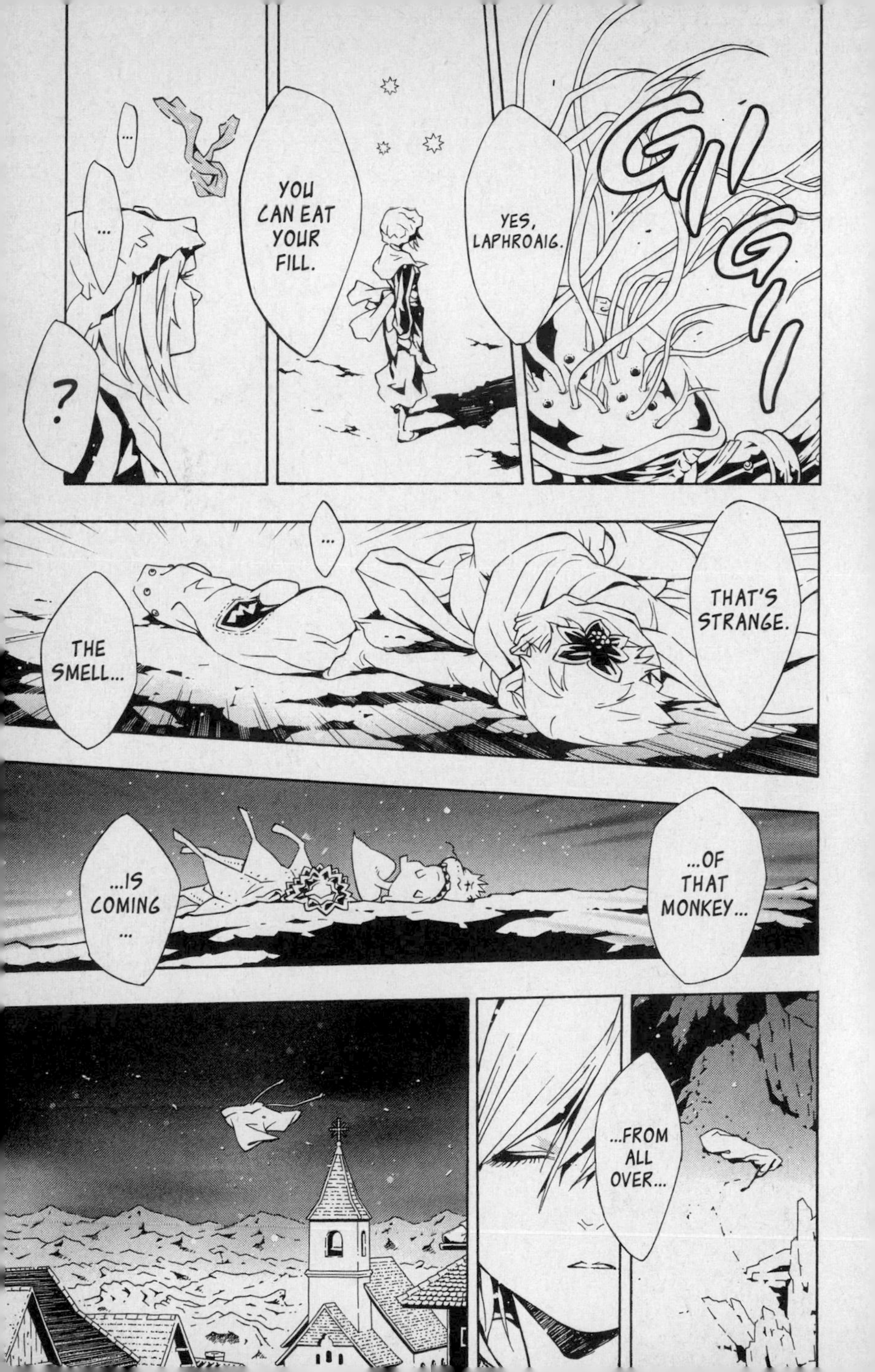
GIGII
YES, LAPHROAIG.
YOU CAN EAT YOUR FILL.
...
...
?
THAT'S STRANGE.
...
THE SMELL...
...OF THAT MONKEY...
...IS COMING ...
...FROM ALL OVER...

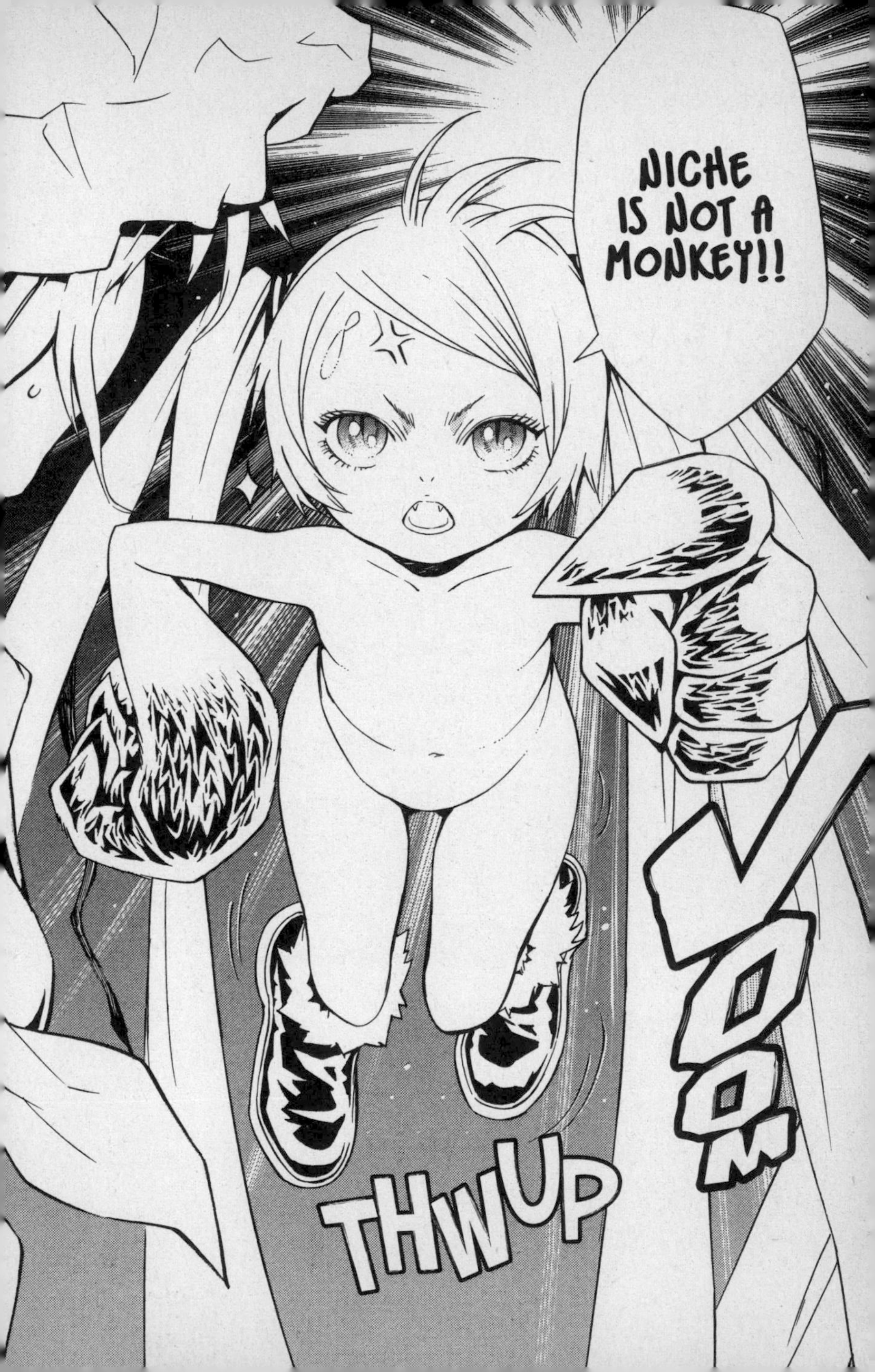
NICHE IS NOT A MONKEY!!
VOOM
THWUP

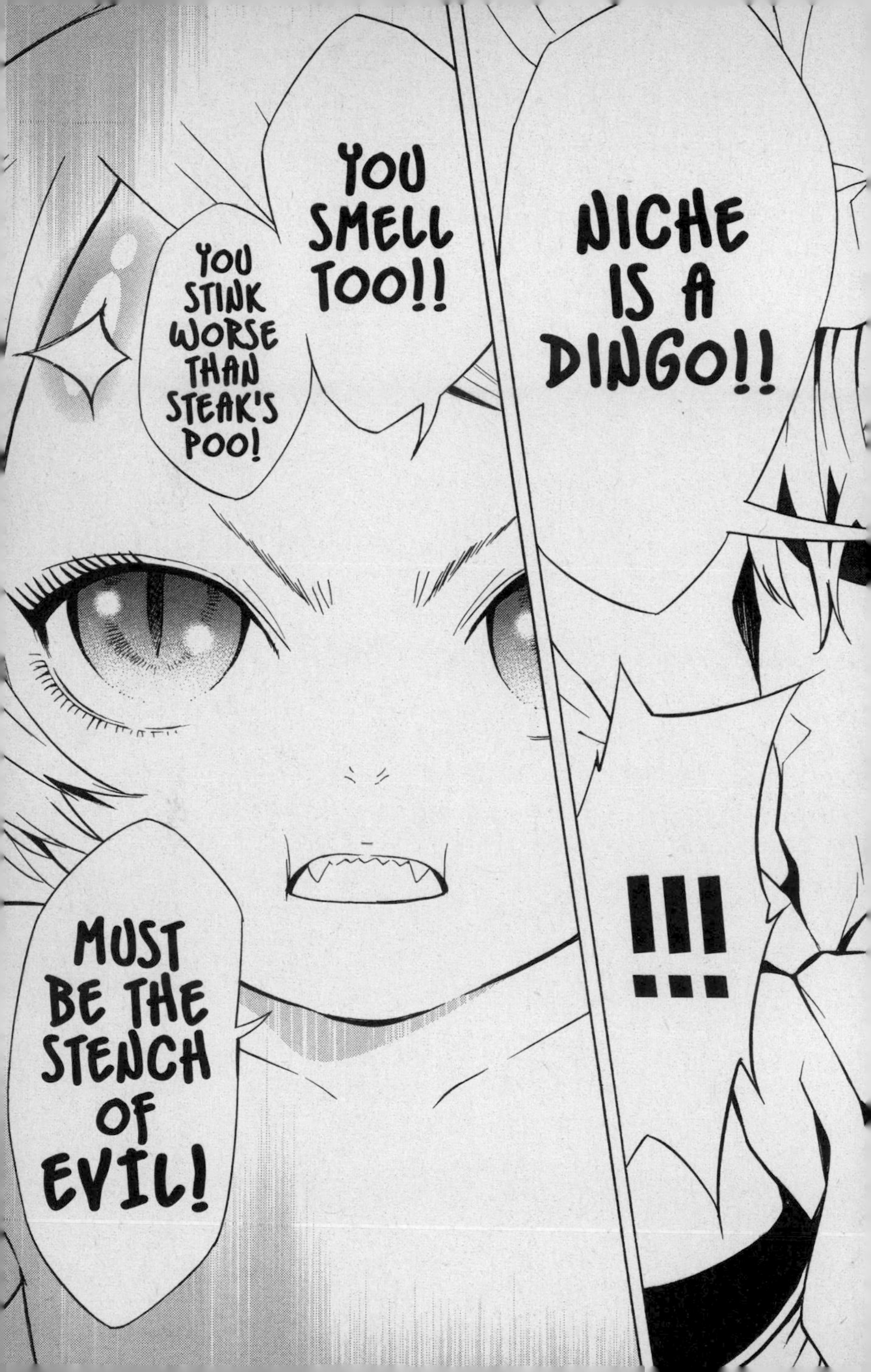
NICHE IS A DINGO!!
!!!
YOU SMELL TOO!!
YOU STINK WORSE THAN STEAK'S POO!
MUST BE THE STENCH OF EVIL!

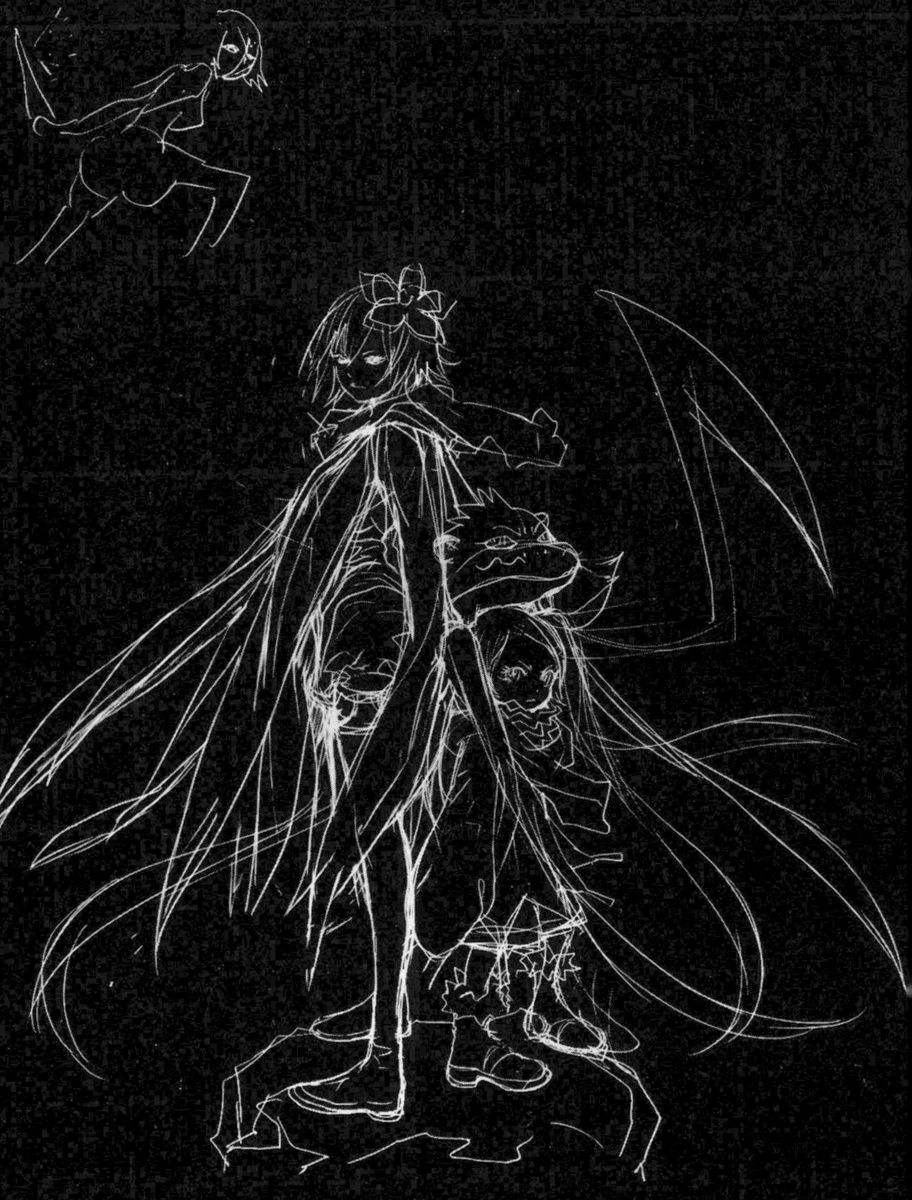

Cover design for Shikao Suga's 2011 CD *Yakusoku.*

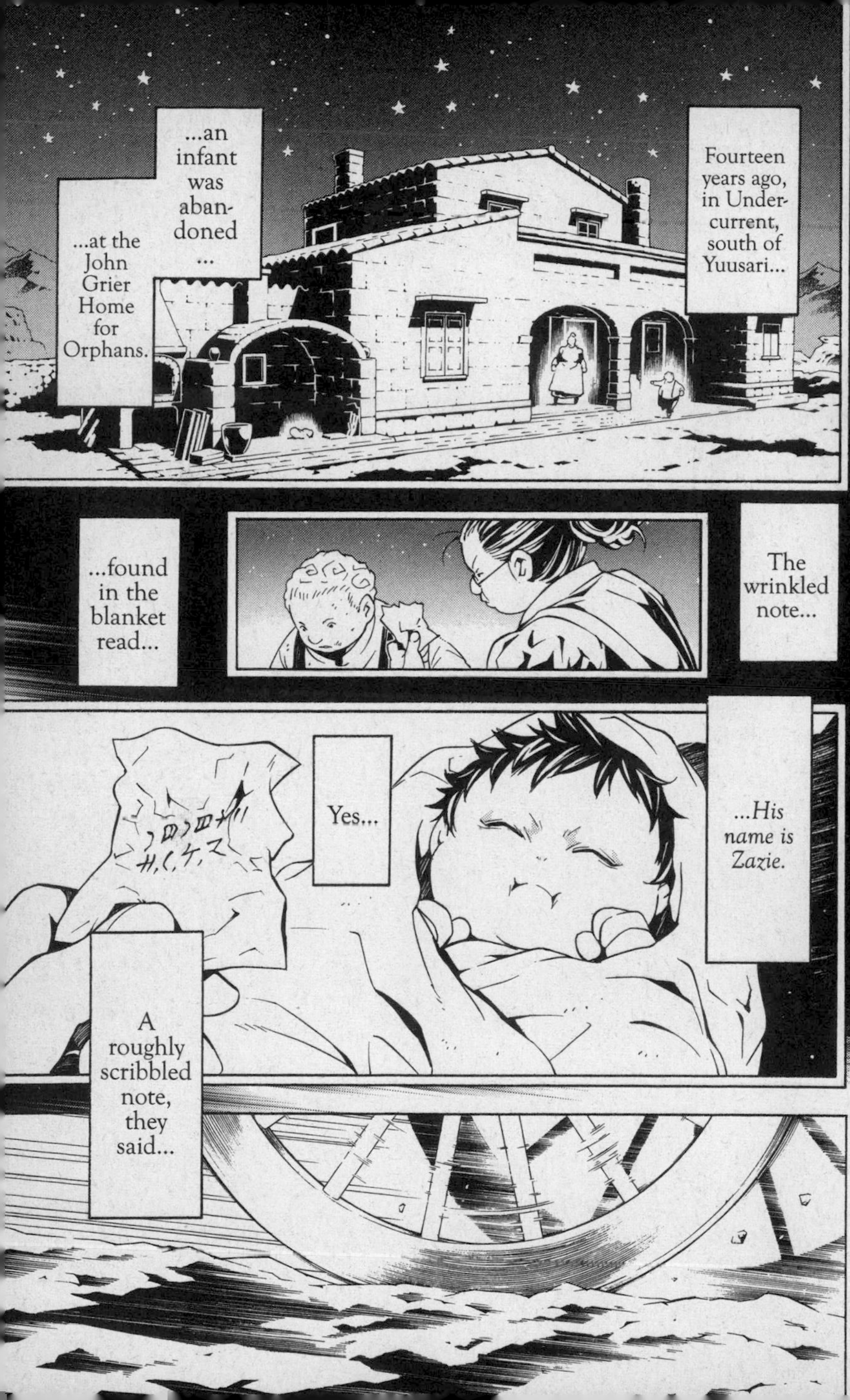
Fourteen years ago, in Under-current, south of Yuusari...
...an infant was aban-doned ...
...at the John Grier Home for Orphans.
The wrinkled note...
...found in the blanket read...
...His name is Zazie.
Yes...
A roughly scribbled note, they said...

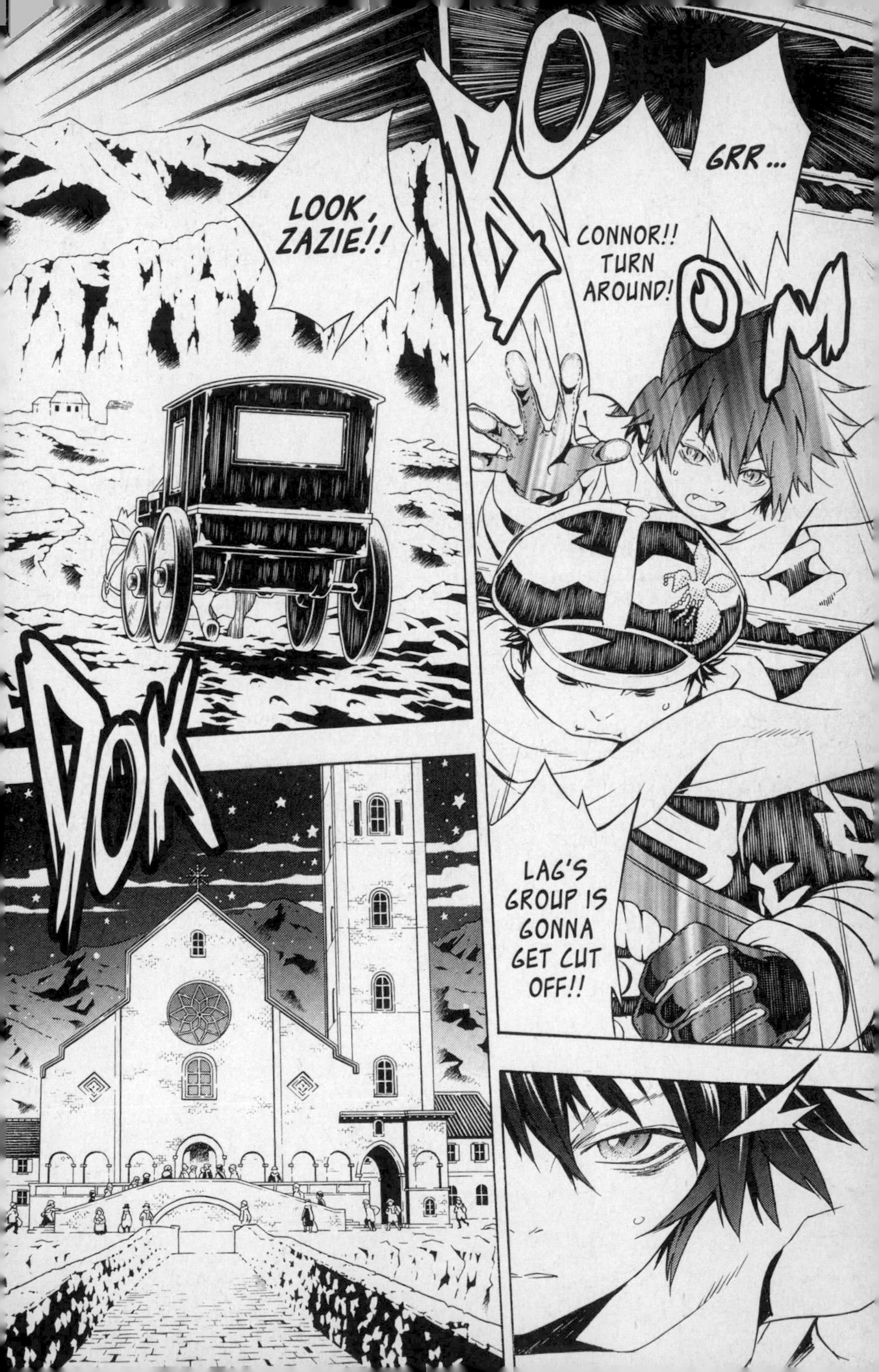
GRR...
CONNOR!! TURN AROUND!
BOOM
LAG'S GROUP IS GONNA GET CUT OFF!!
LOOK, ZAZIE!!
DOK

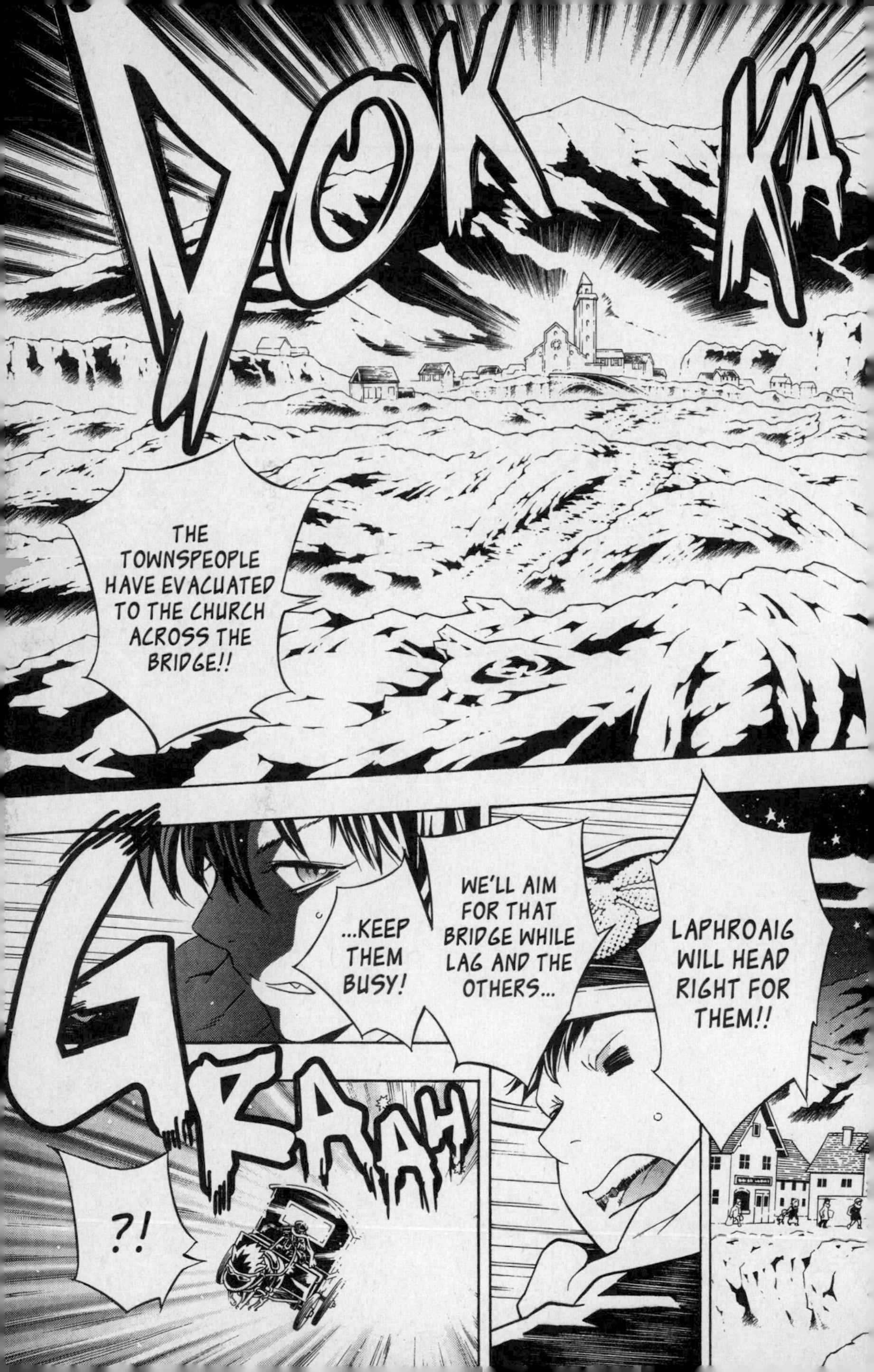
DOK KA
THE TOWNSPEOPLE HAVE EVACUATED TO THE CHURCH ACROSS THE BRIDGE!!
LAPHROAIG WILL HEAD RIGHT FOR THEM!!
WE'LL AIM FOR THAT BRIDGE WHILE LAG AND THE OTHERS...
...KEEP THEM BUSY!
GRAAH
?!

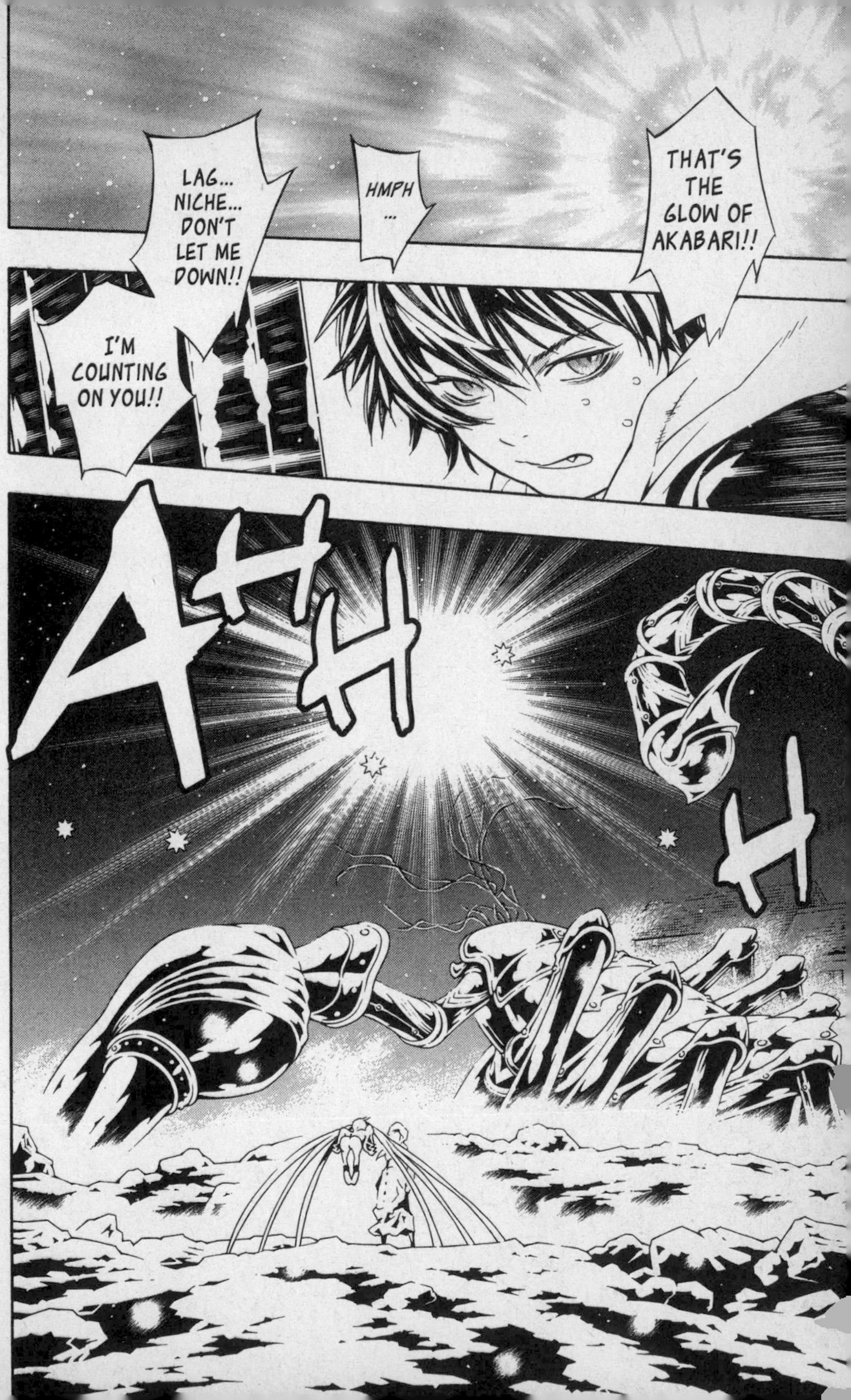
THAT'S THE GLOW OF AKABARI!!
HMPH ...
LAG... NICHE... DON'T LET ME DOWN!!
I'M COUNTING ON YOU!!
AHHH

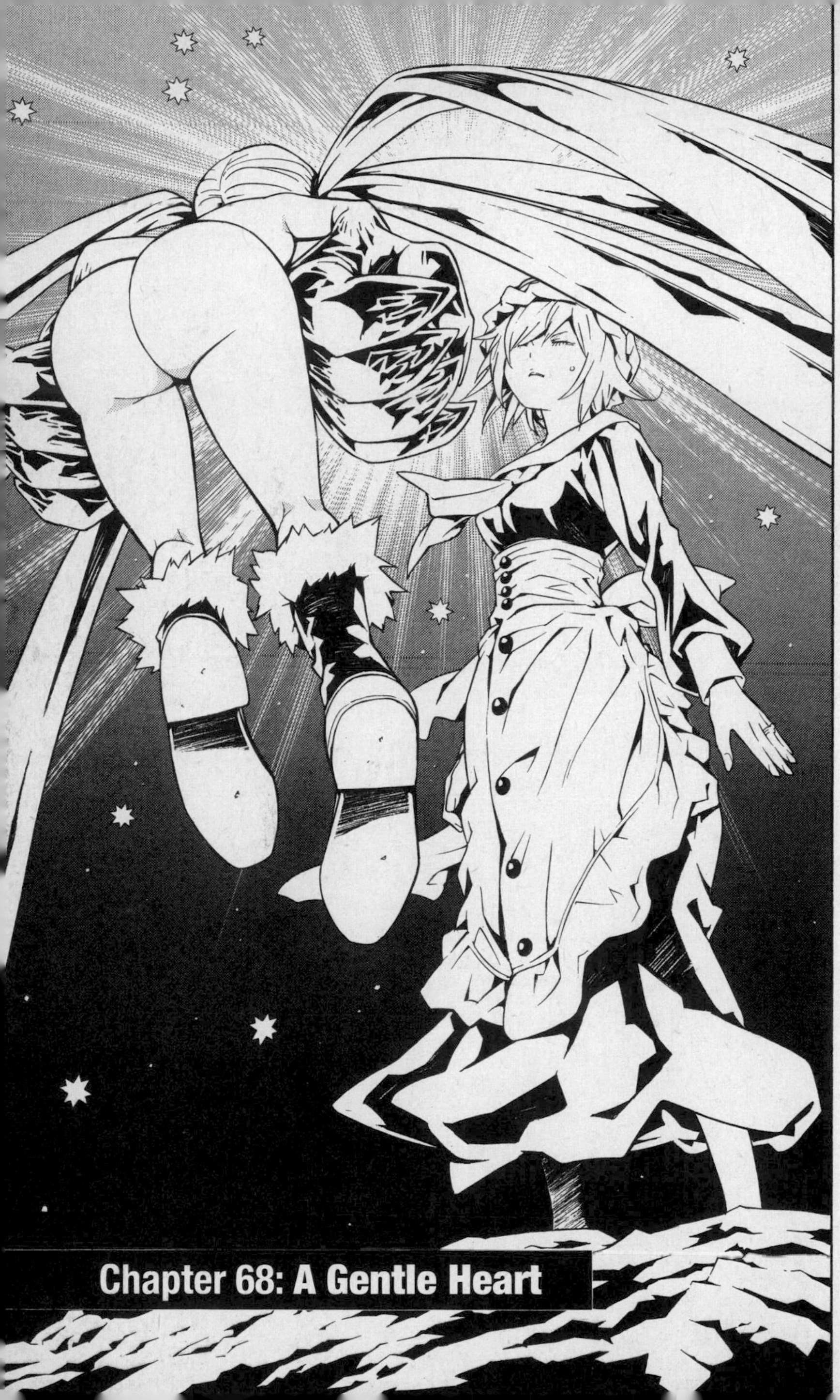
Chapter 68: A Gentle Heart

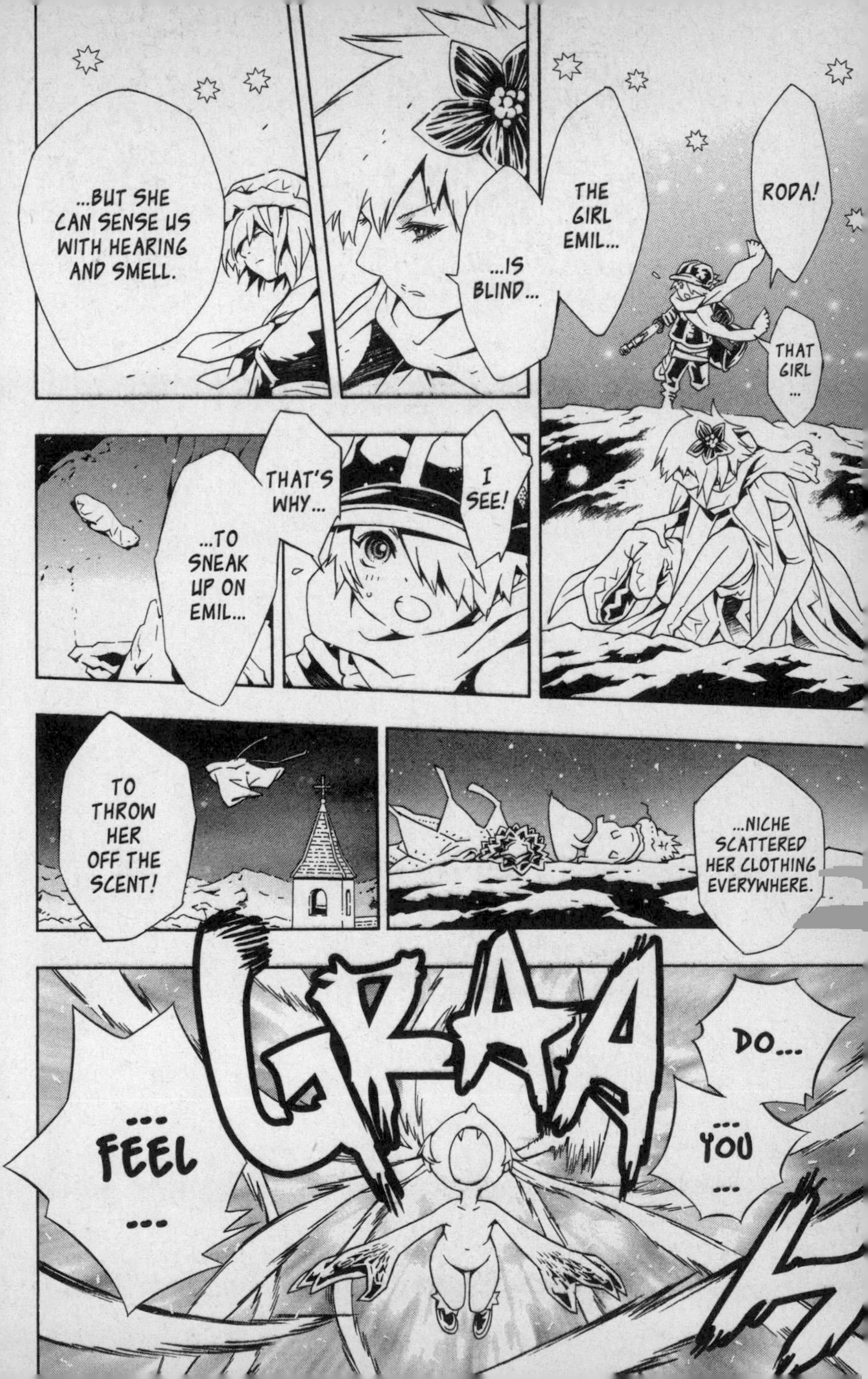
RODA!
THAT GIRL ...
THE GIRL EMIL...
...IS BLIND...
...BUT SHE CAN SENSE US WITH HEARING AND SMELL.
I SEE!
THAT'S WHY...
...TO SNEAK UP ON EMIL...
...NICHE SCATTERED HER CLOTHING EVERYWHERE.
TO THROW HER OFF THE SCENT!
GRAA
DO... ...YOU...
...FEEL...

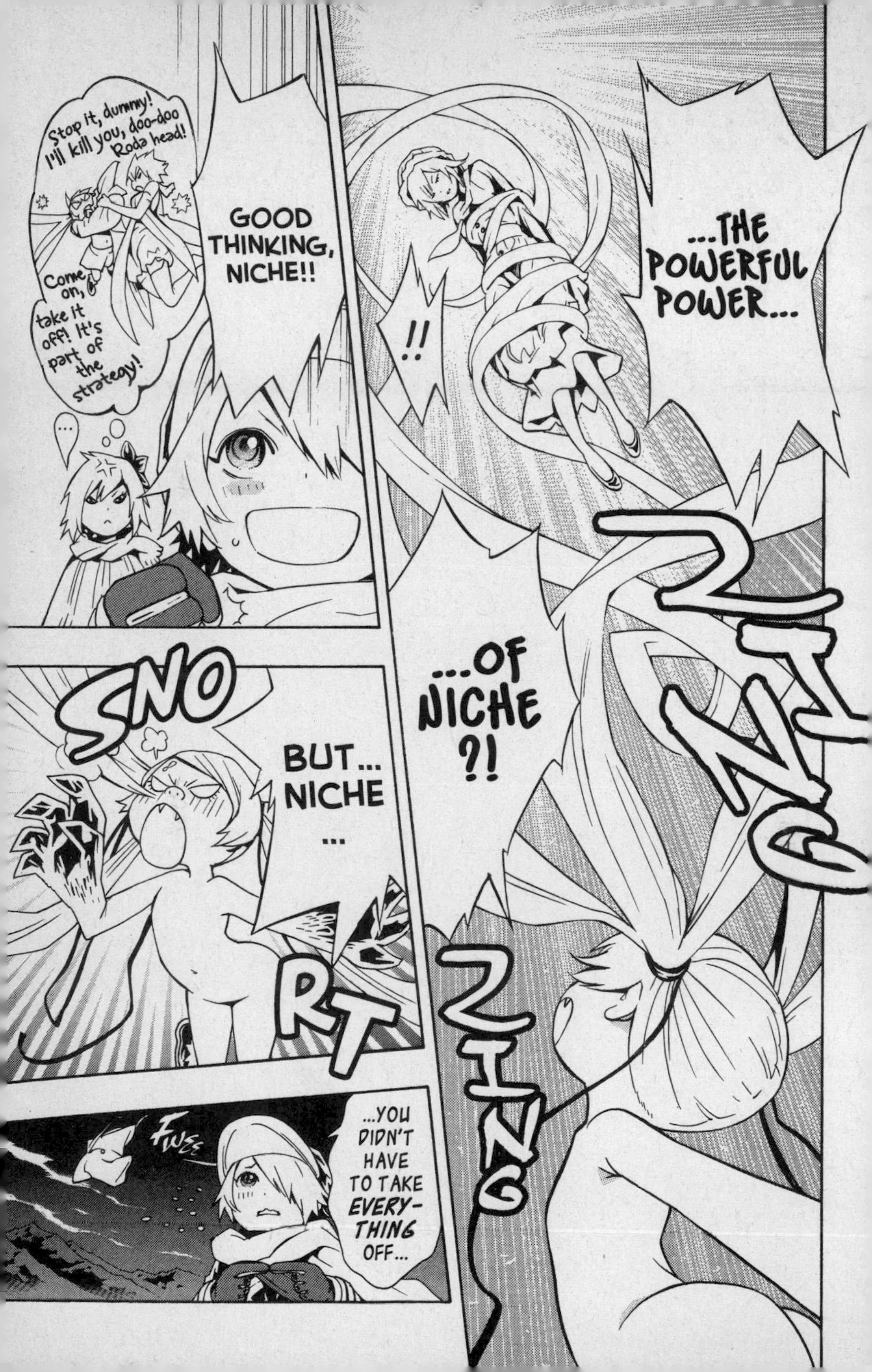
...THE POWERFUL POWER...
!!
...OF NICHE ?!
ZING
ZING
GOOD THINKING, NICHE!!
Stop it, dummy! I'll kill you, doo-doo Roda head!
Come on, take it off! It's part of the strategy!
...
SNO
RT
BUT... NICHE ...
FWEE
...YOU DIDN'T HAVE TO TAKE EVERY-THING OFF...

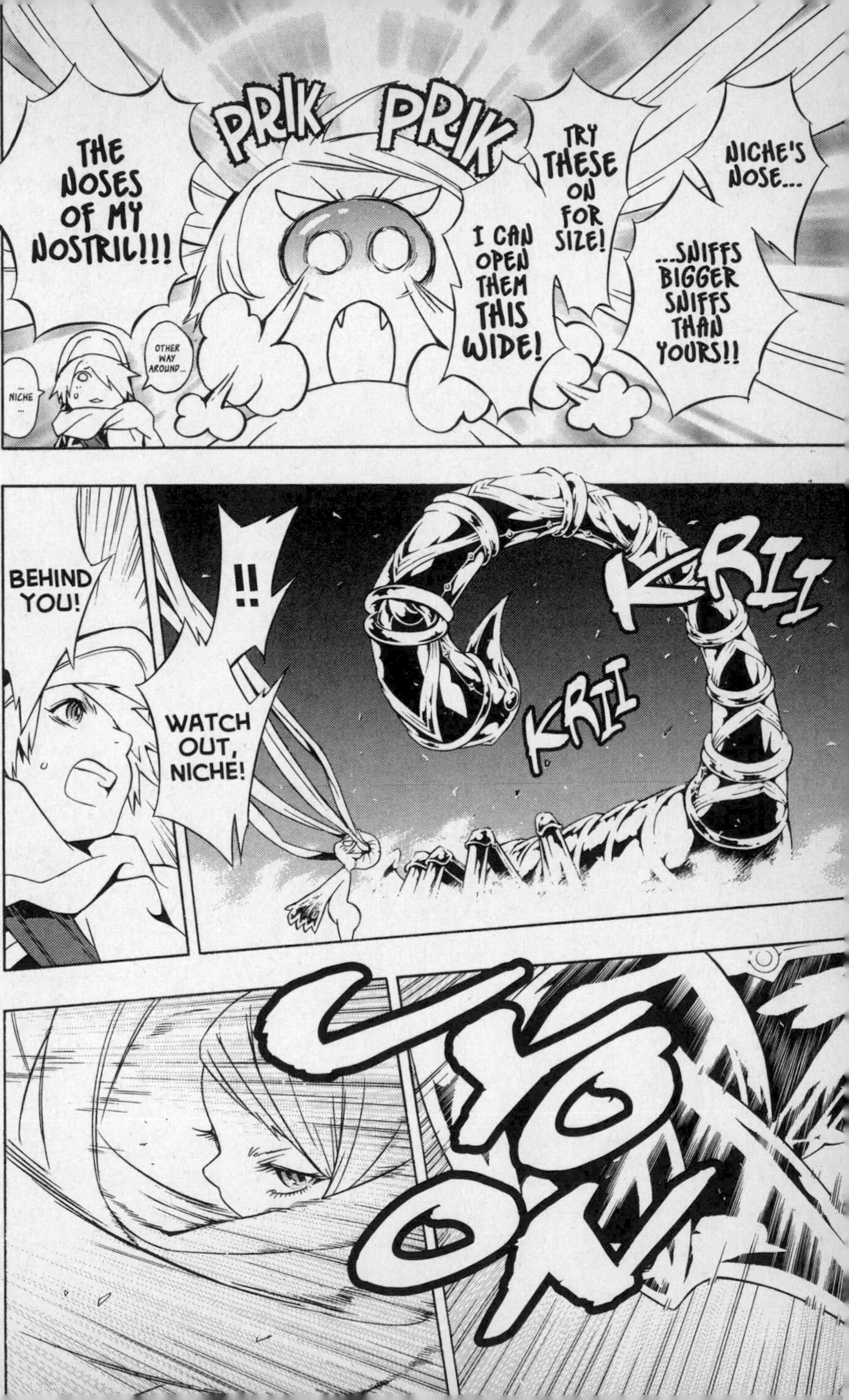
NICHE'S NOSE...
...SNIFFS BIGGER SNIFFS THAN YOURS!!
TRY THESE ON FOR SIZE!
I CAN OPEN THEM THIS WIDE!
PRIK PRIK
THE NOSES OF MY NOSTRIL!!!
OTHER WAY AROUND...
...NICHE...
KRII
KRII
!!
WATCH OUT, NICHE!
BEHIND YOU!

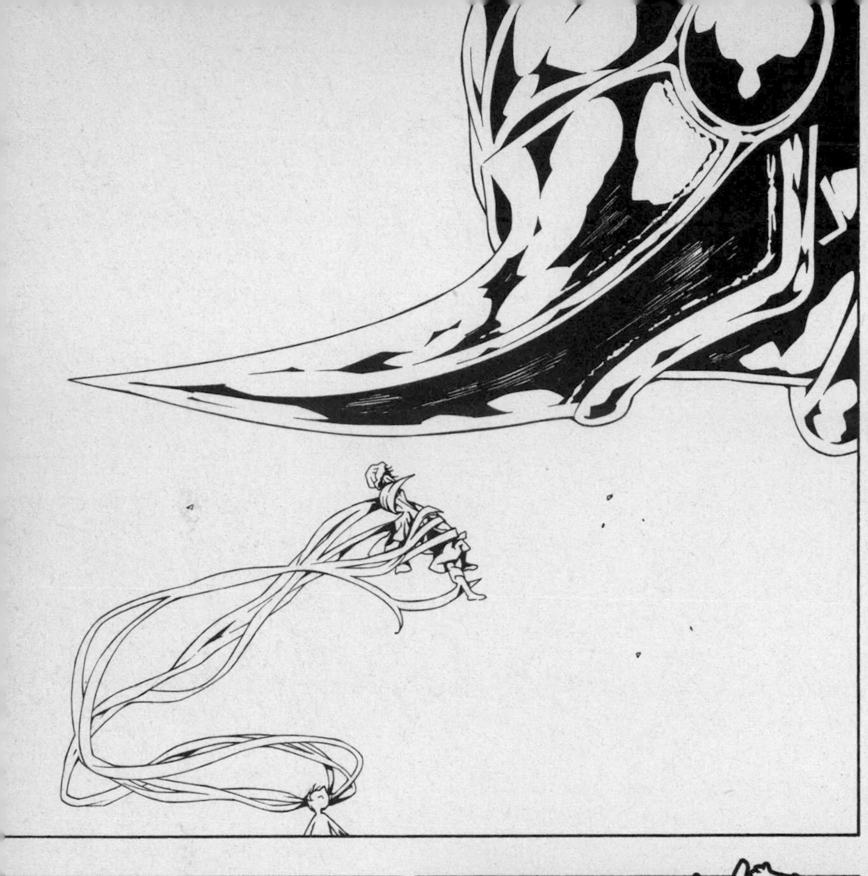

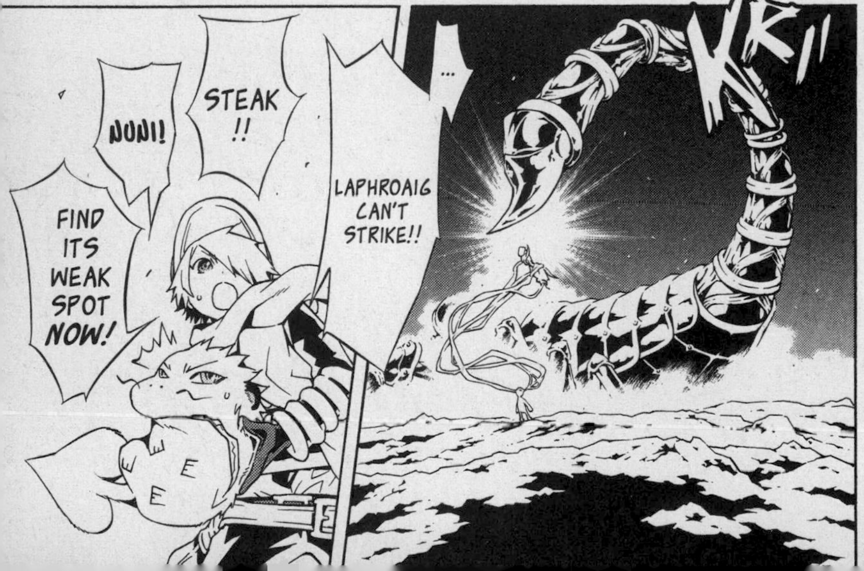
KRI'
...
LAPHROAIG CAN'T STRIKE!!
STEAK !!
NUNI!
FIND ITS WEAK SPOT NOW!

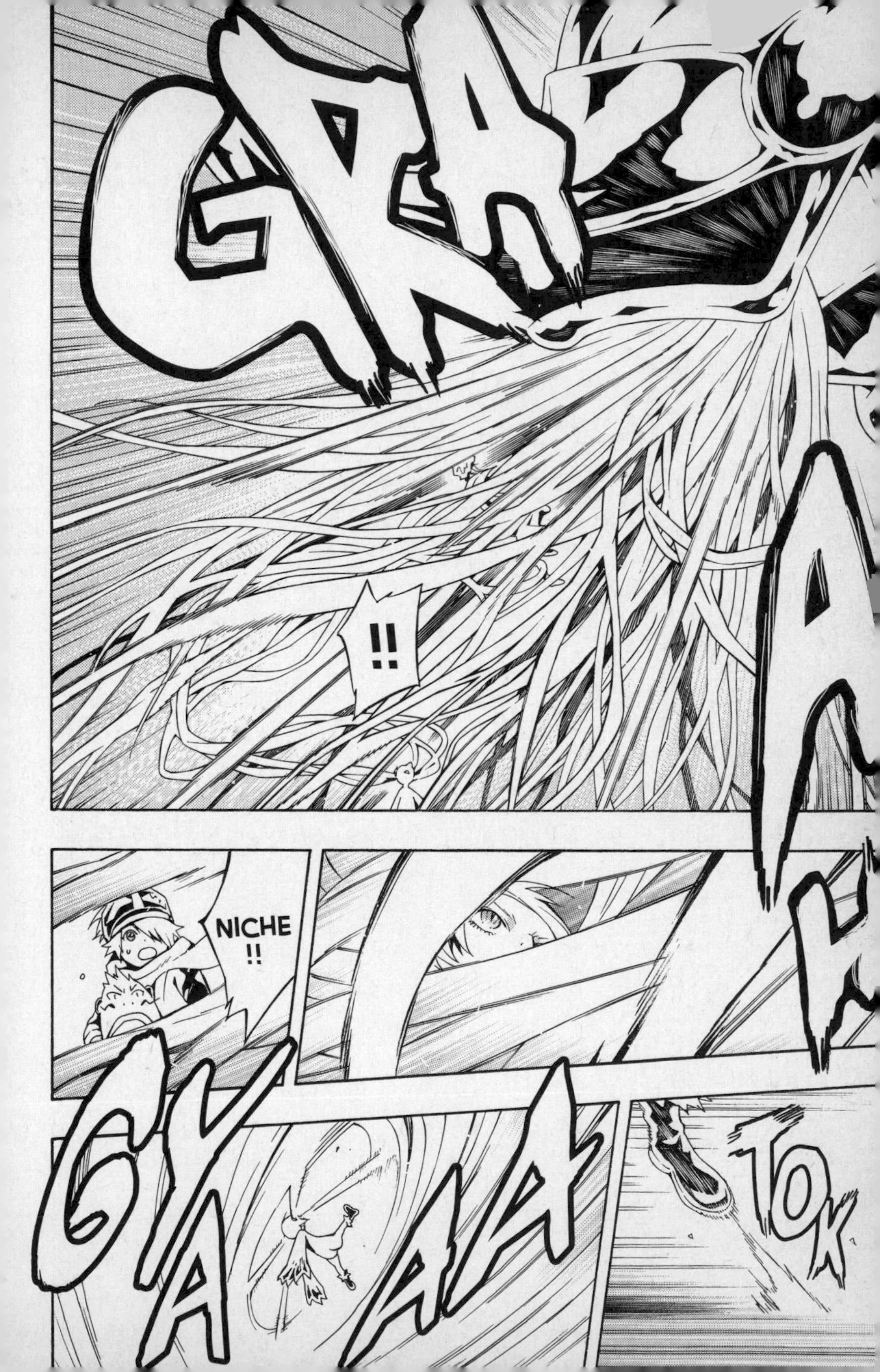
!!
NICHE !!
TOK

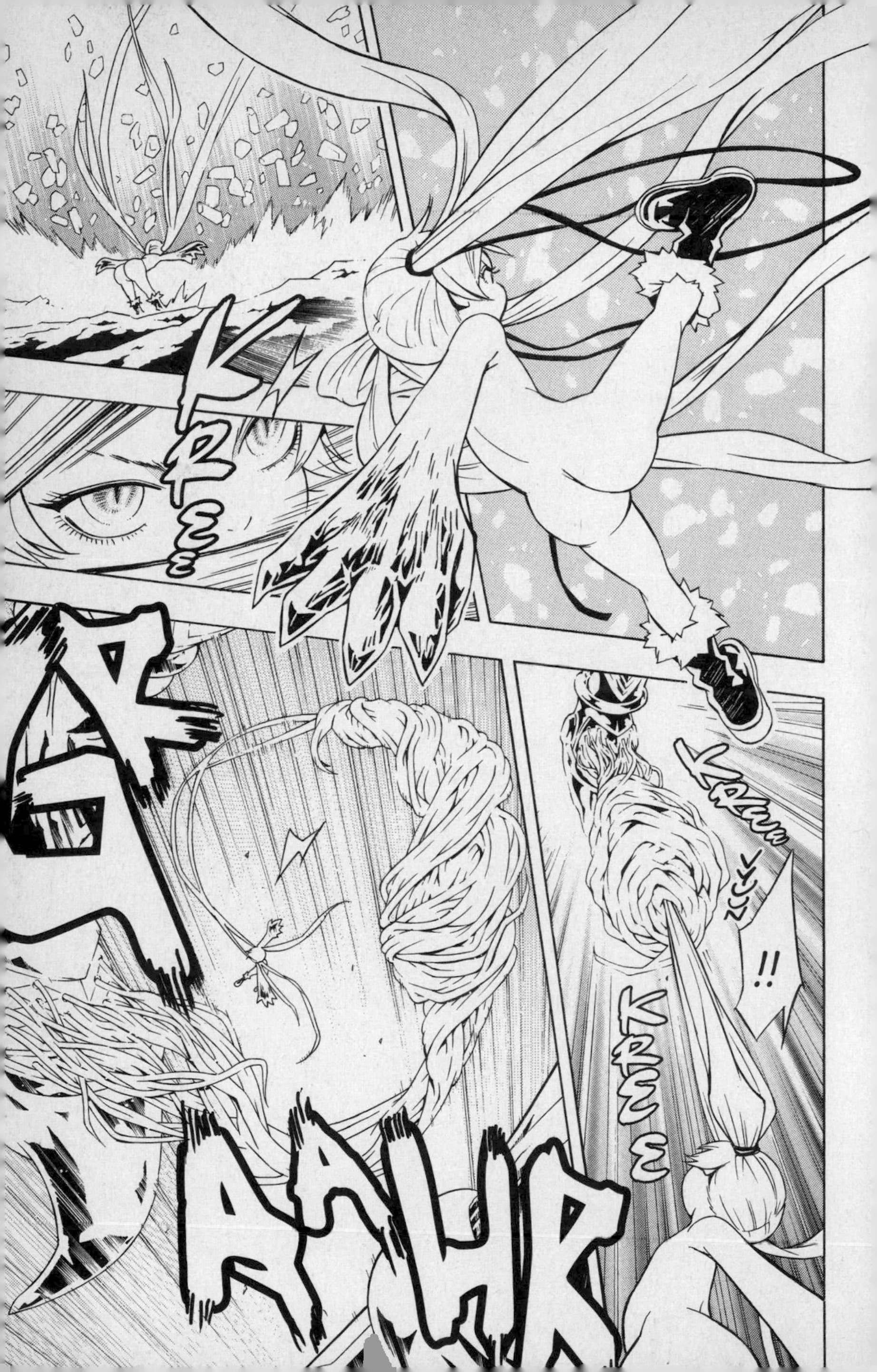
KREE
KRAWW
vvuun
!!
KREE
GRAHR

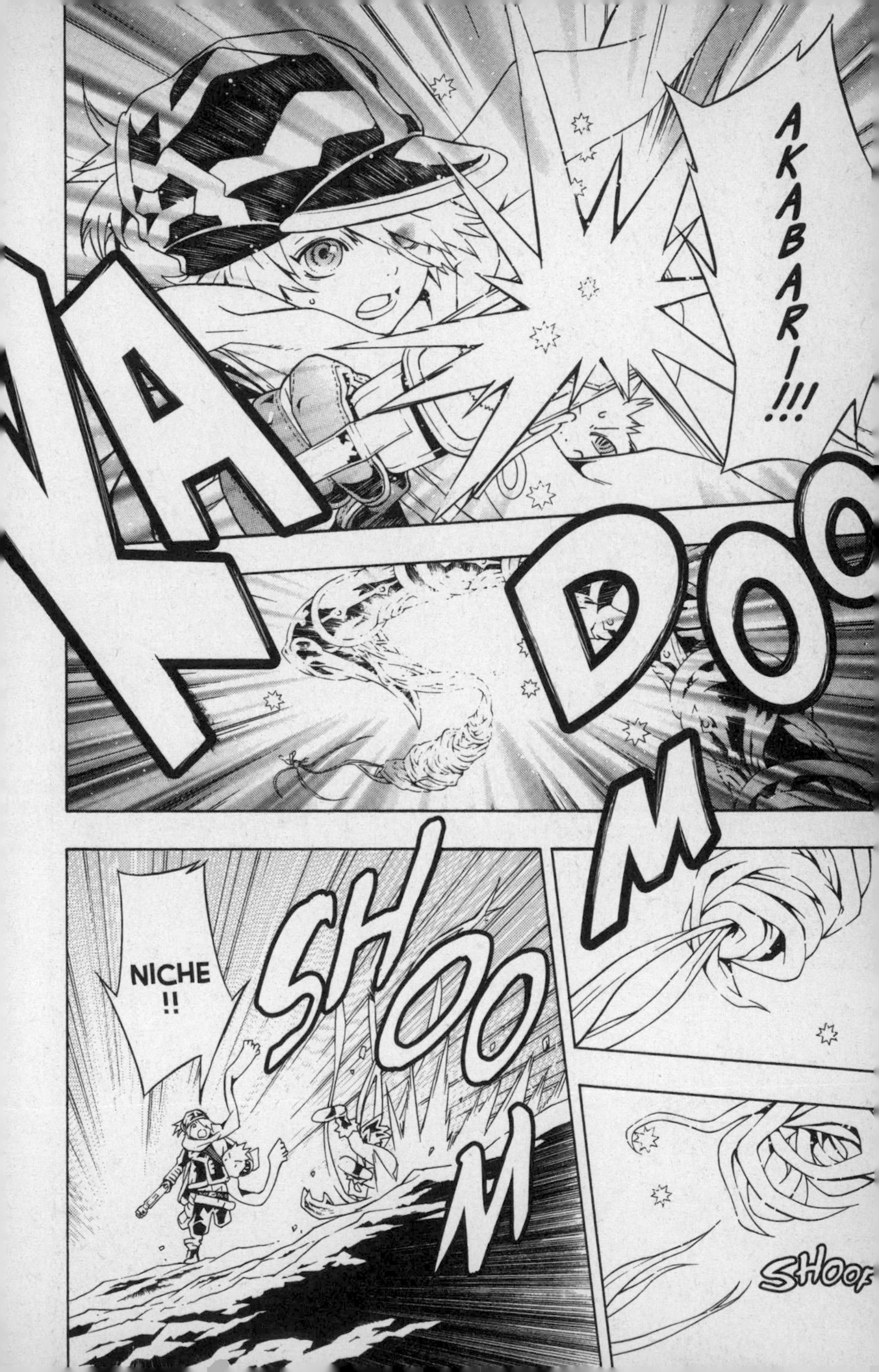
AKABARI!!!
A
DOOM
SHOOF
NICHE !!
SHOOOM

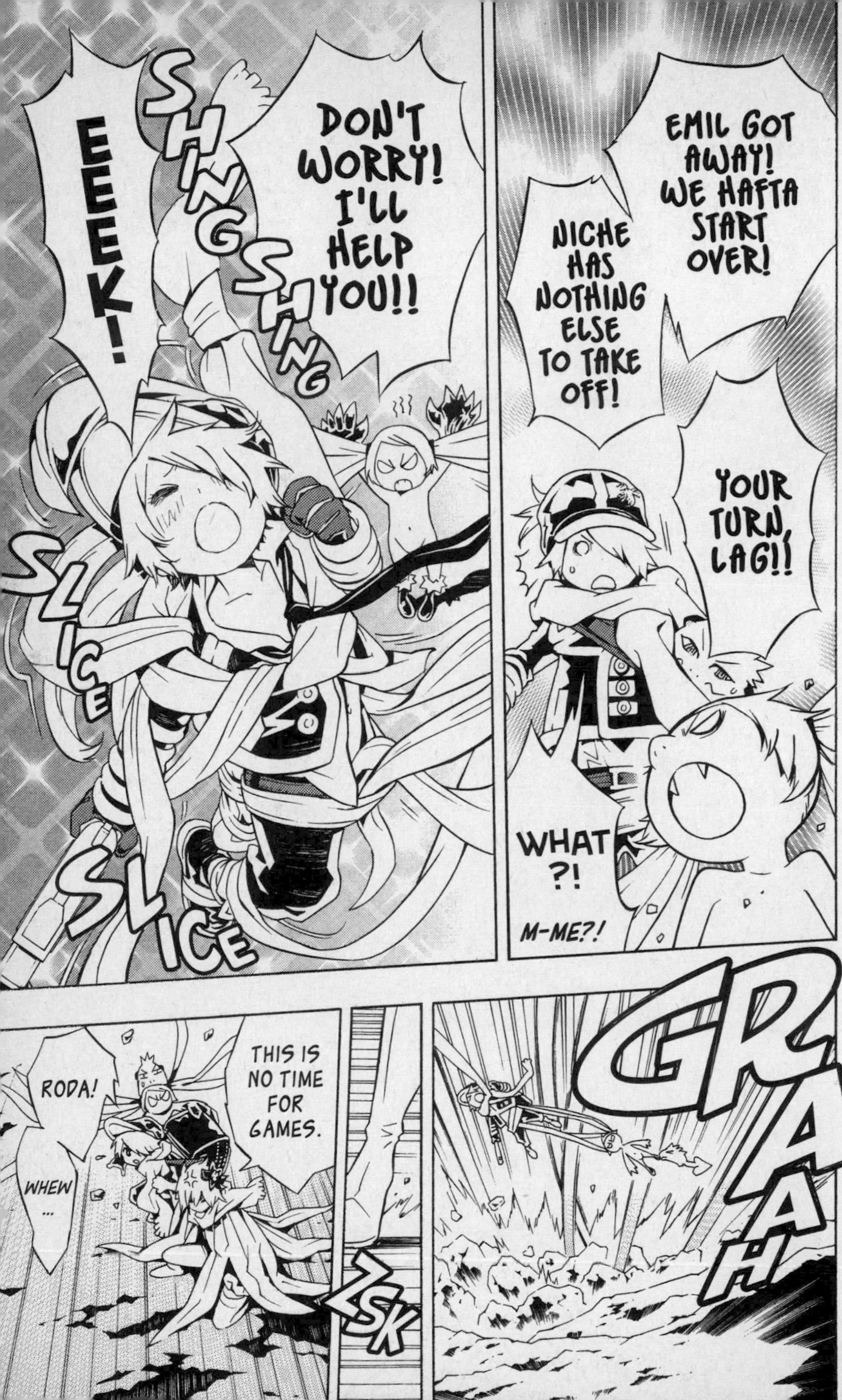
EMIL GOT AWAY! WE HAFTA START OVER!
NICHE HAS NOTHING ELSE TO TAKE OFF!
YOUR TURN, LAG!!
WHAT ?!
M-ME?!
DON'T WORRY! I'LL HELP YOU!!
SHING SHING
EEEK!
SLICE
SLICE
GRAAH
ZSK
THIS IS NO TIME FOR GAMES.
RODA!
WHEW ...

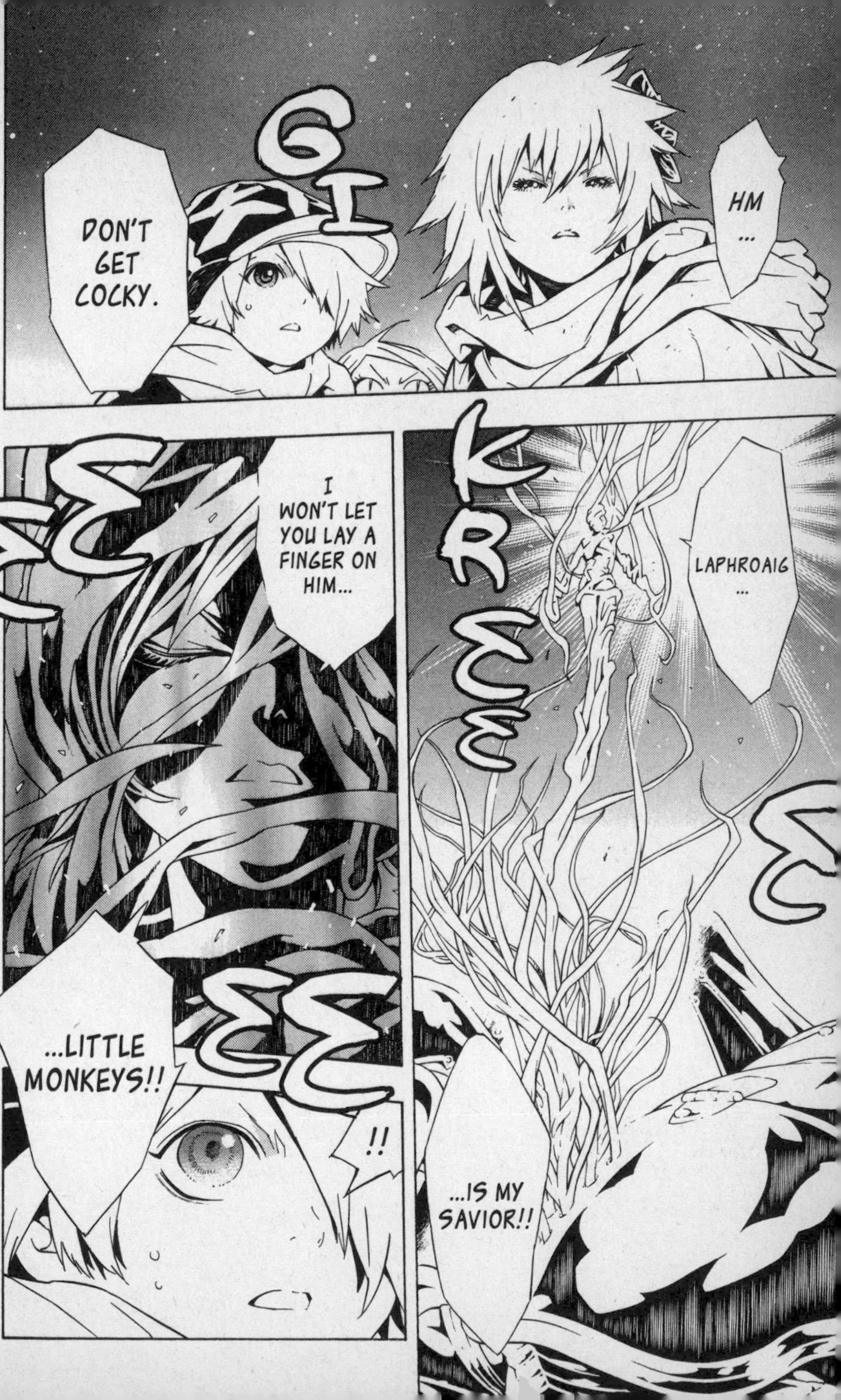
HM ...
GI
DON'T GET COCKY.
LAPHROAIG ...
KREEE
EEE
...IS MY SAVIOR!!
I WON'T LET YOU LAY A FINGER ON HIM...
EEE
...LITTLE MONKEYS!!
!!

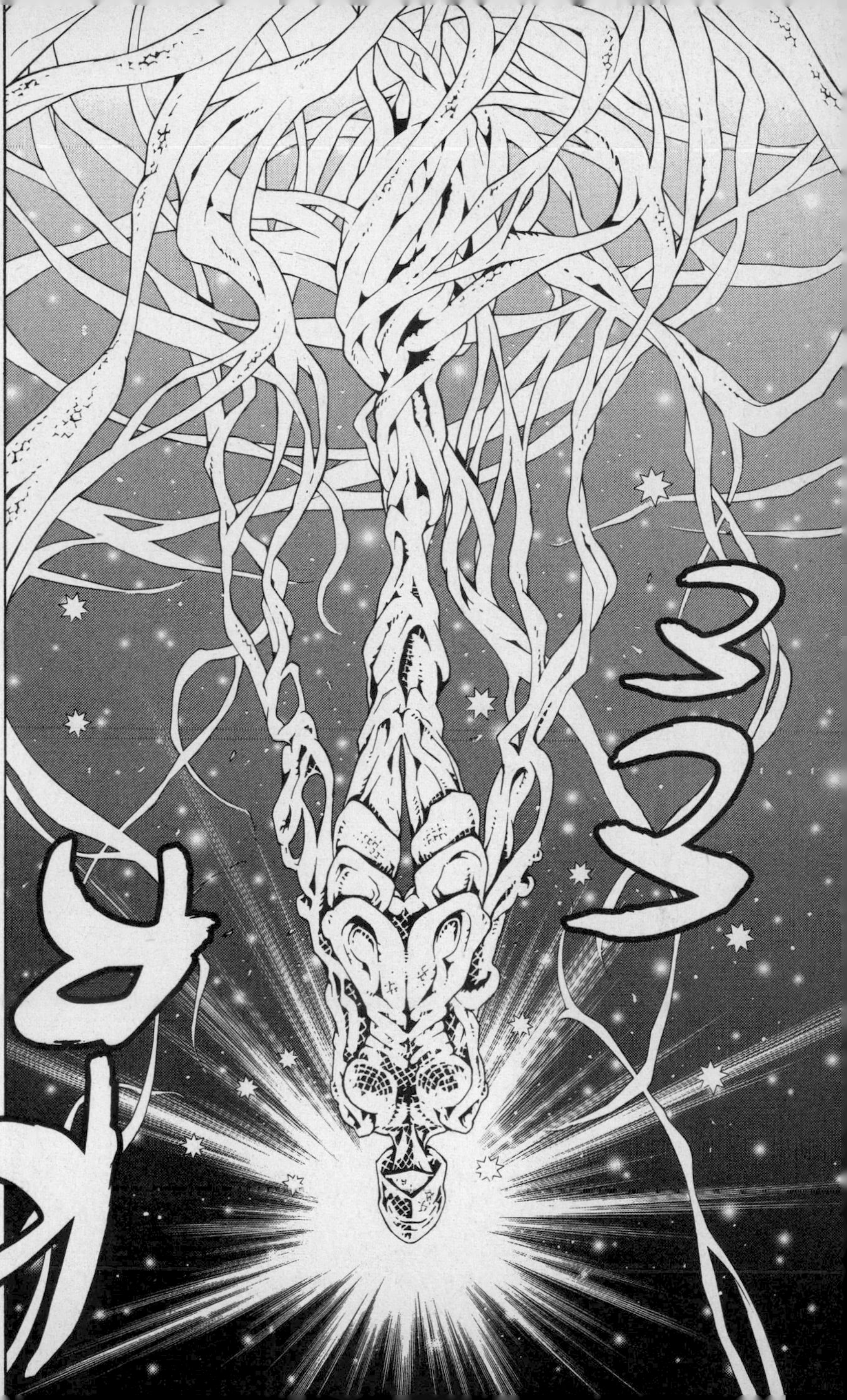

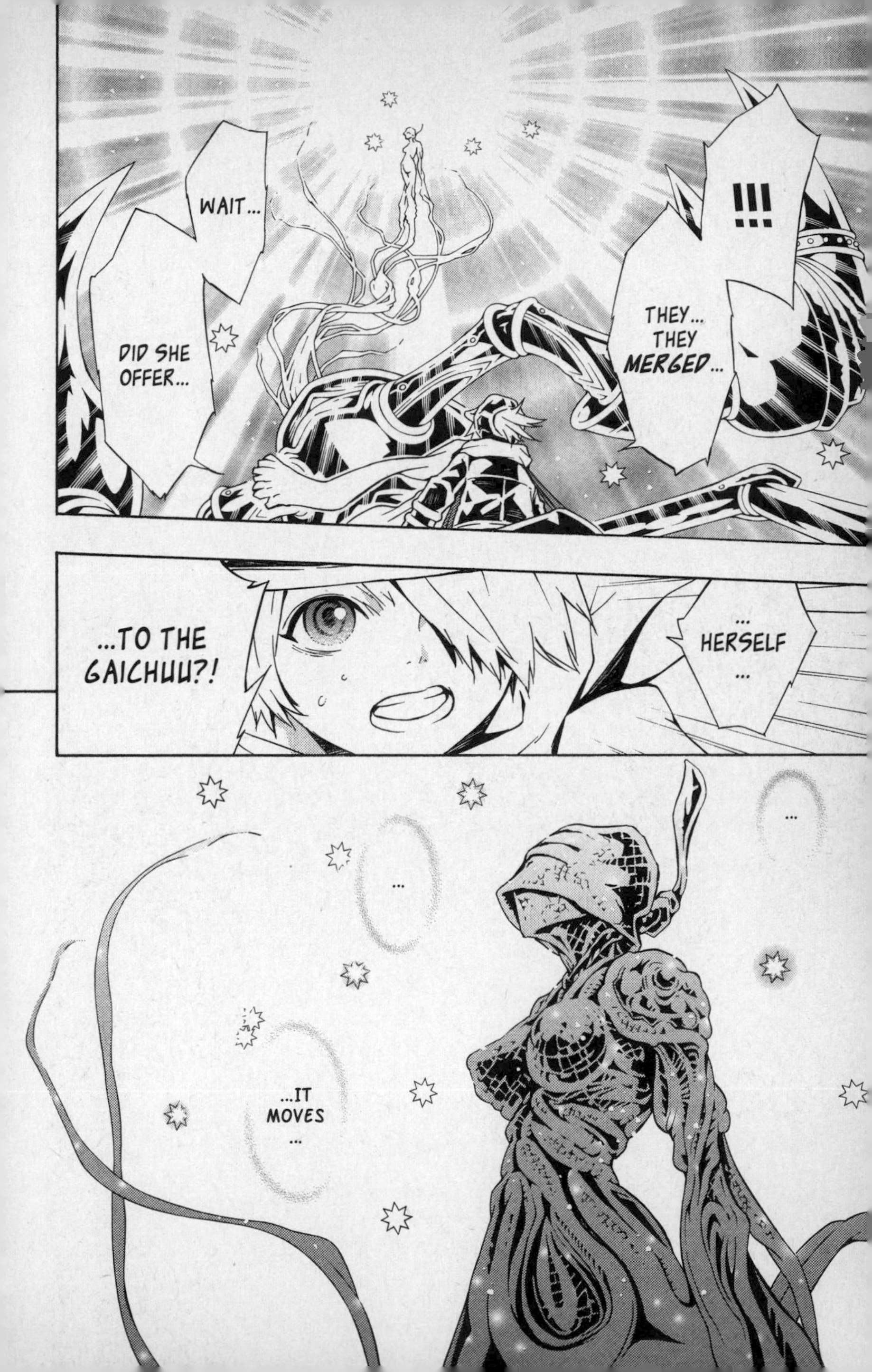
!!!
THEY... THEY MERGED...
WAIT...
DID SHE OFFER...
... HERSELF ...
...TO THE GAICHUU?!
...
...
...IT MOVES ...

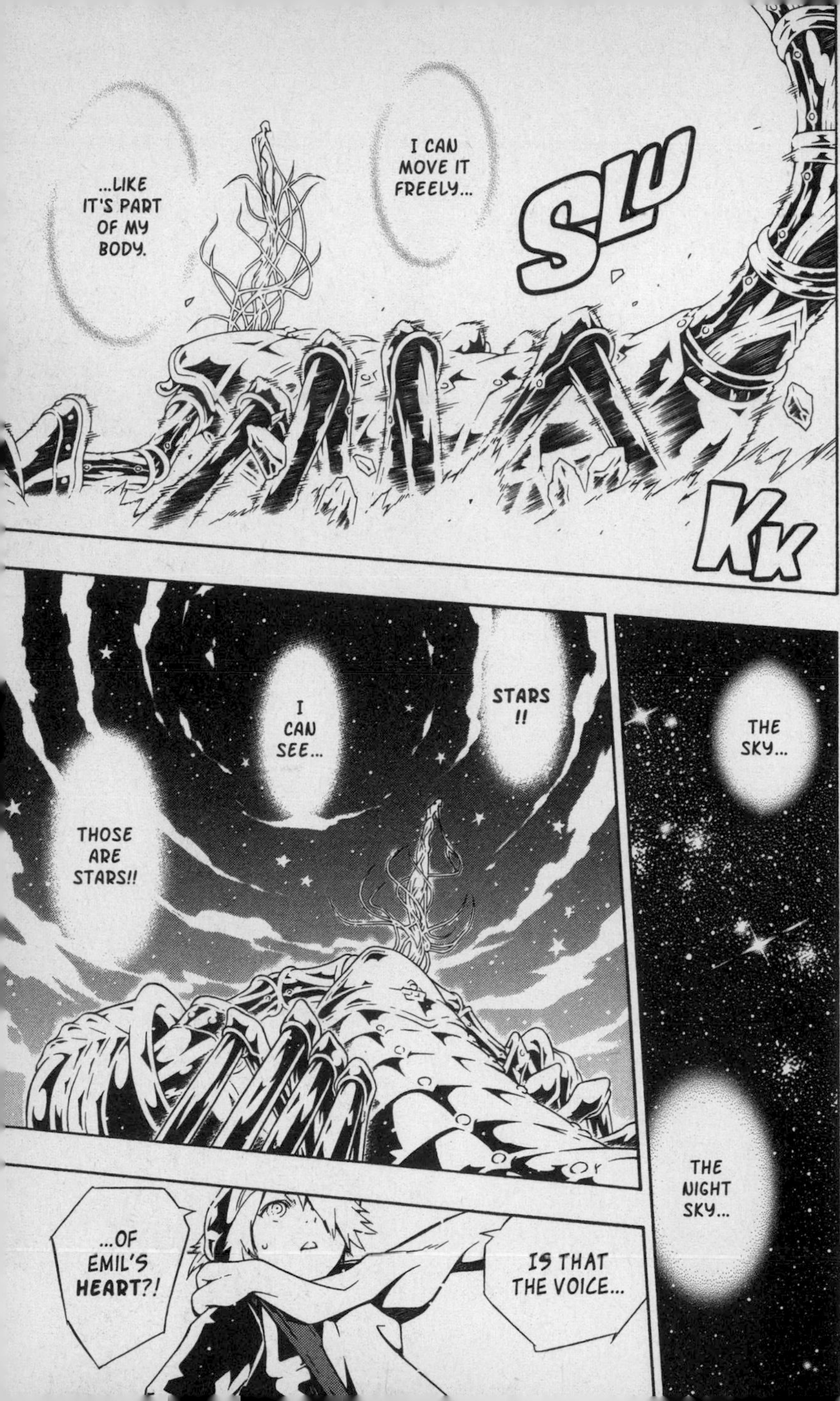
SLU
KK
I CAN MOVE IT FREELY...
...LIKE IT'S PART OF MY BODY.
THE SKY...
THE NIGHT SKY...
STARS !!
I CAN SEE...
THOSE ARE STARS!!
IS THAT THE VOICE...
...OF EMIL'S HEART?!

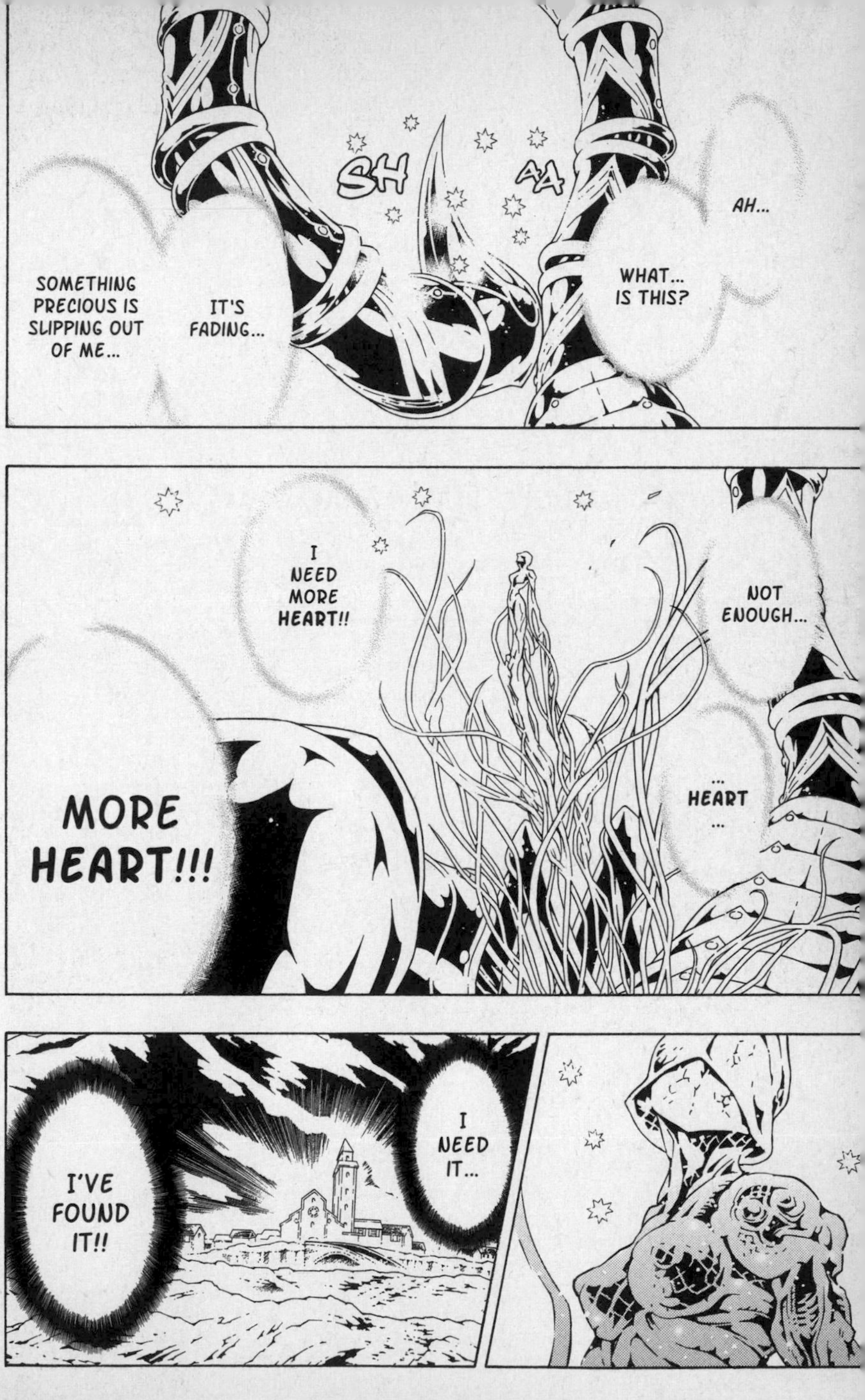
AH...
WHAT... IS THIS?
SHAA
IT'S FADING...
SOMETHING PRECIOUS IS SLIPPING OUT OF ME...
NOT ENOUGH...
... HEART ...
I NEED MORE HEART!!
MORE HEART!!!
I NEED IT...
I'VE FOUND IT!!

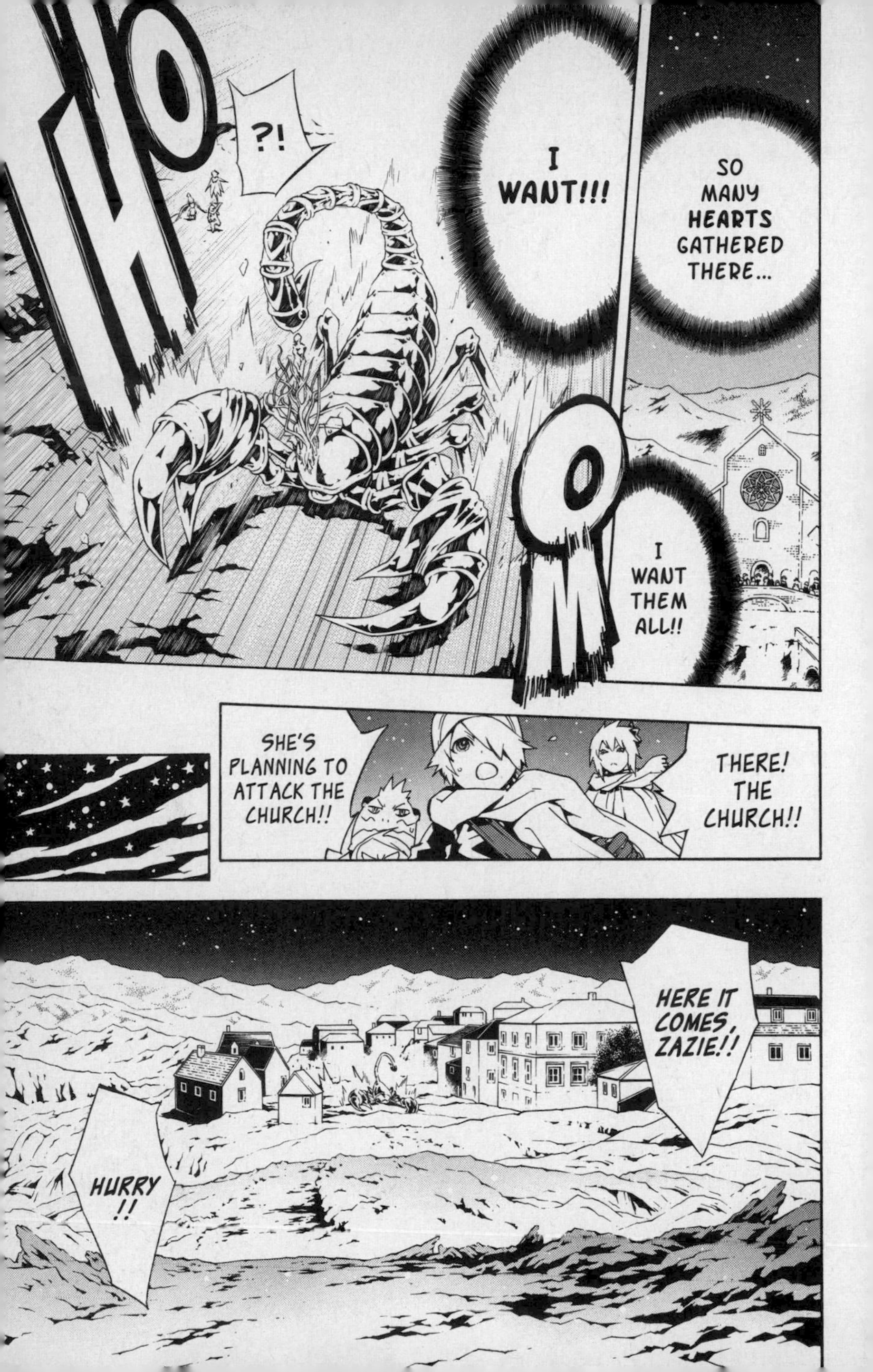
SO MANY HEARTS GATHERED THERE...
I WANT!!!
I WANT THEM ALL!!
OM
?!
THERE! THE CHURCH!!
SHE'S PLANNING TO ATTACK THE CHURCH!!
HERE IT COMES, ZAZIE!!
HURRY !!

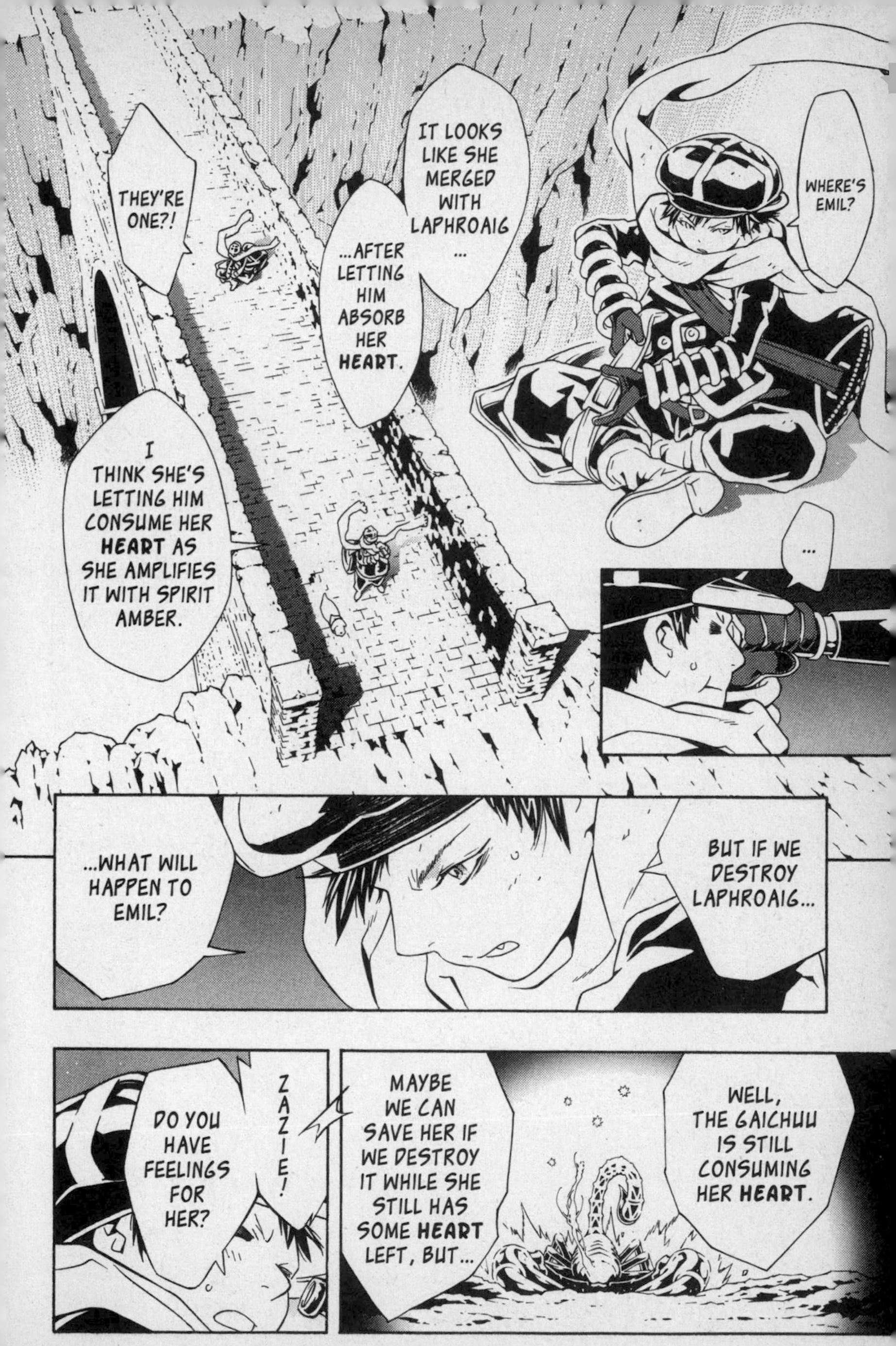
WHERE'S EMIL?
IT LOOKS LIKE SHE MERGED WITH LAPHROAIG ...
...AFTER LETTING HIM ABSORB HER **HEART**.
THEY'RE ONE?!
I THINK SHE'S LETTING HIM CONSUME HER **HEART** AS SHE AMPLIFIES IT WITH SPIRIT AMBER.
...
BUT IF WE DESTROY LAPHROAIG...
...WHAT WILL HAPPEN TO EMIL?
WELL, THE GAICHUU IS STILL CONSUMING HER **HEART**.
MAYBE WE CAN SAVE HER IF WE DESTROY IT WHILE SHE STILL HAS SOME **HEART** LEFT, BUT...
ZAZIE!
DO YOU HAVE FEELINGS FOR HER?

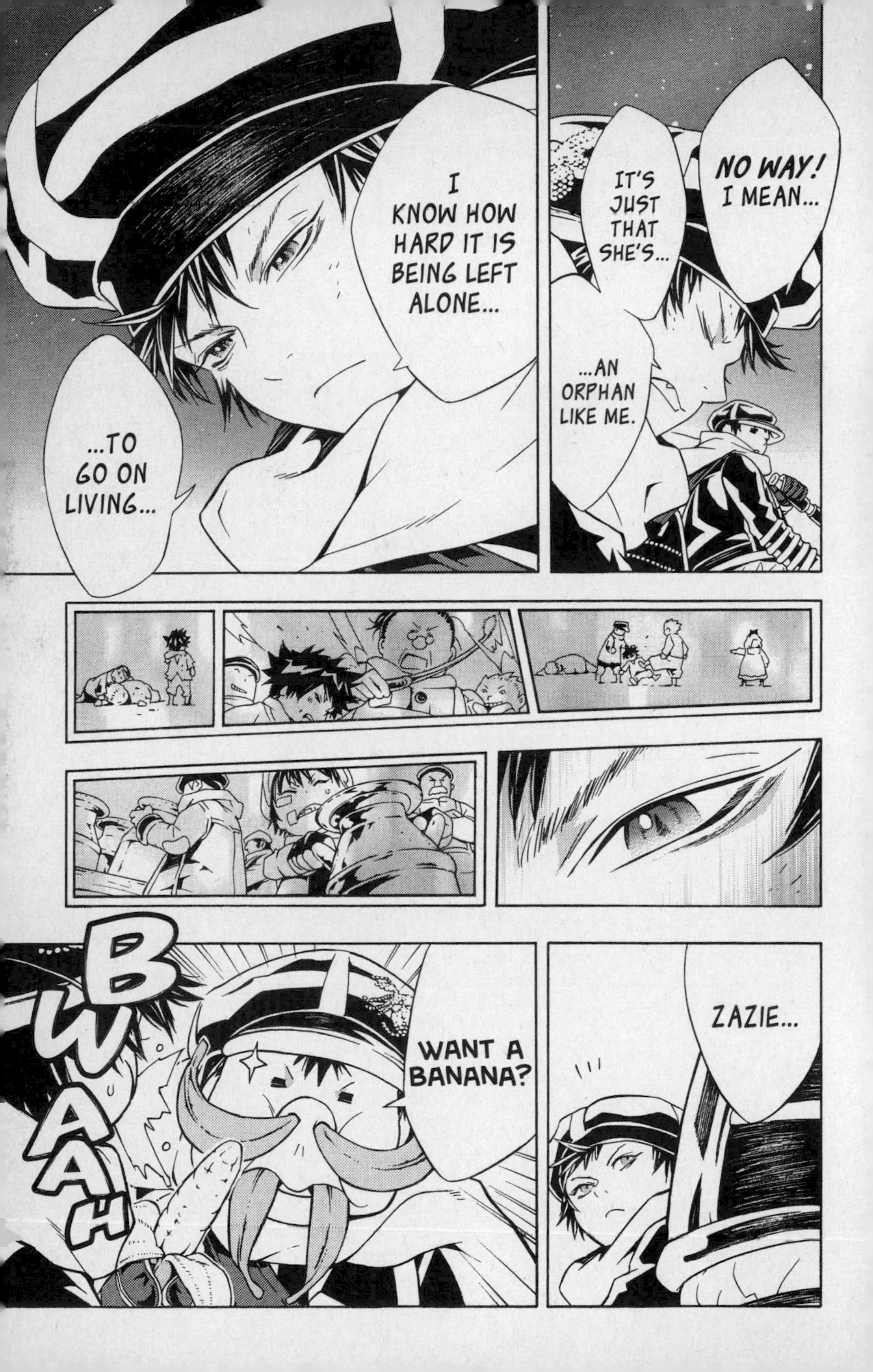
NO WAY! I MEAN...
IT'S JUST THAT SHE'S...
...AN ORPHAN LIKE ME.
I KNOW HOW HARD IT IS BEING LEFT ALONE...
...TO GO ON LIVING...
ZAZIE...
WANT A BANANA?
BWAAAH

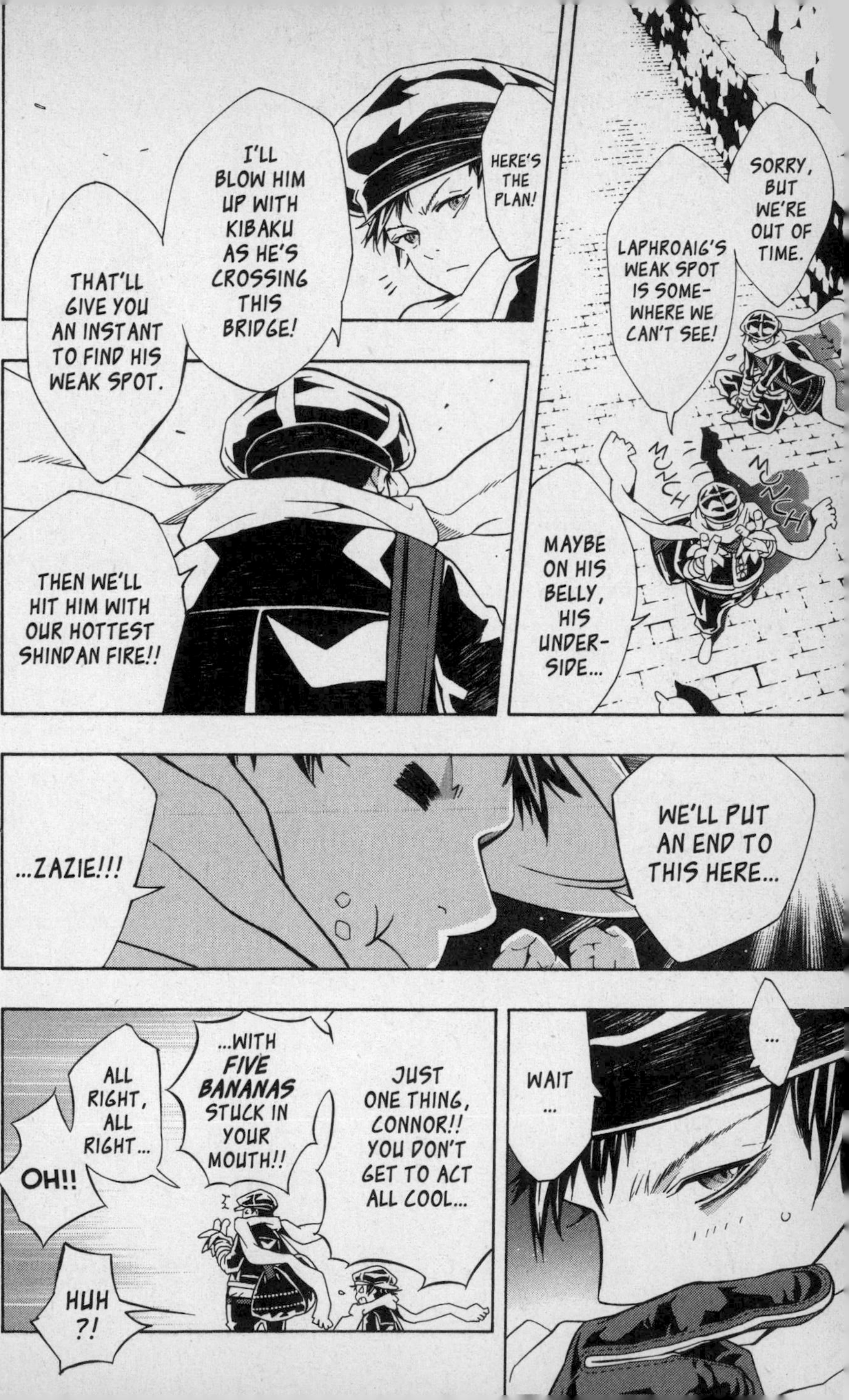
SORRY, BUT WE'RE OUT OF TIME.
LAPHROAIG'S WEAK SPOT IS SOME-WHERE WE CAN'T SEE!
MUNCH
MUNCH
MAYBE ON HIS BELLY, HIS UNDER-SIDE...
HERE'S THE PLAN!
I'LL BLOW HIM UP WITH KIBAKU AS HE'S CROSSING THIS BRIDGE!
THAT'LL GIVE YOU AN INSTANT TO FIND HIS WEAK SPOT.
THEN WE'LL HIT HIM WITH OUR HOTTEST SHINDAN FIRE!!
WE'LL PUT AN END TO THIS HERE...
...ZAZIE!!!
...
WAIT ...
JUST ONE THING, CONNOR!! YOU DON'T GET TO ACT ALL COOL...
...WITH FIVE BANANAS STUCK IN YOUR MOUTH!!
ALL RIGHT, ALL RIGHT...
OH!!
HUH ?!

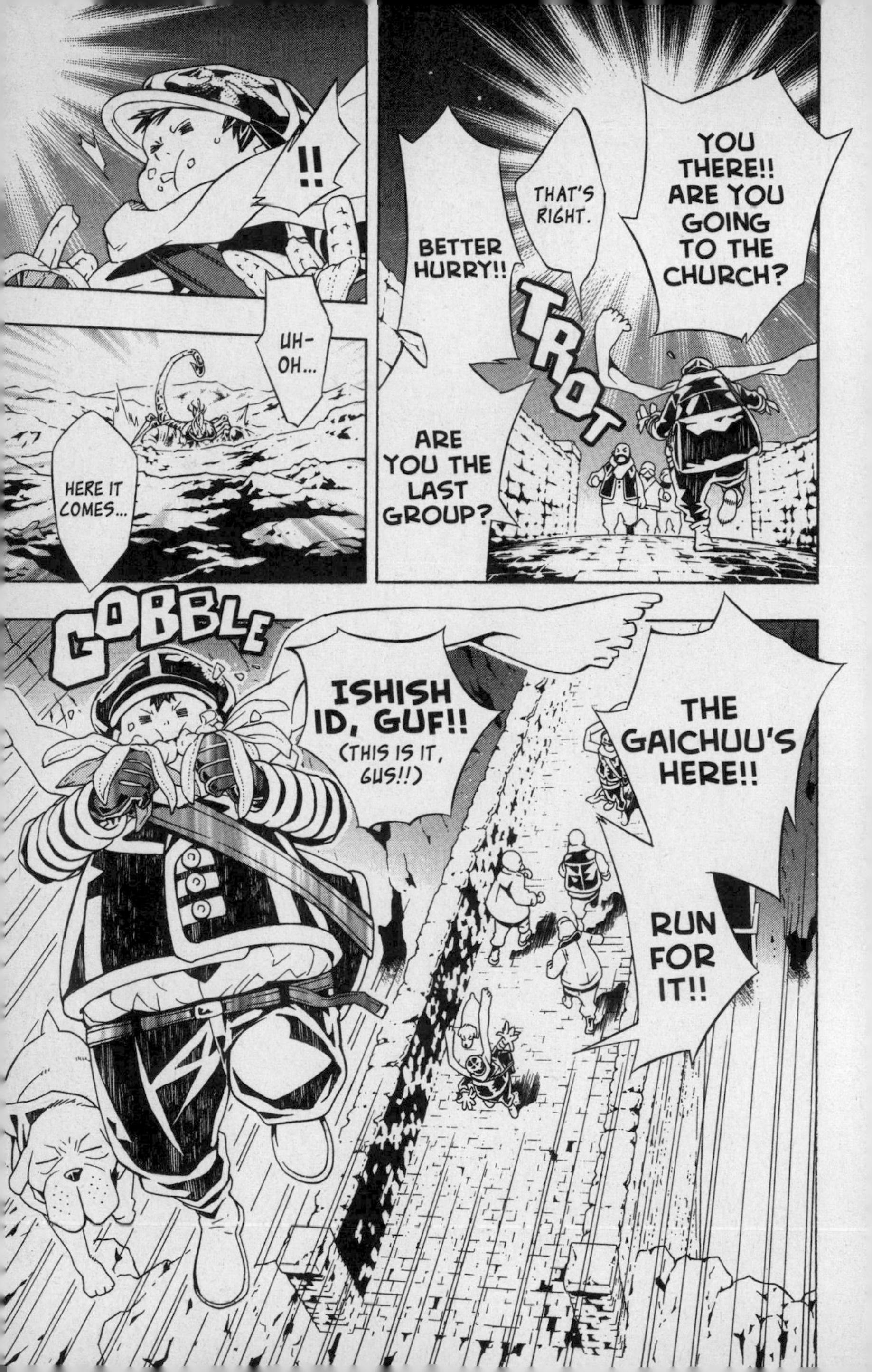
YOU THERE!! ARE YOU GOING TO THE CHURCH?
THAT'S RIGHT.
BETTER HURRY!!
TROT
ARE YOU THE LAST GROUP?
!!
UH-OH...
HERE IT COMES...
THE GAICHUU'S HERE!!
RUN FOR IT!!
ISHISH ID, GUF!! (THIS IS IT, GUS!!)
GOBBLE

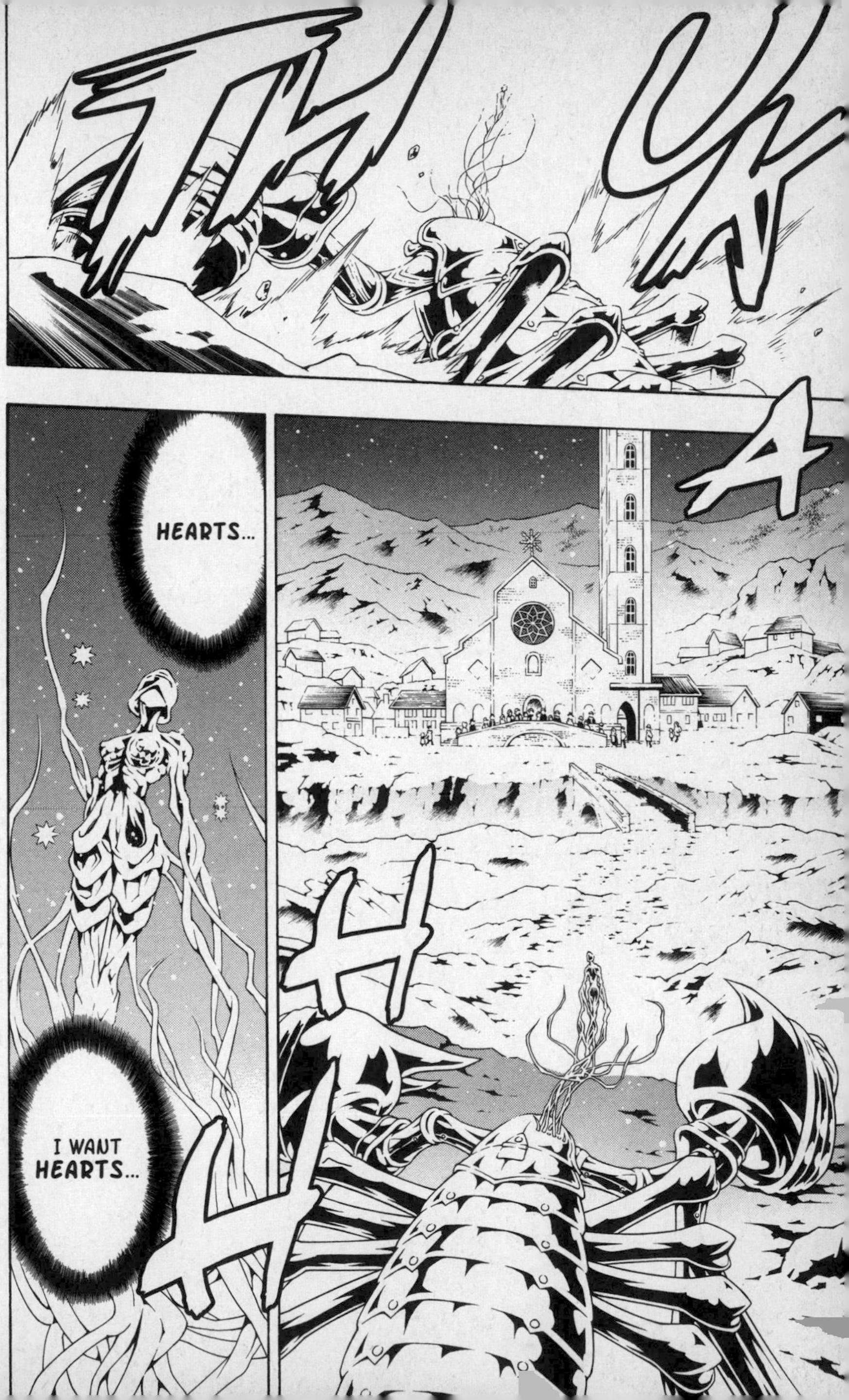
HEARTS...
I WANT HEARTS...

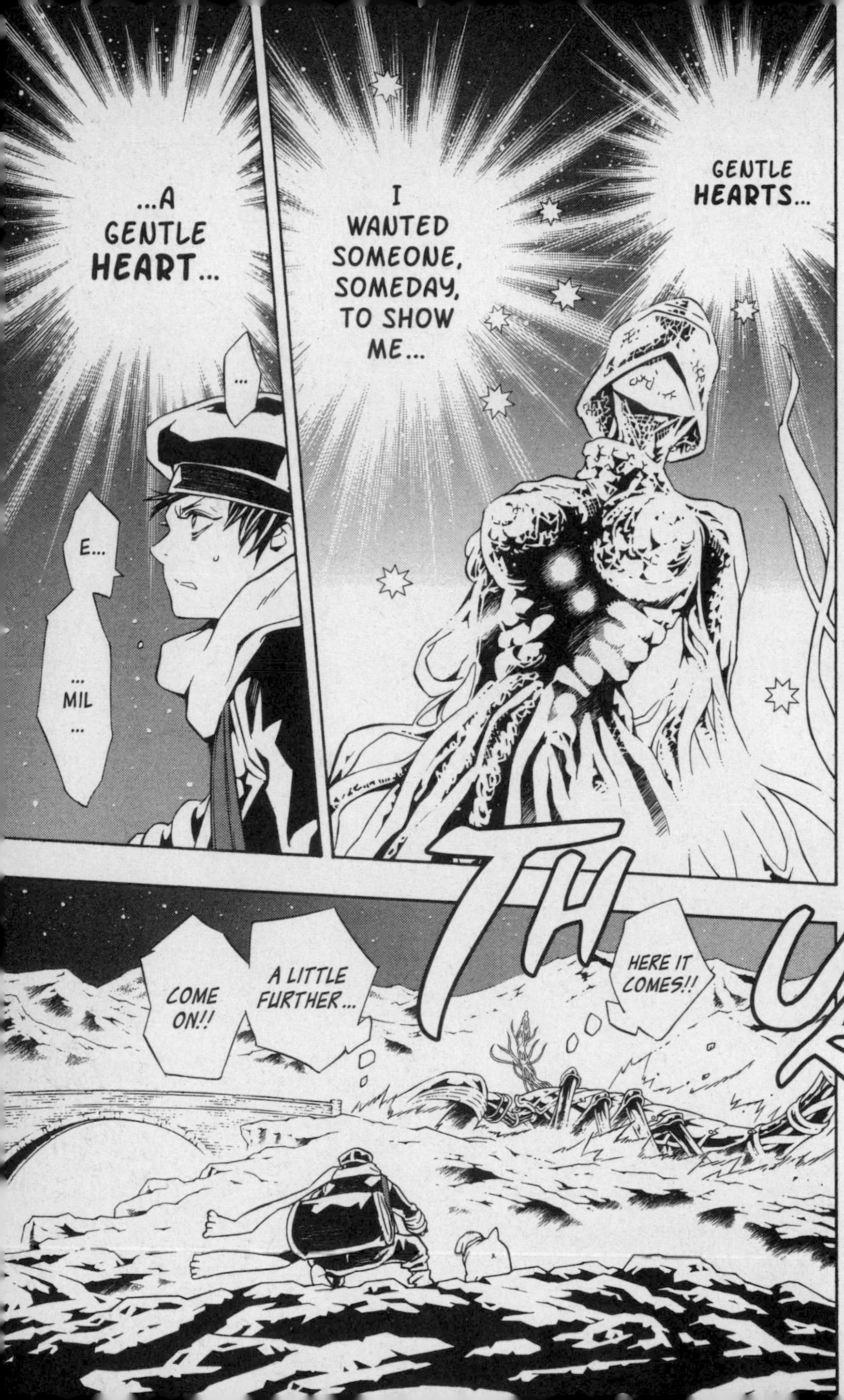
GENTLE HEARTS...
I WANTED SOMEONE, SOMEDAY, TO SHOW ME...
...A GENTLE HEART...
...
E... ...MIL...
THUK
HERE IT COMES!!
A LITTLE FURTHER...
COME ON!!

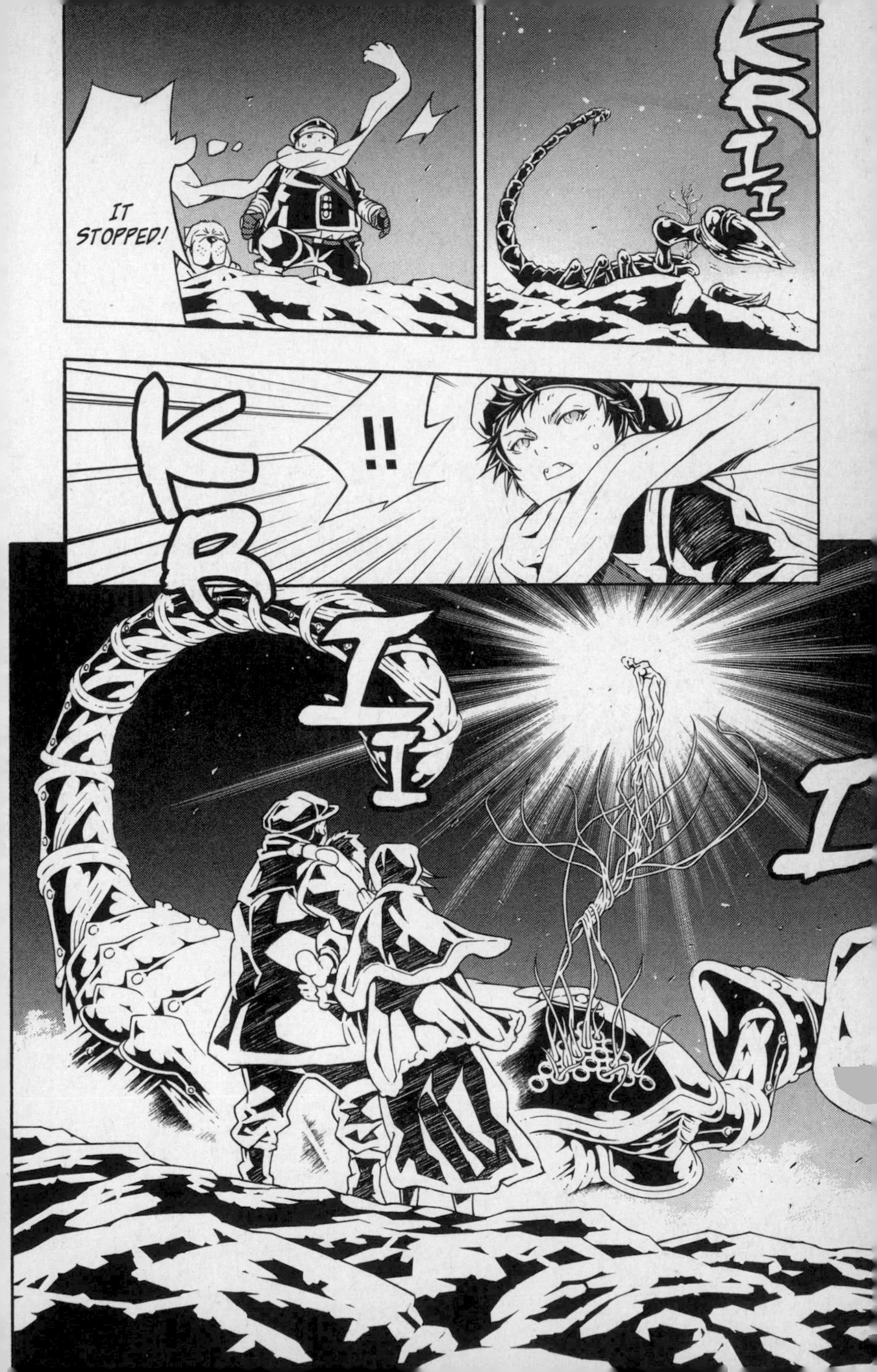
KRII
IT STOPPED!
!!
KRIII
I

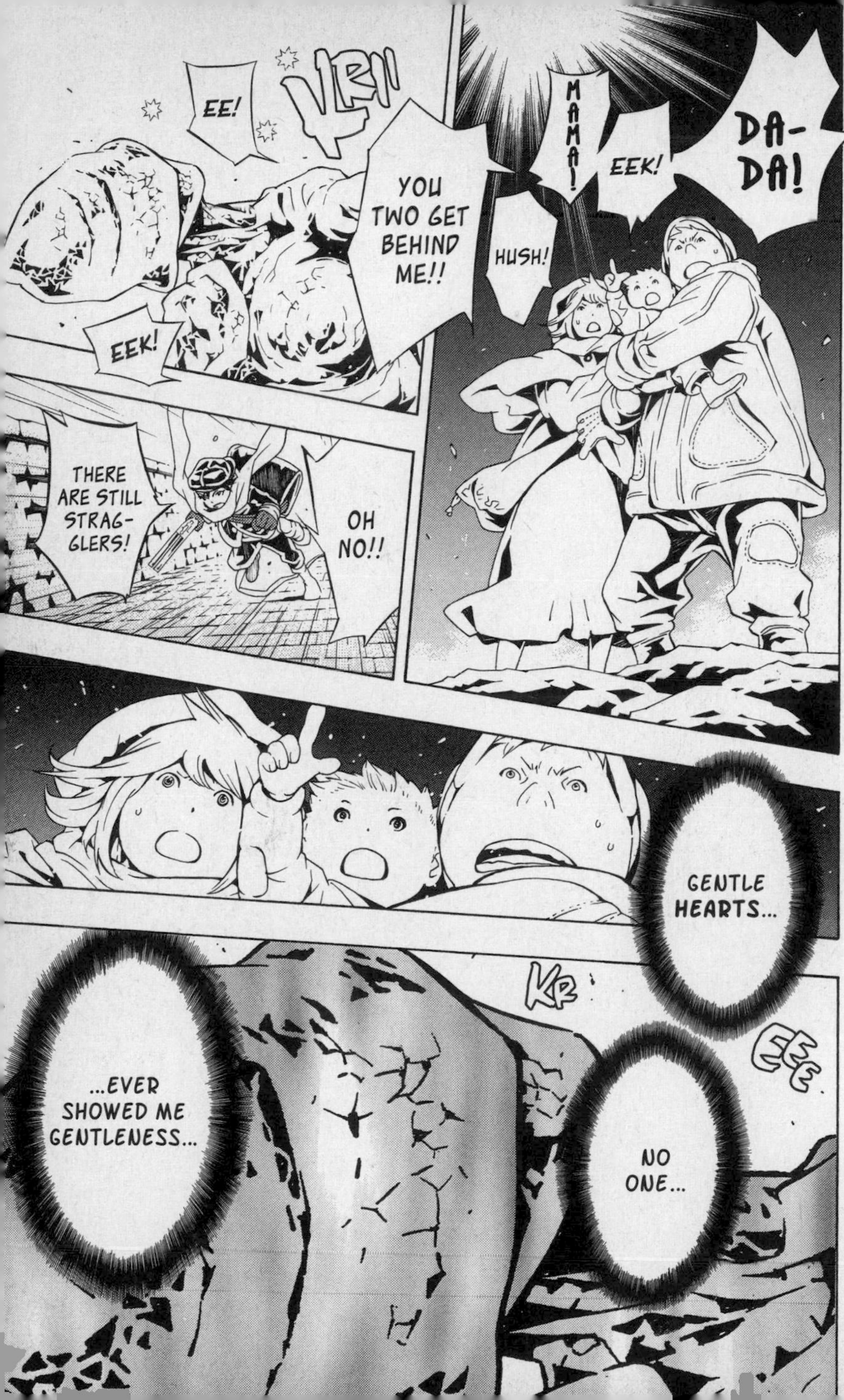
DA-DA!
EEK!
MAMA!
HUSH!
VRI
EE!
YOU TWO GET BEHIND ME!!
EEK!
OH NO!!
THERE ARE STILL STRAG-GLERS!
GENTLE HEARTS...
KR
EEE
NO ONE...
...EVER SHOWED ME GENTLENESS...

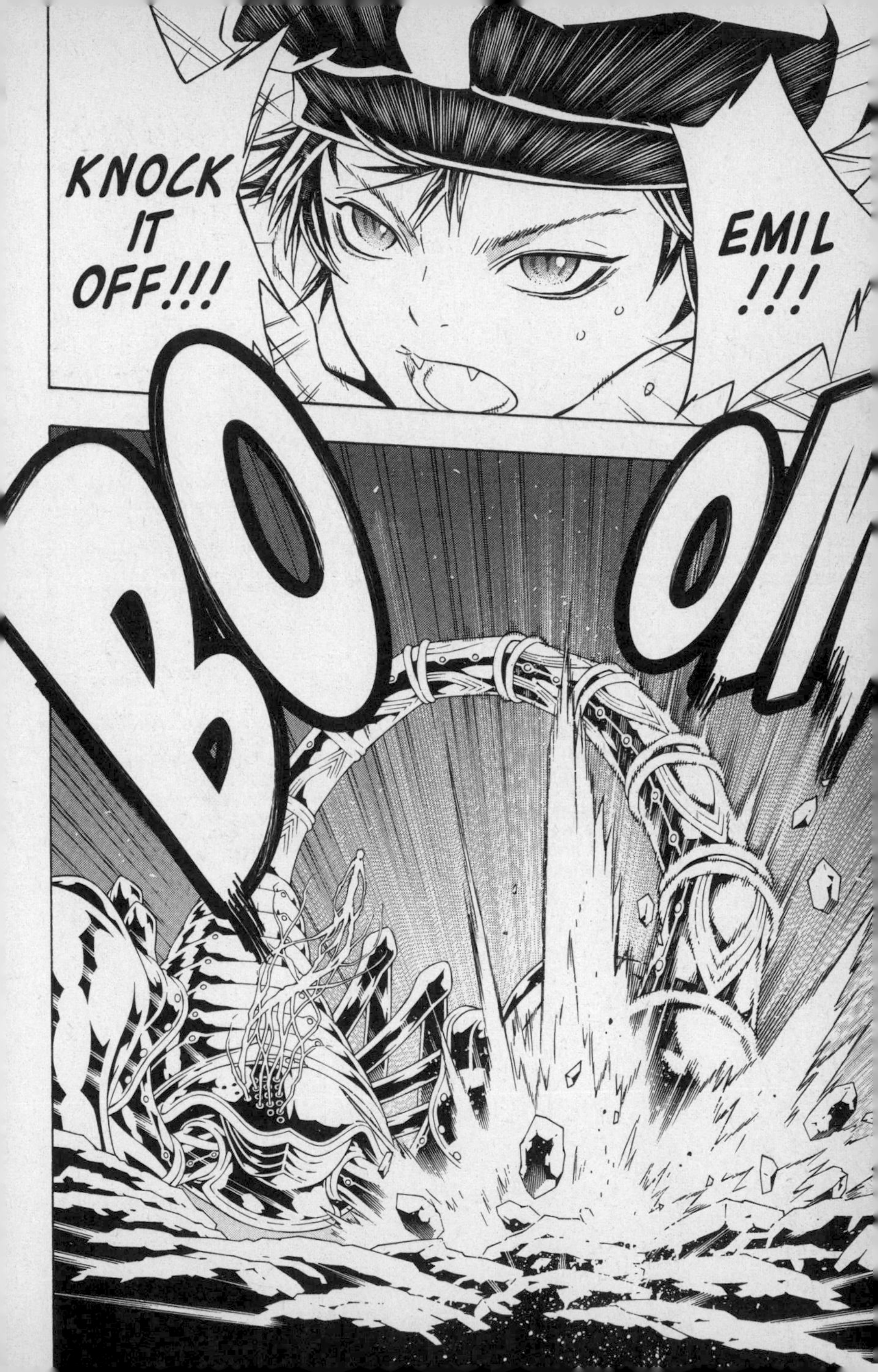
EMIL!!!
KNOCK IT OFF!!!

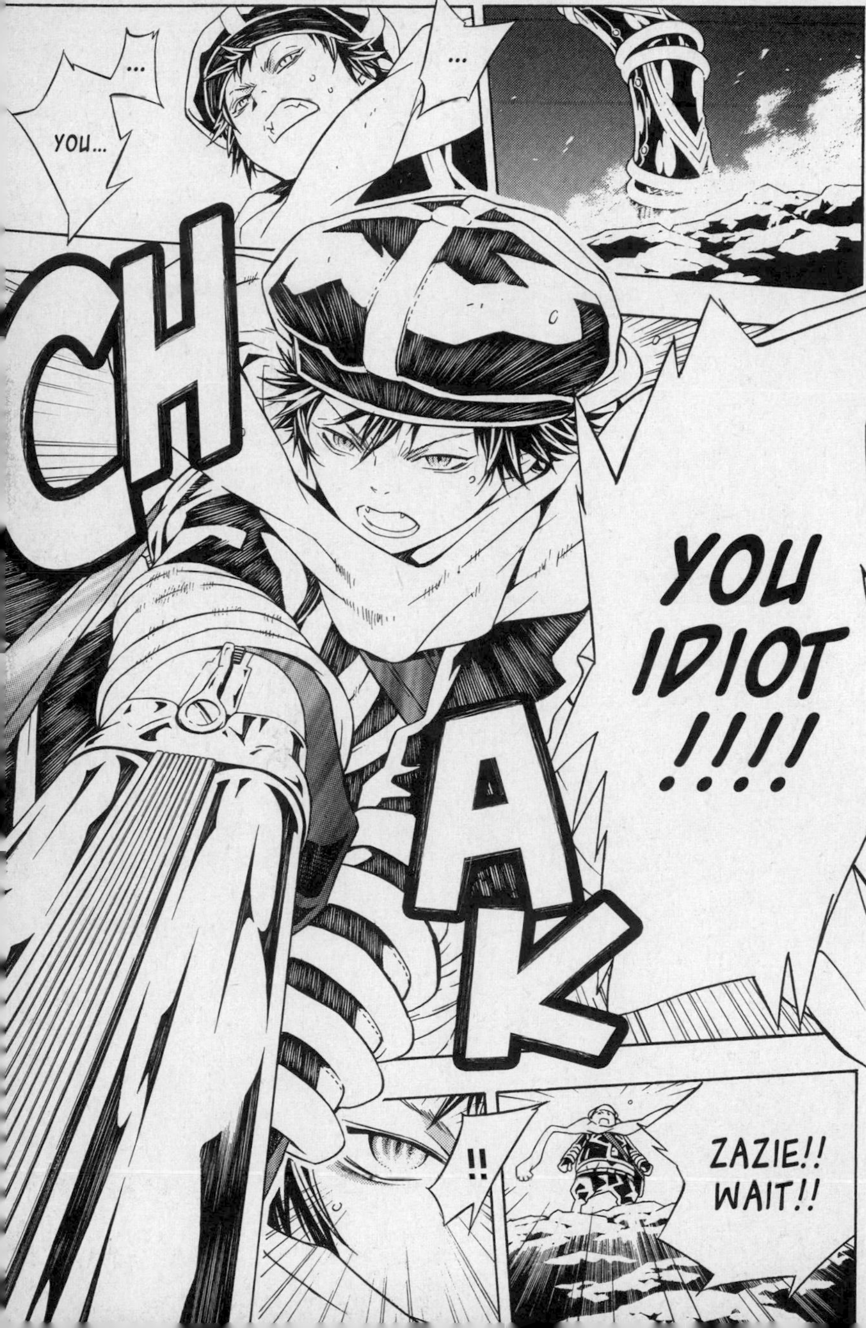
...
...
YOU...
CHAK
YOU IDIOT!!!!
ZAZIE!! WAIT!!
!!

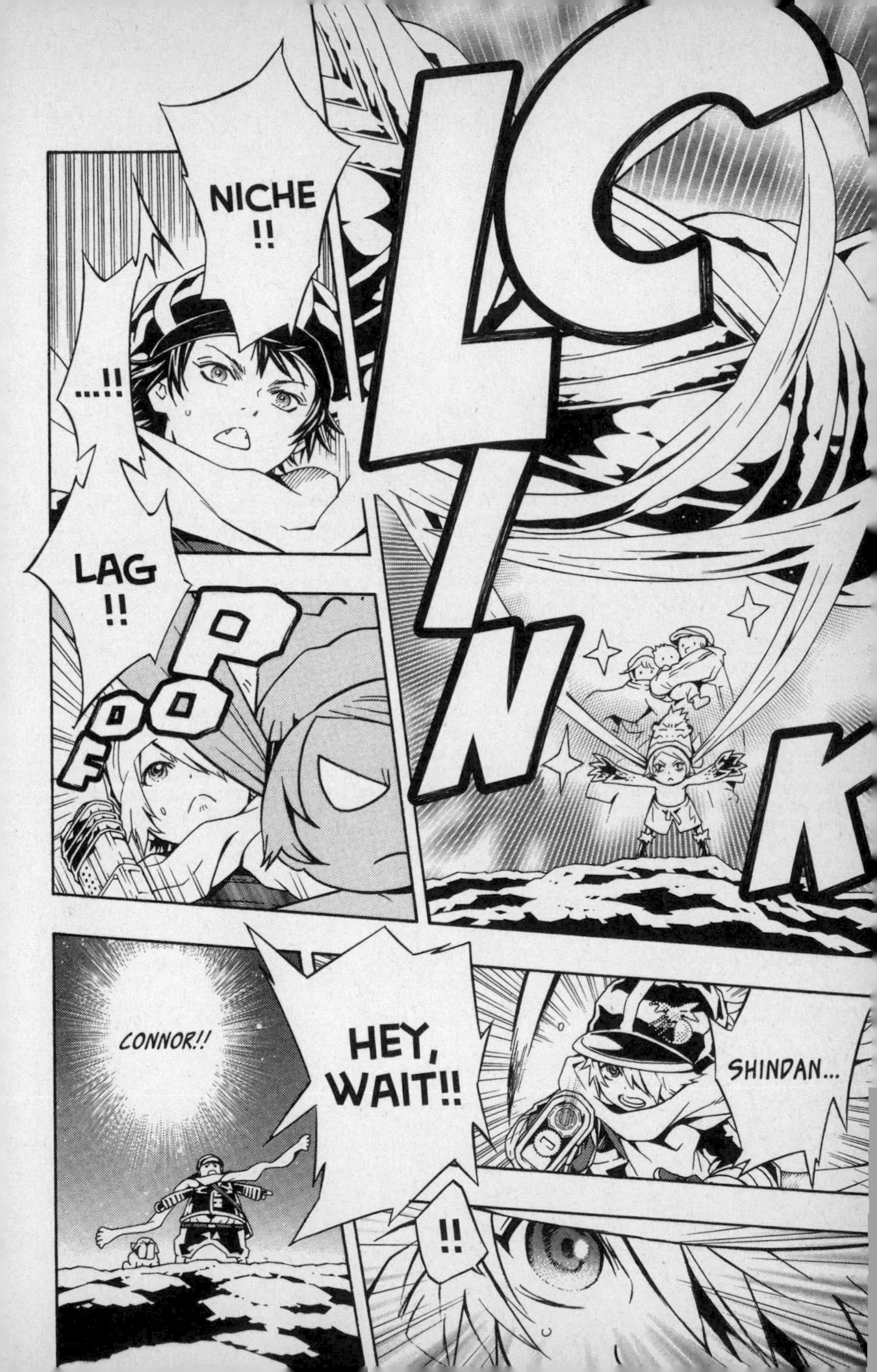
CLINK
NICHE !!
...!!
LAG !!
POOF
SHINDAN...
!!
HEY, WAIT!!
CONNOR!!

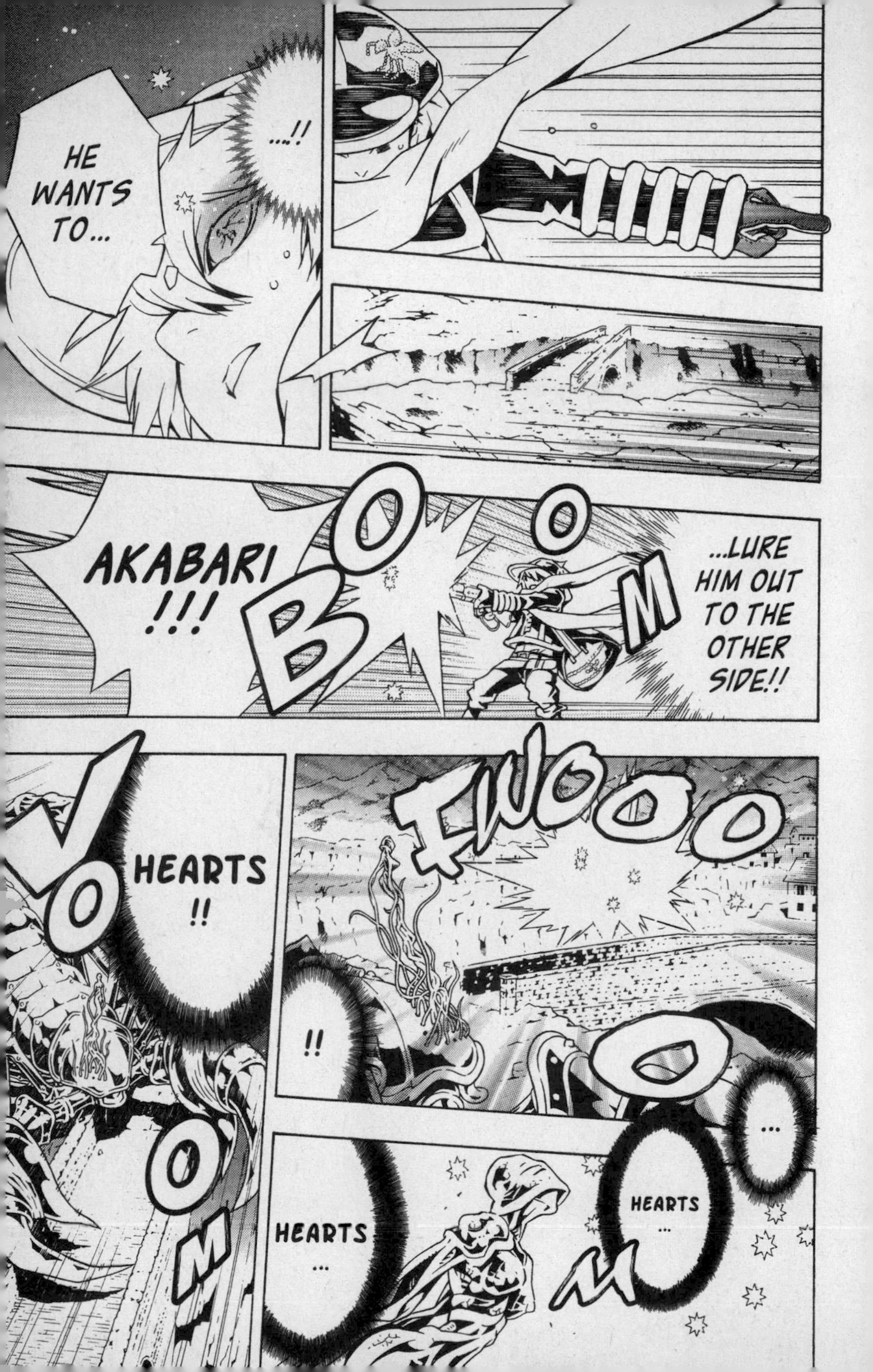
...!!
HE WANTS TO...
...LURE HIM OUT TO THE OTHER SIDE!!
BOOM
AKABARI !!!
FWOOOO
!!
...
HEARTS ...
HEARTS ...
HEARTS !!
VOOOM

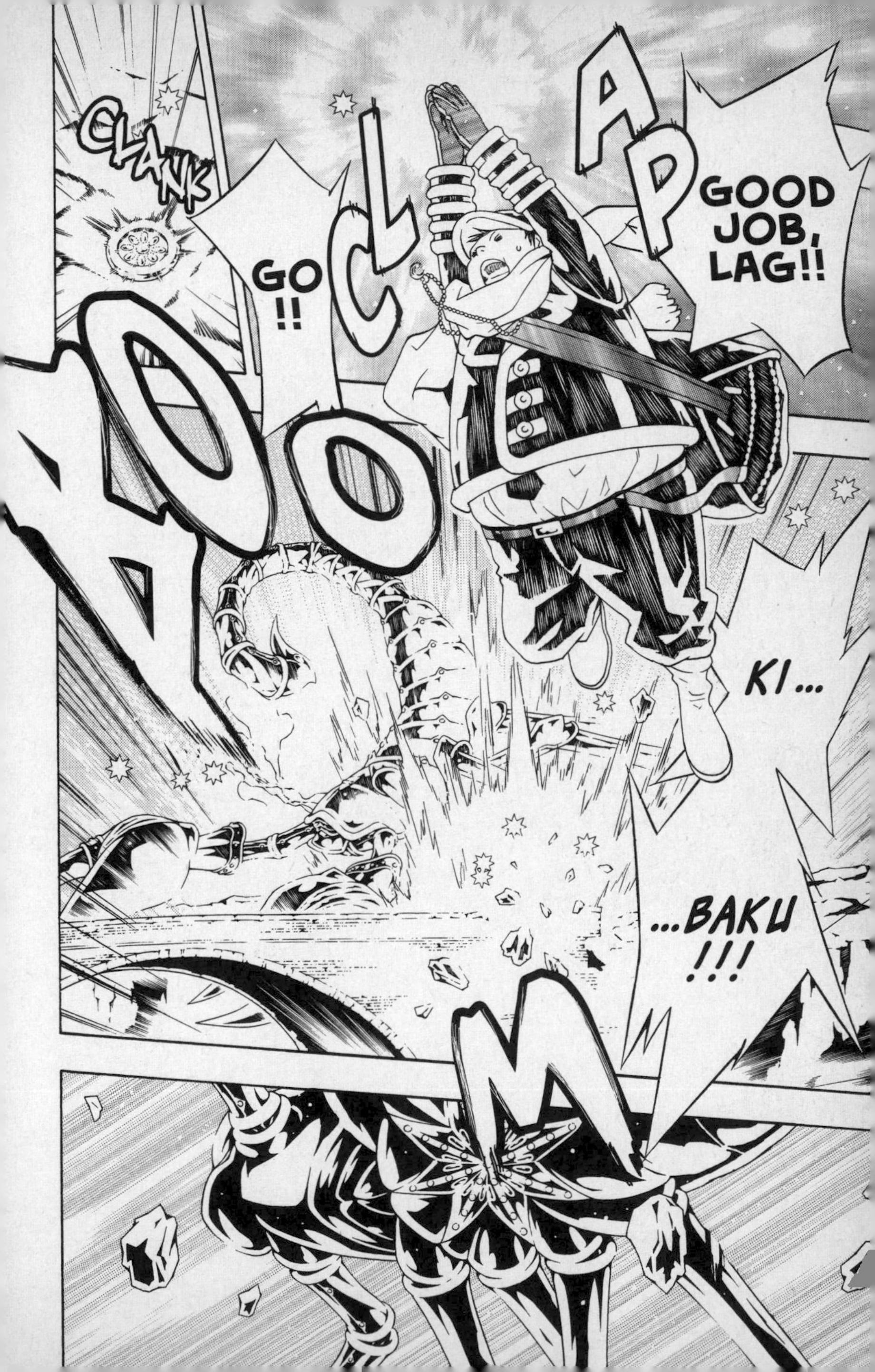
GOOD JOB, LAG!!
CLAP
GO!!
CLANK
KI...
...BAKU!!!
BOOM

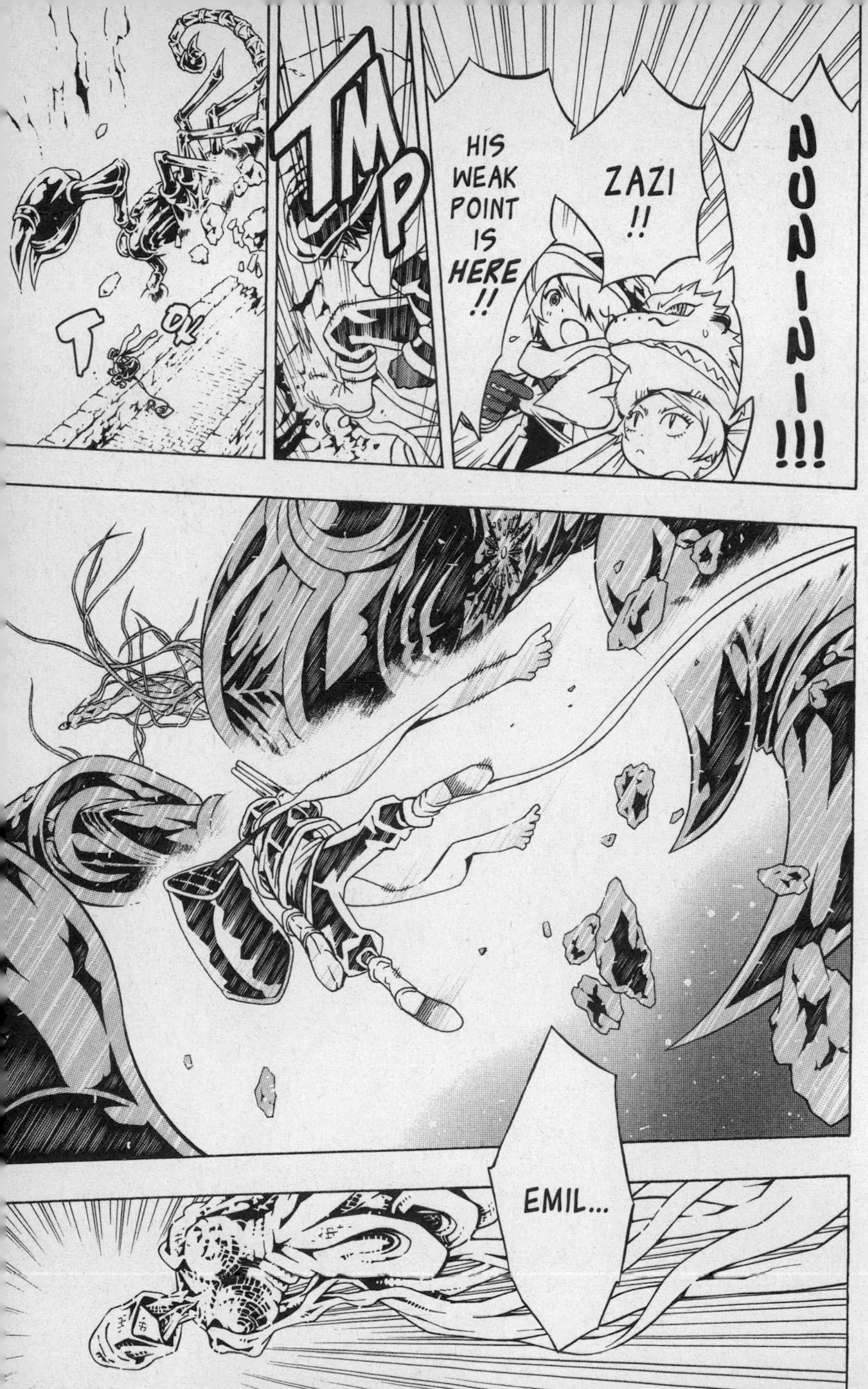
NUN-N-!!!
ZAZI !!
HIS WEAK POINT IS HERE !!
TMP
T
EMIL...

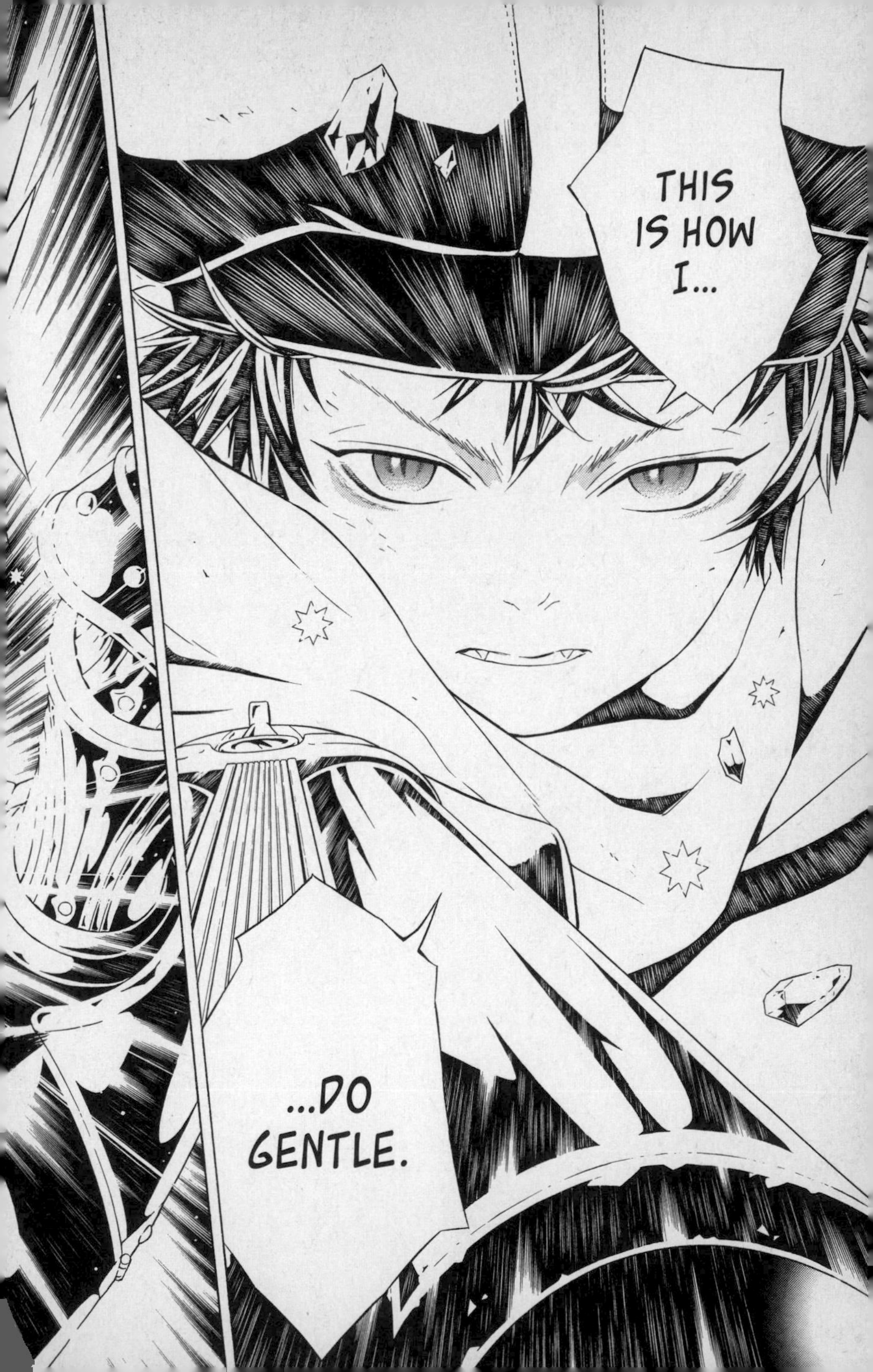
THIS IS HOW I...
...DO GENTLE.

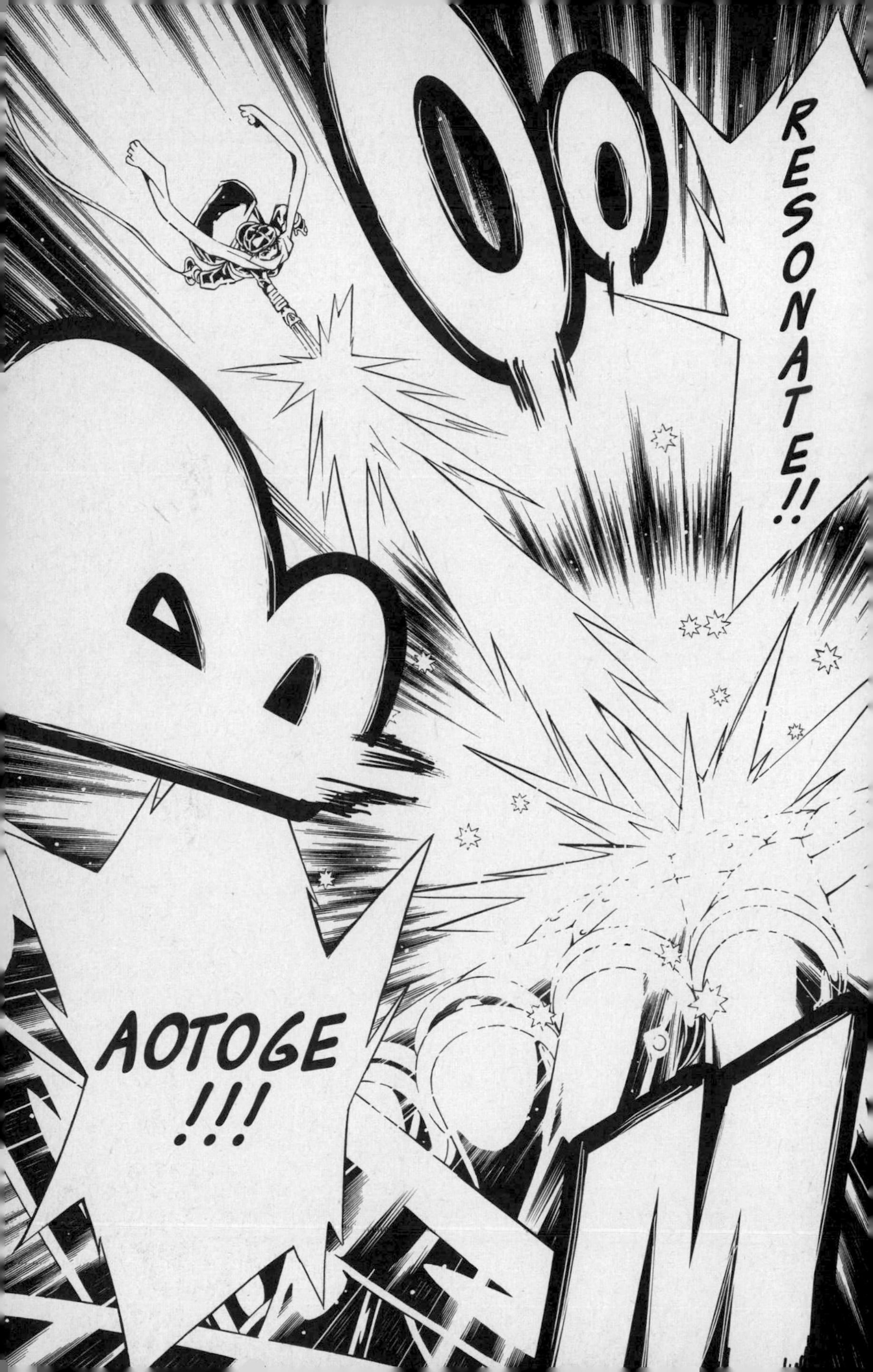
RESONATE!!
AOTOGE !!!

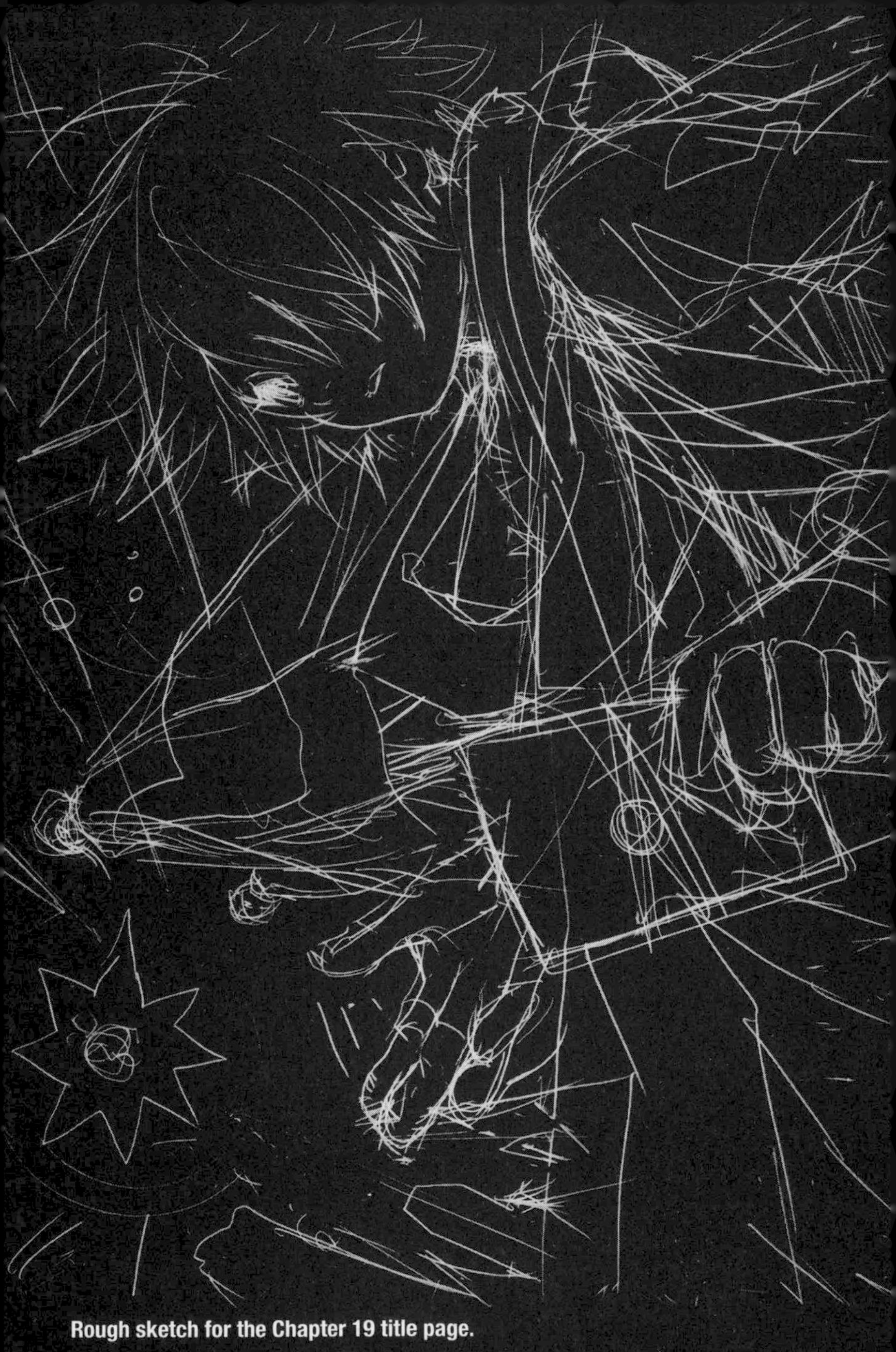

Rough sketch for the Chapter 19 title page.

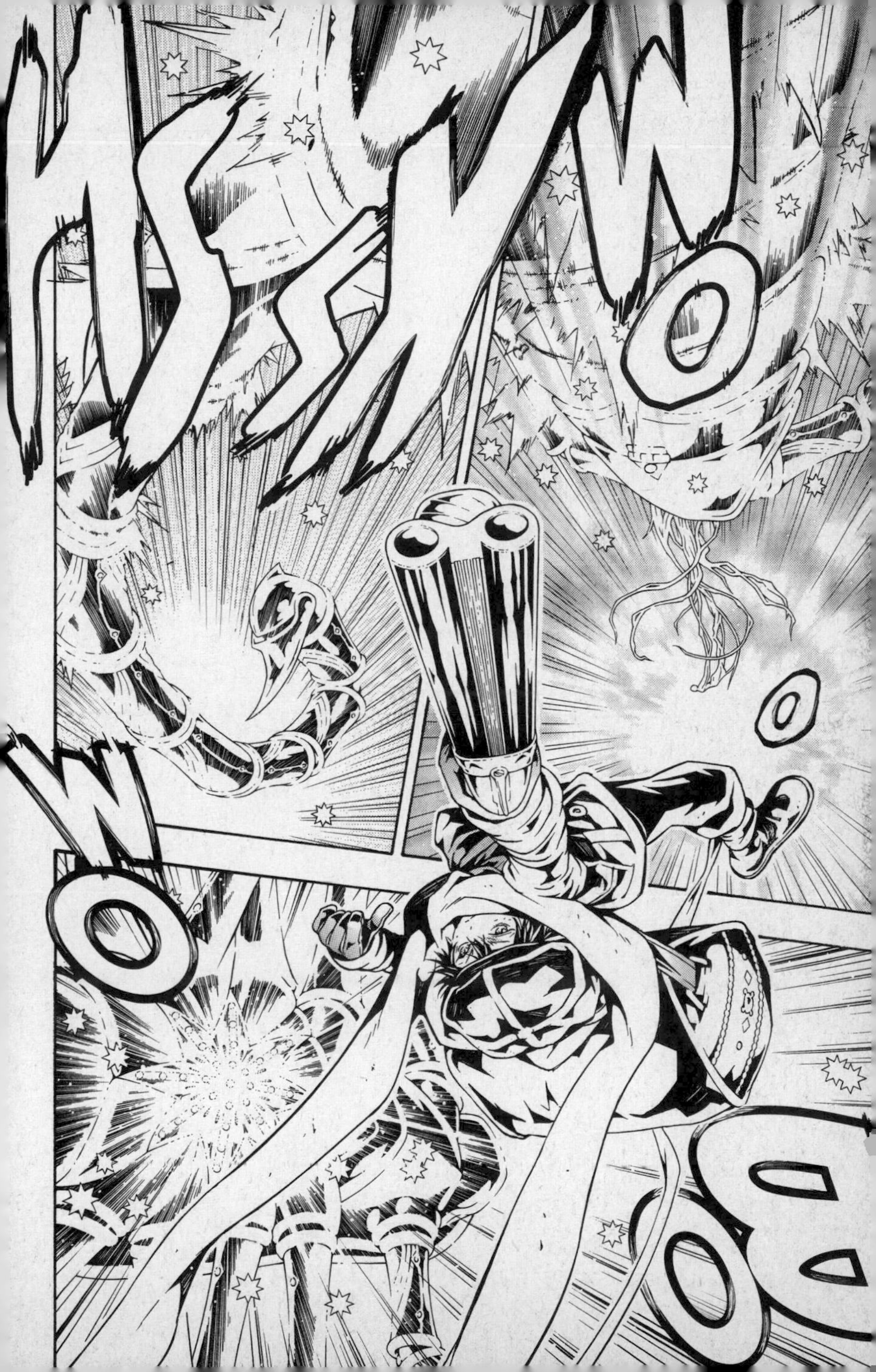

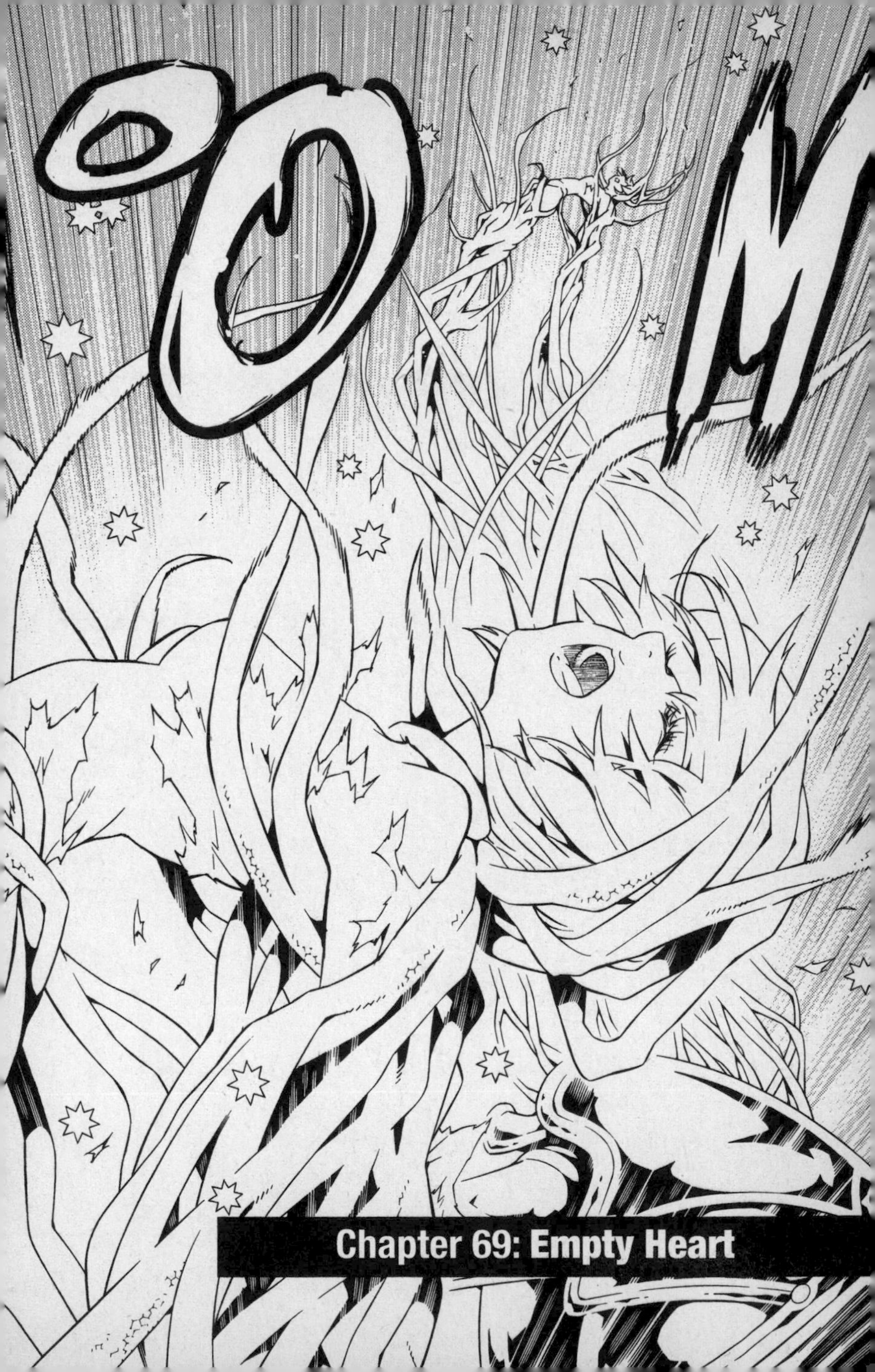
OOM
Chapter 69: Empty Heart

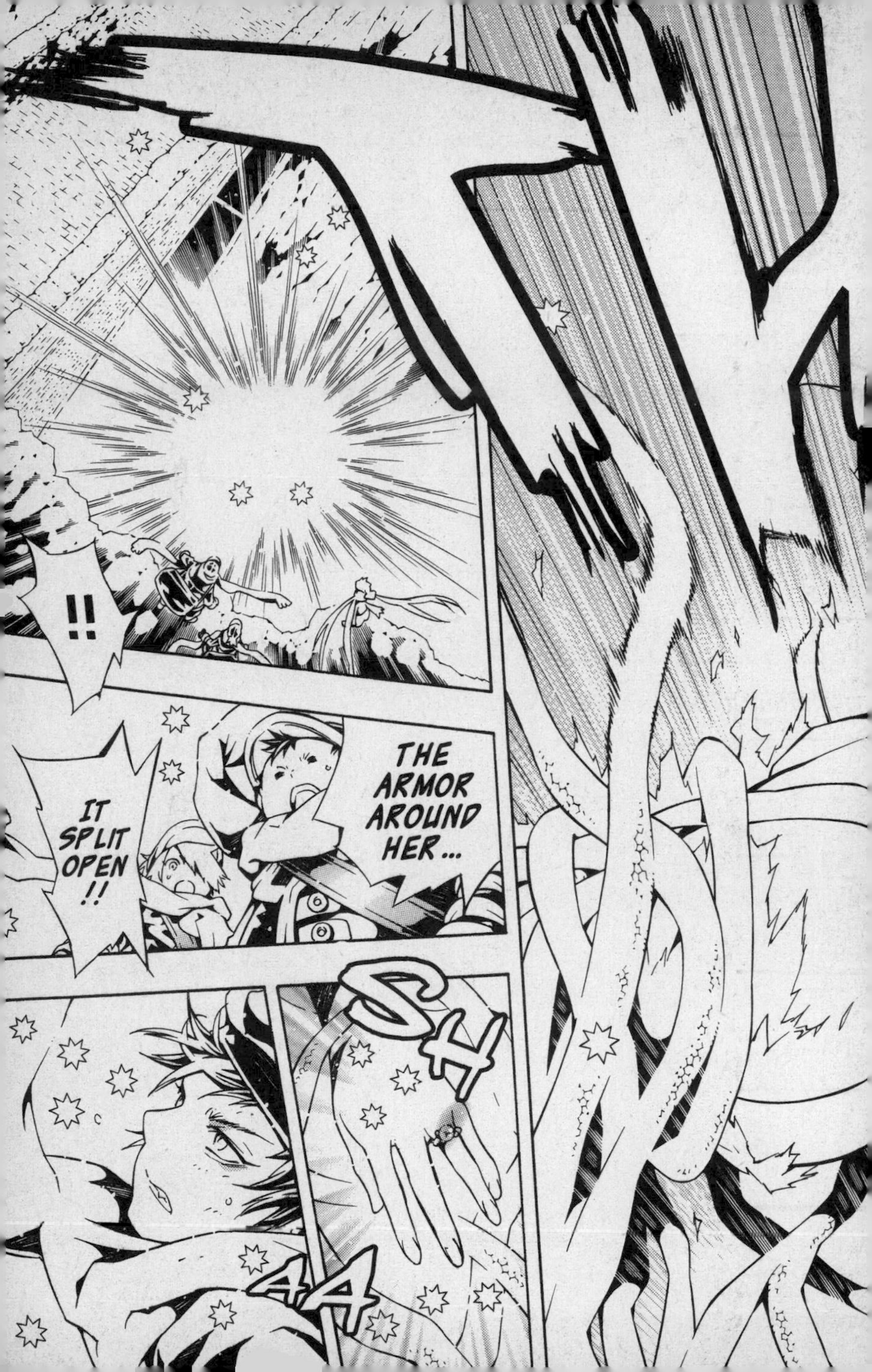
!!
THE ARMOR AROUND HER...
IT SPLIT OPEN!!
SH
AA

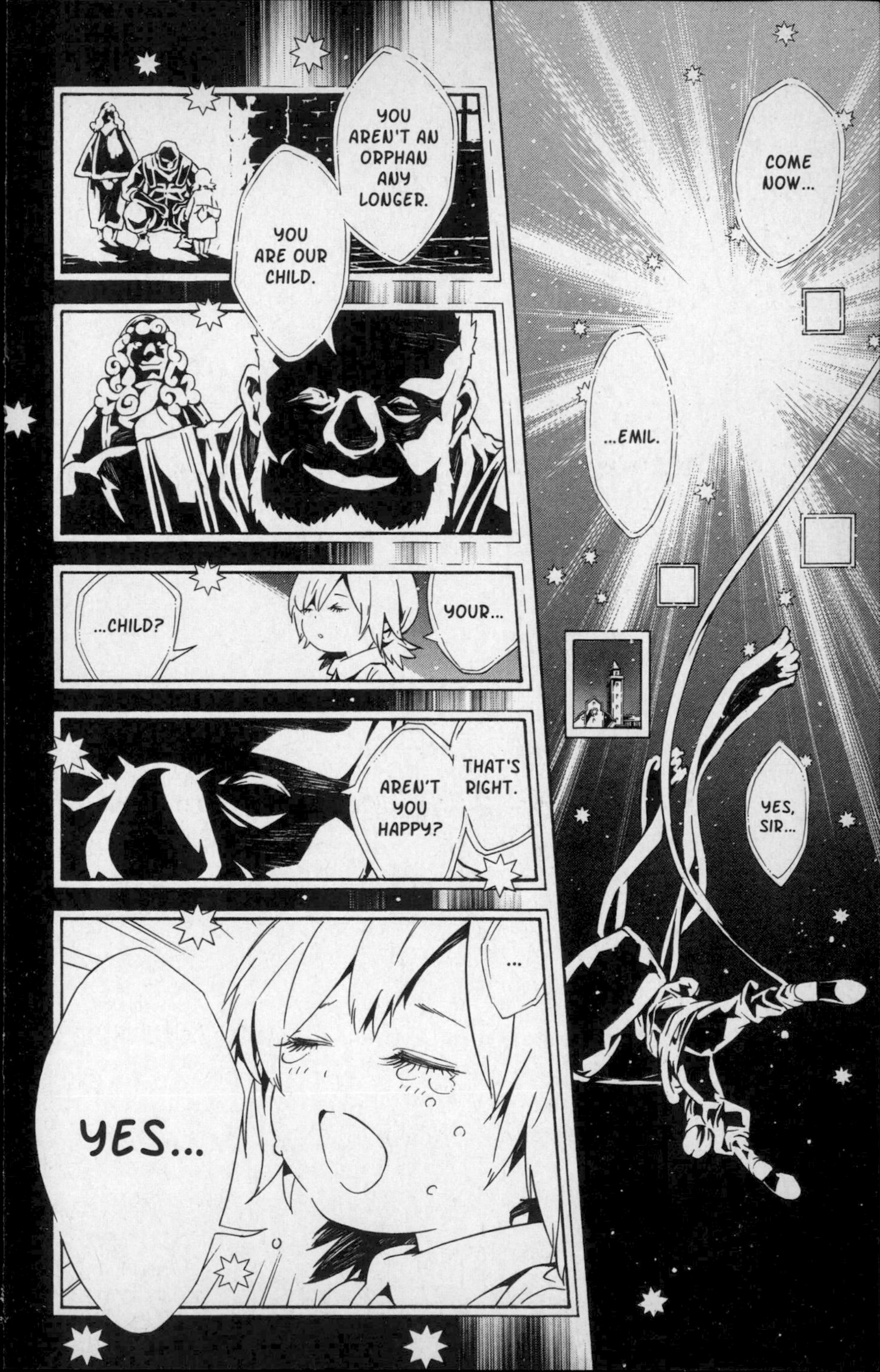
COME NOW...
...EMIL.
YES, SIR...
YOU AREN'T AN ORPHAN ANY LONGER.
YOU ARE OUR CHILD.
YOUR...
...CHILD?
THAT'S RIGHT.
AREN'T YOU HAPPY?
...
YES...

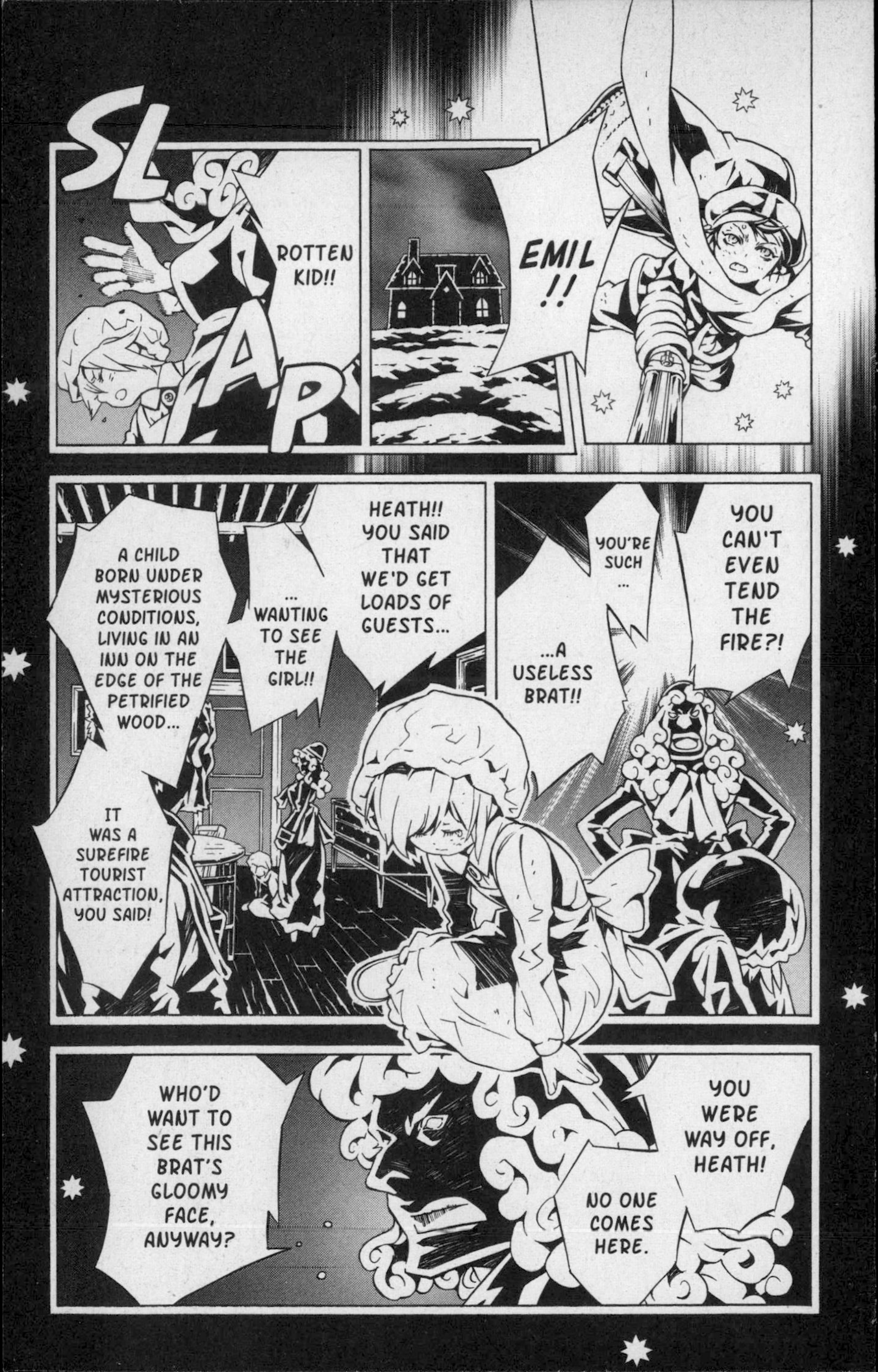
EMIL!!
ROTTEN KID!!
SLAP
YOU CAN'T EVEN TEND THE FIRE?!
YOU'RE SUCH ...
...A USELESS BRAT!!
HEATH!! YOU SAID THAT WE'D GET LOADS OF GUESTS...
... WANTING TO SEE THE GIRL!!
A CHILD BORN UNDER MYSTERIOUS CONDITIONS, LIVING IN AN INN ON THE EDGE OF THE PETRIFIED WOOD...
IT WAS A SUREFIRE TOURIST ATTRACTION, YOU SAID!
YOU WERE WAY OFF, HEATH!
NO ONE COMES HERE.
WHO'D WANT TO SEE THIS BRAT'S GLOOMY FACE, ANYWAY?

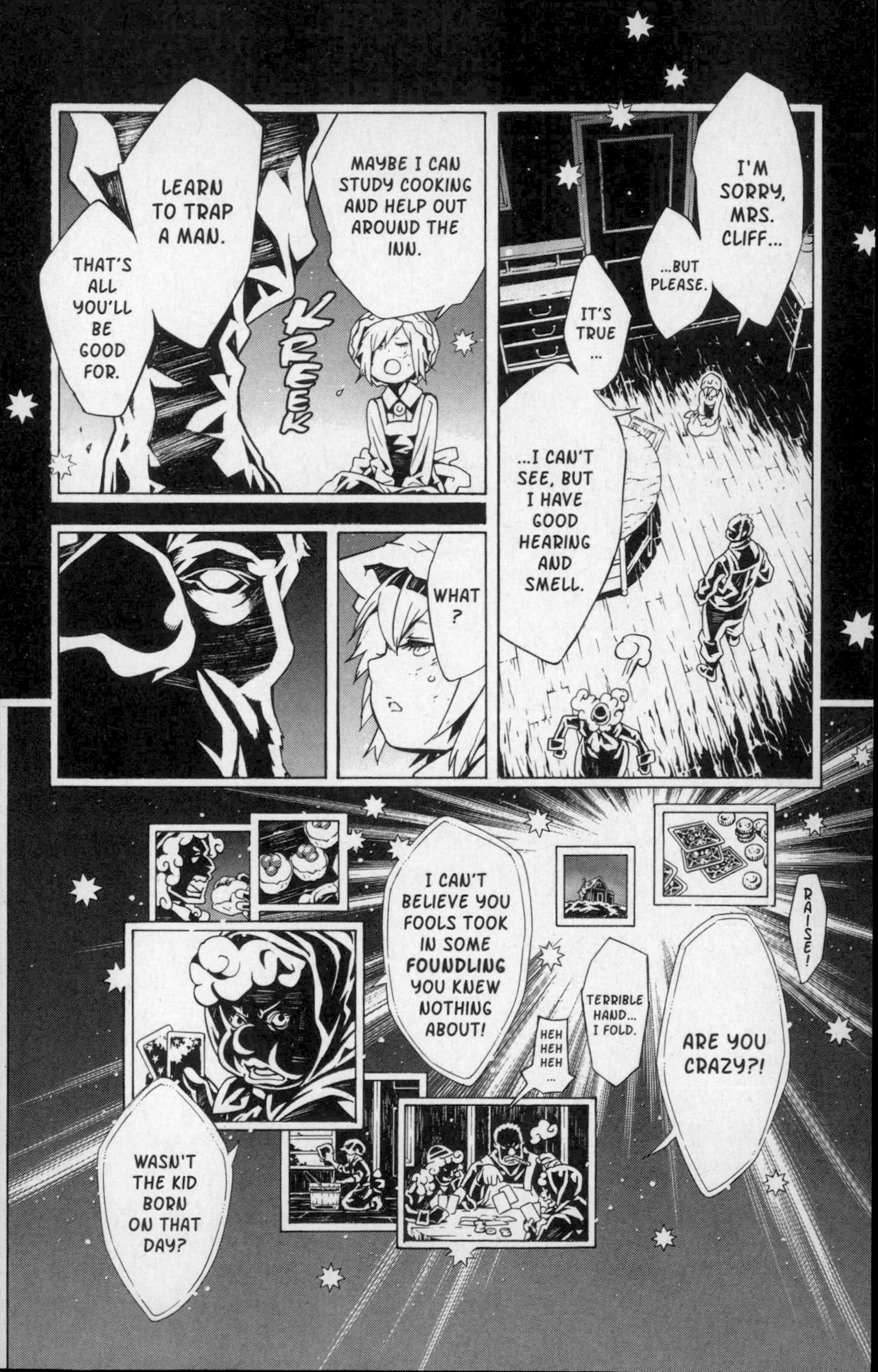
I'M SORRY, MRS. CLIFF...
...BUT PLEASE.
IT'S TRUE...
...I CAN'T SEE, BUT I HAVE GOOD HEARING AND SMELL.
MAYBE I CAN STUDY COOKING AND HELP OUT AROUND THE INN.
KREEK
LEARN TO TRAP A MAN.
THAT'S ALL YOU'LL BE GOOD FOR.
WHAT?
RAISE!
ARE YOU CRAZY?!
TERRIBLE HAND... I FOLD.
HEH HEH HEH...
I CAN'T BELIEVE YOU FOOLS TOOK IN SOME FOUNDLING YOU KNEW NOTHING ABOUT!
WASN'T THE KID BORN ON THAT DAY?

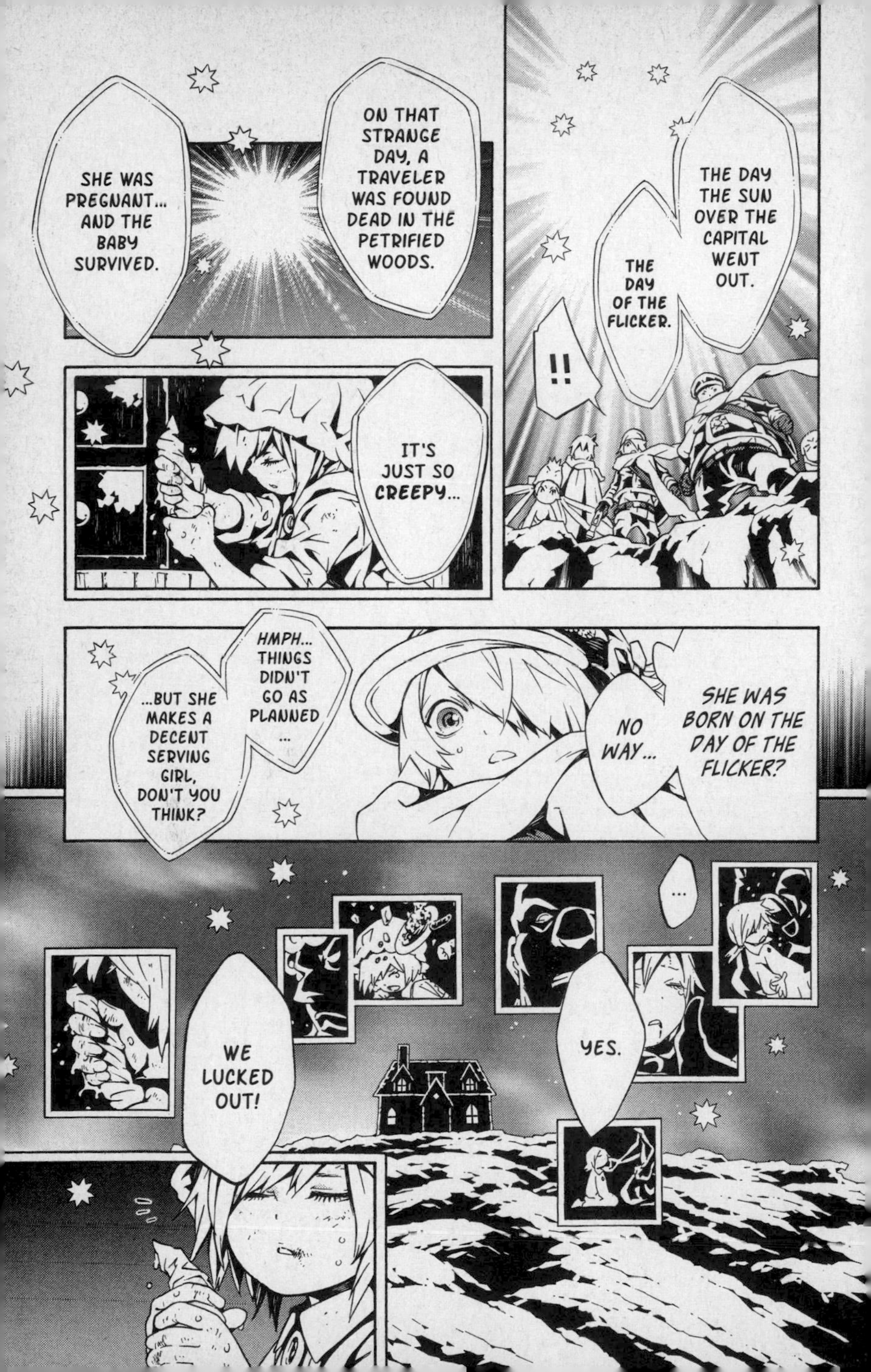
THE DAY THE SUN OVER THE CAPITAL WENT OUT.
THE DAY OF THE FLICKER.
!!
ON THAT STRANGE DAY, A TRAVELER WAS FOUND DEAD IN THE PETRIFIED WOODS.
SHE WAS PREGNANT... AND THE BABY SURVIVED.
IT'S JUST SO CREEPY...
SHE WAS BORN ON THE DAY OF THE FLICKER?
NO WAY...
HMPH... THINGS DIDN'T GO AS PLANNED ...
...BUT SHE MAKES A DECENT SERVING GIRL, DON'T YOU THINK?
...
YES.
WE LUCKED OUT!

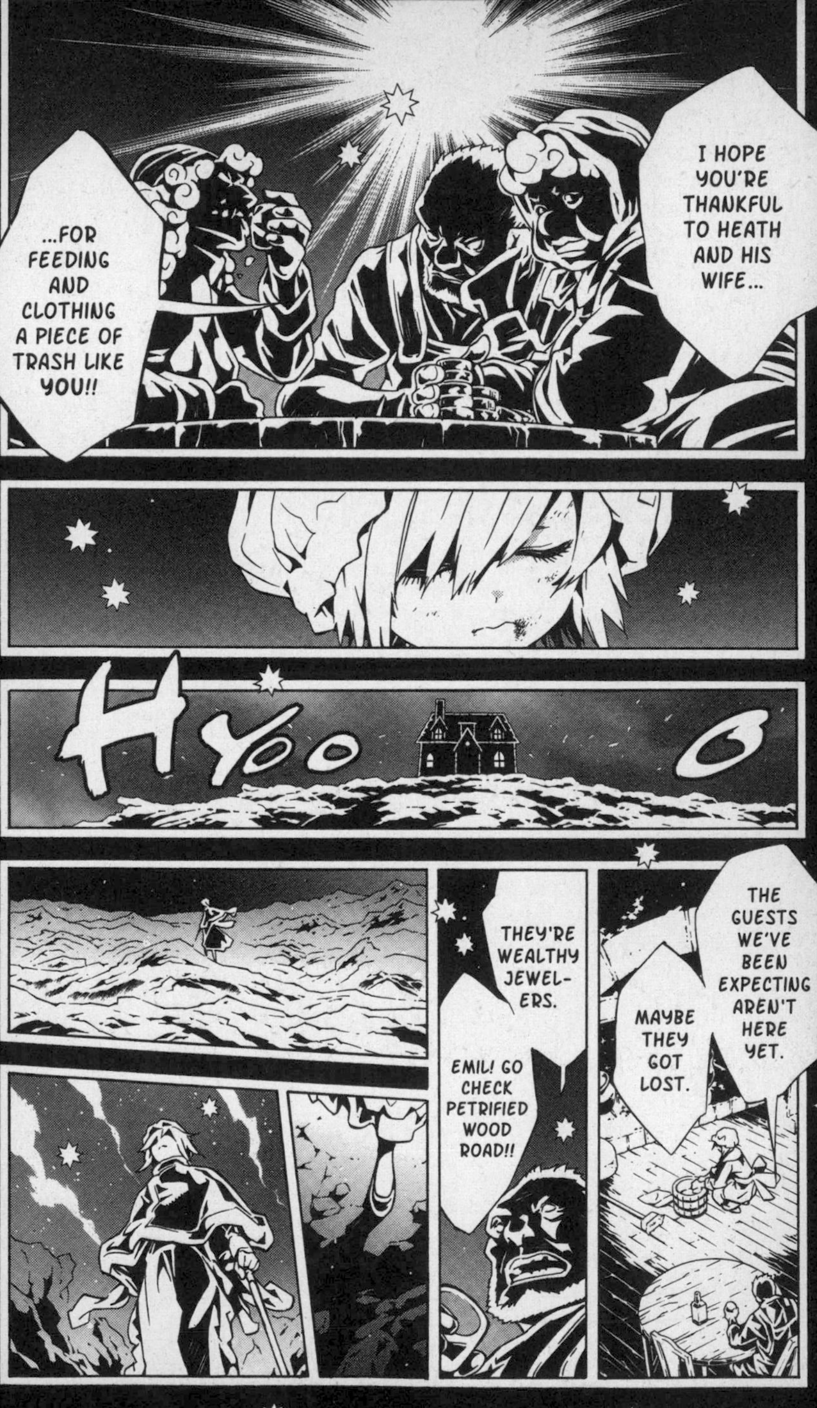
I HOPE YOU'RE THANKFUL TO HEATH AND HIS WIFE...
...FOR FEEDING AND CLOTHING A PIECE OF TRASH LIKE YOU!!
HYOOO
THE GUESTS WE'VE BEEN EXPECTING AREN'T HERE YET.
MAYBE THEY GOT LOST.
THEY'RE WEALTHY JEWEL-ERS.
EMIL! GO CHECK PETRIFIED WOOD ROAD!!

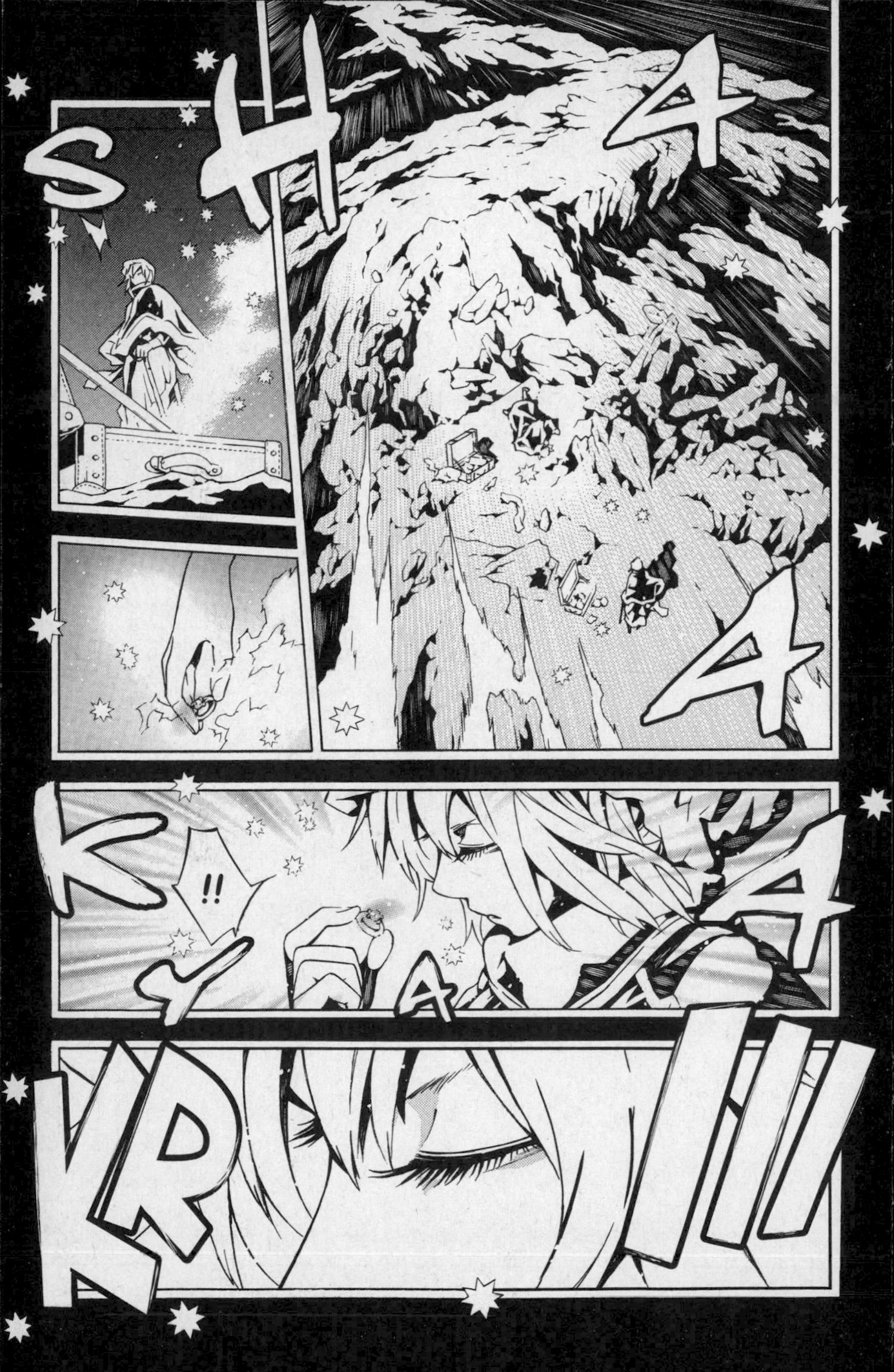
SHAA
!!
KYAA

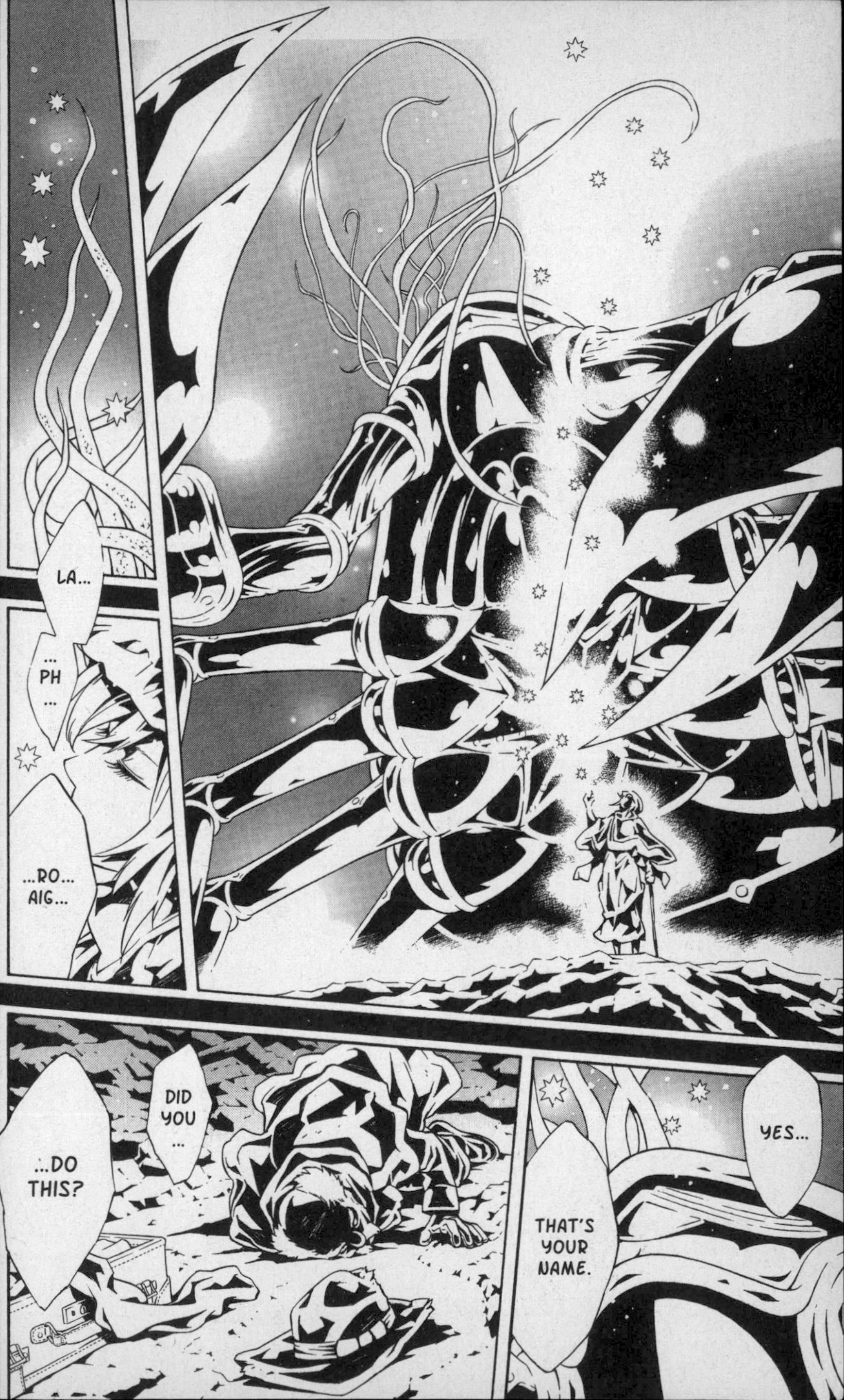
LA...
...PH...
...RO... AIG...
YES...
THAT'S YOUR NAME.
DID YOU...
...DO THIS?

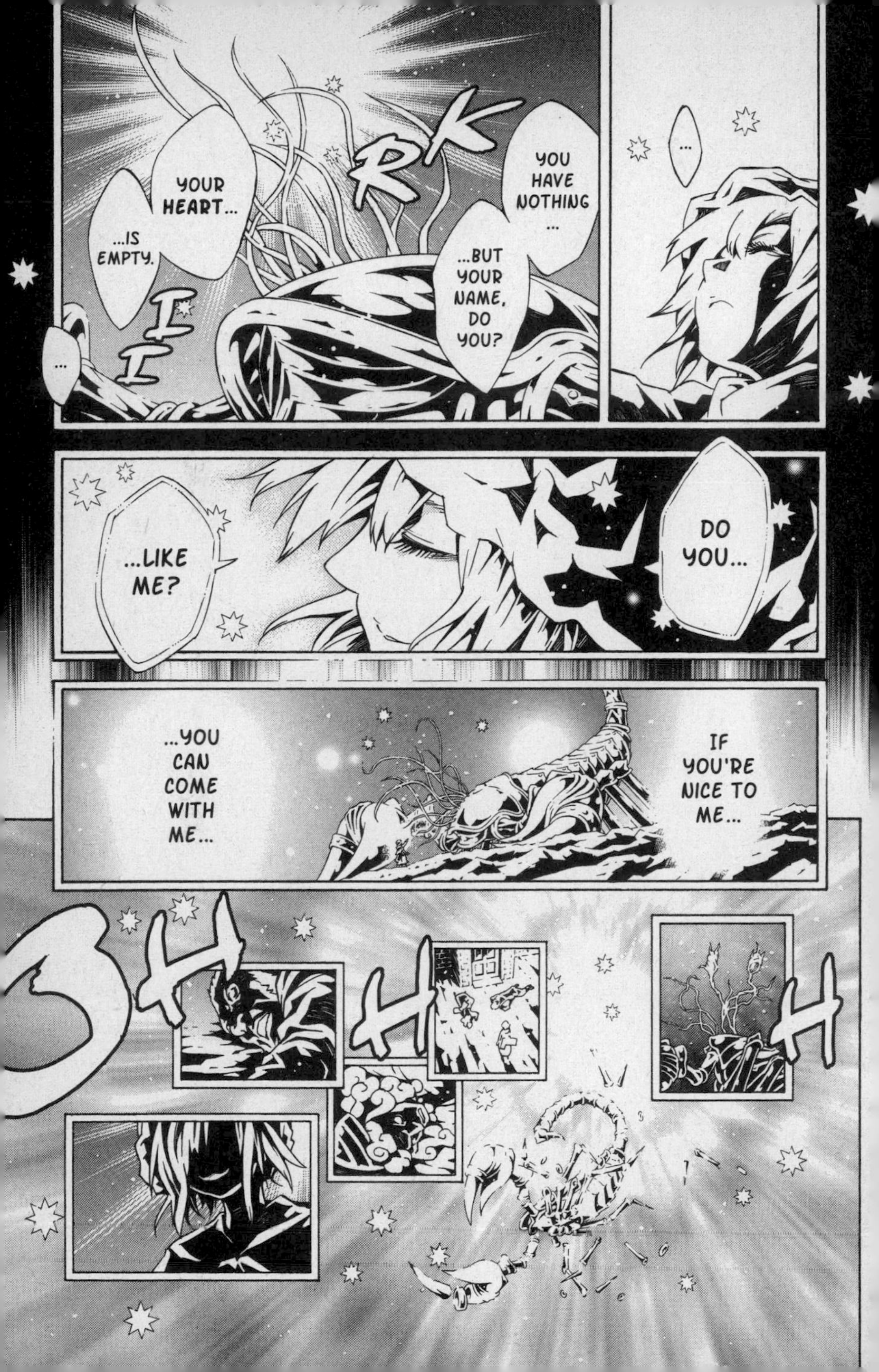
...
YOU HAVE NOTHING ...
...BUT YOUR NAME, DO YOU?
RK
YOUR HEART...
...IS EMPTY.
II
...
DO YOU...
...LIKE ME?
IF YOU'RE NICE TO ME...
...YOU CAN COME WITH ME...

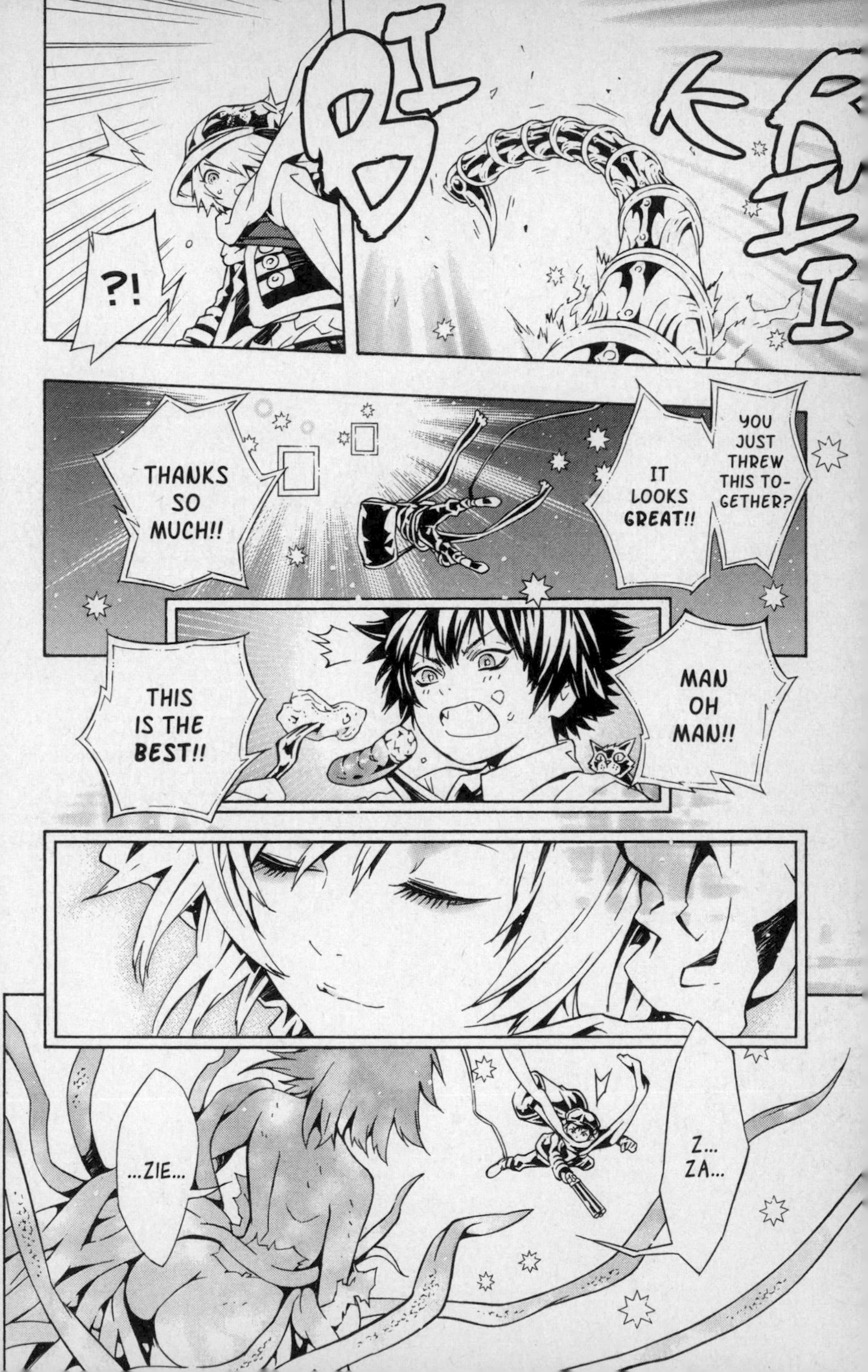
KRII
BI
?!
YOU JUST THREW THIS TO-GETHER?
IT LOOKS GREAT!!
THANKS SO MUCH!!
MAN OH MAN!!
THIS IS THE BEST!!
Z... ZA...
...ZIE...

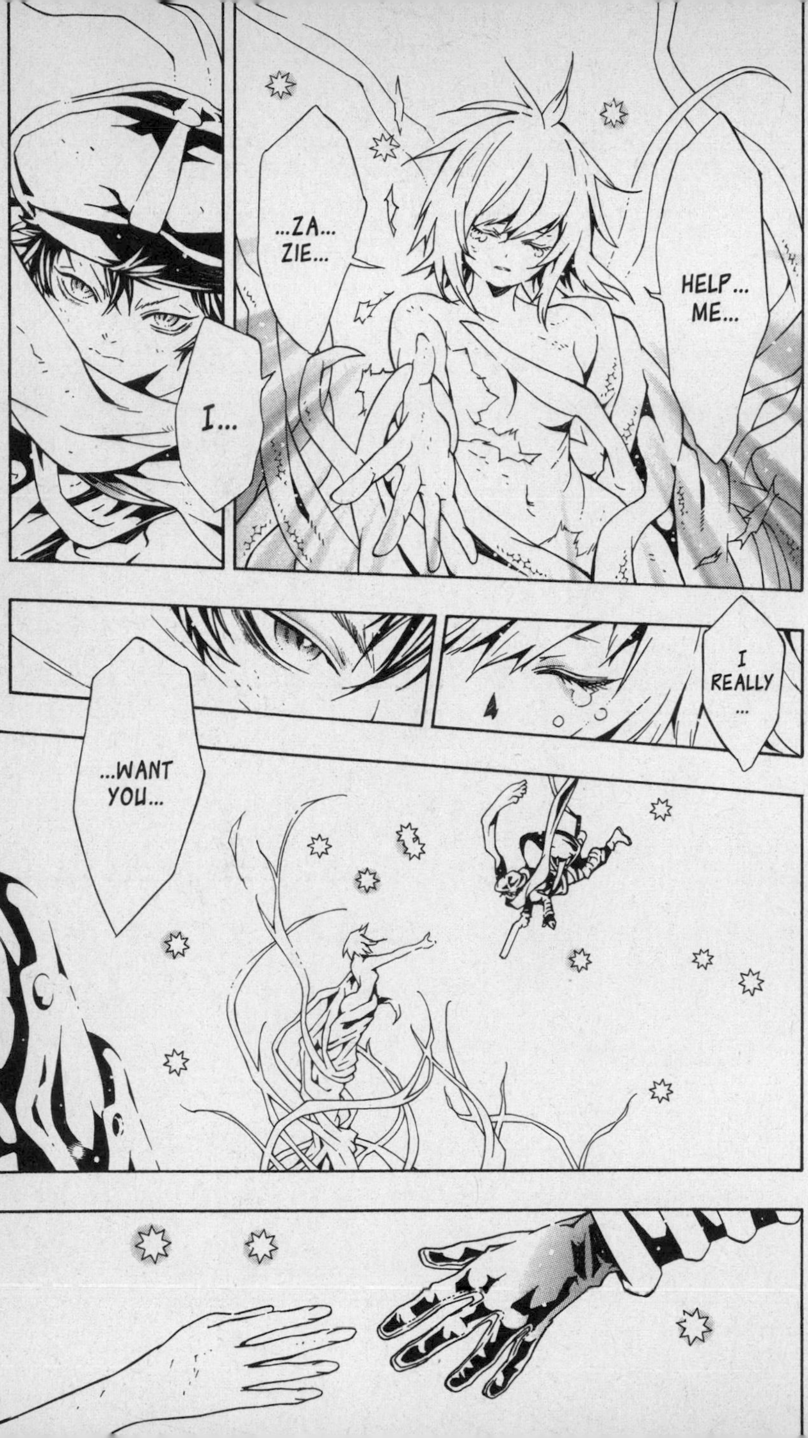
HELP... ME...
...ZA... ZIE...
I...
I REALLY ...
...WANT YOU...

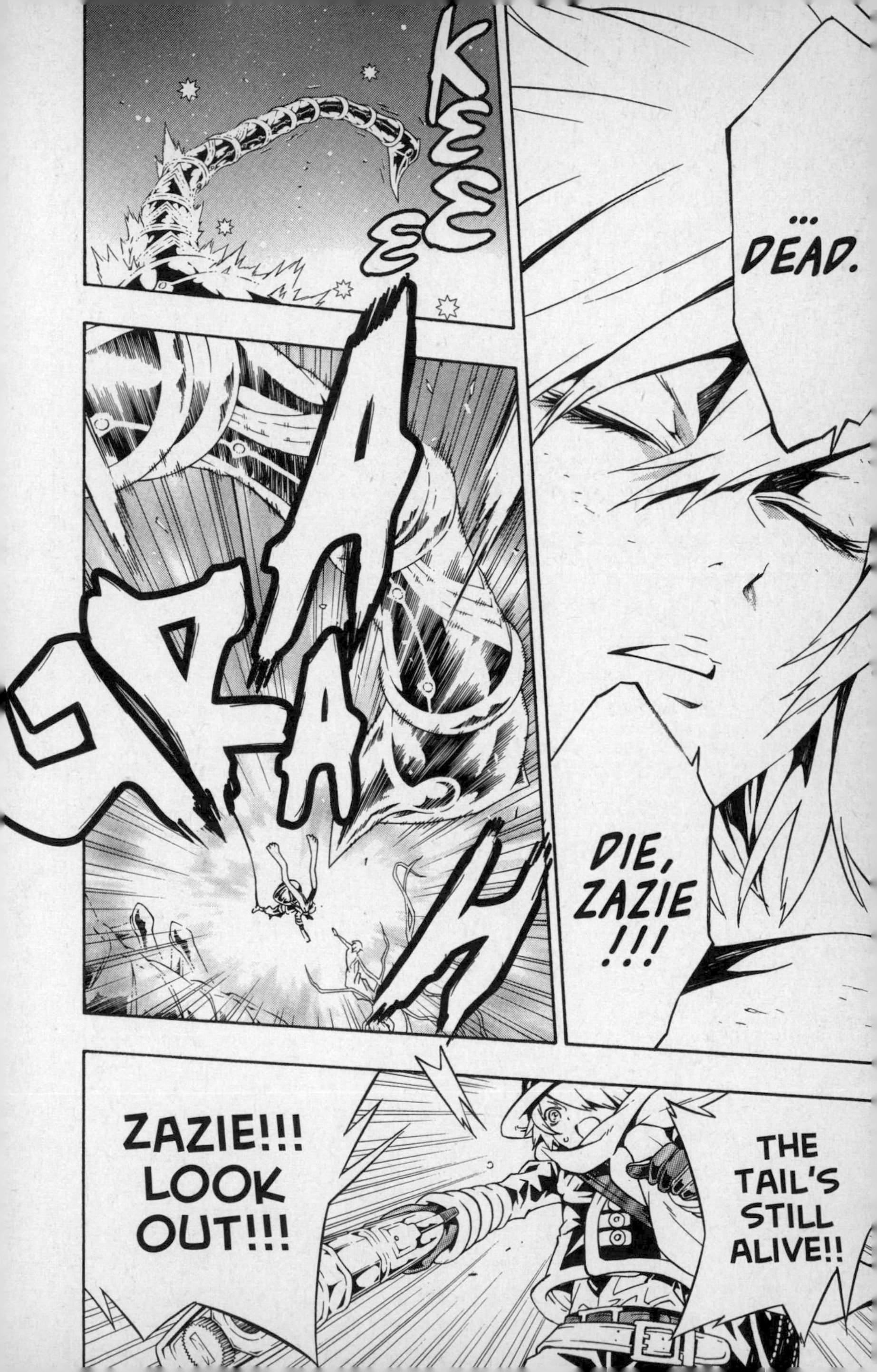
...DEAD.
DIE, ZAZIE!!!
KEEEE
ZAAH
THE TAIL'S STILL ALIVE!!
ZAZIE!!! LOOK OUT!!!

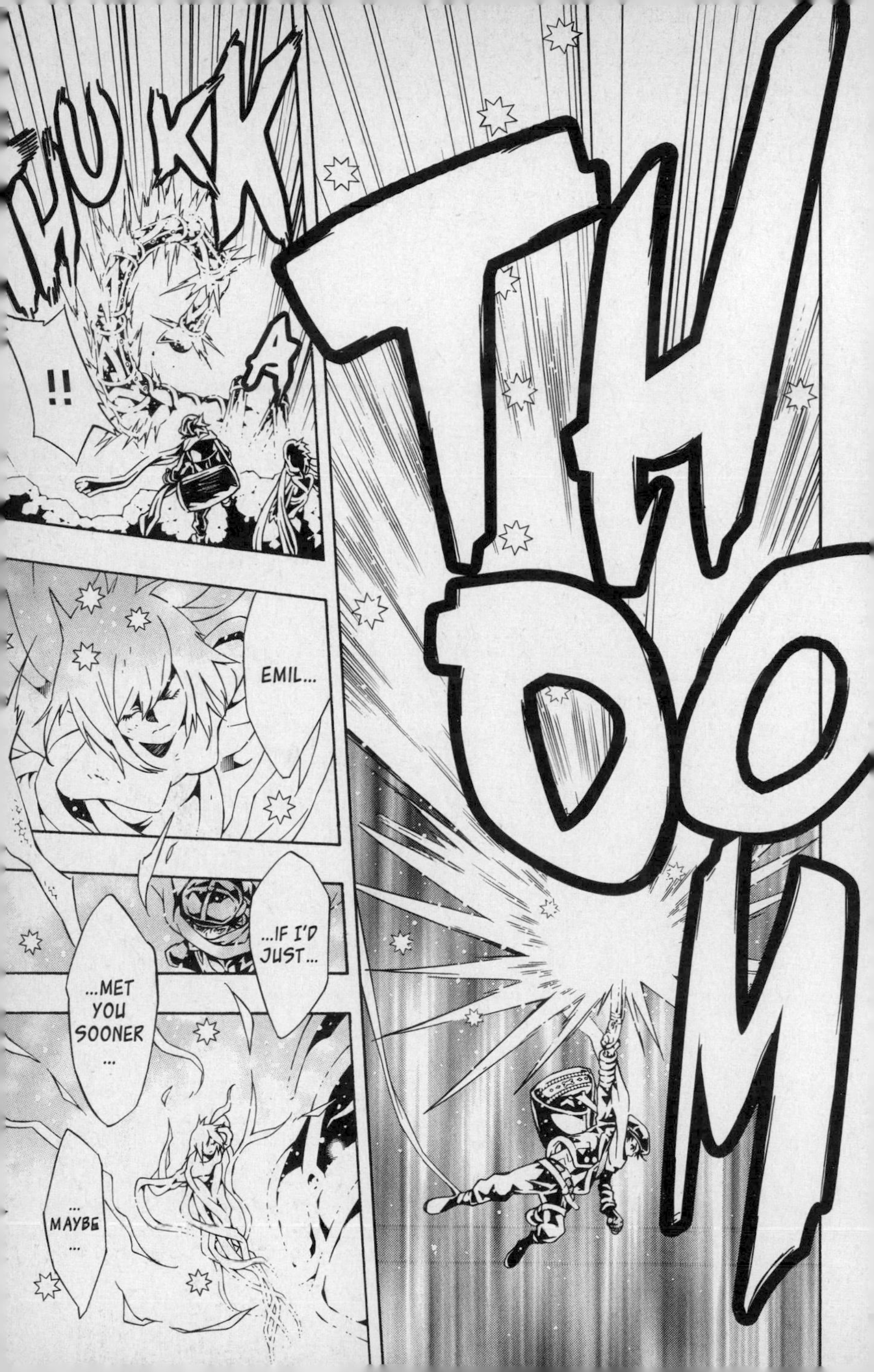
THOOM
HUKK
!!
EMIL...
...IF I'D JUST...
...MET YOU SOONER ...
... MAYBE ...

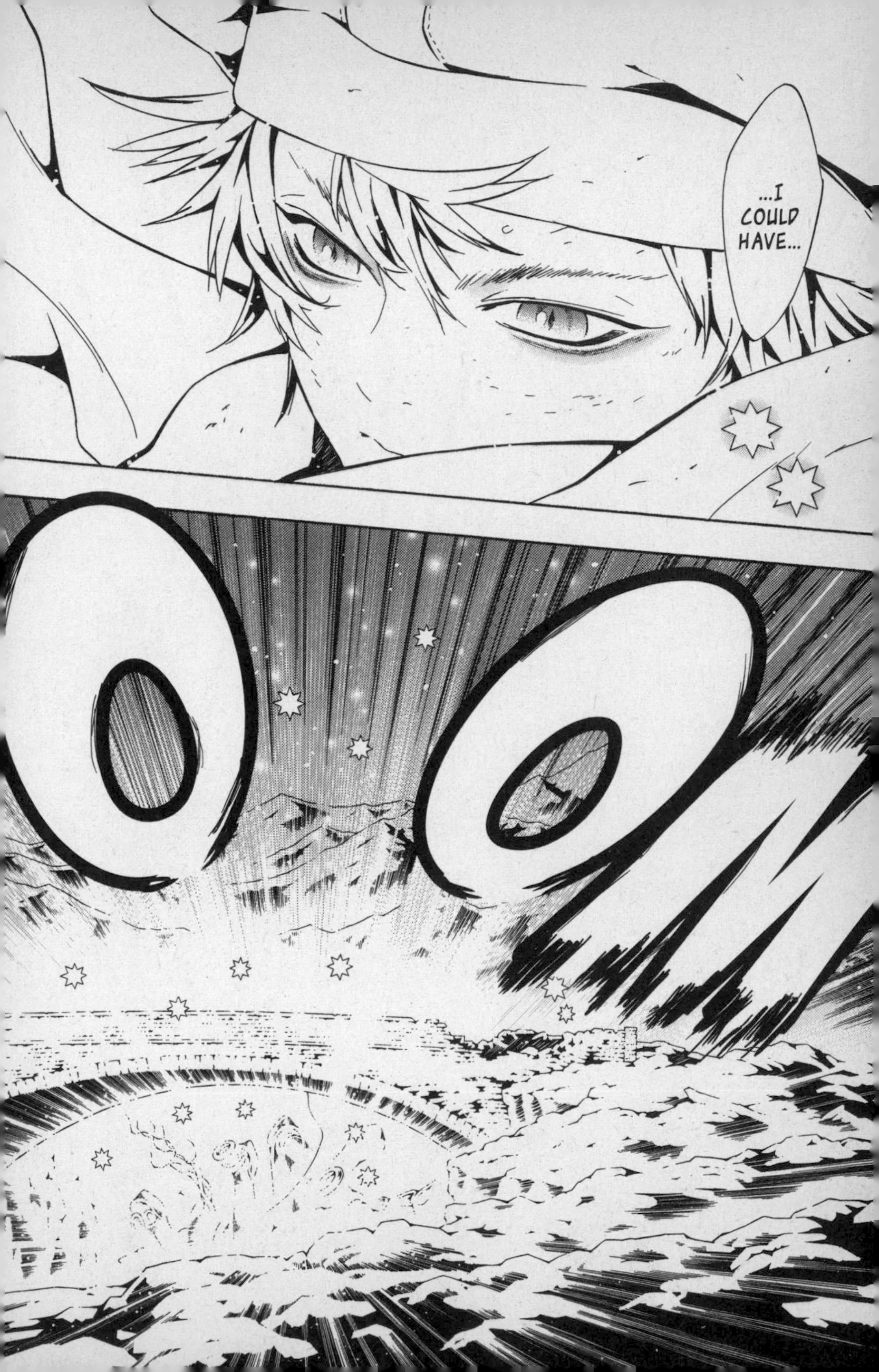
...I COULD HAVE...

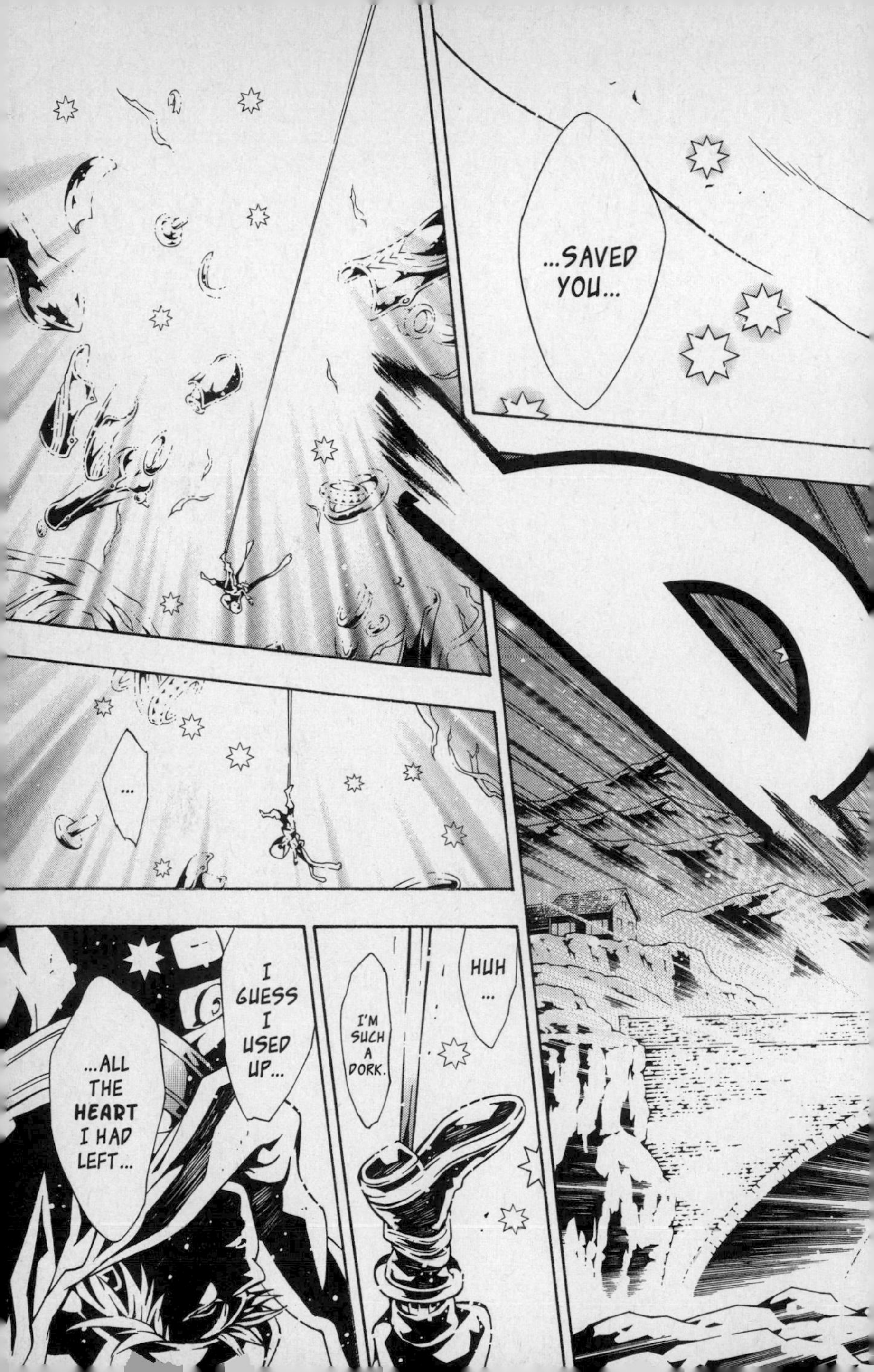
...SAVED YOU...
...
HUH...
I'M SUCH A DORK.
I GUESS I USED UP...
...ALL THE HEART I HAD LEFT...

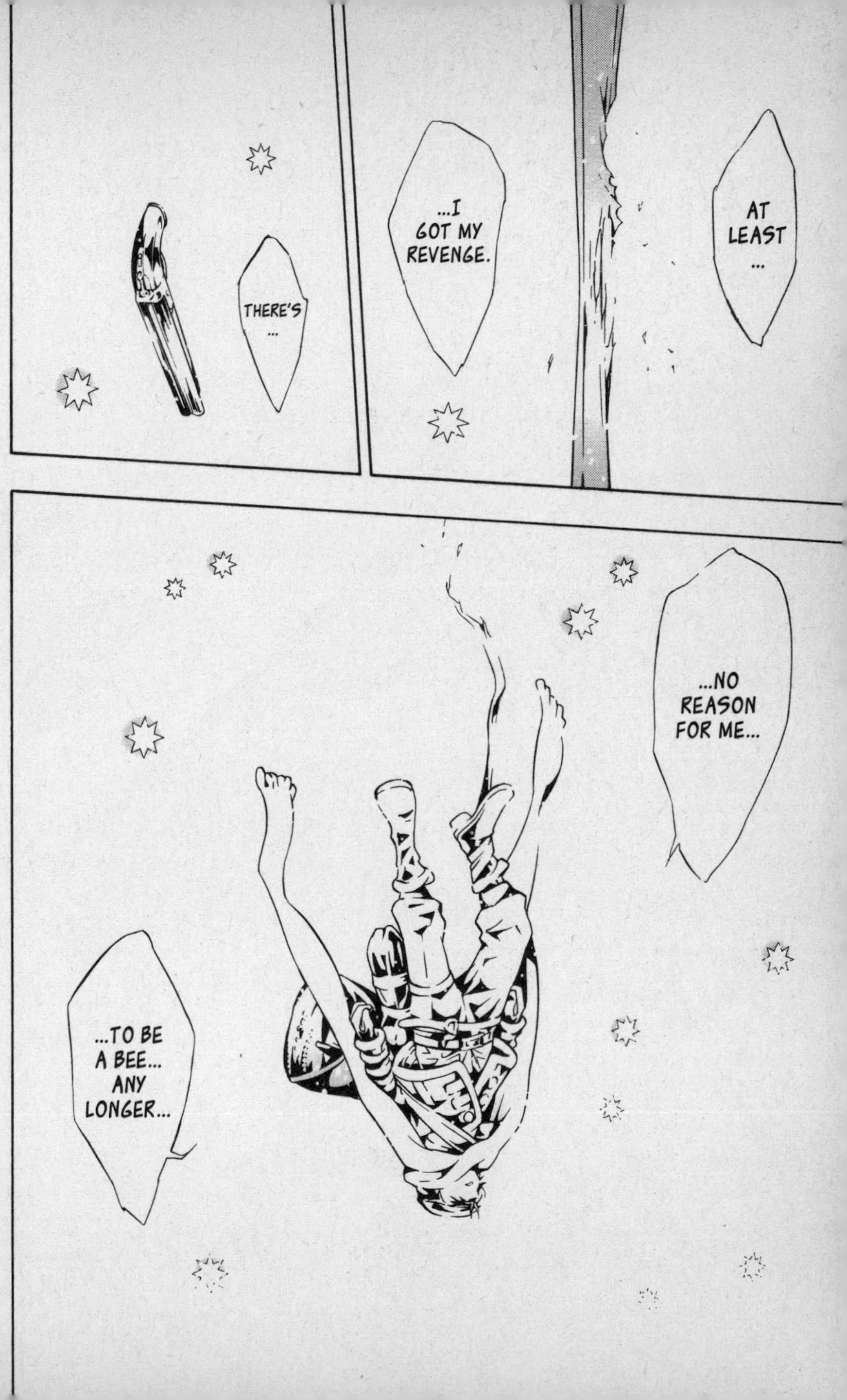
AT LEAST ...
...I GOT MY REVENGE.
THERE'S ...
...NO REASON FOR ME...
...TO BE A BEE... ANY LONGER...

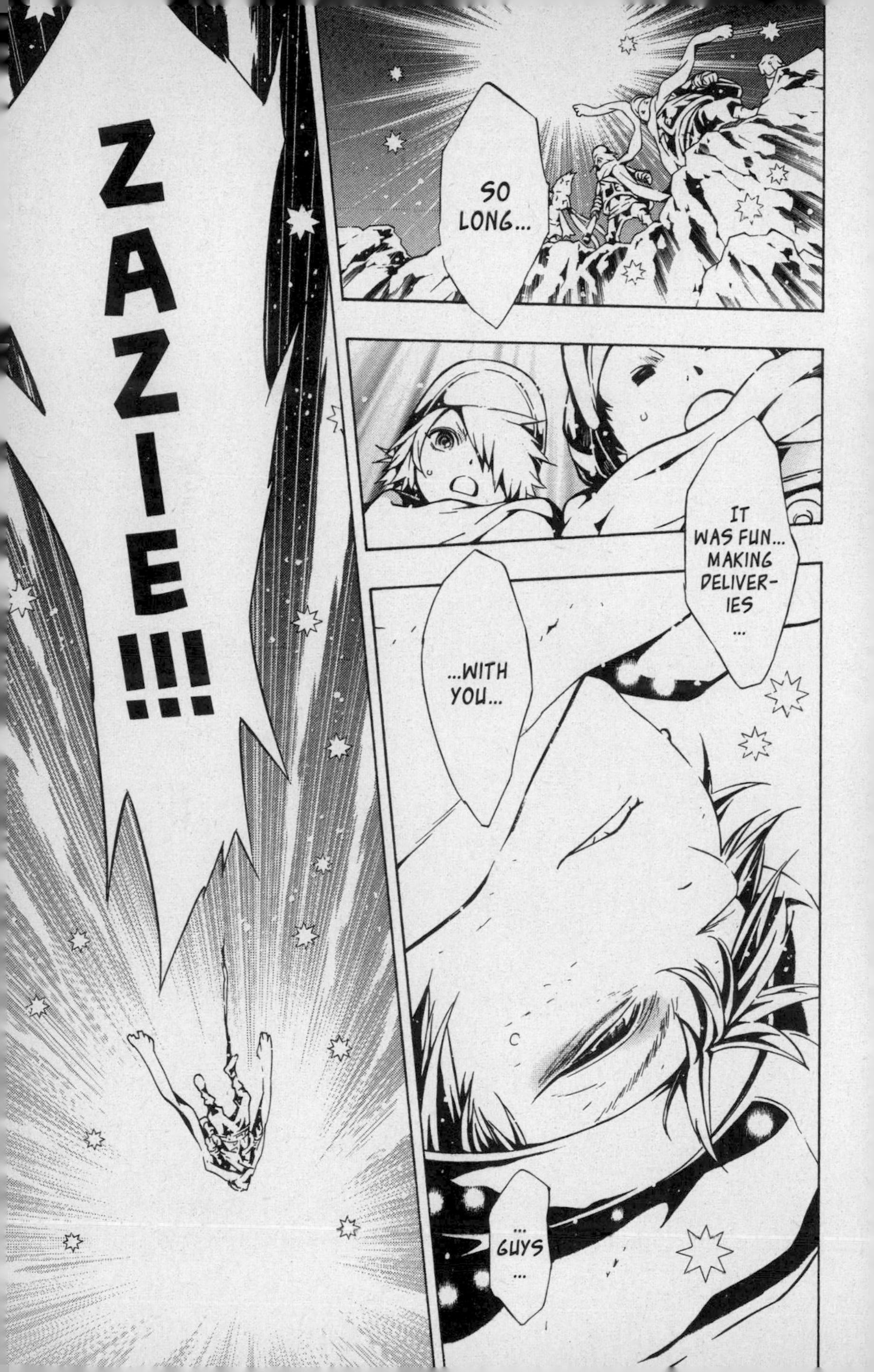
SO LONG...
IT WAS FUN... MAKING DELIVER-IES ...
...WITH YOU...
... GUYS ...
ZAZIE!!!

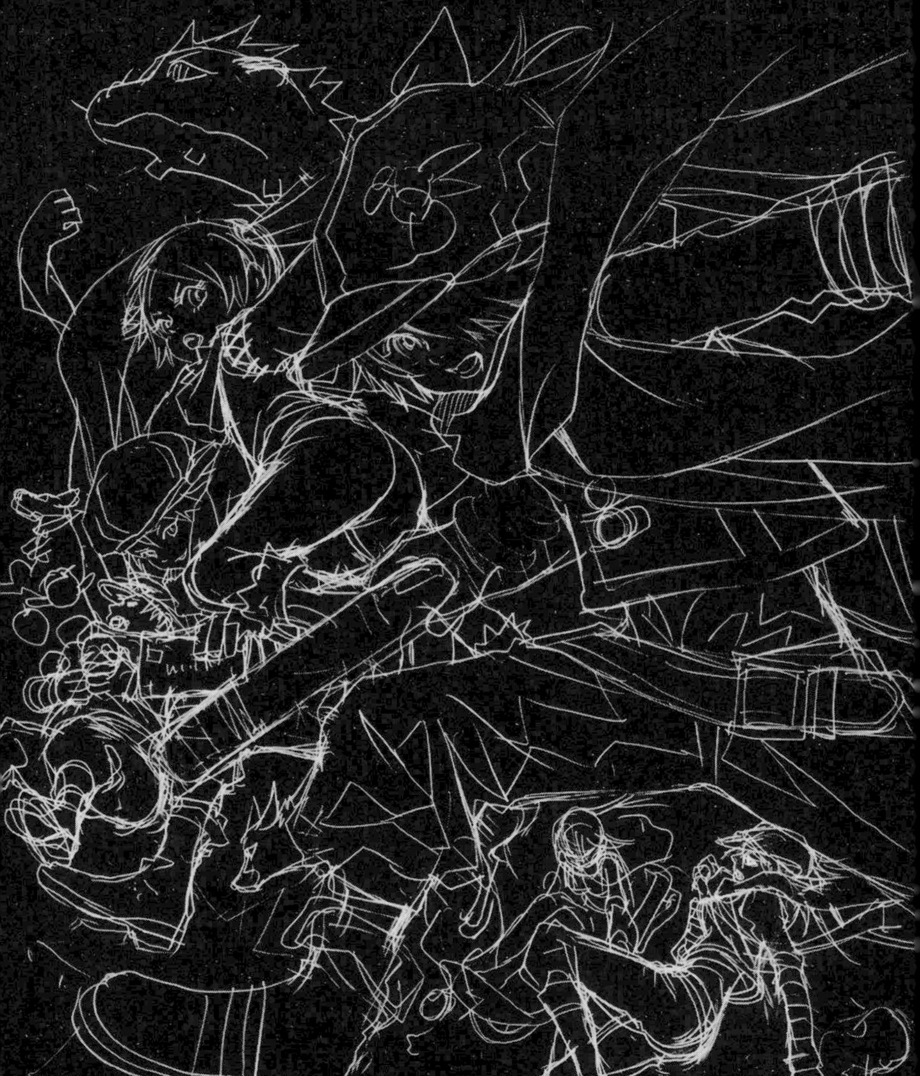

Rough sketch for the cover of the November 2010 issue of *Jump SQ.*

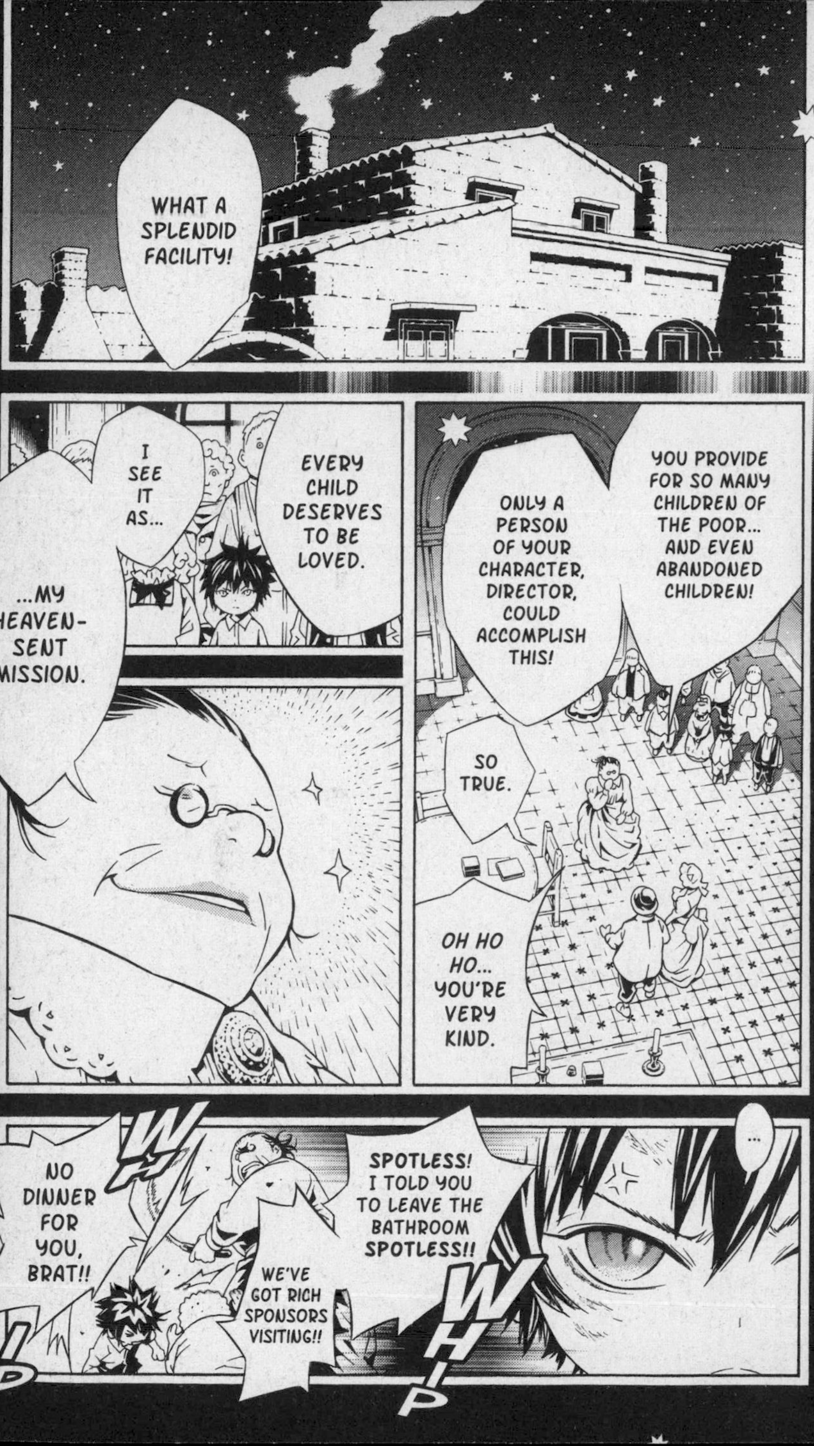
WHAT A SPLENDID FACILITY!
YOU PROVIDE FOR SO MANY CHILDREN OF THE POOR... AND EVEN ABANDONED CHILDREN!
ONLY A PERSON OF YOUR CHARACTER, DIRECTOR, COULD ACCOMPLISH THIS!
SO TRUE.
OH HO HO... YOU'RE VERY KIND.
EVERY CHILD DESERVES TO BE LOVED.
I SEE IT AS...
...MY HEAVEN-SENT MISSION.
...
SPOTLESS! I TOLD YOU TO LEAVE THE BATHROOM SPOTLESS!!
WHIP
WE'VE GOT RICH SPONSORS VISITING!!
NO DINNER FOR YOU, BRAT!!
WHIP

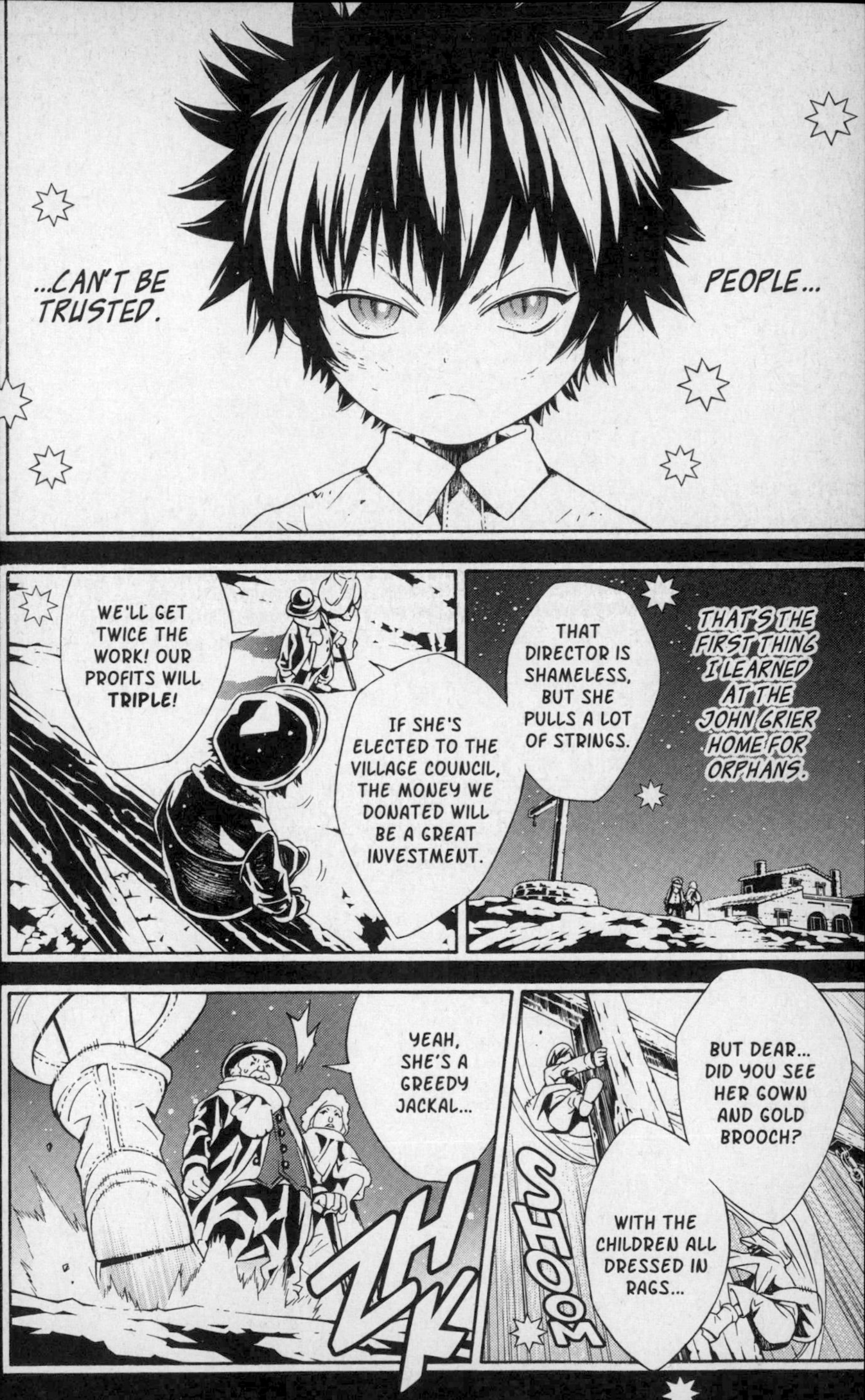
PEOPLE...
...CAN'T BE TRUSTED.
THAT'S THE FIRST THING I LEARNED AT THE JOHN GRIER HOME FOR ORPHANS.
THAT DIRECTOR IS SHAMELESS, BUT SHE PULLS A LOT OF STRINGS.
IF SHE'S ELECTED TO THE VILLAGE COUNCIL, THE MONEY WE DONATED WILL BE A GREAT INVESTMENT.
WE'LL GET TWICE THE WORK! OUR PROFITS WILL TRIPLE!
BUT DEAR... DID YOU SEE HER GOWN AND GOLD BROOCH?
WITH THE CHILDREN ALL DRESSED IN RAGS...
SHOOM
YEAH, SHE'S A GREEDY JACKAL...
ZHK

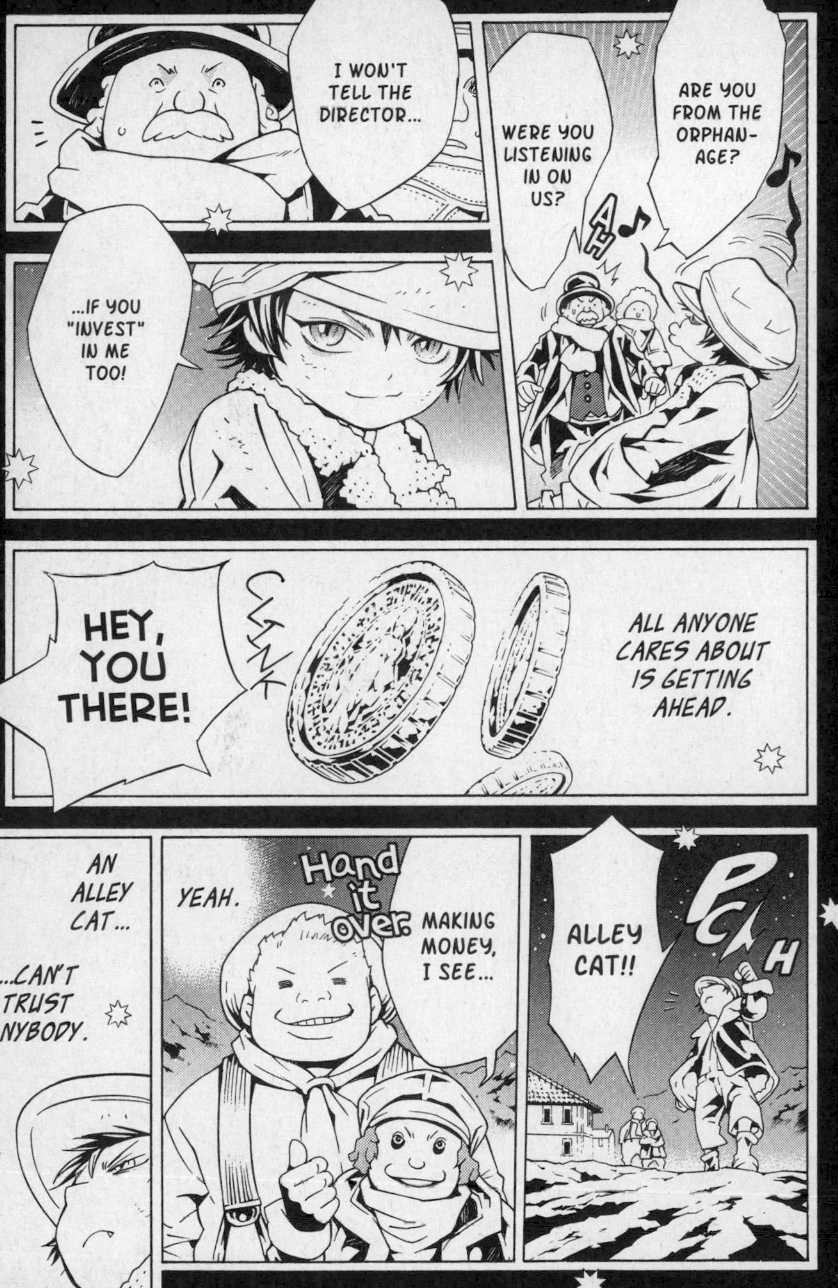
ARE YOU FROM THE ORPHAN-AGE?
WERE YOU LISTENING IN ON US?
AH
I WON'T TELL THE DIRECTOR...
...IF YOU "INVEST" IN ME TOO!
ALL ANYONE CARES ABOUT IS GETTING AHEAD.
CLINK
HEY, YOU THERE!
PCH
ALLEY CAT!!
MAKING MONEY, I SEE...
Hand it over.
YEAH.
AN ALLEY CAT...
...CAN'T TRUST ANYBODY.

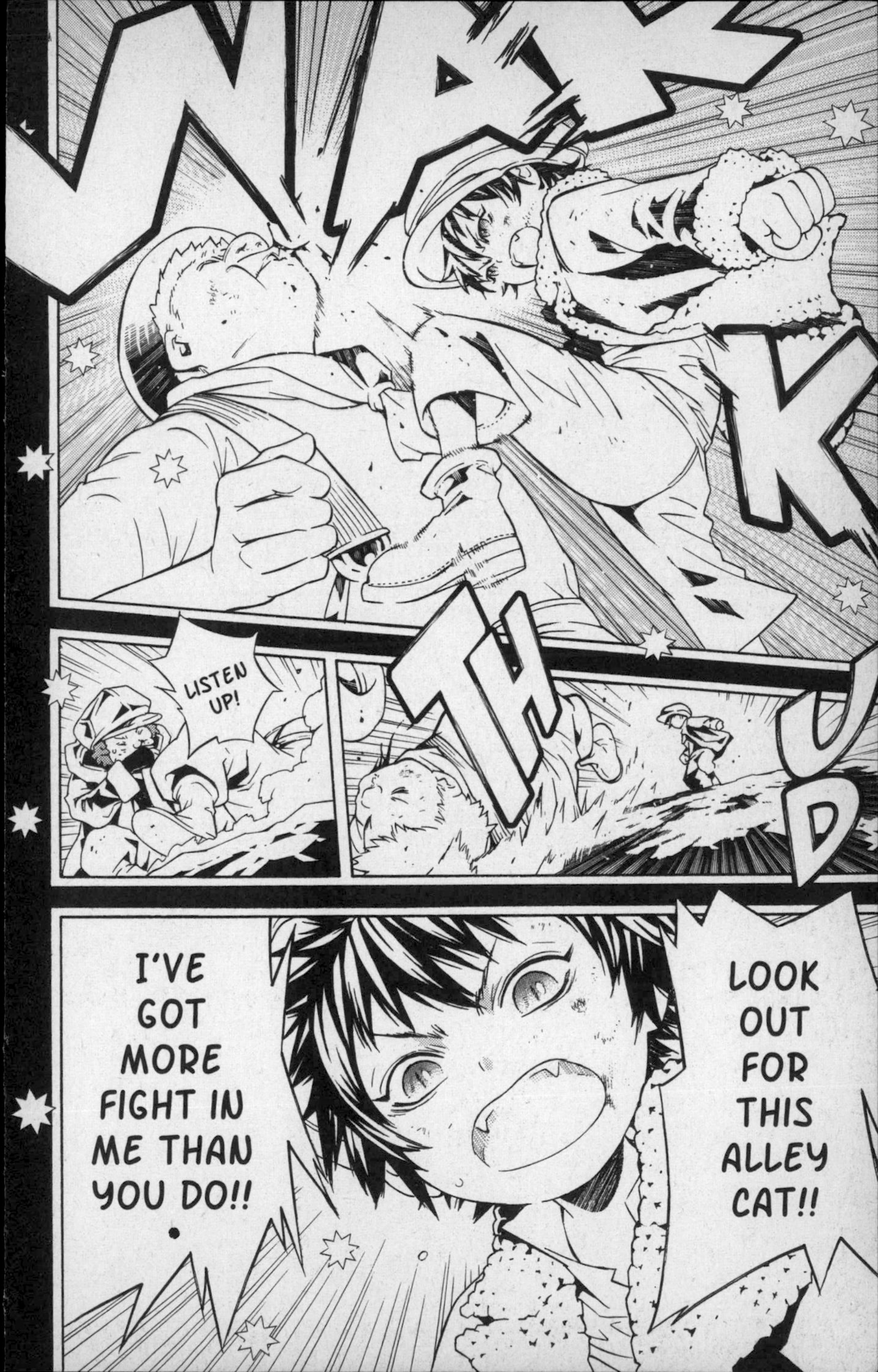
THUD
LISTEN UP!
LOOK OUT FOR THIS ALLEY CAT!!
I'VE GOT MORE FIGHT IN ME THAN YOU DO!!

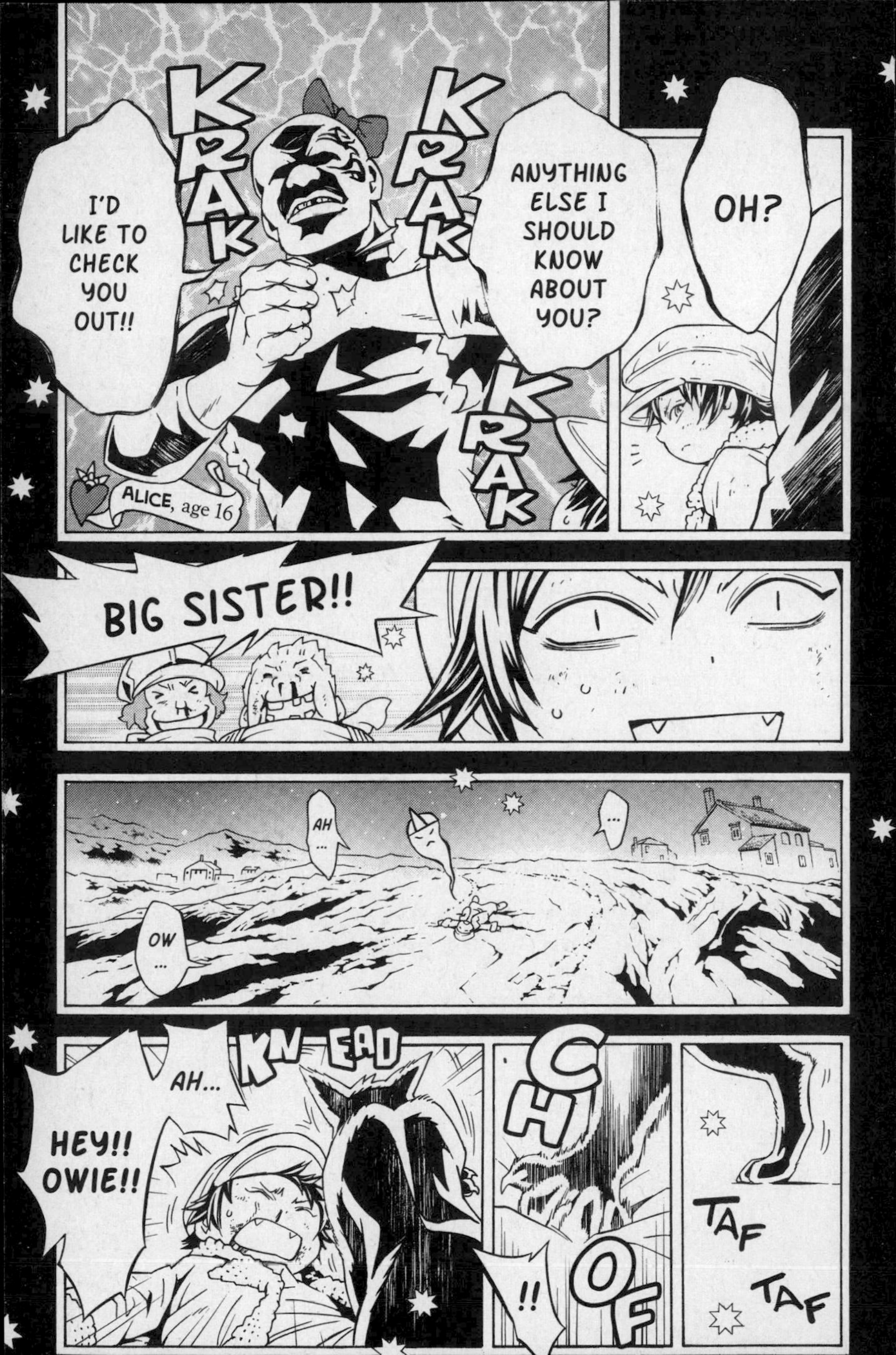
OH?
ANYTHING ELSE I SHOULD KNOW ABOUT YOU?
KRAK
KRAK
I'D LIKE TO CHECK YOU OUT!!
KRAK
ALICE, age 16
BIG SISTER!!
...
AH ...
OW ...
TAF TAF
CH
OF
!!
KN EAD
AH...
HEY!! OWIE!!

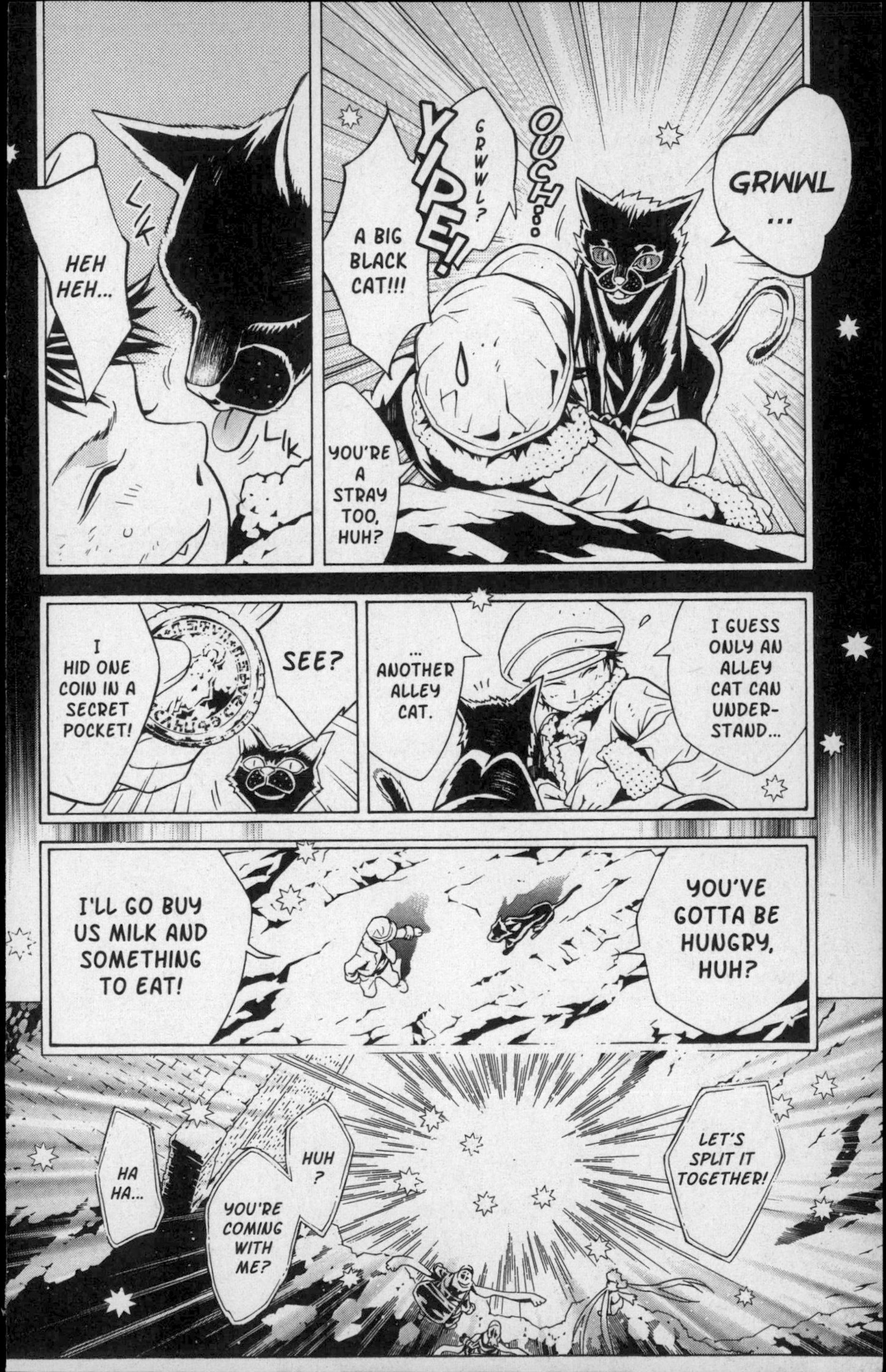
GRWWL...
OUCH...
GRWWL?
YIPE!
A BIG BLACK CAT!!!
YOU'RE A STRAY TOO, HUH?
LIK
LIK
HEH HEH...
I GUESS ONLY AN ALLEY CAT CAN UNDER-STAND...
... ANOTHER ALLEY CAT.
SEE?
I HID ONE COIN IN A SECRET POCKET!
YOU'VE GOTTA BE HUNGRY, HUH?
I'LL GO BUY US MILK AND SOMETHING TO EAT!
LET'S SPLIT IT TOGETHER!
YOU'RE COMING WITH ME?
HUH?
HA HA...

Chapter 70: Name

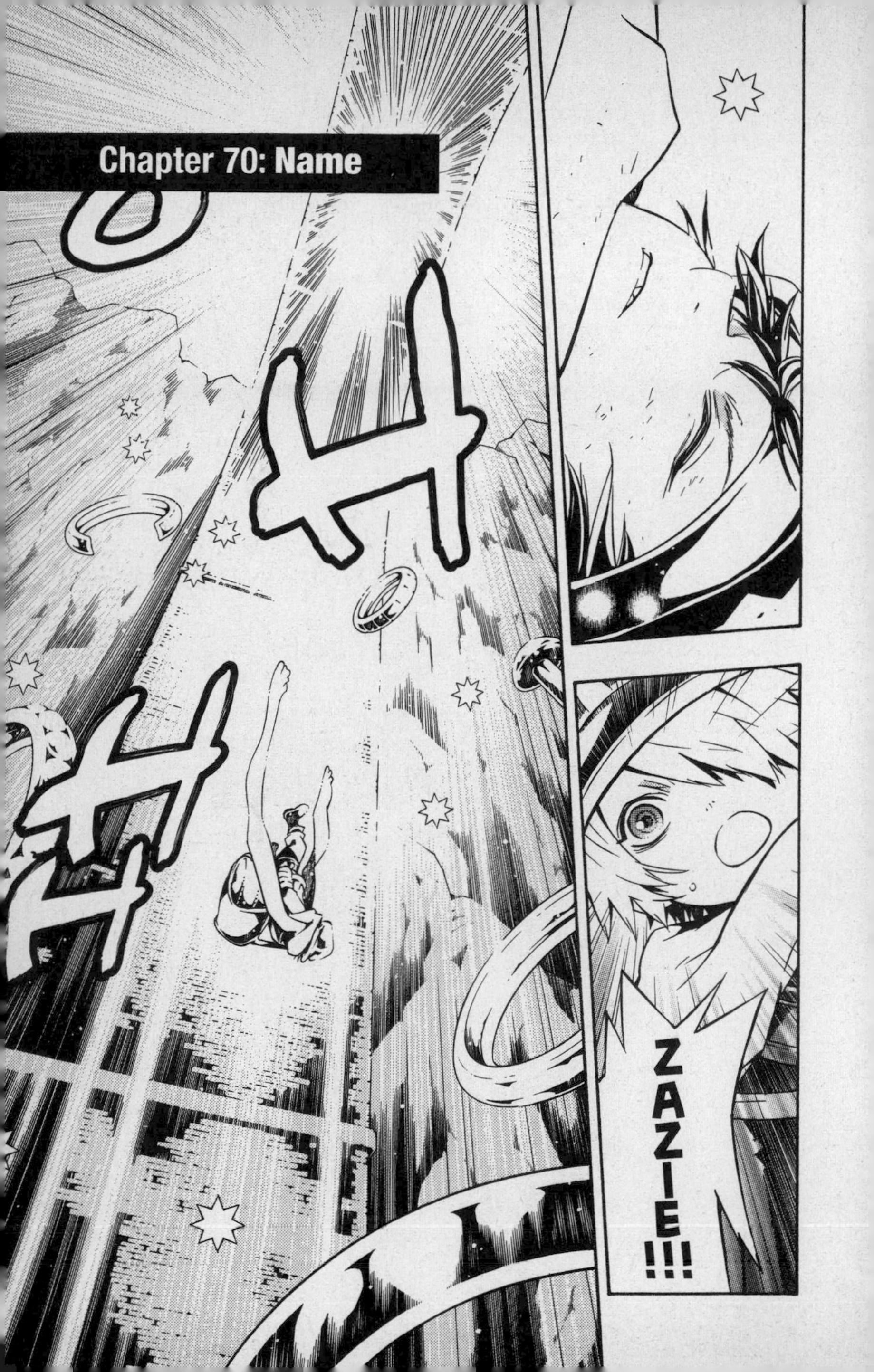
ZAZIE!!!

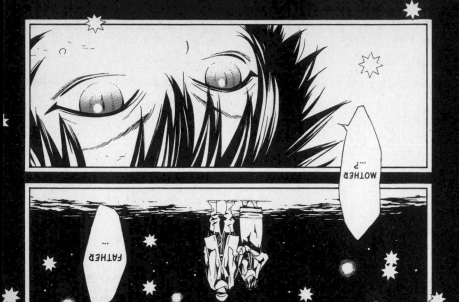

MOTHER...?

...FATHER

...MY PARENTS?

THOSE ARE...

THEY SAY THEY'RE HERE TO FETCH YOU.

NEVER THOUGHT THERE WERE FOOLS WHO'D WAIT TEN YEARS TO COLLECT A CHILD THEY'D ABANDONED!!

I'LL BE SURE TO CHARGE THEM FOR YOUR UPKEEP!

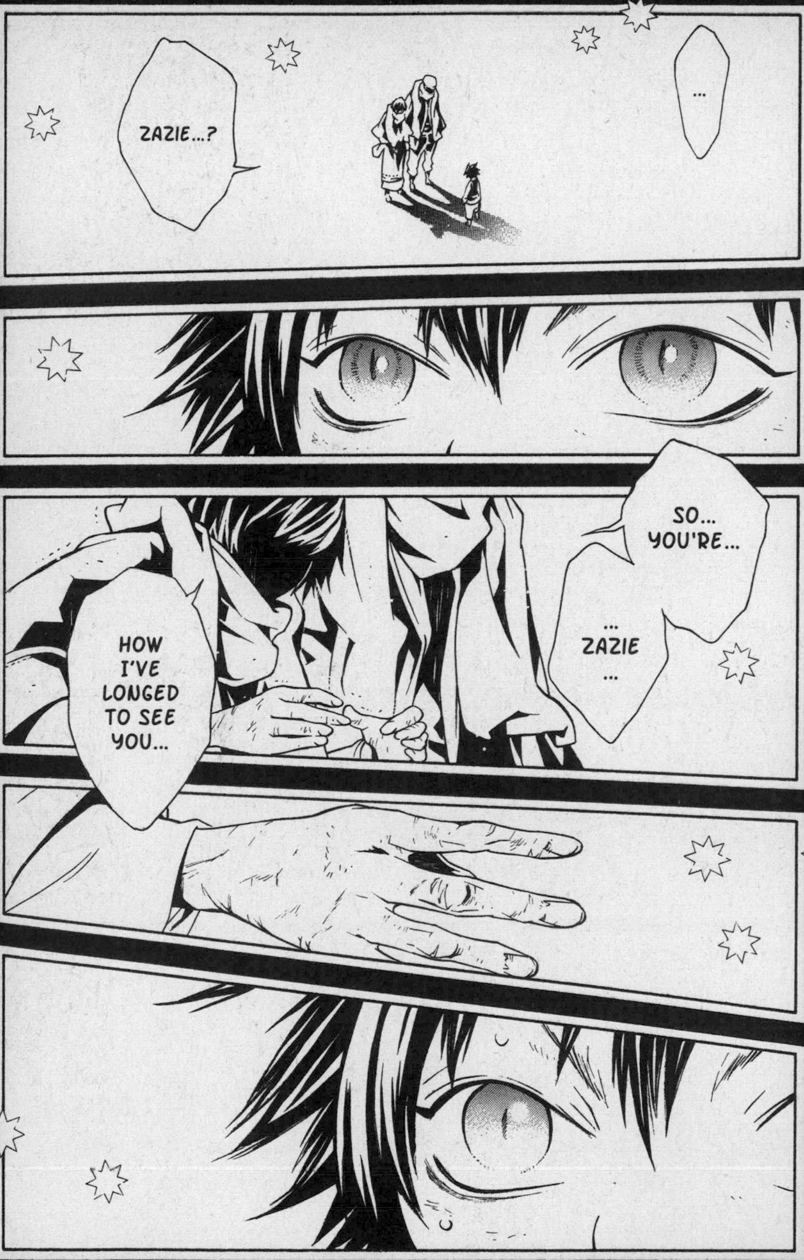
...
ZAZIE...?
SO... YOU'RE...
... ZAZIE ...
HOW I'VE LONGED TO SEE YOU...

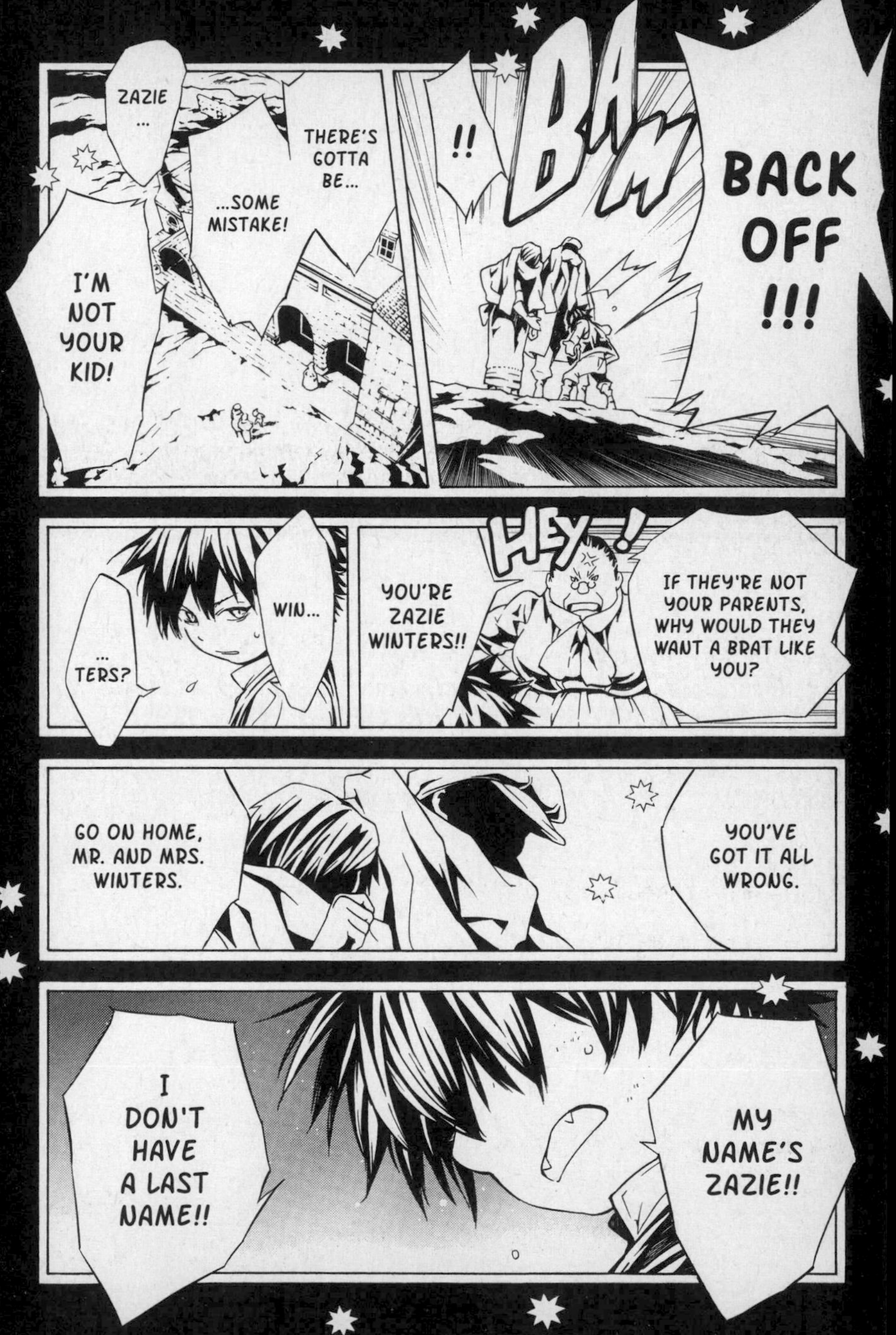
BACK OFF !!!
BAM
!!
THERE'S GOTTA BE...
...SOME MISTAKE!
ZAZIE ...
I'M NOT YOUR KID!
IF THEY'RE NOT YOUR PARENTS, WHY WOULD THEY WANT A BRAT LIKE YOU?
HEY!
YOU'RE ZAZIE WINTERS!!
WIN...
... TERS?
YOU'VE GOT IT ALL WRONG.
GO ON HOME, MR. AND MRS. WINTERS.
MY NAME'S ZAZIE!!
I DON'T HAVE A LAST NAME!!

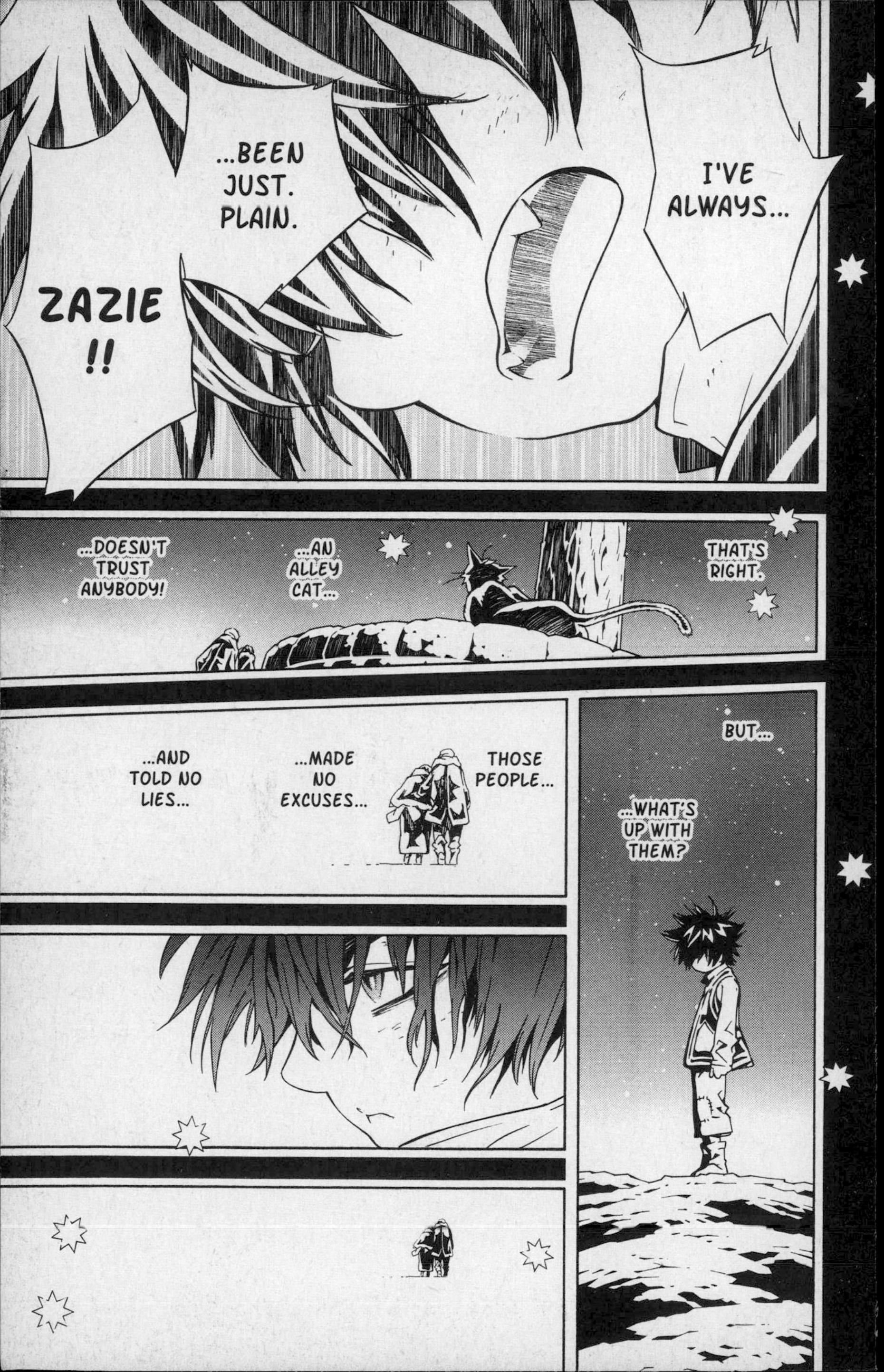
I'VE ALWAYS...
...BEEN JUST. PLAIN.
ZAZIE !!
THAT'S RIGHT.
...AN ALLEY CAT...
...DOESN'T TRUST ANYBODY!
BUT...
...WHAT'S UP WITH THEM?
THOSE PEOPLE...
...MADE NO EXCUSES...
...AND TOLD NO LIES...

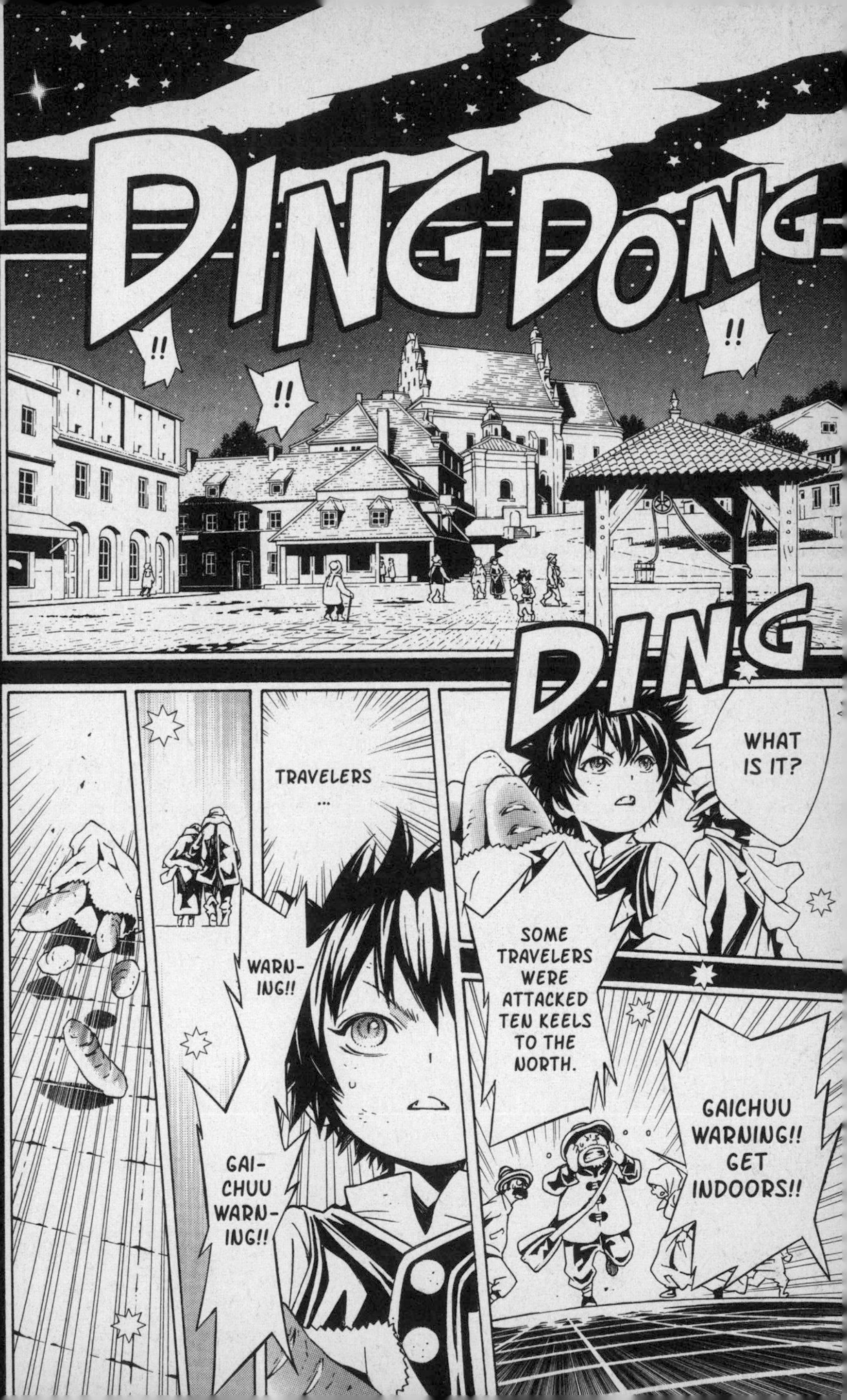
DING DONG
!!
!!
!!
DING
WHAT IS IT?
SOME TRAVELERS WERE ATTACKED TEN KEELS TO THE NORTH.
GAICHUU WARNING!! GET INDOORS!!
TRAVELERS ...
WARN-ING!!
GAI-CHUU WARN-ING!!

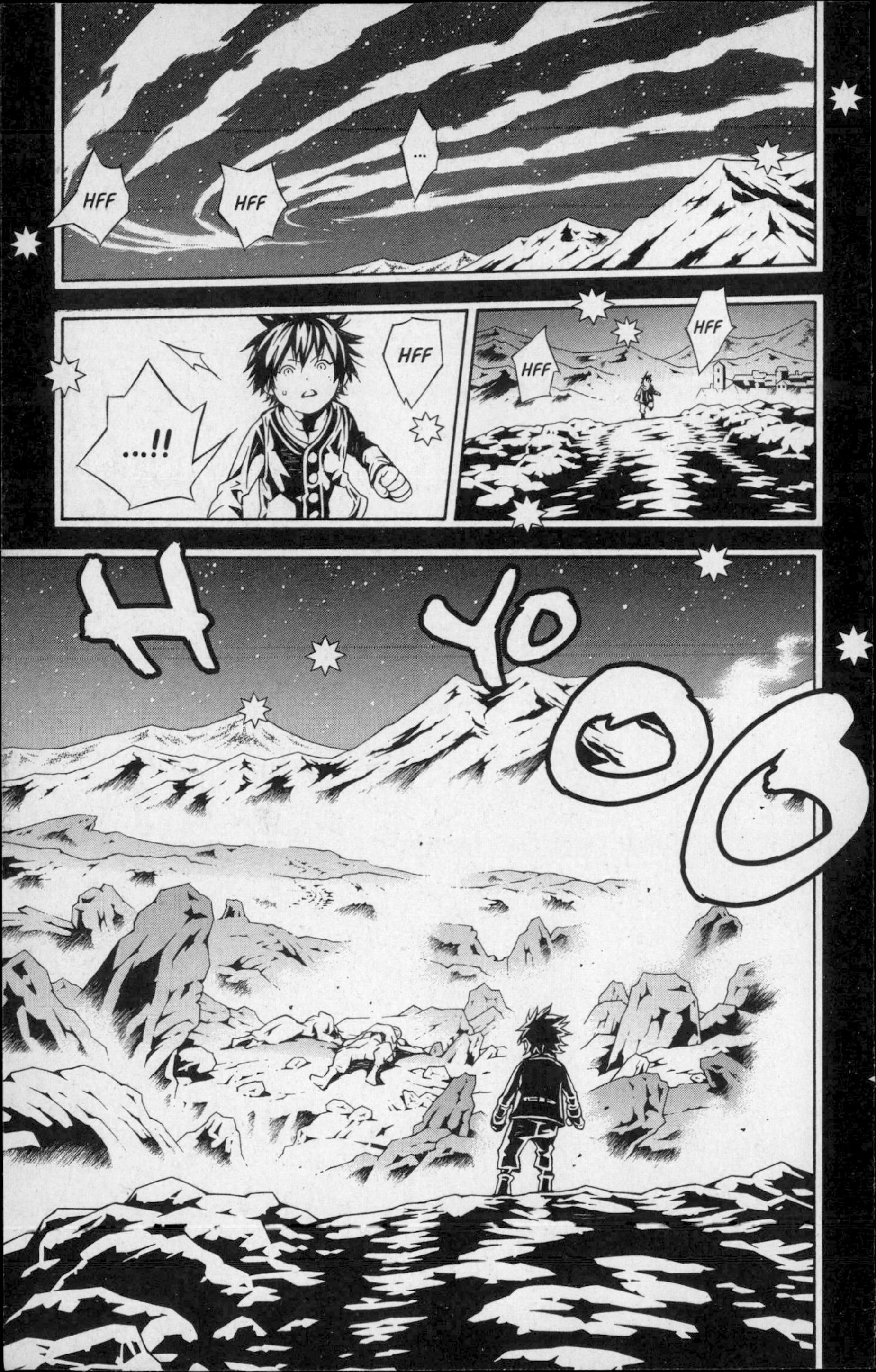
...
HFF
HFF
HFF
HFF
HFF
...!!
HYOOO

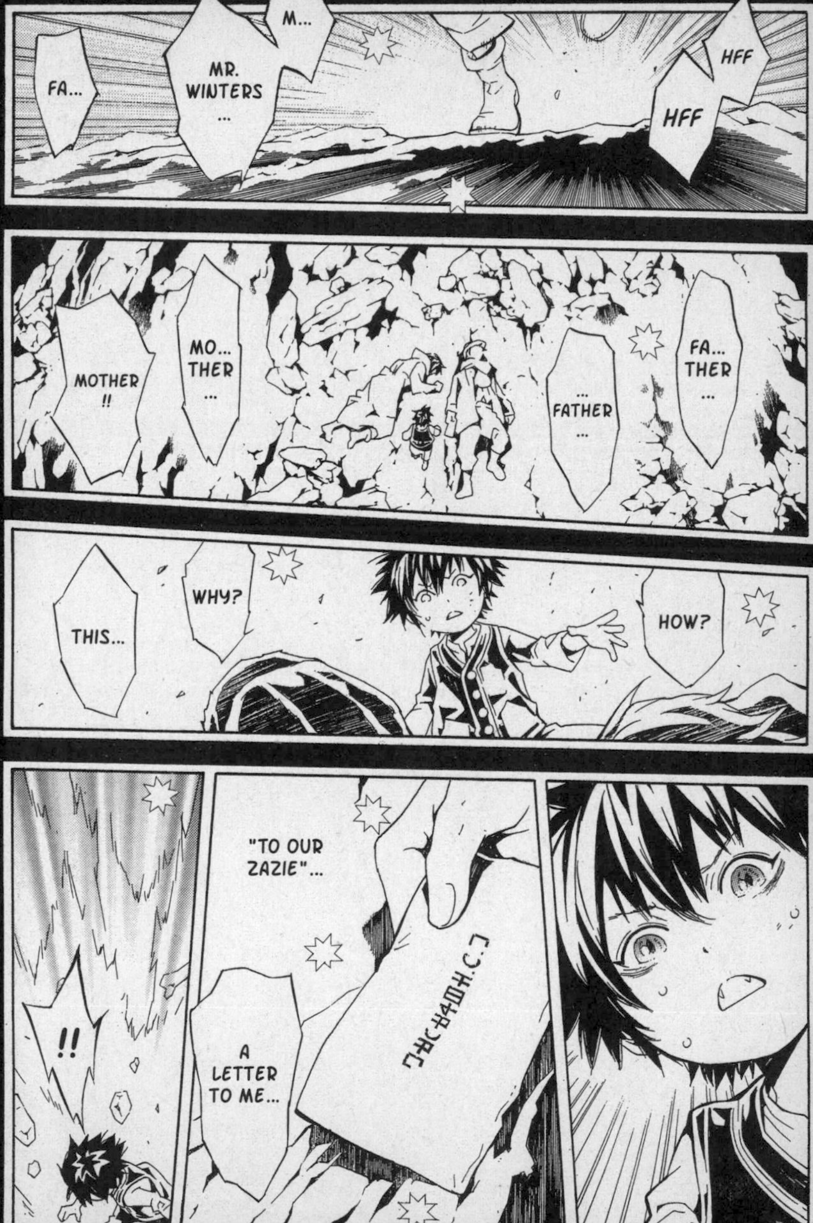
HFF
HFF
M...
MR. WINTERS ...
FA...
FA... THER ...
... FATHER ...
MO... THER ...
MOTHER !!
HOW?
WHY?
THIS...
"TO OUR ZAZIE"...
A LETTER TO ME...
!!

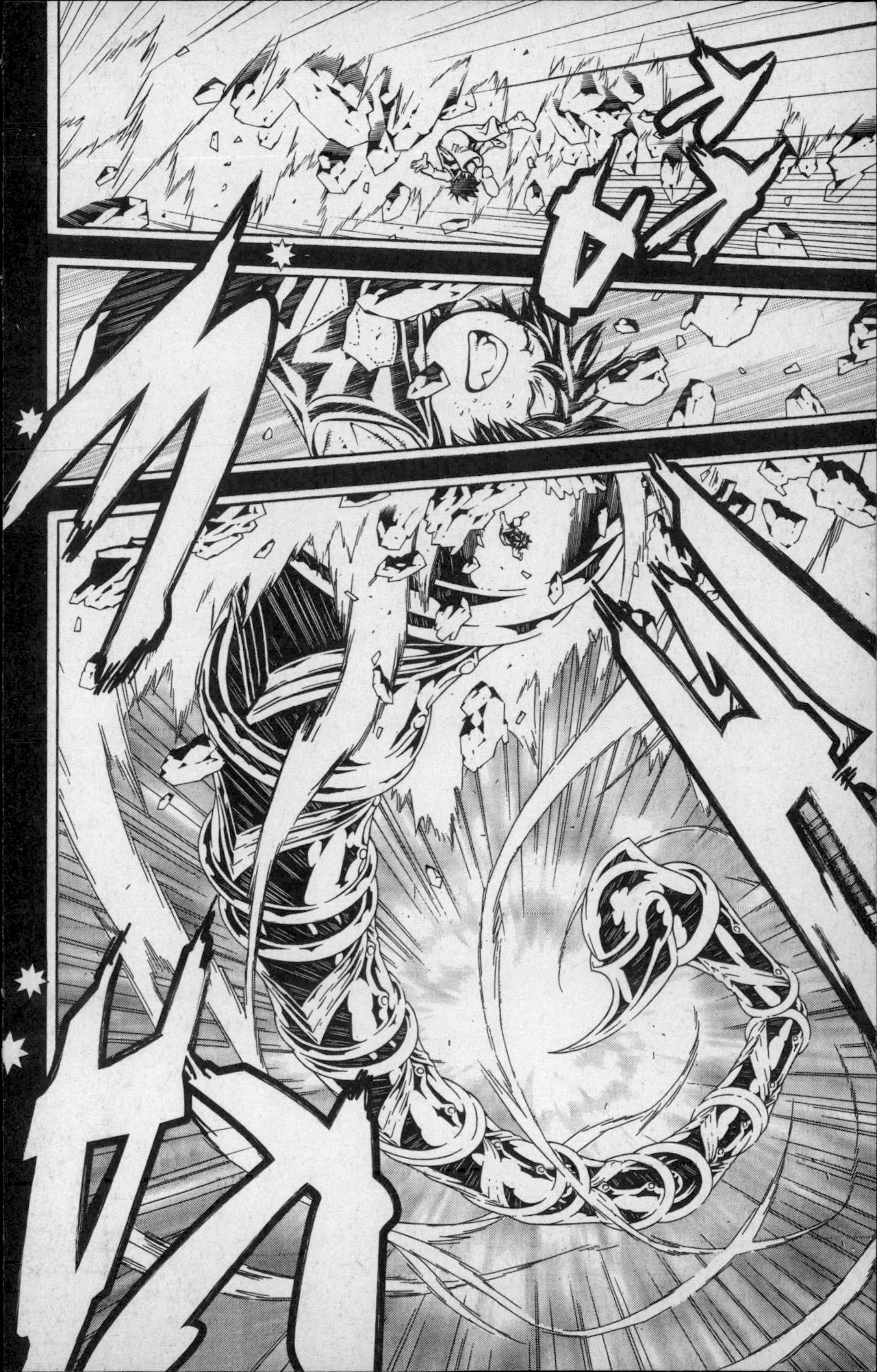

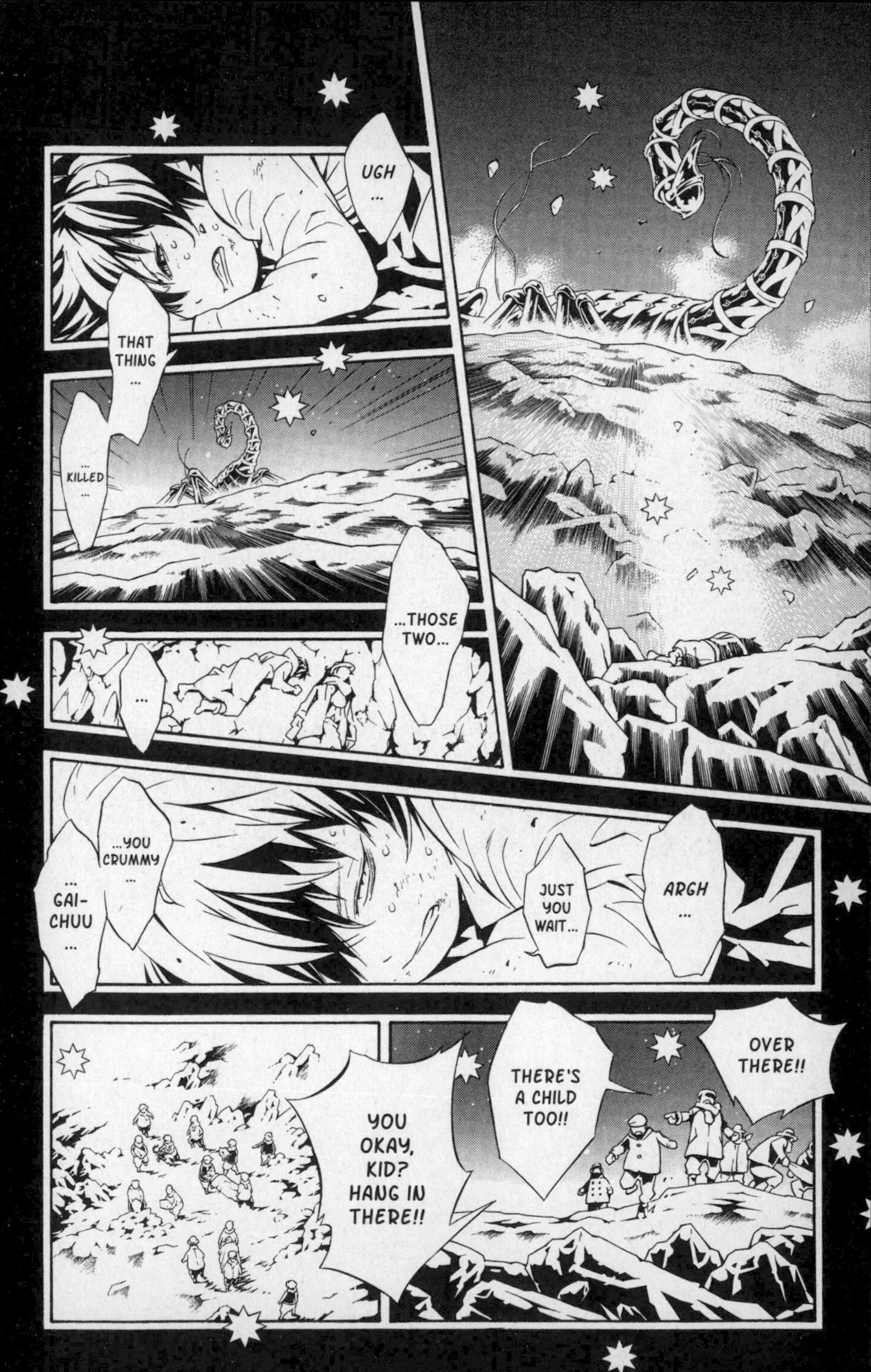
UGH ...
THAT THING ...
... KILLED ...
...THOSE TWO...
...
ARGH ...
JUST YOU WAIT...
...YOU CRUMMY ...
... GAI-CHUU ...
OVER THERE!!
THERE'S A CHILD TOO!!
YOU OKAY, KID? HANG IN THERE!!

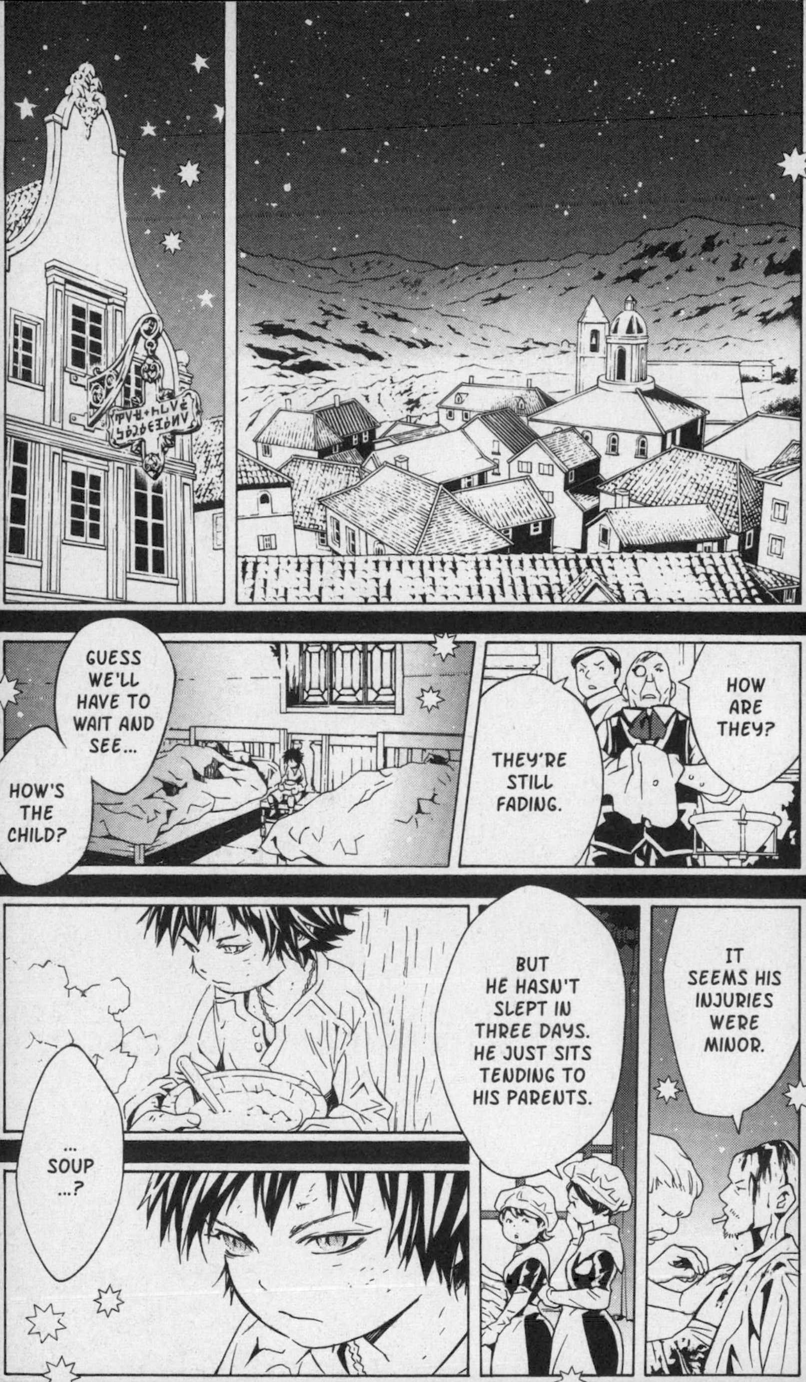
HOW ARE THEY?
THEY'RE STILL FADING.
HOW'S THE CHILD?
GUESS WE'LL HAVE TO WAIT AND SEE...
IT SEEMS HIS INJURIES WERE MINOR.
BUT HE HASN'T SLEPT IN THREE DAYS. HE JUST SITS TENDING TO HIS PARENTS.
... SOUP ...?

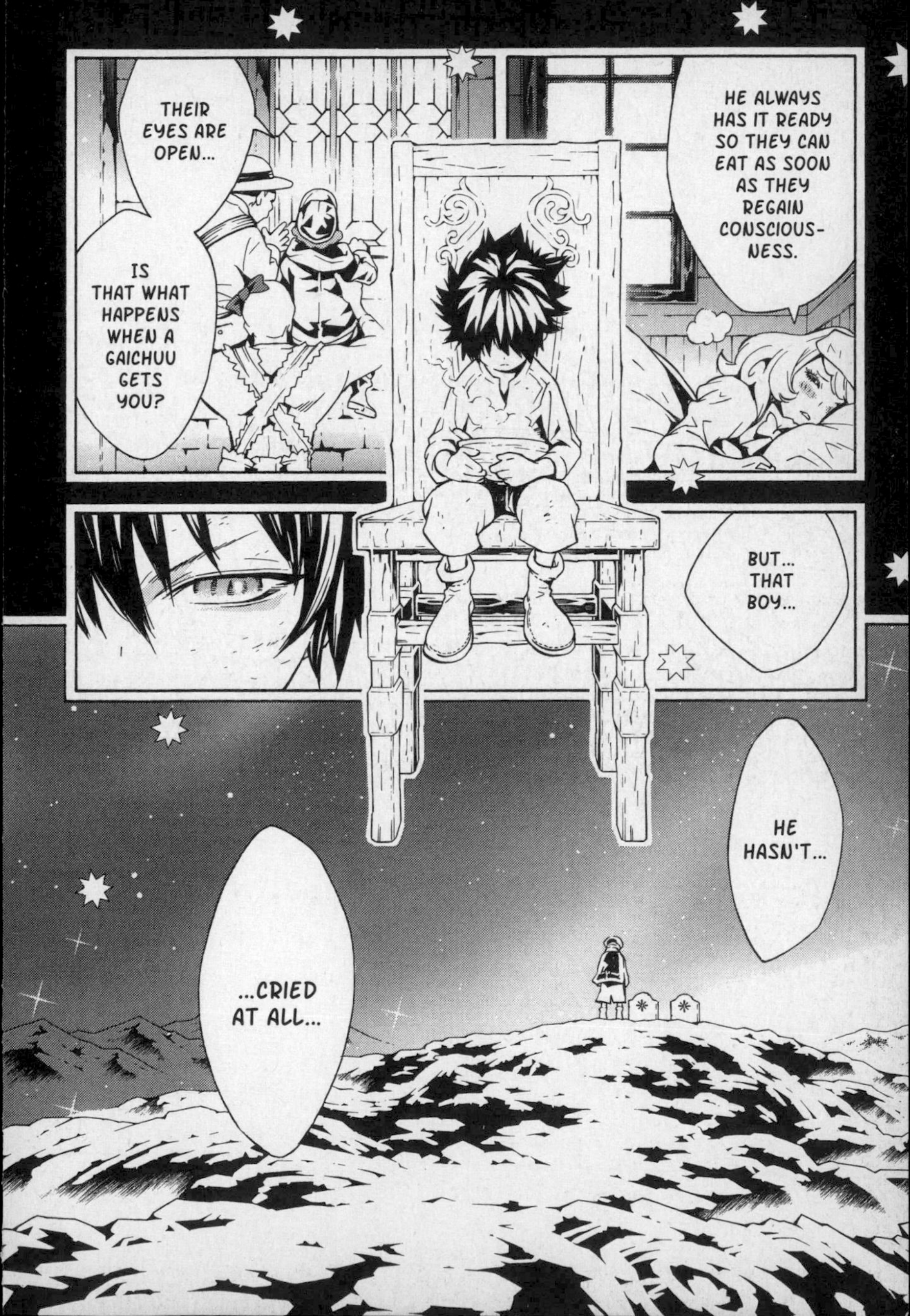
HE ALWAYS HAS IT READY SO THEY CAN EAT AS SOON AS THEY REGAIN CONSCIOUS-NESS.
THEIR EYES ARE OPEN...
IS THAT WHAT HAPPENS WHEN A GAICHUU GETS YOU?
BUT... THAT BOY...
HE HASN'T...
...CRIED AT ALL...

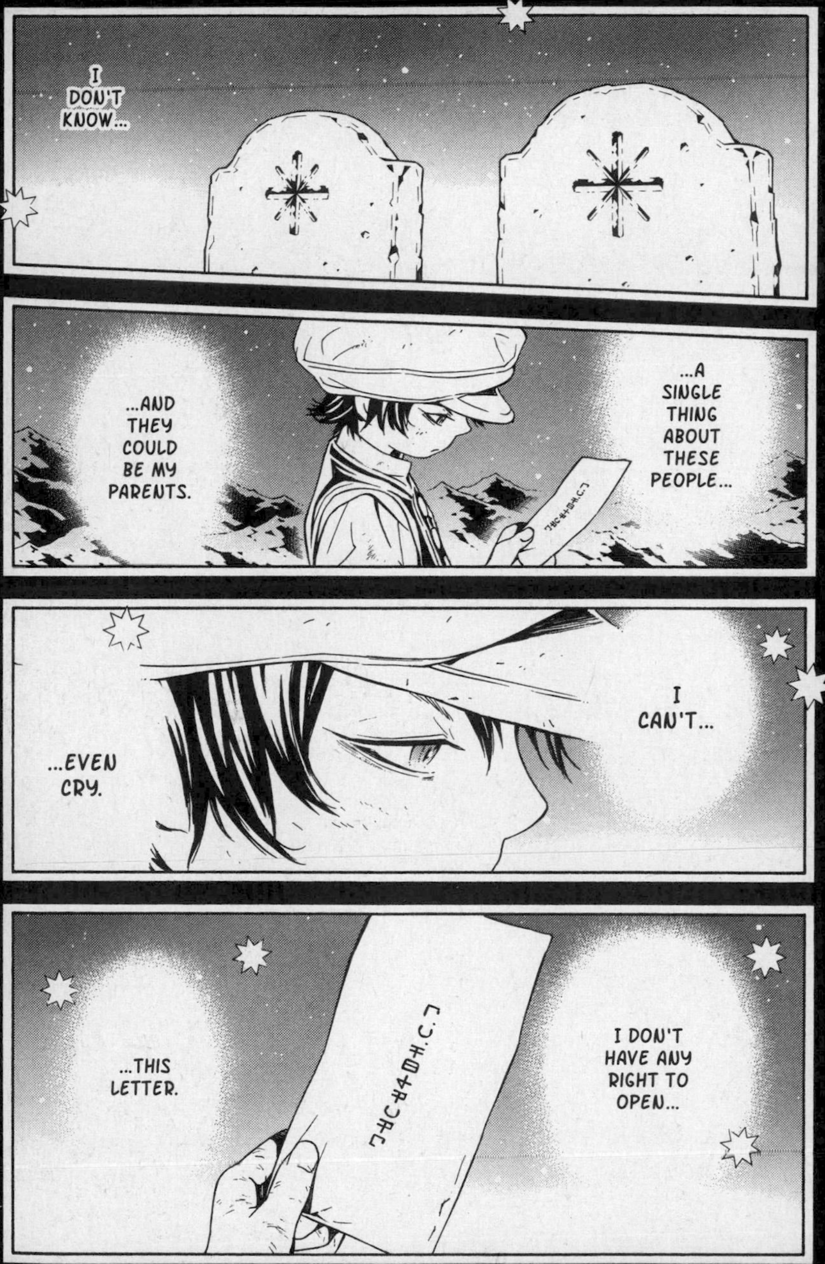
I DON'T KNOW...
...A SINGLE THING ABOUT THESE PEOPLE...
...AND THEY COULD BE MY PARENTS.
I CAN'T...
...EVEN CRY.
I DON'T HAVE ANY RIGHT TO OPEN...
...THIS LETTER.

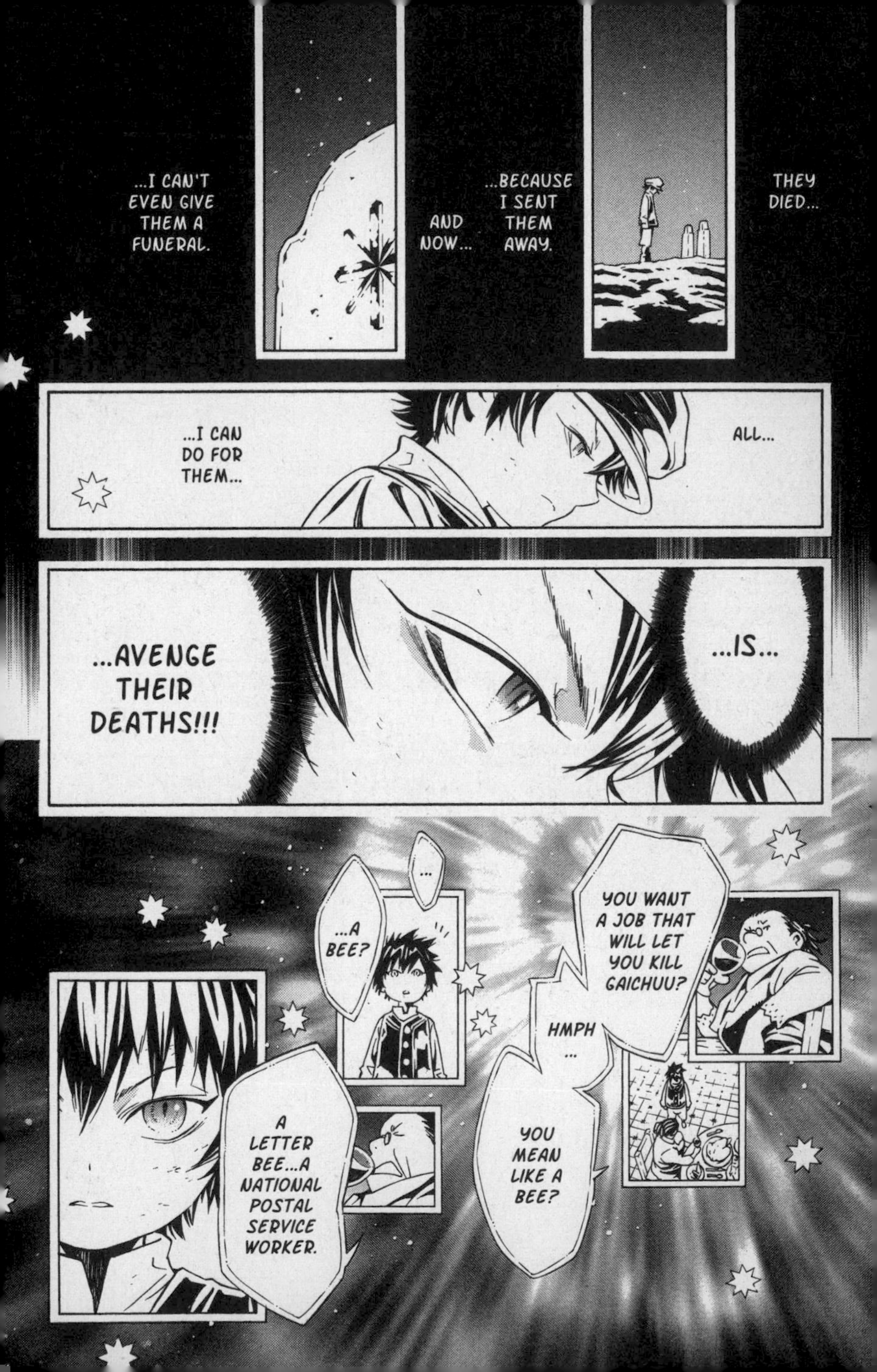
THEY DIED...
...BECAUSE I SENT THEM AWAY.
AND NOW...
...I CAN'T EVEN GIVE THEM A FUNERAL.
ALL...
...I CAN DO FOR THEM...
...IS...
...AVENGE THEIR DEATHS!!!
YOU WANT A JOB THAT WILL LET YOU KILL GAICHUU?
HMPH...
YOU MEAN LIKE A BEE?
...
...A BEE?
A LETTER BEE...A NATIONAL POSTAL SERVICE WORKER.

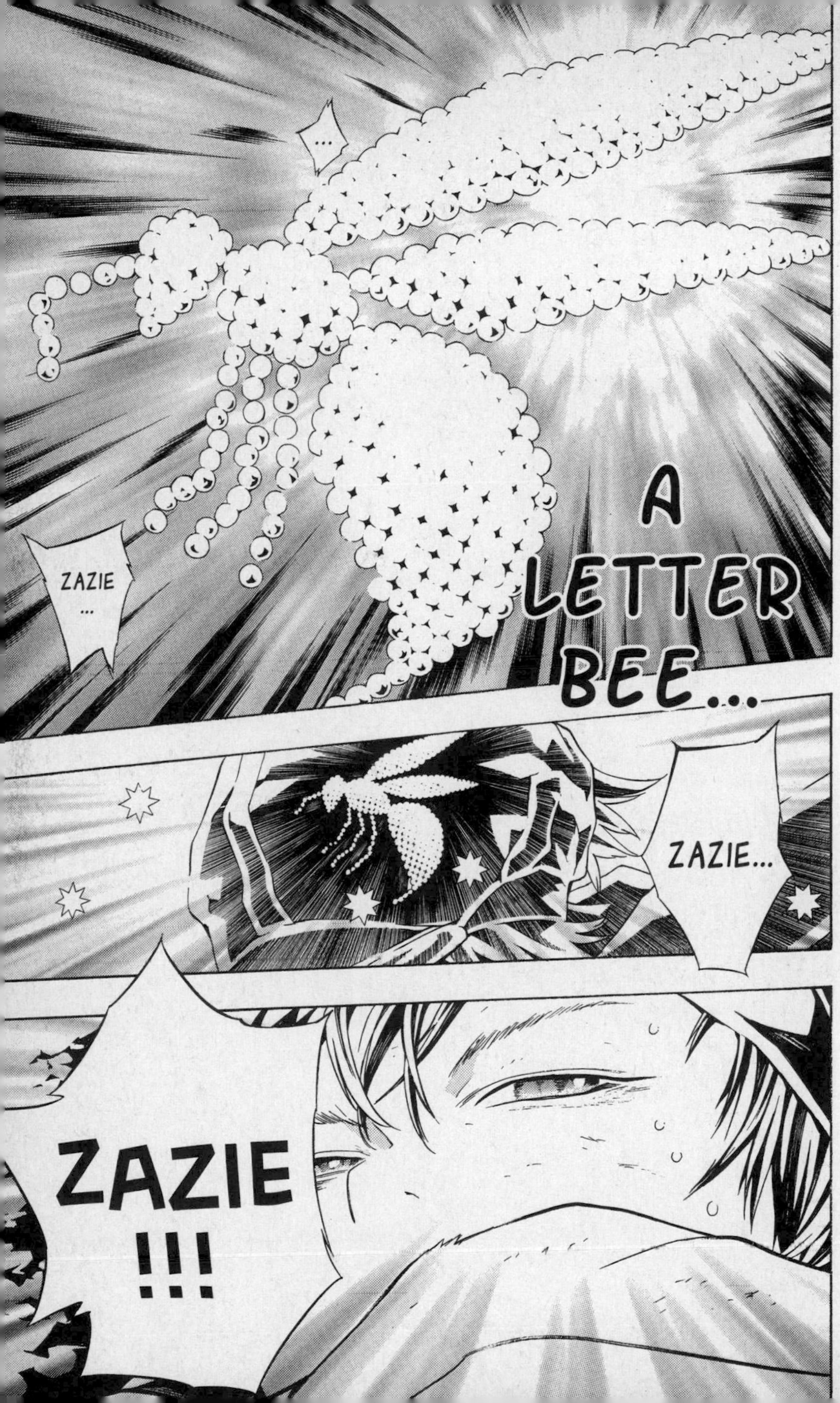
A LETTER BEE...
...
ZAZIE ...
ZAZIE...
ZAZIE !!!

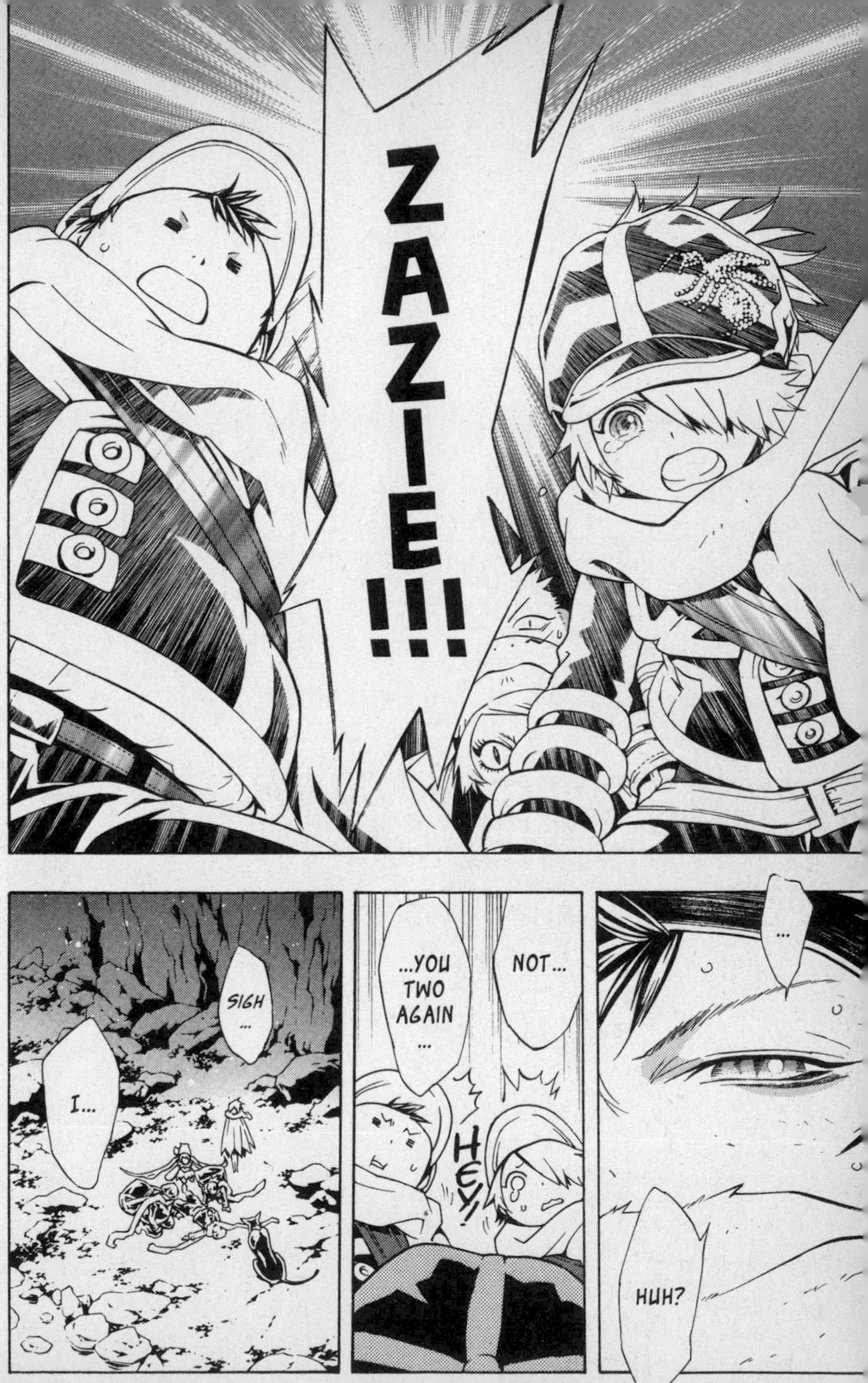
ZAZIE!!!
...
HUH?
NOT...
...YOU TWO AGAIN...
HEY!
SIGH...
I...

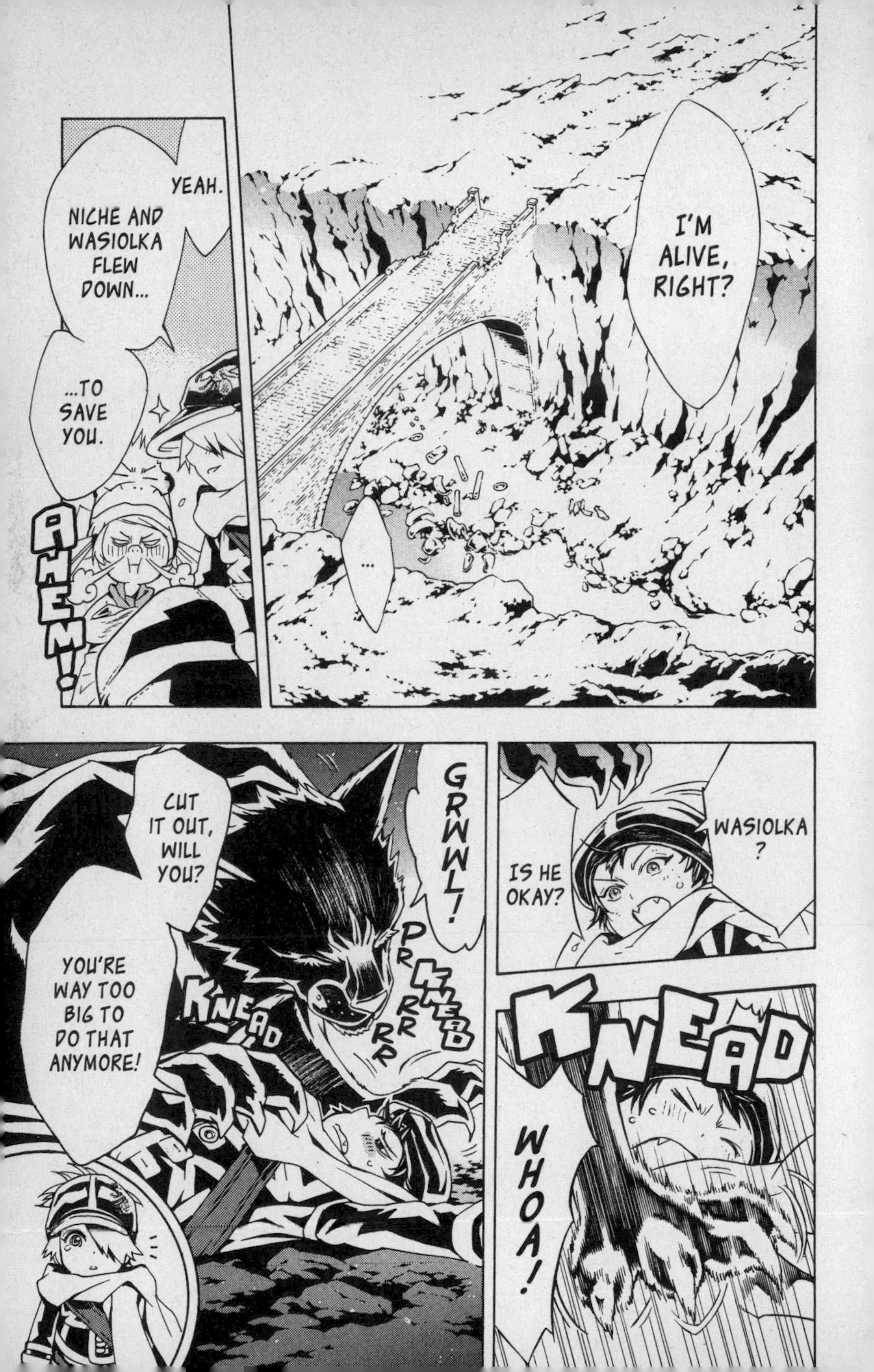
I'M ALIVE, RIGHT?
...
YEAH.
NICHE AND WASIOLKA FLEW DOWN...
...TO SAVE YOU.
AHEM!
WASIOLKA?
IS HE OKAY?
GRWWL!
PRRRRR
KNEAD
KNEAD
CUT IT OUT, WILL YOU?
YOU'RE WAY TOO BIG TO DO THAT ANYMORE!
KNEAD
WHOA!

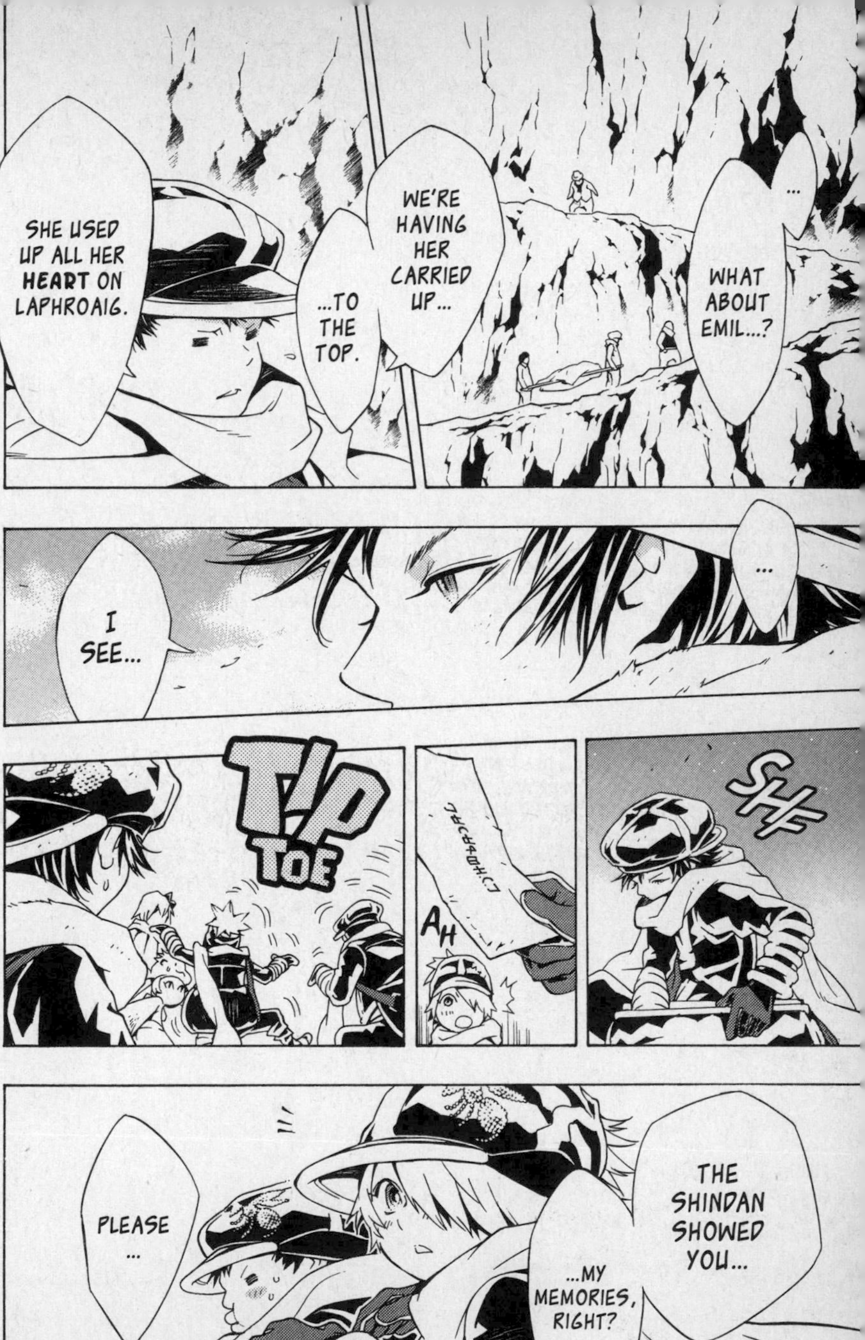
...
WHAT ABOUT EMIL...?
WE'RE HAVING HER CARRIED UP...
...TO THE TOP.
SHE USED UP ALL HER **HEART** ON LAPHROAIG.
...
I SEE...
SHF
AH
TIP TOE
THE SHINDAN SHOWED YOU...
...MY MEMORIES, RIGHT?
PLEASE ...

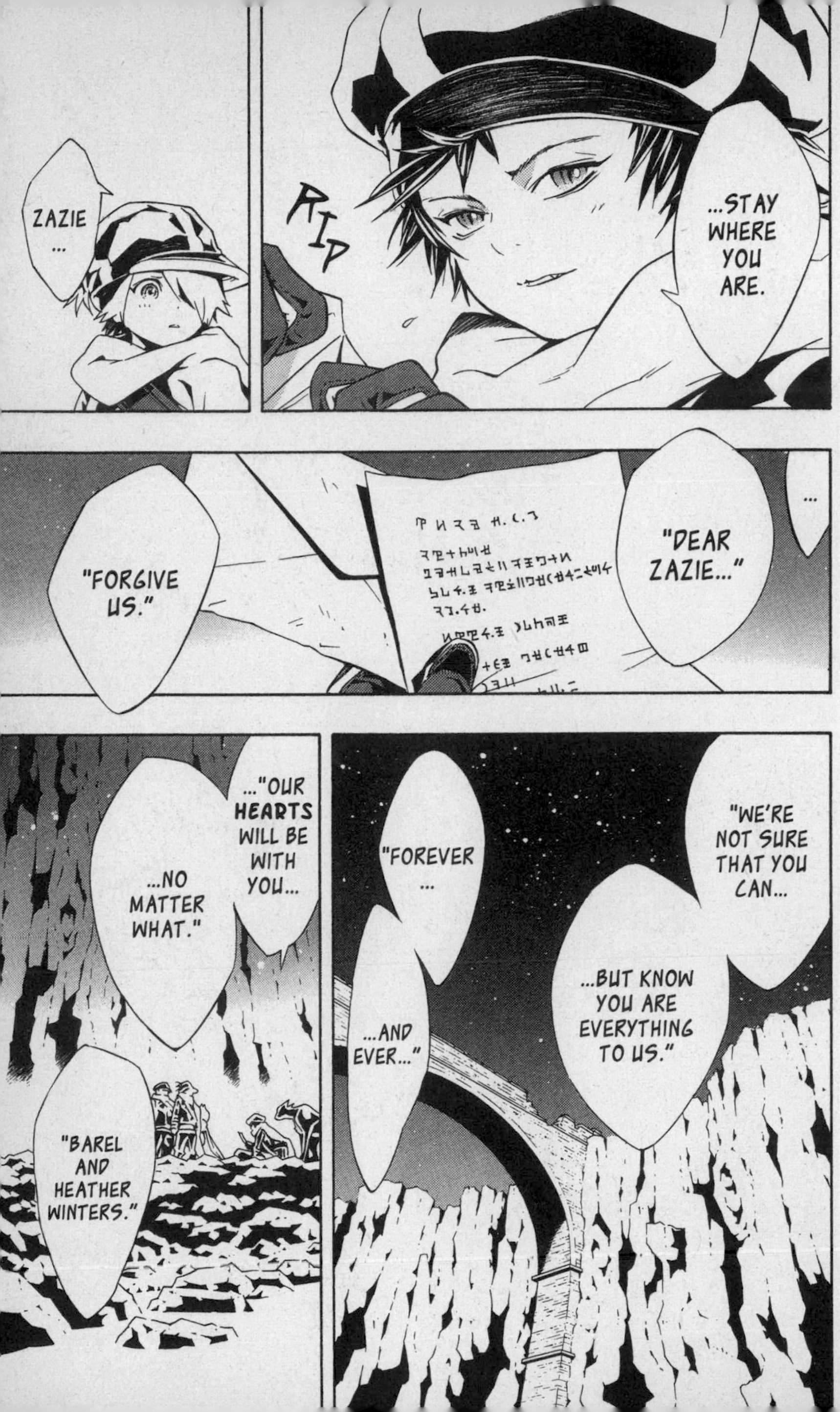
...STAY WHERE YOU ARE.
RIP
ZAZIE ...
...
"DEAR ZAZIE..."
"FORGIVE US."
"WE'RE NOT SURE THAT YOU CAN...
...BUT KNOW YOU ARE EVERYTHING TO US."
"FOREVER ...
...AND EVER..."
..."OUR HEARTS WILL BE WITH YOU...
...NO MATTER WHAT."
"BAREL AND HEATHER WINTERS."

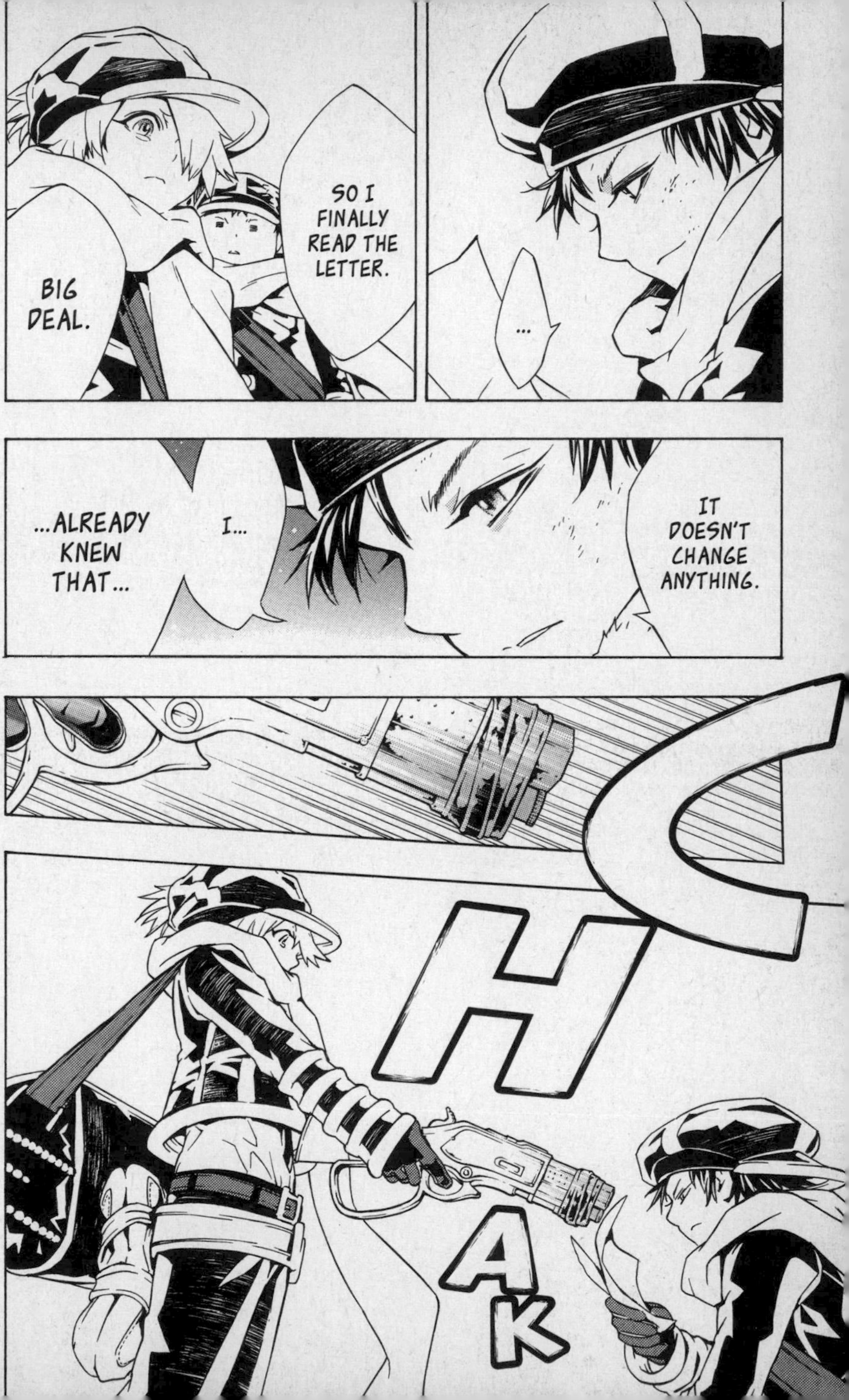
...
SO I FINALLY READ THE LETTER.
BIG DEAL.
IT DOESN'T CHANGE ANYTHING.
I...
...ALREADY KNEW THAT...
CHAK

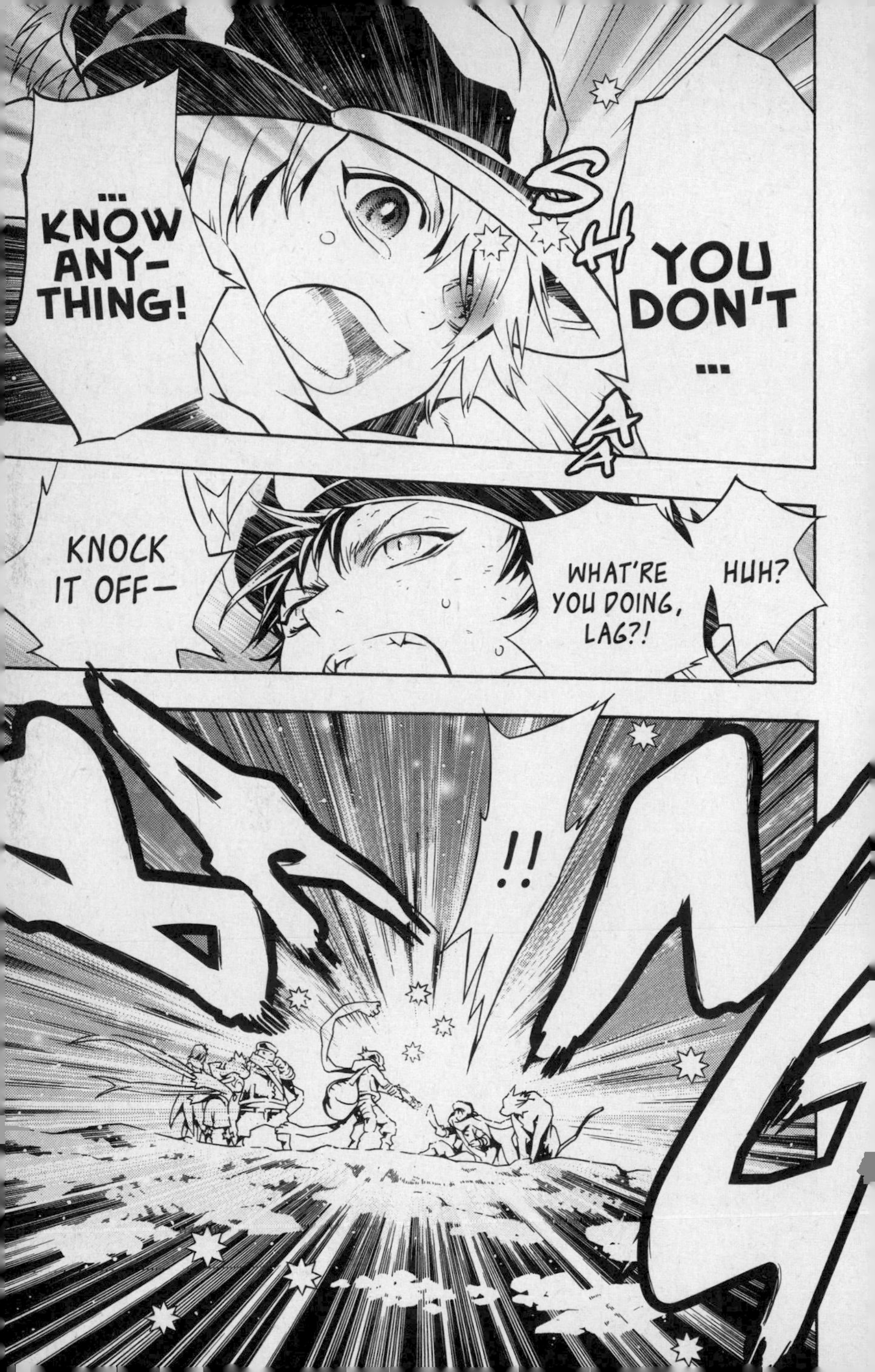
SHA
YOU DON'T ...
... KNOW ANYTHING!
HUH?
WHAT'RE YOU DOING, LAG?!
KNOCK IT OFF—
!!

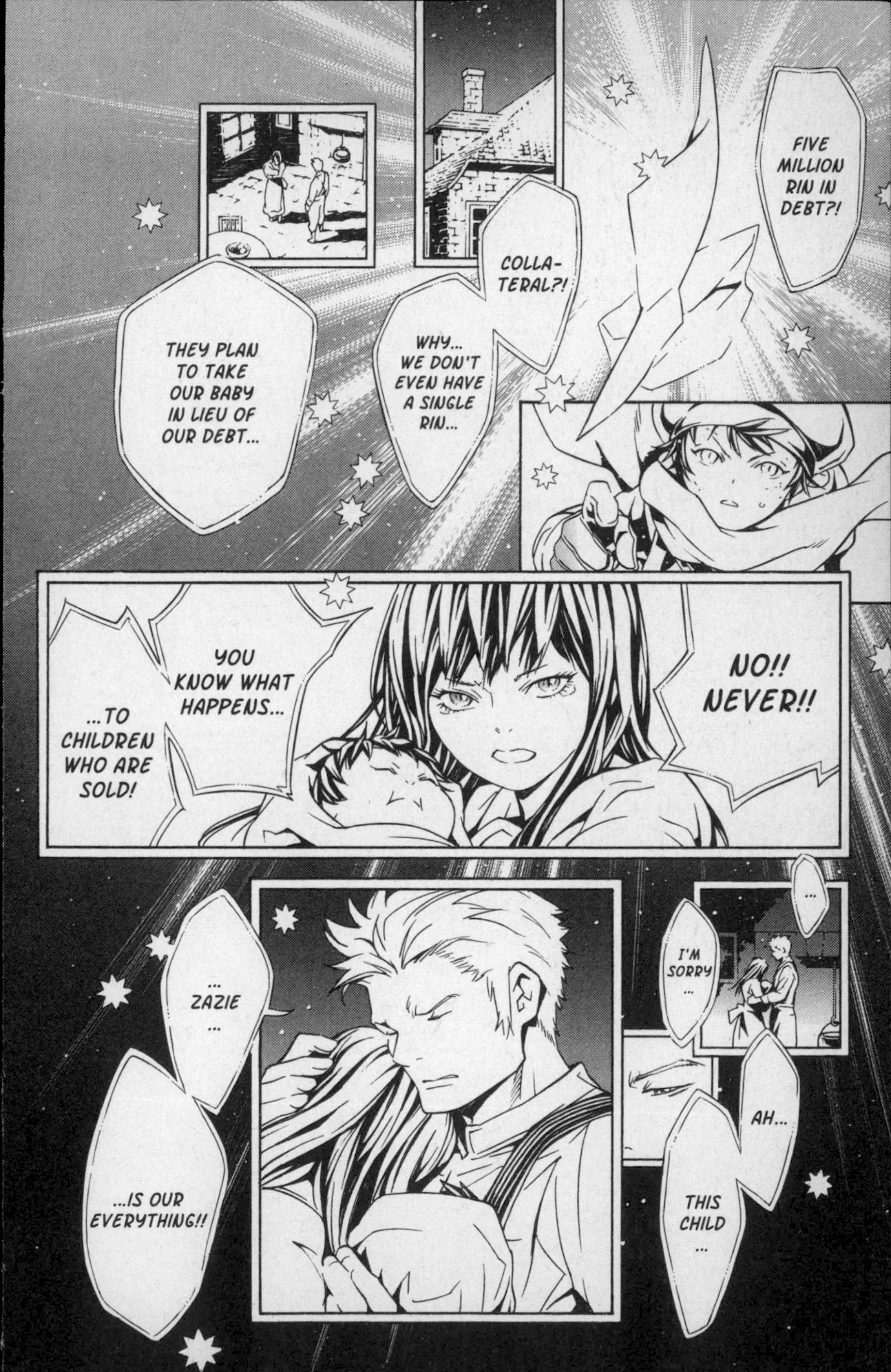
FIVE MILLION RIN IN DEBT?!
COLLA-TERAL?!
WHY... WE DON'T EVEN HAVE A SINGLE RIN...
THEY PLAN TO TAKE OUR BABY IN LIEU OF OUR DEBT...
NO!! NEVER!!
YOU KNOW WHAT HAPPENS...
...TO CHILDREN WHO ARE SOLD!
...
I'M SORRY ...
AH...
THIS CHILD ...
... ZAZIE ...
...IS OUR EVERYTHING!!

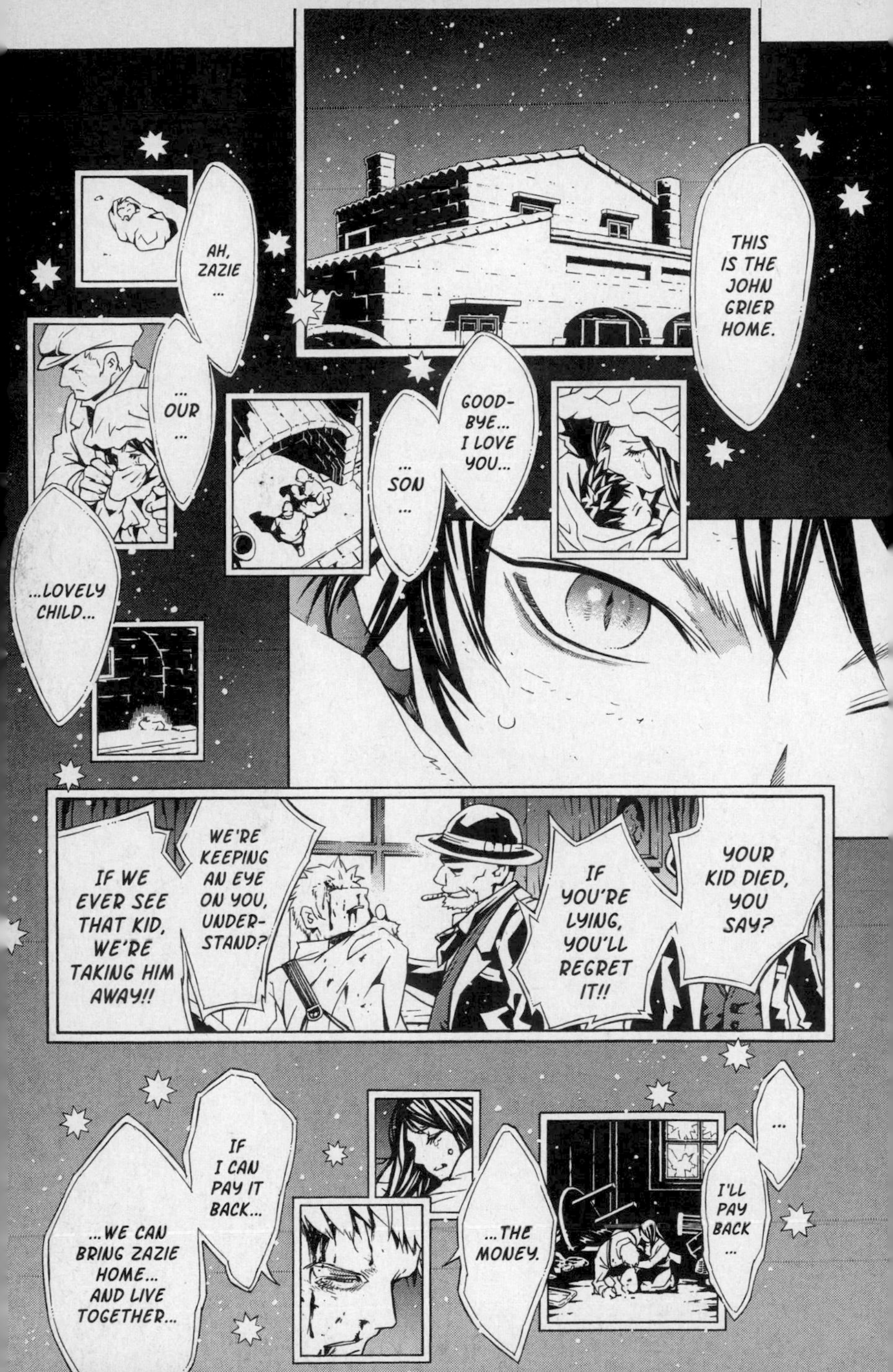
THIS IS THE JOHN GRIER HOME.
GOOD-BYE... I LOVE YOU...
... SON ...
AH, ZAZIE ...
... OUR ...
...LOVELY CHILD...
YOUR KID DIED, YOU SAY?
IF YOU'RE LYING, YOU'LL REGRET IT!!
WE'RE KEEPING AN EYE ON YOU, UNDER-STAND?
IF WE EVER SEE THAT KID, WE'RE TAKING HIM AWAY!!
...
I'LL PAY BACK ...
...THE MONEY.
IF I CAN PAY IT BACK...
...WE CAN BRING ZAZIE HOME... AND LIVE TOGETHER...

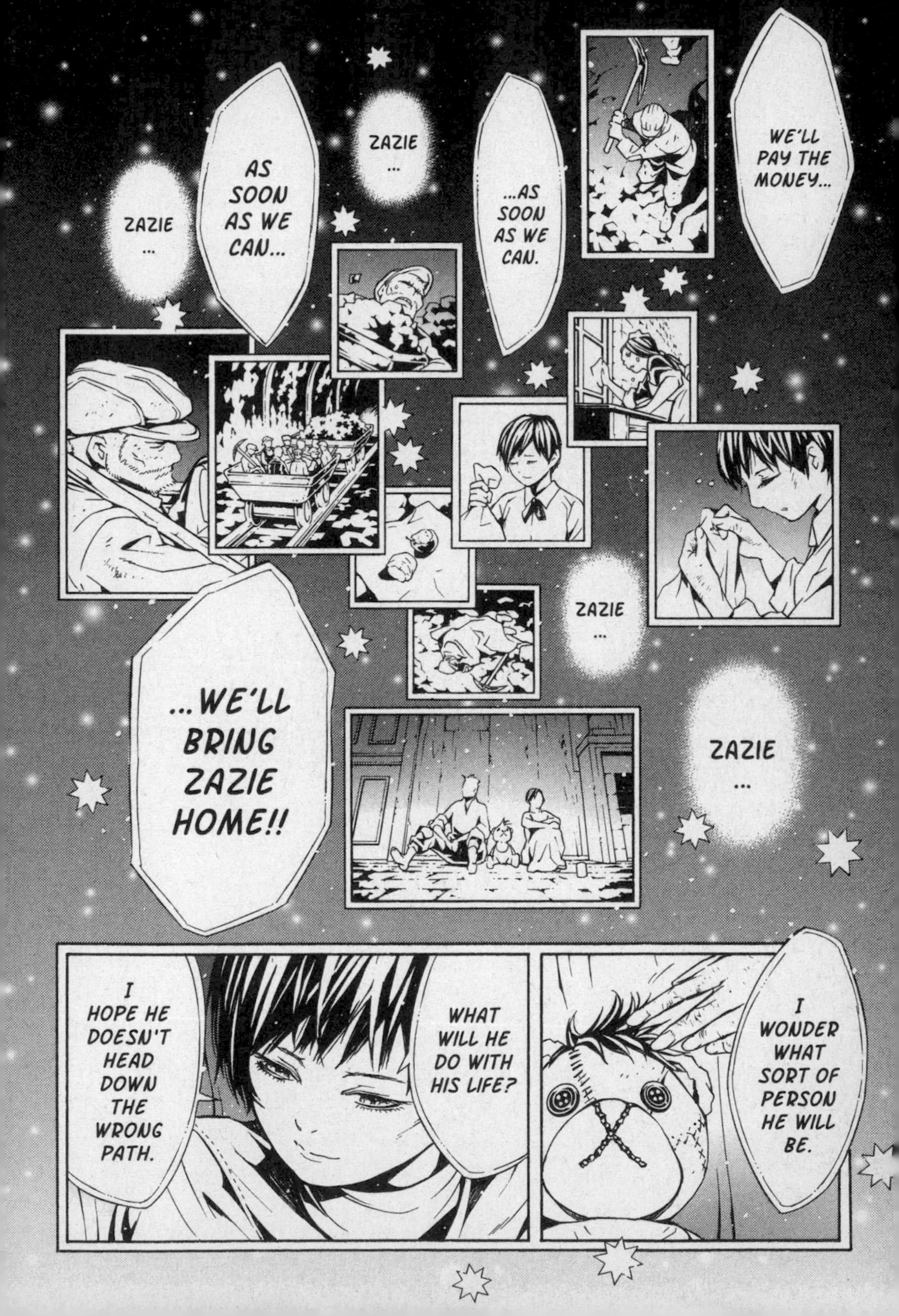
WE'LL PAY THE MONEY...
...AS SOON AS WE CAN.
ZAZIE ...
AS SOON AS WE CAN...
ZAZIE ...
ZAZIE ...
...WE'LL BRING ZAZIE HOME!!
ZAZIE ...
I WONDER WHAT SORT OF PERSON HE WILL BE.
WHAT WILL HE DO WITH HIS LIFE?
I HOPE HE DOESN'T HEAD DOWN THE WRONG PATH.

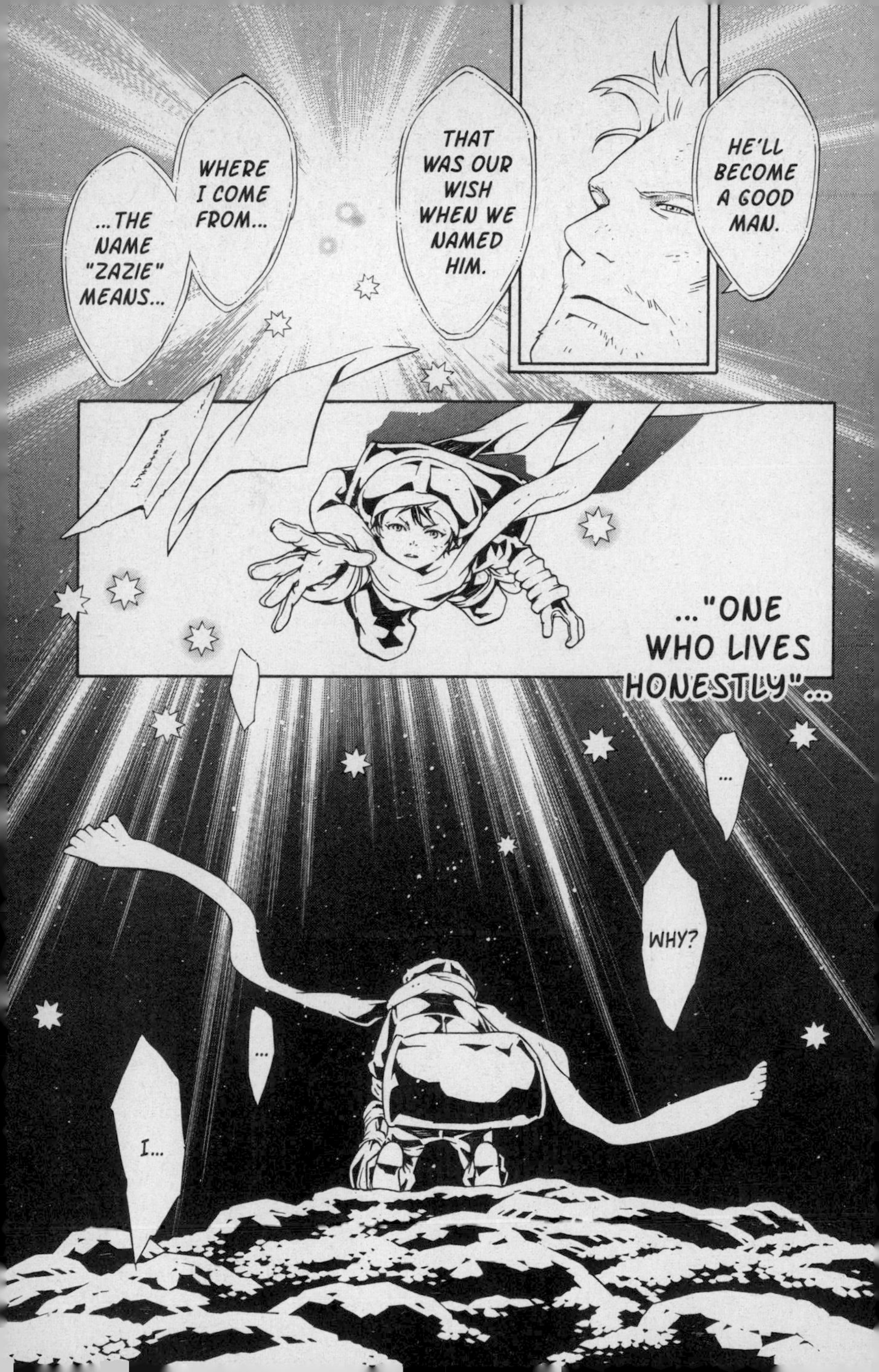
HE'LL BECOME A GOOD MAN.
THAT WAS OUR WISH WHEN WE NAMED HIM.
WHERE I COME FROM...
...THE NAME "ZAZIE" MEANS...
..."ONE WHO LIVES HONESTLY"...
...
WHY?
...
I...

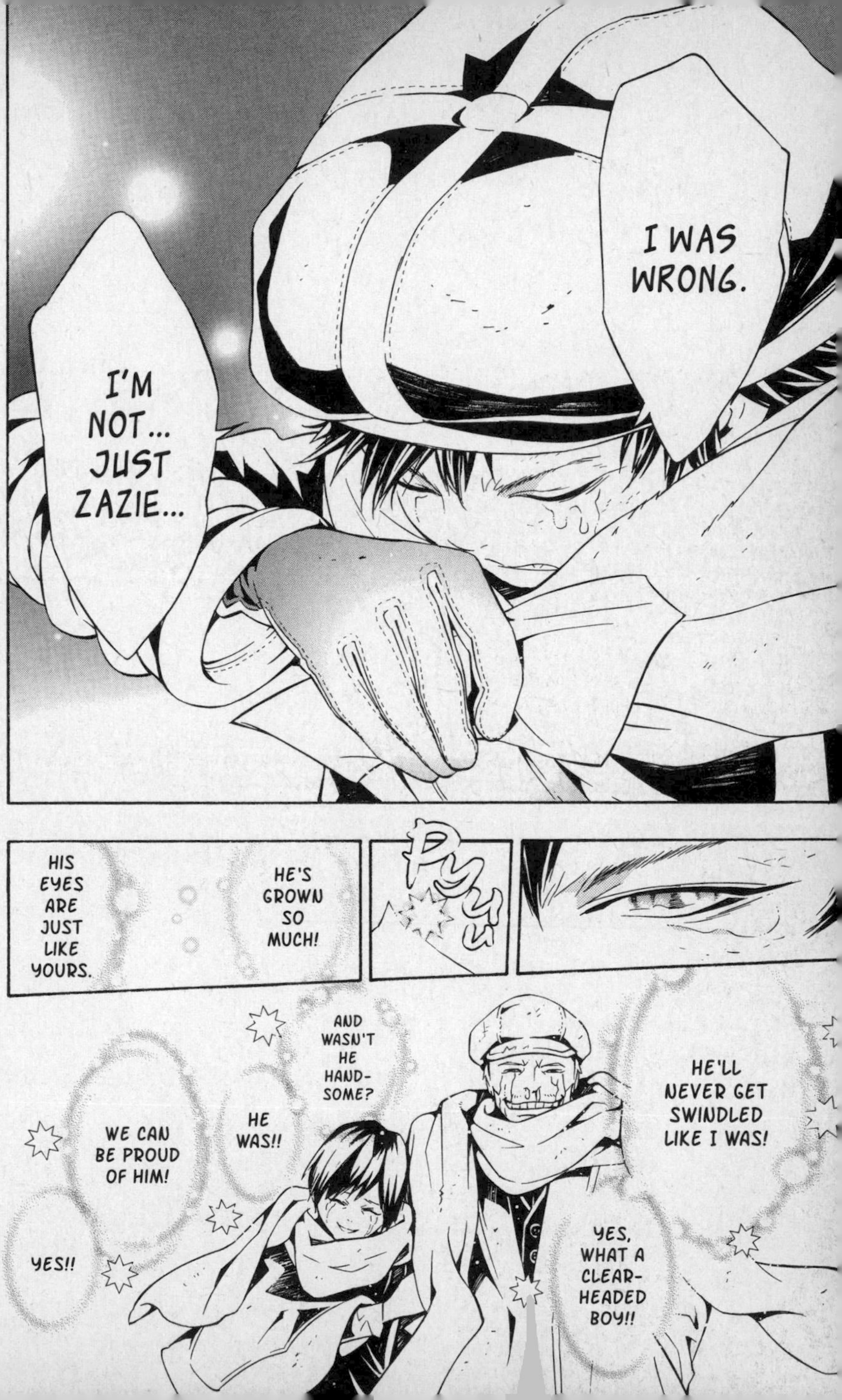
I WAS WRONG.
I'M NOT... JUST ZAZIE...
Pyuu
HE'S GROWN SO MUCH!
HIS EYES ARE JUST LIKE YOURS.
HE'LL NEVER GET SWINDLED LIKE I WAS!
YES, WHAT A CLEAR-HEADED BOY!!
AND WASN'T HE HAND-SOME?
HE WAS!!
WE CAN BE PROUD OF HIM!
YES!!

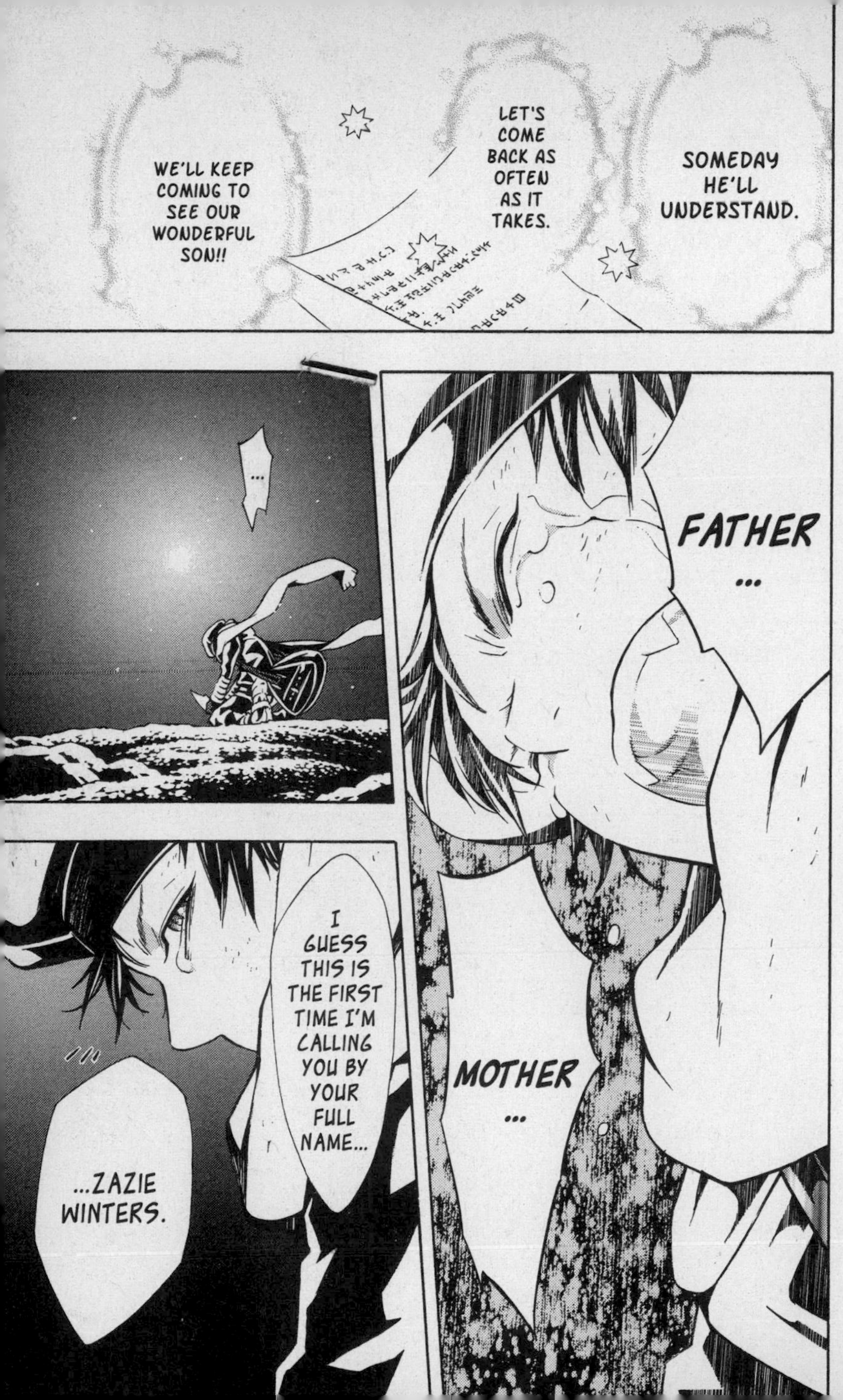
SOMEDAY HE'LL UNDERSTAND.
LET'S COME BACK AS OFTEN AS IT TAKES.
WE'LL KEEP COMING TO SEE OUR WONDERFUL SON!!
FATHER ...
MOTHER ...
...
I GUESS THIS IS THE FIRST TIME I'M CALLING YOU BY YOUR FULL NAME...
...ZAZIE WINTERS.

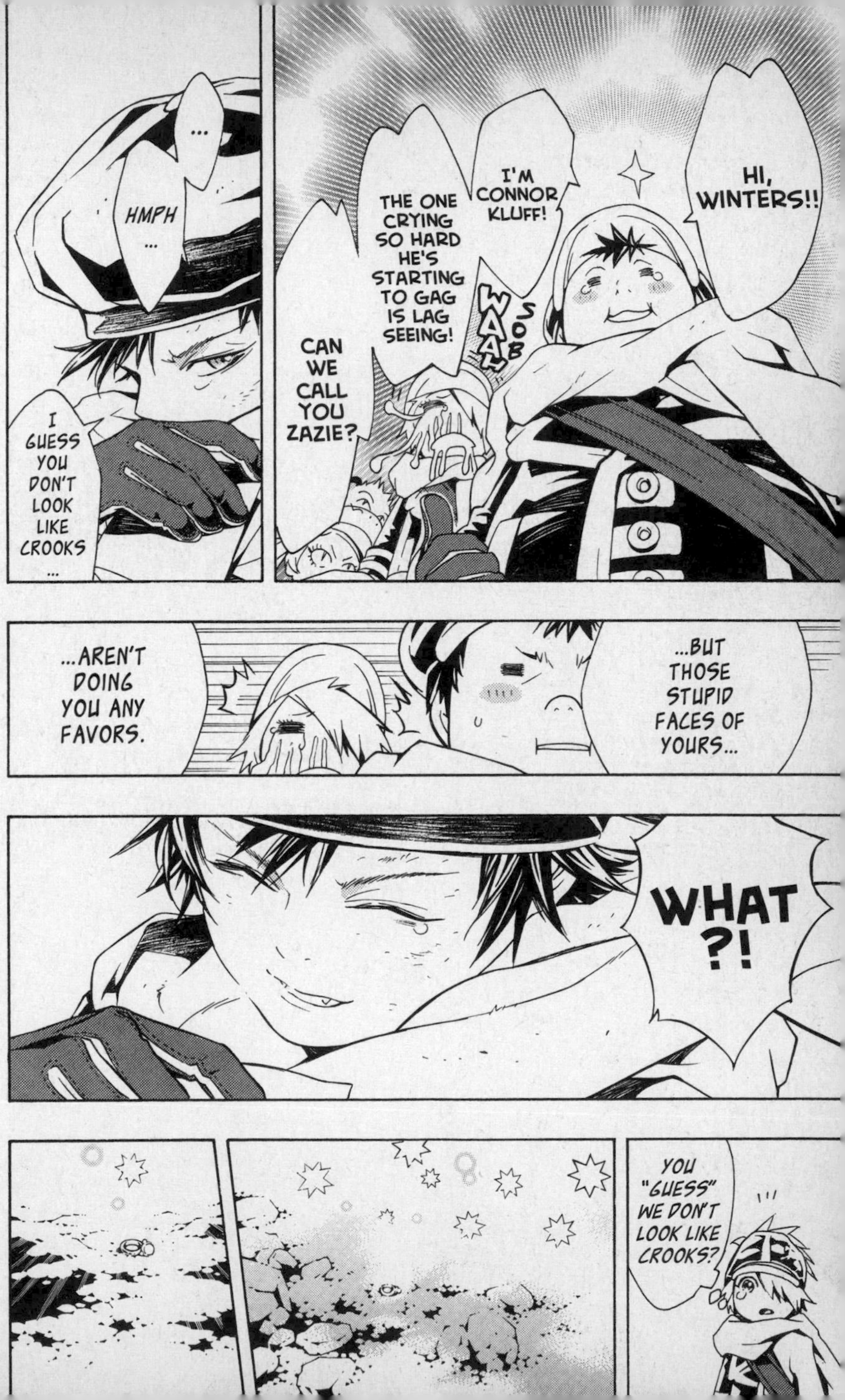
HI, WINTERS!!
I'M CONNOR KLUFF!
THE ONE CRYING SO HARD HE'S STARTING TO GAG IS LAG SEEING!
WAAH
SOB
CAN WE CALL YOU ZAZIE?
...
HMPH
...
I GUESS YOU DON'T LOOK LIKE CROOKS
...
...BUT THOSE STUPID FACES OF YOURS...
...AREN'T DOING YOU ANY FAVORS.
WHAT?!
YOU "GUESS" WE DON'T LOOK LIKE CROOKS?

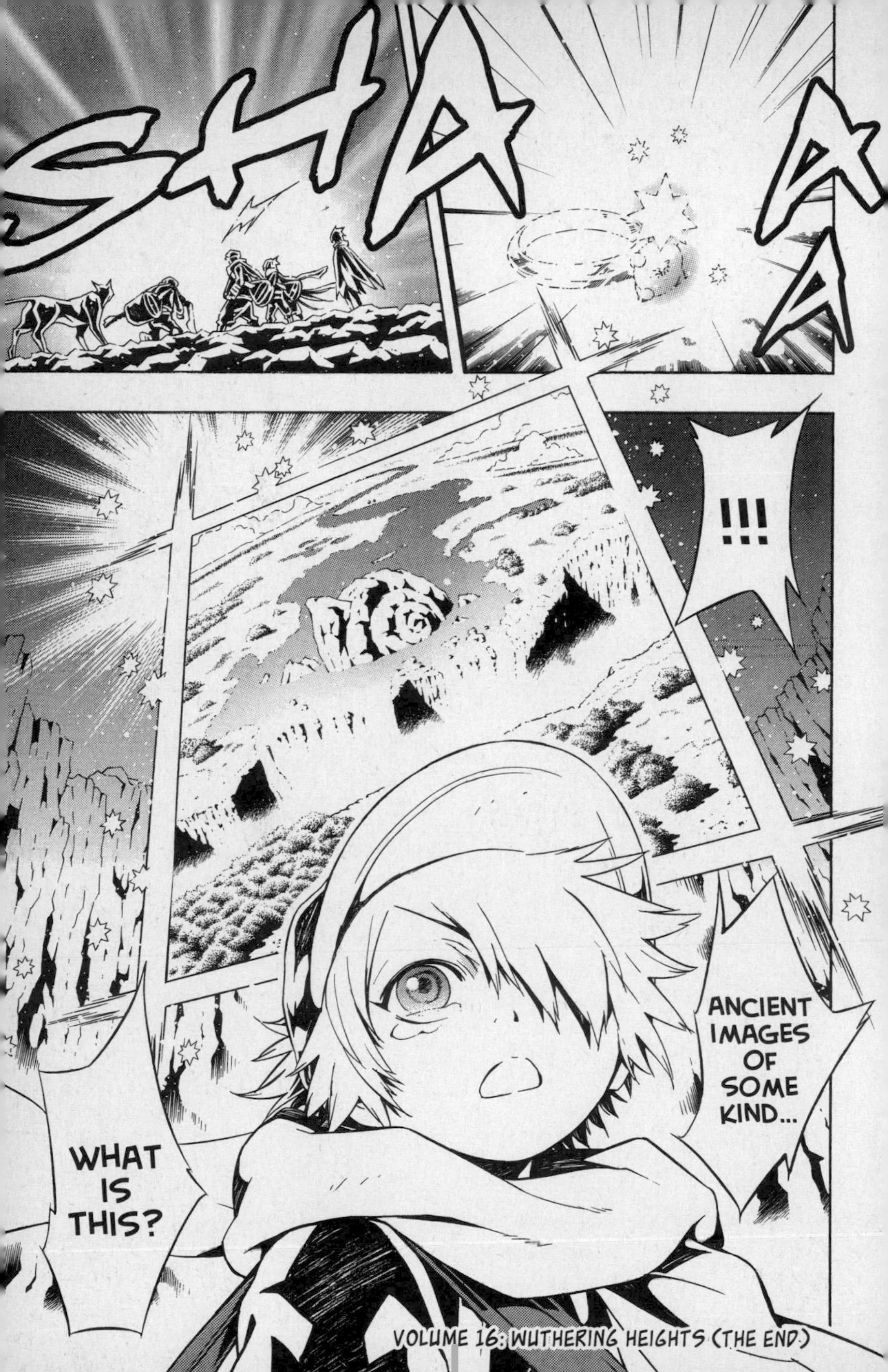
SHAAA
!!!
ANCIENT IMAGES OF SOME KIND...
WHAT IS THIS?

VOLUME 16: WUTHERING HEIGHTS (THE END)

Dr. Thunderland's Reference Desk

To be honest, in the last volume I prudently resolved to stop sulking about my continued failure to appear in this story. But before I knew it I found myself drowning my sorrows in booze from the stress of being prudent. I'd get up in the morning and have breakfast and beer. At noon it was lunch and draft beer. My afternoon snack was tequila. With dinner I'd have wine and sake. After dinner I'd have shochu and a whiskey nightcap. After using the bathroom I did shots of alcohol hand sanitizer.

That'sh not good...that'sh *bad*...heh...

Hurray fer boozhe! I lurrve you...!

*Ahem...*I work at the Yuusari Beehive, researching various subjects each day...while drinking. Here I will review the circumstances of this world presented in this volume...while drinking. *Hic...*

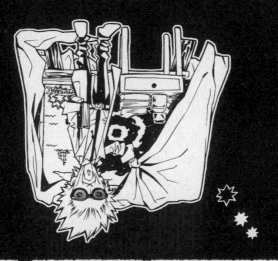

■ EMIL OF WUTHERING HEIGHTS

I think Emil was probably a sweet, innocent little girl when she first came to Wuthering Heights. But during the years of abuse and oppression by the high-handed owners of the inn, darkness was born in her *heart*. When she gained power through Laphroaig, she released her *heart* in the wrong direction. What a pitiable child. Fellow orphan Zazie seemed to feel sympathy for her. He probably wanted to help her. It was unfortunate, but even so, it was Emil's own choice.

That couple was infuriating. Emil said the howling winds were like a lullaby to her. That means she probably heard far worse things on a daily basis. And that cupcake lady! What's with her? I drink from morning to night too, but the more I drink, the sweeter I become! I refuse to admit I have a problem! It's great! Booze is great! Hurray for booze! Drink! Drink! My head is full of drink...*ha ha ha!*

But what goes around comes around, as they say. Someday that lady will get what she deserves.

nb: *Wuthering Heights* by Emily Bronte / Published in 1847 under the name Ellis Bell. Novel of love and revenge set in a run-down mansion in the wilds of Yorkshire.

■ ZAZIE'S PARENTS

We saw them in the memories in the letter, but the fragments of Zazie's *heart* didn't include his parents' faces. That means he doesn't remember them. I don't know if that's because the memory was too brief, or if he consciously tried to erase them from his mind, but it's clear that the event had an effect on Zazie...a big one.

Zazie became a Letter Bee to get revenge. I hope he's come to realize how important his work is. I'm glad Lag and Connor were there for him. Friends are important, aren't they? I don't even have a drinking partner. That's right: poor me will be drinking alone again tonight. I feel like dying. Bartender! Give me another cocktail to wash away my tears!

■ ZAZIE'S NAME

It seems the name "Zazie" means "one who lives honestly." His name says it all, doesn't it? Good or bad, names and natures do often agree. I wonder why. This is something I intend to research thoroughly. Kids nowadays often have such complicated names. They're surprising to old men like me. But listen, everyone, your parents thought long and hard about your name. You've got to try your best to outlive them and keep the name alive.

nb: John Grier Home / Orphanage where the main character, Judy, lives in *Daddy-Long-Legs*, a 1912 novel by American writer Jean Webster.

■ CHILDREN OF THE FLICKER

Emil's mother died in the petrified woods. Only Emil, her unborn baby, survived. But how? It seems plausible that her strange birth is connected to her ability to commune with Laphroaig. Those born on the Day of the Flicker, receiving the memories of the artificial sun, may have a greater ability to utilize their *heart*.

And there we have it: an image from ancient times! We hit it big! Her spirit amber acted as a recorder. So this is what it means to "search your heart." As in Lag's case, these memories may have lain dormant in the depths of Emil's *heart* without her knowledge.

Incidentally, I often lose my memory when I drink too much. I hypothesize that the drinking is causing my brain to shrink. I wonder if it's something like *Whatchamacallit for Algernon.* But they do say, "Ignorance is bliss." Still, my life has been a mess lately. I wonder why. Oh, right, because of the drinking...*heh heh heh...*

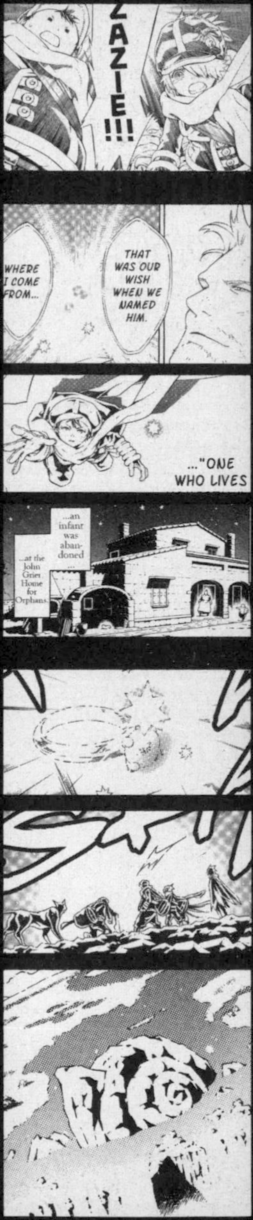
ZAZIE!!!
THAT WAS OUR WISH WHEN WE NAMED HIM.
WHERE I COME FROM...
..."ONE WHO LIVES
...an infant was abandoned ...
...at the John Grier Home for Orphans.

Route Map

Finally, I am including a map, indicating the route of Lag's group since the previous volume, created at Lonely Goatherd Map Station of Central Yuusari.

A: Akatsuki B: Yuusari C: Yodaka

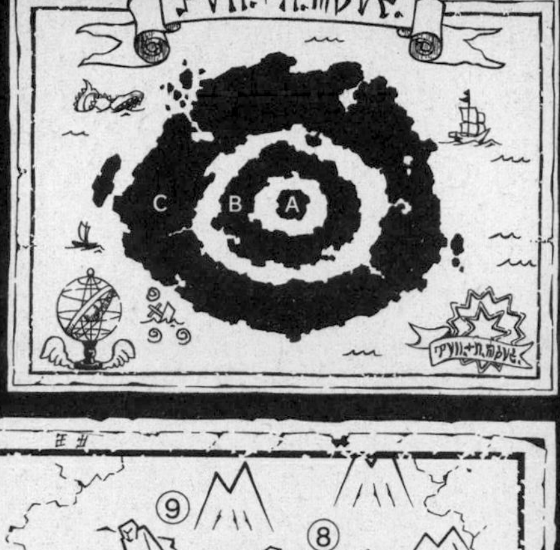

C
B
A

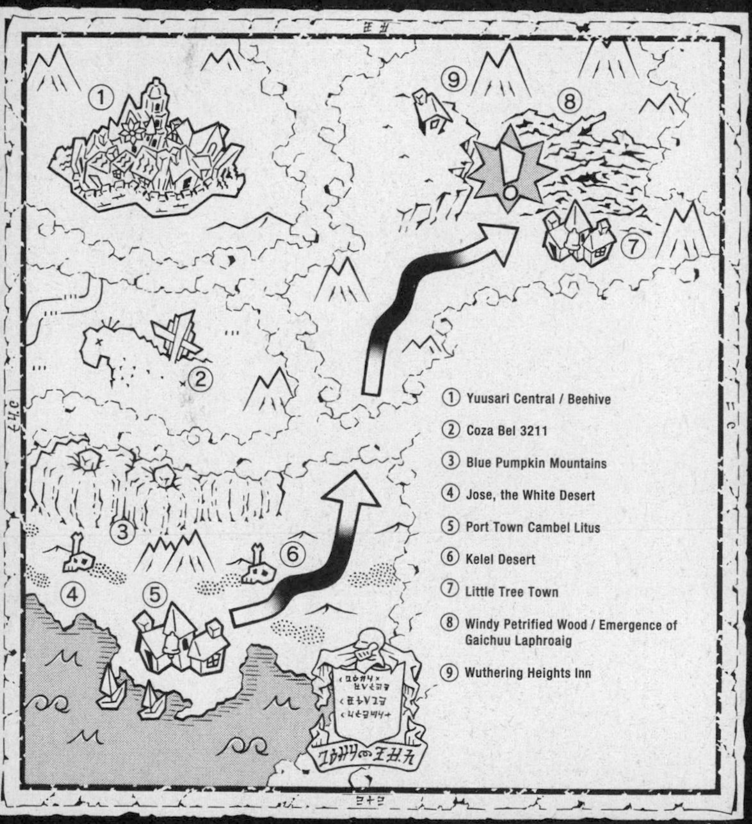

① Yuusari Central / Beehive
② Coza Bel 3211
③ Blue Pumpkin Mountains
④ Jose, the White Desert
⑤ Port Town Cambel Litus
⑥ Kelel Desert
⑦ Little Tree Town
⑧ Windy Petrified Wood / Emergence of Gaichuu Laphroaig
⑨ Wuthering Heights Inn

Snerk...*mm*...I'd better quit drinking sake. Yup...*mph*...I'll stick with beer. And whiskey. Bartender, give me another round of barley shochu, sake and wine...

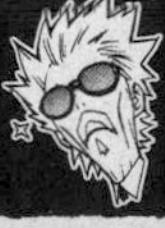

Change Your

From Akira Toriyama, the creator of Dr. Slump, COWA!, and Sandland

Relive Goku's quest with the new VIZBIG Editions of *Dragon Ball* and *Dragon Ball Z!* Each features:

- Three volumes in one
- Larger trim size
- Exclusive cover designs • Color artwork
- Color manga pages
- Bonus content

And more!

DISCOVER ANIME
IN A WHOLE NEW WAY!

www.neonalley.com

What it is...

- Streaming anime delivered 24/7 straight to your TV via your connected video game console
- All English dubbed content
- Anime, martial arts movies, and more

Go to **neonalley.com** for news, updates and to see if Neon Alley is available in your area.

1
2
3
4
5
6
7
8
9
142

Follow the action this way.

THIS IS THE LAST PAGE.

Tegami Bachi: Letter Bee has been printed in the original Japanese format in order to preserve the orientation of the original artwork.

Please turn it around and begin reading from right to left. Unlike English, Japanese is read right to left, so Japanese comics are read in reverse order from the way English comics are typically read. Have fun with it!

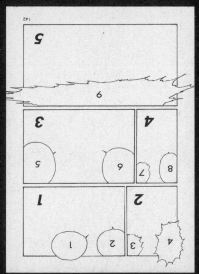